For Craig Mu

from James.

JACKO
WHERE ARE YOU NOW ?

JACKO
WHERE ARE YOU NOW ?

A life of Robert Jackson

Master of Humanitarian Relief
The man who saved Malta

James Gibson

by
James Gibson

PARSONS PUBLISHING

© James Gibson 2006

First published in Great Britain in 2006 by

PARSONS PUBLISHING
PO Box 787
RICHMOND
TW10 7WQ

All rights reserved. No part of this publication may be reproduced, stored on a retrieval system, or transmitted in any form or by any means without the prior permission of the copyright owner. James Gibson is hereby identified as author of this work in accordance with Section 77 of the Copyright, Designs and Patents Act 1988.

ISBN 0-9553968-0-8 Hardback
ISBN 978-0-9553968-1-6 Paperback

Printed and bound by
Martins the Printers Limited
Seaview Works, Spittal
Berwick-upon-Tweed, TD15 1RS
www.martins-the-printers.com

Set in 11/16 Joanna
Design by www.simprimstudio.com

For Maria
in loving memory

Contents

LIST OF ILLUSTRATIONS	iii
LIST OF MAPS	v
LIST OF ABBREVIATIONS	vi
A PERSONAL PREFACE	vii
PROLOGUE	xi

PART ONE   ONE SUCCESS TOO MANY

1	Wilbur	1
2	All at sea	7
3	The Man who saved Malta	15
4	The Middle East Supply Centre (MESC)	37
5	UNRRA - the first UN organisation	63
6	Operation Cool-off	101
7	Disaster at Lake Success	117

PART TWO   WHAT NEXT?

8	Odd job man	147
9	Casey to the rescue	149
10	The Volta River Project	171

PART THREE   BACK TO THE UN

11	Not forgotten	199
12	The Capacity Study	209
13	The Consensus	227
14	The Fountain	237

PART FOUR   THE GREATEST OF OPERATORS

15	Bangladesh	247
16	Africa and Indo-China	281
17	Back to UNDP	297
18	Kampuchea	303
19	The last lap	331
20	Epilogue	345

ACKNOWLEDGEMENTS	351
END-NOTES	353
INDEX	375

List of illustrations

Kofi Annan unveiling Jackson's portrait, 29 January 1997 — xi

PART ONE   ONE SUCCESS TOO MANY

Wilbur Kenneth in his christening robe	Facing page 1
The family at YARALLA, 1927	3
HMAS *Australia* in Sydney Harbour, July 1930	6
Midshipman	8
Paymaster-Lieutenant	9
Peggy and Robert	12
Ohio at rest in Grand Harbour	34
Sheila Collins	39
Director-General of MESC	41
Jackson and staff of MESC	49
Edith and Herbert Lehman	66
Lieutenant-General Sir Humfrey Gale	78
Lieutenant-General Sir Frederick Morgan	78
LaGuardia addressing UNRRA Council, March 1946	81
Cartoon by LOW, September 1946	87
Barbara Ward, December 1946	92
Jackson at Castel Gandolfo, August 1947	98
Jacko at Whispering Sands	104
Sheila at Whispering Sands	104
The table-mat, 4 December 1946	105
Padre Pio, March 1948	112
Robert and Barbara on *Queen Mary*, 15 April 1948	116
Jackson and Trygve Lie, 23 April 1948	118
Robert and Barbara in London, 16 August 1948	138

PART TWO WHAT NEXT?	
The Nuptial Mass, 16 November 1950	156
La Madrina	157
Barbara, Alan (Bill) and Bett, August 1955	175
Jackson and Nkrumah in Delhi, October 1958	182
Anna and Robin at sea, January 1959	183
Jackson, Kaiser, Lodigiani and Nkrumah, 23 January 1962	195
PART THREE BACK TO THE UN	
Joan Anstee	201
Joan, James and Maria at Trélex	217
Jackson presenting the Capacity Study to Hoffman, 24 November 1969	224
Thomas sitting on the Capacity Study	234
The Fountain	236
PART FOUR THE GREATEST	
Subhas Dhar	259
Joan, Maria, James and Jacko at Petersham, summer 1978	298
Jackson addressing donor governments in New York, 26 March 1980	306
Jackson briefing press after donors' meeting in New York, 26 July 1982	320
The Investiture, 13 November 1986	336

List of maps

The Fortress	14
The Volta River Project	170
The Mekong River Basin	198
Bangladesh: Main railway supply routes	246
Zambia isolated	280
Kampuchea	302

Abbreviations

ACC	Administrative Committee on Coordination (of UN)	SDDG	Senior Deputy Director-General (of UNRRA)
ASG	Assistant Secretary-General (of UN)	SITREP	Situation Report
		UN	United Nations
CIA	Central Intelligence Agency	UNAC	UN Appeal for Children
CID	Committee of Imperial Defence	UNBRO	UN Border Relief Operation
DDG	Deputy Director-General (of UNRRA)	UNCTAD	UN Conference on Trade and Development
DP	Displaced person	UNDP	UN Development Programme
DSIR	Department of Industrial Research	UNEPRO	UN East Pakistan Relief Operation
ECOSOC	Economic and Social Council (of UN)	UNESCO	UN Educational, Scientific and Cultural Organisation
EPTA	Expanded Programme of Technical Assistance	UNHCR	UN High Commission for Refugees
ERP	European Recovery Plan	UNICEF	UN International Children's Emergency Fund
FAO	Food and Agriculture Organisation	UNIDO	UN Industrial Development Organisation
HMG	His/Her Majesty's Government		
IACB	Inter-Agency Consultative Board	UNROB	UN Special Relief Office, Bangladesh
IBRD	International Bank for Reconstruction and Development, also known as The World Bank.	UNROD	UN Relief Operation in Dacca
		UNRRA	UN Relief and Rehabilitation Administration
		UNZAP	UN Zambia Aid Programme
ICRC	International Committee of the Red Cross	VALCO	Volta Aluminium Company
		WFP	World Food Programme
ILO	International Labour Office	WHEB	Who Else But?
IPF	Indicative Planning Figure	WHO	World Health Organisation
MESC	Middle East Supply Centre		

A personal preface

I FIRST MET JACKO in January 1969 when he and Joan Anstee were working on the Capacity Study. Mary, my wife, had known Joan from their days at Newnham College, Cambridge, where they had struck up an immediate and lasting friendship. They had adjoining rooms and were both reading French and Spanish; before long Mary was *Maria*, and Joan *Juanita*.

Jacko had invited the three of us to dinner in London, not at *The Garden*, a frequent haunt of ours in a Covent Garden basement when I was working on the music staff of the Royal Opera House, but, by mistake, at *The Royal Garden*, a hotel with a large airy restaurant high up above the trees, with views over half London. This turned out to be a far more appropriate venue for our first encounter with the great man, accustomed to dealing with prime ministers and presidents, definitely a VIP in our book. He was a commanding figure: very tall and slim, with wavy auburn hair and smiling blue eyes, impeccably dressed and extremely courteous, with just a trace of an Australian accent. Not that he was on his dignity; the ice, if there was any, was soon broken, but it was an occasion when we were all on our best behaviour.

That Easter Joan invited us to stay at the little house she had taken at Trélex, near Geneva, where Jacko and his team were based. He came for the week-end too, and that was when we really got to know him; 'we clicked' as he would say, and soon he too was calling Mary *Maria*, which she will remain throughout this book.

His UN work involved a great deal of travelling and he, like Joan, would often stay with us in Petersham, near Richmond and not far from Heathrow airport. He was a most considerate guest, bringing his own supply of Remy Martin, his regular tipple (he didn't drink whisky), and leaving a bottle of 'medicine' (Veuve Clicquot) in the fridge when he left. He often took us out to meals. He brought chocolates for our children, and when they were small he would make up stories for them about Crispin, the crocodile on his shirt. He soon became a much-loved friend. If he arrived when we were out he knew where to find the front door key, and whenever he had to leave very early in the morning he crept out of the house so quietly that we never heard. He was often under great pressure of work, and I think he found our home a haven, where he could unwind and relax, free from tensions of every kind. He didn't talk much about his work and we didn't ask him. Occasionally he had to go into action and there was one day when we nearly came to blows to get at the phone, he to find a thousand tons of rice for Bangladesh, and I to find a replacement soprano for the next night's performance!

Of an evening he often talked about his childhood and his early years in the Navy, especially his time in Malta during the war; the fact that in those days he was unhappily married was something he never revealed, though he often said that he had made a mess of his personal life and spoke of his first love, Relda, the woman in New Zealand 'whom he should have married'.

Being Australian he often gave people nick-names. Maria acquired hers when the four of us were on a journey over the Atlas Mountains in 1971, a great holiday for us, but hard work for Joan who had just taken up her post as Resident Representative of UNDP in Morocco. The night we stayed at Zagora there was a muddle over our hotel bills which not only defeated my attempt to pay for the dinner, but charged Jacko 48 dirhams for Maria's bed! From that day she was known as *48 Dirhams* – *Dirhams* for short.

Later that year when he invited us all out to dinner in a London hotel, I was determined to pay, so I squared the head-waiter in advance. Jacko's discomfiture when he asked for the bill was all the greater for his having suggested a second bottle of champagne, and I became *Double-Crosser*, sometimes with two stars, sometimes four! As I later discovered, being double-crossed was for Jacko a serious business, and I found myself in the company of two UN Secretaries-General, but unlike them soon forgiven.

Jacko was often urged to write his memoirs and always refused, saying no-one would be interested. Nevertheless he left all his papers in good order; his 'faithful secretary Sheila' who was with him through MESC, UNRRA and LAKE SUCCESS, had filed the carbon copies of his letters meticulously, even labelling one of the boxes 'Boswell'. The story that he always wanted to tell, but never did (except to a few of his friends, who heard it more than once!) was that of his time in Malta at the start of World War II. Fortunately he left two accounts of it, for these, it seems, are virtually the only record of the part he played in bringing about the survival of 'The Fortress'.

After he died Joan Anstee – now Dame Margaret – who was his professional and personal partner for over twenty years, and Robert, his son, asked me to write his biography, putting all his papers at my disposal. I am most grateful to them for their advice, encouragement and, above all, patience. My thanks to the many others who have helped me are recorded at the end of the book.

I have told much of the story in Jacko's own words; I hope that in so doing I have not earned any more stars.

JG 2006

Prologue

KOFI ANNAN was unveiling Jackson's portrait during his first visit to the *Palais des Nations* as UN Secretary-General in January 1997. It was one of those times when the UN was in crisis and calls for reform were in the air, as they still are.

'Jacko', he cried, 'where are you now when we need you?'

Kofi Annan unveiling the portrait of Robert Jackson by Judy Cassab, 29 January 1997

Two years previously, when the UN was celebrating its fiftieth anniversary, Brian Urquhart, the doyen of the secretariat, calling to mind some of the UN's distinguished servants, had asked: 'Who remembers Robert Jackson, the greatest of humanitarian relief operators?'[1] We must not leave it entirely to Kofi Annan.

Wilbur Kenneth, aged six months, in his christening robe.

Part One – One Success Too Many

1 Wilbur

WILBUR? YES – WILBUR. The man we knew as RGA Jackson was given the names Wilbur Kenneth, after his godfather, the American doctor, WK Bouton, who had assisted at his delivery and was a friend of his mother.

Both his parents had been brought to Australia as children. Archibald, born in Scotland in 1858 was only two at the time. He had very little education, was apprenticed as a blacksmith/engineer to a firm of boiler-makers in Melbourne and worked for the Victoria Railway workshops. With ideas of becoming a journalist he engaged a tutor and travelled widely, staying for several months in the Holy Land. On his return he resumed his career as an engineer, became an active member of the Presbyterian Church and keen supporter of its Sunday School. He later became a director of several companies and finally chairman of the board of The Mutual Store, one of Melbourne's biggest general stores. A shrewd businessman with a social conscience, he maintained his connection with the church as a lay reader and elder.

Kathleen Williams, his second wife, was born in 1872, one of twelve children of an Anglo-Irish family who came to Australia in about 1880. She worked in the Homœopathic Hospital in Melbourne for eight years, becoming head nurse in the male surgical ward, where she was 'valued and liked for her thoughtful and gentle treatment of her patients'.[1]

She and Archibald were married by his elder brother James on 21 November 1900 at the Presbyterian Church in Hawksburn, a suburb of Melbourne comprising small terrace houses and workmen's cottages alongside a railway line, now part of South Yarra. Trains still stop at Hawksburn station.

After their first child, Alan, was born in 1901 Kathleen devoted herself to her family and to charities, especially the Red Cross. Like Archibald she was a devout church-goer, but with liturgical tastes higher than his preferred to worship at the Anglican Church. On 8 November 1911 they had a second son; though they christened him Wilbur Kenneth they always called him Rob.

In 1914 they moved to Cheltenham, a small town about 20 miles down the eastern side of Port Phillip Bay, where the houses mostly stood in their own grounds. STOKEAVELY was situated near the top of a gentle hill a mile and a half along Park Road, then little more than a track. It was a substantial single-storey house with spacious well-furnished rooms. Archibald made a huge vegetable garden, kept horses and drove to the city in a pony and trap. It was the establishment of a reasonably prosperous man. The house still stands, and beside it a splendid silky-oak tree (*grevillea robusta*), planted by young Rob. Archibald later built another house, YARALLA, on part of the ground and sold STOKEAVELY.

Also in the household was Beryl, not a Jackson, but a relative of Archibald's by his first marriage, born in 1909 and orphaned shortly afterwards. The three children got on well enough, and Rob never missed a chance to tease her.

He once threw a hammer through the dining room window with much damning and blasting when his mother was entertaining the vicar to lunch. His father, after beating him, would always give him an orange.

Rob attended Cheltenham State School from 1918 to 1920 – a fact he was reluctant to admit, claiming later that he was educated privately between 1919 and 1924.[2] He missed school for the whole of 1921 due to illness, and had to spend several months in the dark. Whatever the illness was, no permanent damage was done to his sight, though this did not prevent him claiming later that 'he was blind for quite a part of his younger years'.[3] As we shall see, he was not so much 'economical with the truth' as over-generous with it.

As more people moved into the area a new Anglican grammar school for boys opened in nearby Mentone in 1920. It was a modest establishment funded by private subscription, with only 29 pupils in its first year. Rob went there in February 1922. The head-master, Mr JA Ball, was a good athlete and popular with the boys. They did well in inter-school sports, and he liked to celebrate their successes by giving half-holidays – on days which had a way of coinciding with the Mentone Races. He was not a good administrator and by the end of 1922 the school was in financial difficulties and its future uncertain. During the Christmas holidays a group of dissatisfied parents including Archibald drew up proposals for a new school, and it was decided at a public meeting (by 27 votes to 14) to set up a reconstituted Mentone Grammar School.

The headmaster withdrew and the school council, of which Archibald was a member and later president, quickly got the man they wanted: H.L. Tonkin, aged 39, a schoolmaster for 17 years with an excellent reputation. Having previously taught at Melbourne Grammar School he did what he could to emulate its style of education in the hope of getting better academic results; he had a hard struggle, and in most years fewer than half the pupils got their intermediate certificates. Even the sports results were poor at first. There were rarely more than 100 pupils and never more than four in the top class; in Rob's final year there were only two, working at the billiard table at the end of the dining hall.

Tonkin's ability and enthusiasm brought out the best from his abler pupils, of whom Rob was one, finishing up as School Captain and Dux (a Scottish word meaning top scholar) and distinguishing himself at cricket and tennis.[4]

Beryl, Alan, Kathleen, Archibald and Rob at YARALLA, 1927.

Putting pen to paper came easily to him and he wrote pieces for the school magazine, The Mentonian. When the British Empire was renamed the British Commonwealth of Nations in May 1928 (in the days when Empire Day was celebrated as a public holiday) he wrote:

> The British Empire was not made in a decade, but in centuries, and with many long wars which cost England dear. Until 1914 no test had been made of the vows of alliance of the self-governing colonies, but when the clarion trumpet of war sounded, England felt her need and called for help. ...
>
> In 1914 many thousands ... answered the call – from every British Dominion and Colony they came, and proved the Empire's worth when 'They lived and died for England, and gladly went their way.'
>
> Now in peace, we reap the benefits of the 'Brotherhood of the Empire'. ... The new title is admirable in all respects and though the words 'British Empire'

have associations dear to many, one must not fail to remember that many changes have occurred, and that some of the colonies that were dependent on Great Britain twenty years ago are today self-governing dominions.

Not bad for a boy of 16. His final piece was entitled 'The Ideal Captain':

The ideal captain has yet to appear... He should be tactful, self-reliant, resourceful, and be able to keep his temper under perfect control, no matter what circumstances may arise. ... The ideal captain, however, must, as well as possessing the above-mentioned qualities, be prepared to sacrifice himself for the benefit of the school, and be firmly resolved to 'play the game'. WKJ (Capt.1928).

It was an ideal he lived up to; it also brings to mind a nickname he acquired much later in life – WHEB – 'Who Else But?'!

At the end of his final term he passed his leaving examination with distinctions in all five subjects. He had expected to go to Melbourne University, but because of Archibald's death and the Wall Street crash there was not enough money. Alan's career also suffered a setback; having hoped to become a doctor he had to be content with running a pharmaceutical business.

Rob's cousin, James Dunlop Jackson, was a Paymaster-Commander in the Royal Australian Navy. A son of the Reverend James, he was considerably older than Rob, and had joined the RAN in 1911. He suggested that Rob should take the examination for special entry into the Navy as a Paymaster-Cadet (without having to go through the Naval College at Jervis Bay.) He took the exam in early 1929 and won his cadetship against the competition of 120 others.

'What an honour to be chosen from so many!' wrote Tonkin to Kathleen. 'How proud his father would have been! It really is a great achievement and Bob has a position that is lucrative and of a high social order. I am very pleased.'[5]

Praise from his father would have meant much to him at that stage. As a dutiful son Rob had loved his father, but stood in awe of him and feared his displeasure. Archibald was a great ox of a man, a muscular Christian who attached much importance to physical fitness and expected the boys to emulate his example of the good Christian life and service to others. Although popular with the boys at Mentone, he must have been rather alarming as a father.

It was very unfortunate that Rob could not go to University, and for that matter that he had not been sent to Melbourne Grammar School. Archibald evidently did not realise that his son's abilities at the age of ten were special enough to justify such a step, particularly when there was a promising new school at hand which he had helped to found. He took pride in Rob's talents as a star pupil in 'his school'. While Mentone (and particularly Tonkin) undoubtedly did much for Rob, Melbourne would have done even more.

His misfortune was to be a big fish in such a very tiny pool, where success came to him so easily. At Melbourne Grammar School he would not have been the only bright boy in the class, and a few corners might have been knocked off. At Melbourne University he would have encountered other first class minds and learnt to respect other opinions, and to write essays with fewer words; more importantly, he would have had time to find himself, to become a more rounded young man and to gain the inner confidence which he still lacked. If he went out into the world with a slightly inflated sense of superiority and self-importance, the fault was hardly his; as it was he was over-anxious to impress his superiors. This would show itself in the Navy, where his senior officers positively encouraged him to make sure he was noticed, and also much later in his life, when he would strive to impress people he was meeting for the first time by dropping names, as if to prove that even if he hadn't been to a university he was as good as they were.

When Rob was born his father was 53 and his mother 39. Her devotion to her family was by now beginning to wear thin and she and Archibald tended to go their separate ways. Whenever they were both away at the same time Rob would be dumped on one of her sisters. He was Kathleen's favourite, but she could be difficult and demanding, so while his boyhood could not be called unhappy, neither was it particularly happy. He was very fond of his brother Alan, 10 years his senior, to whom he looked for help and advice. Alan for his part did not mind taking charge of 'the young 'un', even to the extent of beating him when he caught him smoking a cigar. When Rob won his cadetship Alan, himself a good boxer, arranged for him to have coaching before joining the navy.

Rob often discussed religion with his school-friend John Crotty, whose father was an Anglican Canon, very high church and a close friend of Kathleen's. (Crotty later became a Roman Catholic and finally a Benedictine monk.) Given his background and the different theological tastes of Rob's parents one can imagine the two boys having earnest conversations about God.

HMAS *Australia*, July 1930

2 All at sea

ON 1 MAY 1929 PAYMASTER-CADET W K JACKSON RAN arrived in Sydney by the night train to report for duty on HMAS *Australia*, the flagship of the Australian Naval Squadron. Her Captain and Commander of the Squadron was Rear-Admiral ERGR Evans CB, DSO, RN and British. (He had been with Scott on his second Antarctic expedition.)

Wilbur was put to work in the Admiral's office to learn about paymastering – the duties of the Ship's Officer and the General Accountant Officer. Like the other cadets from naval college he took part in the general training activities of the ship's company such as drill and rowing, but apart from that most of his time at sea would be spent in the Admiral's Office.

On his second day he was invited to lunch with the Admiral and the Flag Captain, WS Chalmers, DSC, also RN. The dessert was a chocolate soufflé, and he was served first. 'I took a spoonful and it was liquid metal. I can remember the tears coming down my eyes and I felt my mouth burning, but I held on to the bloody stuff. Chalmers took one mouthful and spat it out on the table. 'You poon, boy, you bloody poon, boy!' I'd never heard the word before. I couldn't speak for three days.' Apparently he could take it, so Evans and Chalmers gave him a good mark.[1]

On 26 May *Australia* left harbour in wet stormy weather. He didn't much enjoy the first few hours; then he felt fine. After they reached Hervey Bay, in Queensland, he wrote to his old school:

> The skies here are things of wondrous beauty, especially at sunset – deep tones of blue, purple, orange, crimson, silver, together with wonderful clouds, all united in a glorious confusion of colour. The moon is a big red fellow, and looks very jolly as he climbs over the thickly wooded hills. This bay is a little larger than Port Phillip, and affords splendid fishing. Yesterday I caught 24 large silver bream, which were much appreciated by the officers.

The band plays every morning when the flag is hoisted and the tune is that of our old school song – quite a bit of home.²

The flagship had an annual routine, cruising and exercising along the eastern and southern shores of Australia, making occasional visits to New Guinea and other islands in the Pacific; February and March were regularly spent around Tasmania with short spells in harbour at Hobart, much to the delight of the local debs and the young officers. In June and July she returned to Sydney.

Midshipman

In May 1931 Jackson, now Paymaster-Midshipman, was posted to the new flagship, HMAS *Canberra*, sister ship to *Australia*. Chalmers wrote in his report

A young officer of great promise. Intensely enthusiastic and keen but of excitable temperament which he will probably overcome later. Did very well on the upper deck and in boats. Recommended for promotion in the ordinary course.³

He was promoted to Sub-Lieutenant in May 1932 and Lieutenant in November 1933.

The Commander of the Squadron was now Rear-Admiral R C Dalglish, CB, RN, (but Australian). 'He gave me two of the best bits of advice that anyone could ever have; he was an enormous man, very heavily built but light on his feet – he won a gold medal for fencing at the Olympics in his forties. He had an enormous voice and said 'Boy, boy, never be out of the flagship, always let the Admiral see you'. His other advice was probably Talleyrand all over again ['*Surtout, messieurs, point de zèle*'], but it was Talleyrand in a much more sophisticated form: 'Boy, boy, never forget there is a world of difference between scratching your bottom and tearing chunks of flesh off your arse.' That was probably as good advice as anyone ever gave me.'⁴

Three others serving on *Canberra* were his cousin, James Dunlop Jackson, who as Secretary to the Admiral could keep an eye on the youngster, Eric Creal with whom he had worked in *Australia* and Victor Smith, a year his junior, who remembered him as 'a first class organiser with a very good brain and keen on physical fitness, often to be seen running round the quarter deck when he had a spare half hour. He was intolerant at times and did not suffer fools gladly. He generally got on well with his shipmates, but could be condescending; he had a slight chip on his shoulder – probably because he was a pay-bob'.[5] There were two chaplains on the *Canberra* and he sometimes thought about becoming a Roman Catholic.

In April 1934 Dalglish was succeeded by Rear-Admiral Ford RN. Wilbraham Randall Tennyson Ford was English, a grand-nephew of the poet, and another heavyweight; he had boxed and played rugby for the Navy. 'He had only two interests in life – tennis and bridge. He virtually exhausted me (and I played good tennis) because wherever it was, it was tennis, tennis, tennis, and I was his doubles partner. And he played bridge every night; it was all right for him, he could lie in in the morning, but I was up at six doing rifle drill. After Ford I never played bridge again.'[6]

Paymaster-Lieutenant

He continued to get good reports, but his marks for power of command and judgement – 6 or 7 out of 10 – were never as high as those for professional ability, zeal and energy, reliability and initiative, for which he got 8 or 9. He was recommended for accelerated promotion and specialisation in a secretarial capacity. 'Very much to my satisfaction' wrote Ford; 'a slight tendency to rate his own abilities so high as to convey an attitude of superiority does not affect his loyalty or tact'.[7] If some of his shipmates were less enthusiastic about the Admiral's blue-eyed boy, who enhanced his image by adopting the habit of wearing a handkerchief in his sleeve in the manner of his English superiors, that would not have worried him!

If his seven years at sea can be reckoned highly promising, the same cannot be said of his brief periods of shore-leave, which would lead to thirteen years of unhappiness. In February 1932 he met Peggy Dick in Hobart. She came from a well-respected family and was fresh from a finishing school in Switzerland. She was very popular locally, not a great beauty, but vivacious and pretty; not sophisticated or intellectual, but 'a good sort', who enjoyed life to the full. Victor Smith remembered her as 'a wonderful girl'.

Her father, a successful grazier, had died young, and her mother, to help pay for her and her younger brother's education, wrote short stories and serials for the papers; she was quite a celebrity in Hobart. She lived in Sandy Bay and kept open house for young officers.

Wilbur went there regularly and spent more time discussing religion with Mrs Dick, who was then a Christian Scientist, than with Peggy. He liked Peggy well enough, but he was by no means smitten. When he went back to sea it was her mother who wrote to him frequently.

In March 1933 she told him that Peggy was in love with him and he was breaking her heart. After their next dance, assuming that it was expected of him, he kissed her. From then on he confused friendship and affection with love.

Mrs Dick's stream of letters continued, about faith and how he could help her, and about him and Peggy. Their meetings and the talks went on, and the three of them were often joined by his shipmate Eric Creal. Mrs Dick's influence became increasingly dominant and she began to think of Wilbur as her other son.

In June 1936 she demanded that his engagement to Peggy be announced. This worried him, for he saw Peggy as a good friend, and knew he was not in love with her, but the announcement was made and he went back to sea.

A year later in Sydney there was 'a great explosion one night' when he made his feelings clear to Mrs Dick that he was not in love with Peggy. She replied that having gone so far, if he did not marry her he would wreck Peggy's life and her own, furthermore he would be letting down the navy and its tradition of service. For those two reasons, especially the latter, he decided to go through with it. He saw it as 'an act of service'.

It seems astonishing that he had not turned to his brother for advice, but he may have had a reason. Back in 1931 Alan had written him a letter on the subject of girl friends which he had found 'hurtful and offensive. It was unjust, unfair and probably inspired by their mother'; perhaps this was the one subject which he would not discuss with his brother. Eleven years later he had to raise it when he needed Alan's help to divorce Peggy so that he could marry Barbara Ward. On 3 December 1946 he wrote him a long letter giving the whole story, on which the account given above is based.[8]

Dr Bouton, his rich American godfather, had promised to leave money to both the Jackson boys in his will. When it transpired that he had not done so his namesake decided to have done with Wilbur Kenneth and to take names with military associations from his mother's family. On 14 July 1937 he changed them by deed poll to Robert Gillman Allen. (Kathleen's mother, Minerva, was an Allen, descended from a commander in Cromwell's army; Minerva's sister had married Major-General Sir Webb Gillman DSO CB, who had distinguished himself in South Africa in the early 1900s and later in the Great War.) The following day he went back to sea for three months and wrote reassuring letters to Peggy.

She next met Rob, as she was now to call him, two days before the wedding. He had spent two nights in Melbourne with his brother, who was still unaware of his unhappy situation, and took his mother to Hobart on Saturday 16 October 1937.

It was the time of the agricultural show and the hotels had kept their best rooms for regular visitors. The only room Peggy had been able to secure for Mrs Jackson was not up to the standard she expected. When she exploded in an Irish rage he directed the full force of her anger and his own at the unfortunate Peggy. She was so hurt that she told her mother that she didn't know if she wanted to go on with the wedding, but for Mrs Dick to call it off at that stage must have been unthinkable.

The next day, Sunday 18 October, the bridegroom gave a luncheon party for the three bridesmaids and his own three attendants, who included his best man, Eric Creal. In the afternoon he wrote to his mother:

> My dearest Kathleen, In about three hours time I shall be marrying Peg. ... I hope that I shall do you credit as your son ... With my marriage there must be no change towards you ... you know that ... I remain your son always. And for you

may God give his Peace, His understanding, and all things which go to make our life so wonderful. And always there will be the true love and gratitude of your son – Robert.

Peggy and Robert

That evening they were married in St David's Cathedral. The service ended with the hymn 'O perfect Love, all human thoughts transcending …'

He knew he had made a terrible mistake. Peggy did not. The thought of a honeymoon alone with a wife with whom he was not in love was too much, so he invited Eric Creal to join them.

Afterwards they rented a flat in Sydney close to the harbour where the flagship, HMAS *Sydney*, was in dock. He worked office hours from eight o'clock until four and attended Communion regularly at the Cathedral. When the Squadron left harbour in February 1938 he remained ashore; Admiral Ford had been appointed to take command of the naval dockyard in Malta and wanted to have Jackson on his staff; Jackson agreed and in May he and Peggy sailed to Naples. From Capri he wrote to his mother:

> 28 May. We came over here this morning for the week-end – we return to Naples on Monday, and then catch a ferry to Malta on Tuesday – it arrives on Thursday. And then work begins!!

Back in September 1933 the Flagship had called at Lyttleton, the port for Christchurch, New Zealand, where he met Relda, a beautiful girl of 19. In March 1935 they met again, but when his ship called there in April 1937 she was abroad. Had she been at home how different all their lives might have been. He always said that Relda was the woman he should have married; she felt the same about him. They remained in touch for the rest of his life, and from time to time he saw her in New Zealand and Australia. Maria and I met her in 1993; then in her eighties she was still a very good-looking woman. In her youth she must have been stunning.

The Fortress

3 The man who saved Malta

JACKSON REPORTED FOR DUTY on board HMS St Angelo – Fort St Angelo, the dockyard headquarters, to be precise, but like all naval shore establishments deemed to be a ship – which the Germans later claimed to have sunk! His intended post – Secretary to the Chief Staff Officer, Captain Durnford – was already filled, so he was assigned to other duties, including tennis with Admiral Ford. At least this gave him and Peggy a chance to settle into their new home, Villa Sunshine, a two storey house in Tax Biex, a village overlooking Marsamxett Harbour.

He bought a car to get to work and promptly collided with a bus; while the car was being repaired they lived quietly, planning the garden and enjoying the antics of Roger, their Maltese kitten, as he skidded around on the marble floors. They had a gem of a maid – Nina – who came every day and cooked for them.

The political situation in Europe was getting steadily worse: Hitler had already annexed Austria, and on 29 September Chamberlain signed the Munich pact. About then the Secretary to the Chief Staff Officer went on leave and Jackson took over temporarily, or so he thought.[1] He was asked to re-write the 'Malta Command Defence Scheme'. At that time it was the view of the Committee of Imperial Defence (CID), in effect that of the British Government, that Malta, for all its importance as a naval base, could not be defended against attack from the air.

How he did this was the story he liked to tell, and many years later, probably during a flight in 1987, he put it on paper, straight off the cuff on two SWISSAIR notepads, without making any corrections. For all its racy style this is an important document. The occasional inaccuracy is hardly surprising, since it was written 50 years after the events described:

> Late October 1938: Munich – and a great crisis. What of the Malta Command Defence Scheme? Couldn't be found!!! Said to be in six or seven Parts.

Part I, Introduction. When discovered, simply a general description of what might be done. Useless.

Part II. Army. Said to be in London with the Governor and Commander-in-Chief.

Part III. Navy. Said to be with Admiral Sir Dudley Pound, Commander-in-Chief of the Mediterranean Fleet, then on a shooting holiday in Greece.

Part IV. Air Force. Never found, but irrelevant since there were no aircraft in the fortress.

Part V. Passive Defence, i.e. protection of the civil population from air raids. Also irrelevant — there were no facilities.

Part VI. Internal Security Measures against subversion within the fortress. Superficial.

During the crisis — late October and first half of November 1938 — key staff officers from the Navy, Army, Air Force and Government of Malta are called together by Captain Durnford. I act as rapporteur. Every thing we might do to defend the fortress from our own resources within the fortress was recorded. (The Mediterranean Fleet has withdrawn [to Alexandria].) I rewrite a Malta Command Defence Scheme based on actualities in 88 hours — longest virtually non-stop effort ever made in my life.

Mid-Nov 1938. With Captain Durnford's approval I met almost continuously with anyone who might have ideas on how the fortress could be defended — the three Services, the staff of the Naval Dockyard (invaluable) and the civil government. I became convinced Malta could be defended — if the Royal Navy could keep it supplied.

First reason? One of the earliest of Robert Watson-Watt's radio-location sets had come to us [and] we could discern Italian aircraft flying in and out of Catania and Syracuse [in Sicily]. This meant that if the RAF had good fighters (reports of the development of the Spitfires and Hurricanes were available to us) then they would have sufficient time to get satisfactory operational altitudes (as well as providing short range cover for the fleet).

(That is not quite correct: the site for the radar had been chosen, but the set — the first outside Britain — was not installed until March 1939 when it did make it possible to detect aircraft taking off from Sicily.[2])

Second reason? Malta was made of limestone, very easily worked. This of itself represented some defence against bombing, and incendiaries would have very little effect.

Basic strategy? The civilian population must be protected and provided with essentials. Without their co-operation and support (for the Dockyard and support services to the Army and RAF in particular) no defence would be possible.

Start with protection and basic food – bread and water. Put them underground whenever necessary – build tunnels in deliberate stages – first so they could stand / then sit / then lie down / then sleep / marry / have babies / die natural deaths.

(And so it happened, 23 miles altogether at the end).

Seven great underground oil storage tanks were already being excavated, each with 10,000 tons capacity – each like a cathedral, about 300' long, 90' high, 70' span. Fresh water was available if it could be pumped. Therefore, build an underground generating station, run it on oil, and lay a strategic power circuit around the entire fortress so power could flow either way if bombing cut a particular point. Put pumps for the water underground.

Two thousand years before, the Romans had stored grain in large FOSSES – excavations some 30 to 40 feet deep shaped like wine bottles, with very heavy circular stone covers on them. Store grain there. Put a flour-mill underground.

(It was not the Romans, but the Knights of St John who had used them during the Great Siege of 1565. Now known as 'The Granaries' they were used again during the siege of the 1940s.)

Result – IF the Navy could bring essential supplies we could protect the population and keep them alive on bread and water (plus, of course, their essential foods and medical supplies etc.)

Each Service and the Civil Government stated its basic needs. For the latter, it was clearly a matter of protecting the population. For the RAF it was more and improved airfields, fighter and reconnaissance aircraft when they became available, more radar and so on. The Army needed reinforcements, and, in particular anti-aircraft guns (preferably 3.7", the 4.5" were not well regarded).

Armoured vehicles and many other items of equipment were required, and the intelligence services would need to prepare effective and internal security plans, especially if Italy became a belligerent. Searchlights, facilities for illuminating the entrance to Grand Harbour etc were all on the list. For the Navy, the Dockyard and its facilities were of critical importance; facilities for submarines – not enough time to put them underground, but much could be done to give them overhead reinforced protection. Communications facilities must go underground, for Malta was a key link in the Admiralty's world-wide network. So too with medical facilities and supplies, wherever possible. Boom defences and many other facilities would either need to be modernised or provided.

After several days and nights of intense work an impressive programme of defence and rearmament was produced. There was general agreement that the best chance of the British Government giving serious consideration to this revolutionary change in policy would be for the RN to advance it, since in the final analysis, Malta was a naval base.

I therefore prepared a submission from Admiral Ford to Admiral Sir Dudley Pound and agreed it with the other two services and the Civil Government. One morning, about the middle of November, I took this fairly large document to Admiral Ford, Captain Durnford having given it his blessing, and placed it on his desk.

'What's this balls, boy?'

'Proposals to defend the fortress, Sir.'

'Where do I sign it?'

'Here, Sir.'

'Tennis at 1530.'

'Yes, Sir.'

He never read the paper, but he knew perfectly well what was in it. It was sent as quickly as possible to the C-in-C.

Ataturk dies. Admiral Pound attends his funeral. BBC announces soon afterwards that Admiral Pound has arrived in London. A few days later, Admiral Ford receives a signal from the Admiralty which read roughly:

'Your submission so-and-so to C. in C. Med. All proposals approved. Parliament has not voted any money for these works but proceed with all despatch and where necessary quote MED 107 as authority.'

Naturally the receipt of that signal remains one of the great moments of my life. From that moment onwards everyone worked flat out.[3]

The most remarkable feature of Jackson's paper was his perception that without the cooperation and support of the civilian population no defence would be possible. It was indeed a curious and paradoxical idea – that notwithstanding the need for military armaments and equipment it was the civilian population on which Malta's defence must ultimately depend – but it was correct. This was the first demonstration of Jackson's logistical skills which would be the hall-mark of so many of his later undertakings.

Searches in the National Archives in London (formerly the Public Record Office) failed to reveal the signal from the Admiralty, or for that matter any other papers relating to the Malta Command Defence Scheme of 1938, which are conspicuous by their absence. Jackson's own accounts of these events are therefore all the more important.

The signal 'proceed with all despatch' was an order from the Admiralty; it did not indicate any change of policy by the CID at that time and it is not even mentioned in the CID records. Nevertheless on the island that signal was the turning point – the moment when defence preparations were begun in earnest. Had they not started when they did perhaps Malta might not have survived the siege which was to come.

> After London had approved our rearmament proposals, I was given a free hand and a roving commission 'to get things done', and the title of 'Local Defence Officer' on the Naval Staff. Support from all the Senior Officers was wonderful, and all my colleagues in the Army and Air Force and Government could not have been more co-operative.
>
> So it was too in the Dockyard where there were many officials of outstanding ability. One in particular, Bill Bolton, who had won an MC in the first World War as a gunner, and who was Superintending Electrical Engineer, proposed that a Dockyard Defence Battery should be formed, using Bofors guns (when we could get them) and manned by dockyard workers. Admiral Ford doubted whether there would be any volunteers, but Bill and I persuaded him to put it to a vote. Of a staff of between 8500 and 9000 practically every man volunteered.[4]

By June the strain of working non-stop for nine months was beginning to tell; Durnford had been posted in March, his successor was not up to the job, and the responsibility was too much for one man. 'Everything in my life – home life, sport and hobbies – has been sacrificed to work. Whatever happens, I shall be content – the change in our defences in the last nine months is almost unbelievable.'[5]

It was not until July, seven weeks before the outbreak of World War II, that the CID squarely addressed the problem of Malta. At its root was a difference of opinion between the Navy, which had long recognised its importance as a naval base, and the other services, particularly the RAF, which considered that if war came in the Mediterranean the island could not be adequately defended.

The Joint Defence Sub-Committee, which advised the CID, was asked to review the scale of air defence in Malta with the object of deciding whether the repair and docking facilities of the base could be made adequately secure for the navy to use in time of war with Italy. When it met on 20 July it agreed that the existing approved scale of anti-aircraft defences would not be adequate to prevent the destruction of the dockyard. As to whether a suggested increased scale would be adequate, (112 AA guns as against 48, 60 light AA guns as against 16, four fighter squadrons as against one) it was unable to agree. The Admiralty pointed out that these measures would cost less than one battleship – and the use of Malta would be worth far more than that. The Air Ministry entirely agreed on the absolute necessity of securing the use of Malta for the Fleet – if this were reasonably possible – but in their view Malta could be rendered unusable whatever scale of defence was provided. Once again unable to put forward any agreed recommendations, the Sub-Committee referred the problem back to the CID.[6]

The CID considered it on 27 July. Admiral of the Fleet Lord Chatfield, who was also Minister for Coordination of Defence, took the chair. Sir Dudley Pound, now First Sea Lord and Chief of Naval Staff, explained the strategical considerations: the fleet could not at present operate from Malta, but Malta was far preferable to Alexandria for exerting pressure on Italian communications; he emphasised the importance of doing everything possible to enable Malta to be used by the fleet. The members of the CID then spoke in turn; they were overwhelmingly in favour of the increased scale of anti-aircraft defences. Only Air-Chief-Marshal Sir Cyril Newall (Chief of Air Staff) spoke against.[7]

The view of the Navy had finally prevailed, and Ford believed that Jackson's paper had been very largely responsible for this (see page 32 below). Even so, it would be a long time before these armaments and aircraft would arrive; a note from the

Admiralty dated 1 March 1940 stated that 'the ultimate provision of defences on this increased scale would depend on the priority which could be accorded from time to time to Malta. It was not at present possible to forecast a date by which they might be expected; but the question was being kept under constant review.'[8] In the meantime work on the island continued without ceasing.

It is impossible to overstate the importance of HMG's reversal of its earlier policy. In THE BATTLE FOR THE MEDITERRANEAN the historian Donald Macintyre wrote:

> The contest revolved largely round the ability of the British to build up and preserve the little island of Malta as an offensive base in the midst of waters otherwise dominated by enemy air and sea power. This involved, on the one hand, the supply and replenishment of the fortress; on the other, the efforts by the enemy to eliminate it. It led to the principal clashes by sea.
>
> On the outcome depended, absolutely, the success or failure of the campaign in North Africa and hence, it can be said, of the whole war.[9]

The Admiralty's order eight months previously – 'proceed with all dispatch' –may have jumped the gun, but that too was crucially important in getting work on the fortress started eight months earlier than otherwise.

Peggy, like most service wives, went to England in June, then she returned to Australia with her mother. He moved into a flat in Guardamangia, just outside the walls of Valletta, and wrote a will leaving everything to her, which he sent to his brother: 'Dear Bill' (he always called him Bill) 'Try and get in touch with Peg sometime – I don't expect that she'll be feeling too pleased with life at present. Pity we didn't have a longer and more normal time together ... she didn't have much fun.'[10]

It is difficult to be sure what his real feelings towards Peggy were at that time. Perhaps he didn't even know himself. Although he laid the blame for the breakdown of his marriage on the pressure of work, he would say later that he had welcomed the work as an escape. She had no reason to think that their parting was anything more than an interruption to their marriage and looked forward to the time when they would be together again.

Bess Manisty arrived in Malta at the beginning of August, sent by the Foreign Office to work in the Defence Security Office. She was in her mid-twenties, gentle and unassuming, and very good at her job. She spoke several languages, was a rapid and skilled stenographer, could encipher and decipher messages, and was utterly discreet. If anything especially intricate or secret had to be done, she usually did it.[11] She lived in a small house in the centre of Valletta, and Nina sometimes saw Jackson setting off to visit her. Bess enjoyed the tranquility of those early days:

> One was particularly fortunate to be in such a place at such a time. War was declared within five weeks of my arrival – for a little while the shadow of fear fell on the Island; most people were nervous and on edge. But during the months of the 'phoney war' that followed, and until the reports of Dunkirk broke the spell, danger seemed to recede and life to return to normal. When spring came there were walks along the cliffs, there was sunbathing on rocky shelves above water translucently blue; there was tennis, dancing, sailing, moonlight picnics. That was a rich, halcyon time in spite of the background of war.[12]

At that time Hitler was not interested in this small island in the Mediterranean. The passive defence preparations were able to continue without interruption and merchant traffic in the Mediterranean remained normal. By the end of May 1940 over 600 ships, large and small, had brought supplies to the island. Sufficient reserves of food, fuel and other essential commodities were built up to last for at least six months. The harbour was not yet ready to be used as a naval base, and work to provide naval facilities in and around Alexandria was still continuing.

> 26 April 1940: Kathleen darling, Just a scrawled note – in the midst of my usual flap. Work still going on at the same wild rush. Now it has been like this for two years: it has become the most important thing in my life and unfortunate for my marriage. However war is war and nothing else matters. ...
>
> I have been working until 2, 3 and 5 in the morning. Give my love to Alan. Explain to him. People don't know the pace at which we're going these days. As long as it contributes to our victory nothing matters. God bless you, Kathleen – what ever my faults I have loved you. Your tired and rather sad son, Rob.

According to Bess it would be wrong to think that he never stopped work; he could switch off and relax completely for an afternoon or even for an hour. He was good company and much sought after.[13]

On 28 April a new Governor and Commander-in-Chief was appointed: Lieutenant-General Sir William Dobbie.

> He was a man of extraordinarily strong Christian belief, and of great physical stature – about six feet four in height and built proportionately. There can be no possible doubt of his extraordinary contribution to the defence of Malta, and of the effect of his profound faith that undoubtedly the Almighty and the Trinity were always on the side of the good.[14]

By then the war in France was going badly: the Germans were advancing in the north and Italian troops were massing against the border in the south. The British Government briefly considered offering Italy concessions – handing over Malta was one – if she would keep out of the war, but Churchill was now Prime Minister and would have none of it. On 28 May the British evacuation at Dunkirk began; on 11 June Italy declared war, and on 24 June France surrendered. The situation in the Mediterranean was transformed.

> As soon as Italy entered the war General Dobbie and the three Service Chiefs set up a Chief Staff Officers' Committee – together with Sir Edward Jackson [the Lieutenant Governor] and his Senior Assistant [Andrew Cohen]. I was made Secretary of that Committee, and early on suggested that the defence of Malta should always be compared to a four-legged stool and that it could never stand up unless all four legs were on the ground at the same time. I wanted to do everything possible to keep the three Services constantly aware of the fact that in the first and last analysis, our defence depended on the civil population. This concept appealed especially to General Dobbie and Sir Edward who repeated it in public again and again. We always had the people of Malta and Gozo with us.[15]

The people of Malta and Gozo, faced in 1802 with the prospect of the islands being restored to the Order of the Knights of St John, decided that they would prefer to be governed by Britain, and under the Treaty of Paris in 1814 Malta became a British dependency. Whether or not Britain recognised during the years preceding World War II that she had a duty to defend Malta (probably not) there is no doubt that the loyalty of the Maltese people, the fourth leg of the stool, was to prove indispensable when the war came.

By the end of May merchant traffic in the Mediterranean had virtually ceased and no supplies reached the island for four months. During that time the reserves previously established proved more than sufficient, but thereafter it would become increasingly difficult to keep the island supplied.

At the end of August the first convoy to Malta, three merchantmen with a close escort of four destroyers forming part of OPERATION HATS, sailed from Alexandria. It was heavily attacked by the Italian Air Force and one of the merchantmen, SS *Cornwall*, was severely damaged, but her heroic crew got her into Grand Harbour, listing heavily, just two hours after the other two. During the last four months of 1940 five convoys got through with little loss.

A new authority was created to co-ordinate supplies: known as COSUP, its task would be to establish all needs on the island, both civil and military, and to combine supplies whenever possible. Jackson was put in charge of COSUP in August and promoted to the rank of Acting Paymaster-Lieutenant-Commander with the temporary rank of Commander. His time was divided between the services and the Government; he had one office in the combined Navy and Army Headquarters in Lascaris Barracks overlooking Grand Harbour, and another with General Dobbie in his headquarters in the Palace in Valletta.

> The naval convoys carrying the vital supplies generally came from Alexandria, escorted by the Mediterranean Fleet under the command of Admiral Cunningham, but sometimes additional ships came from Gibraltar, escorted by Force H under the command of Admiral Somerville. Those convoys and those going north to Russia became the greatest operational convoys of the war. This does not underrate the vital importance of the Atlantic convoys, but those in the Mediterranean and those bound for Russia were specific naval operations involving fleets every time a convoy took place. ...
>
> I was able to merge into one single supply line all the essential military and civilian requirements of a common nature such as steel, cement, wheat, lubricating oil and things like that. You also had the specialist requirements of the services and of the civil population. Thus when you arranged the convoys, usually composed of four to ten ships, the cargo in each ship was split up into equal proportions of the essential imports. Thus if one ship was lost then you lost only one quarter, or one tenth, of that particular item. Before the Italians came into the war imports into Malta were about 400,000 tons a month; within three months of Italy's entry, we had reduced that figure to about 40,000 tons.

I would fly to England or to Alexandria to inspect the cargoes before the operations started, and when the convoy arrived in Malta I was there to receive it. In Alexandria we were very lucky in having a most capable Canadian, Colonel E C Barron, in charge of arranging the cargoes. He was the Chairman of Egyptian Bonded Warehouses and we could lay out in his warehouses, allocating one warehouse to each ship, the precise proportion of the essential requirements that each ship would carry. The authorities in London soon developed a similar arrangement at a railway depot at Didcot. There they laid out the cargoes in fields under covered tarpaulins, and subsequently loaded them in separate trains which then proceeded to the appropriate port for loading into the ships.[16]

On 11 November planes from *Illustrious* devastated the Italian fleet in Taranto harbour, putting out of action three battleships, two cruisers and two fleet auxiliaries. By mid-December General Wavell's Army of the Nile had the Italians on the run in North Africa. Things were looking good, and when Admiral Cunningham, flying his flag in *Warspite*, visited Malta a few days before Christmas he was given a rapturous reception: 'I went all over the dockyard next morning with the Vice-Admiral and was mobbed by crowds of excited workmen singing 'God Save the King' and 'Rule Britannia' ... It was a very moving experience, and once again I realised what a great acquisition we had in Sir Wilbraham Ford.'[17]

The mood of optimism on the island was not to last long. Having defeated France, Hitler now turned his attention to the Mediterranean. He moved his crack unit of Stuka dive-bombers – Fliegerkorps X – to southern Italy and Sicily, with the order '*Illustrious müssen sinken*'. They practised on a floating mock-up.[18]

In January 1941 OPERATION EXCESS was proceeding according to plan. This was a convoy of six merchant ships from Gibraltar, three bound for Malta (where they duly arrived) and three for Greece. *Illustrious* was one of the escorting vessels. On the morning of 9 January when they were less than 100 miles from Malta the convoy was spotted by Italian planes. Shortly after noon the next day waves of Stuka dive-bombers launched a ferocious onslaught on the aircraft-carrier; it was a brilliantly executed operation lasting six and a half minutes and leaving Illustrious severely damaged; but for her armoured flight deck she would almost certainly have been sunk. Her main engines were just kept going and she struggled on towards Malta. When a second attack followed in the afternoon her own fighters, having flown to the Island to refuel and rearm, were ready. Only one bomber got through but its single bomb fell through a lift shaft and burst inside the ship. Assisted by tugs she managed to limp into Grand Harbour later that night.[19]

Bess was waiting to welcome her brother, a Captain of Marines serving on board. She learned that he had been killed in action the previous day. The halcyon time had ended.

On 16 January the Fliegerkorps returned. Over seventy bombers came in to be met by a barrage from every gun and ship in the harbour. (Among the few serviceable aircraft available that day, with orders to keep away from the harbour and pick off stragglers, were two of the immortal trio of Gloster Gladiator biplanes known as *Faith*, *Hope* and *Charity*.) Although the attack was directed at *Illustrious* as much as the island, the ship was only slightly damaged by one bomb. Many people were killed and many buildings demolished in Valletta and the towns surrounding the dockyard. For the next few days work to make *Illustrious* seaworthy continued non-stop, and on 23 January she was able to slip away in the night to Alexandria, and thence to the USA for a complete refit. Though the Luftwaffe had suffered serious losses, the air-raids continued by day and night throughout January, February and March.

By the beginning of 1941 much of the underground work had been done; the fuel tanks were completed and filled, the generating station, the strategic circuit, the pumps and the flour mill had all been brought into operation.[20] The provision of public shelters, however, had not progressed very far. Buildings had been strengthened, slit trenches had been dug near airfields and main roads, many windows and doorways were protected by sandbags, and a disused railway tunnel was converted into a shelter, but the fortress was not prepared for the heavy bombing by the Luftwaffe which now began. Dobbie explained in a broadcast that the government was doing all it could to provide shelters, but hewing them out of rock took time, and there was a shortage of miners and tools.[21]

Jackson was still living in his flat near the dockyard, looked after by the faithful Nina, who recalled a lunch for twelve being interrupted by an air raid warning.

When he said 'Down to the shelter!' she said 'No – God, when he wants you, will find you' and they all stood there holding hands while she said a special prayer in Maltese. A bomb fell right through the building but failed to explode. After that Nina stayed at home with her mother, Jackson moved into the barracks and Roger went to live with Bess.[22]

In January 1941 General Wavell, C-in-C Middle East, pushed back the Italian Army and took Tobruk; he urgently needed reinforcements, but they were sent to Greece instead. During February and March Rommel was able to get large numbers of his Afrika Korps across to Tripoli with virtually no hindrance from British forces based in Malta; there were not enough planes or ships to attack them. The British were driven back to Egypt, leaving Tobruk as an isolated garrison. A counter-attack by Wavell in mid-June failed and the situation in the desert would remain unchanged until November.

Four powerful new destroyers reached Malta in April and soon sank an entire German convoy off the Tunisian coast – five transports bringing troops and supplies to North Africa, and two of their escorting destroyers. More planes and submarines arrived and inflicted serious losses on the enemy shipping. Thus as the war in North Africa was dragging on the importance of Malta was increasing.

Given the damage which ships and aircraft based on the island were now able to inflict it may seem surprising that the Axis powers never attempted to invade it. This was twice considered by Hitler and rejected; his aim was rather to bomb and starve it into submission. Even so, between January and September 1941, twenty-nine supply ships, as well as submarines bringing fuel for aircraft, reached the island. One of the biggest convoys from Gibraltar – OPERATION SUBSTANCE – arrived on 24 July. All six merchantmen got through, though one was damaged; of the escorting vessels one cruiser and one destroyer were damaged and one destroyer sunk; despite the losses this operation was reckoned a success.

In the hope of preventing these supplies being used, on the following night the Italian Navy attempted to sink the ships in the harbour. It was a daring operation which depended on the bravery of a few men, some in explosive motor-boats with a one-man crew and ejector seat, some in manned manoeuvrable torpedoes (known as 'pigs') with detachable warheads and time-fuses. The intention was that the pigs would blow up the outer defences of Grand Harbour to create a way through for the motor-boats to sink the six merchant-men inside. It went disastrously wrong: the explosion of the first motor-boat brought down the defences and blocked the harbour entrance completely; the attackers were spotted on the radar, picked up by searchlights and sunk within two minutes. The operation failed, but it left Jackson in no doubt of the desperate lengths to which the enemy was prepared to go – and the courage of the Italians.

By September 1941 sufficient stocks of essential commodities to last for seven months had been built up; during the next ten and a half months no substantial convoy got through; the supplies which arrived in small convoys and single ships were enough for only two months.

According to Bess, who knew Dobbie's daughter, not all the service chiefs liked him, and he relied on Jackson to keep him informed about what was going on. He explained his predicament to Ford: he needed a staff officer in the know to keep him *au fait* and the obvious person was Jackson. 'He has, with your kind connivance, come and seen me most days and has told me a lot, and has been a great help to me. But that has all been on an unofficial basis, and the arrangement for that reason has been limited in its usefulness. I think it is desirable now that it should be regularised, and I would like, if you agree, to nominate him to my personal staff for coordinating duties (we can devise a suitable title). It would I feel be a help to him and put him on a better wicket in his dealings with heads of other services when he collects information for me. Can you see your way to agreeing to this suggestion?'[23]

Ford agreed, and 'being on Dobbie's staff' enabled Jackson to say that he had been in the Army as well as the Navy! Unhappily for both of them the arrangement turned out to be short-lived.

By April Wavell's area of command covered not only North Africa, it extended from Ethiopia in the south to Greece in the north. He was also burdened with political and logistical problems in the Middle East. The British Cabinet was concerned about the problem of keeping this vast area supplied, and in order to lighten Wavell's load Churchill appointed an 'Intendant-General' – a kind of super Quartermaster-General – based in Cairo, to be responsible for organising supply services for the Army. This arrangement did not work well and Churchill's son Randolph, then serving in the Middle East, sent his father a telegram on 7 June saying that what was really needed was a Minister of Cabinet rank (which Wavell had always wanted). Churchill immediately appointed Oliver Lyttelton as Minister of State in the Middle East, with Cabinet rank. As President of the Board of Trade he had been in charge of clothes rationing and civilian supplies generally. Now he was to represent the War Cabinet on the spot and settle questions which previously had to be referred to London; he could give the Commanders-in-Chief political guidance and supervise the activities of the Intendant-General.

Lyttelton arrived in Cairo in July and made a preliminary tour during which he saw Dobbie in Malta; he also met Jackson and asked if he had any ideas about the Middle East. In fact Jackson had already expressed his views in Cairo in April, but he did not reveal them to Lyttelton. When Lyttelton made a second visit, having seen the situation himself, Jackson spoke more freely, telling him that what he had seen in the Middle East Command had convinced him that the Army were going about the supply job in the wrong way. They had identified the primary bottlenecks as shipping, but even more critical was the capacity of the ports, the 'throats' to the Middle Eastern theatre and to the Persian Gulf. Then came the problems of the interior lines of communication. He was certain that what should be done in the Middle East was to cut out all unnecessary imports and make much better use of the existing ports, ships and lines of communication. This would be a much more effective and economical solution than building new facilities. Since the Americans and British virtually controlled all shipping, if they controlled what went into them at their point of loading they would control what came out at the other end.

If, he continued, Lyttelton could arrange for imports into the Middle East to be controlled it would be possible to eliminate all non-essential imports into the area, while preserving the peoples' lives, internal security and so forth. Non-essential activity should be eliminated, and the entire area made self-supporting as quickly as possible. The volume of imports would drop sharply, as it had in Malta, and the ports and lines of communication would carry virtually all that was needed in the Middle East, and the Aid to Russia route via the Persian Gulf could be developed to its maximum capacity. Brilliant logistical thinking again, but this time he was talking himself out of the job he loved.

One thing which I didn't like, the thing that shocked Dobbie most, was Lyttelton saying to him, almost in a throwaway fashion, before he went on to London 'Oh, do you mind if I borrow Jacko for three weeks?' Dobbie agreed but had no idea that I would be taken away from him permanently, any more than I did. In simple terms, he was double-crossed.

Shortly afterwards, so I was told later by Sir Edward Bridges, Secretary to the Cabinet, a Cabinet meeting was held at which Lyttelton said what he felt should be done in the Middle East. He had been much influenced by our Malta experience and what I'd said to him, and a decision was taken that I should be literally taken out of the Navy and removed from my job with Dobbie in the Army and transferred to the British Treasury. Lyttelton was certain there would be reactions from the Navy and the Army, and that General Dobbie would go through the roof when he learned that he was losing his right arm, and, according to Bridges, took an exceedingly tough line about my appointment to his staff. There was to be no argument in the matter; it was marching orders and that was that.[24]

Minutes of Cabinet meetings do not go into such details; they merely recorded that Lyttelton attended a meeting on 24 September, and on 2 October the Prime Minister said that his visit 'had been of great advantage and had facilitated the settlement of a number of important matters.'[25] An annex to the minutes contains a brief account of what Lyttelton said, but makes no mention of Jackson.[26] No doubt Bridges informed Dobbie and Ford in terms that brooked no argument. It didn't occur to him to tell the Australian Navy!

Jackson made one more trip to England[27] and on 8 November – his 30th birthday – he was in a flying boat on his way to Alexandria.

I didn't know whether Dobbie was more upset or I was, because I loved him, and Malta was my life. As far as I was concerned, Malta was the war. It was the only experience I ever had in the war where the concept of the fortress, as something in itself, was totally above all personal considerations. In other circumstances, and in other Army formations and naval commands there were always personalities. But in Malta it was always 'The Fortress', just 'The Fortress'. Personalities never came into our lives in the usual sense. I knew that I was in a unique atmosphere, and undergoing a unique experience, and I also knew that I was in a unique position in the fortress. So if Dobbie was upset I was equally upset.[28]

Bess, too, was upset – devastated by his sudden departure. He had never formally proposed to her, but had said that he would have no difficulty in getting his first marriage 'untied' and she believed they had reached an understanding. When they met by chance in Cairo two years later she realised she had been wrong, and wisely concluded that their relationship was over. Many years later, clearing out his belongings in New York, he came across a piece she had written about Roger the cat and sent it to her. 'It was as if a rusty gate had been opened into an overgrown garden which was long forgotten and had been beautiful.'[29] They would meet again.

'Before you go to Egypt', wrote Dobbie, 'I should like you to know how very deeply indebted I am to you for all the really magnificent work which you have done for Malta. Everything which you have turned your hand to has been a success and nobody could possibly have worked harder or more uninterruptedly than you have. Nothing has been too large or too small for you to tackle, but the things which stand out are the co-ordination of our defences, the organisation of supplies and the planning of re-armament. I am very glad indeed that you were able to go to London to explain the re-armament plans to the Departments there; it was a fitting conclusion to your efforts in this direction. On the supply side I do not know how we could have got on without you. The successful supply of the Fortress was absolutely essential if we were to maintain ourselves, and quite apart from the obvious local benefits which we have obtained from your work, it has directly affected the strategical position in the Central Mediterranean.'[30]

Ford concluded his official report on Jackson:

> When he took over the duties of Secretary to the Chief Staff Officer his immediate task was the revision of the Malta Command Defence Scheme which was in a very chaotic and out-of-date state. Previous efforts to reduce this chaos had been only partially successful due to the lack of liaison and co-operation amongst the other two services. He was able to eliminate this to an astonishing degree and to obtain concurrence in the important items of the defence scheme by sheer force of personality and extremely hard work.

Shortly after the Munich crisis he wrote an appreciation of the situation in Malta which I forwarded to the Commander-in-Chief, then Admiral Sir Dudley Pound, which was, I believe, very largely responsible for the re-shaping of the Imperial Defence Committee's policy with regard to Malta which they had hitherto described as being 'undefendable'. From that moment onwards there was no item in the re-arming of Malta with which he did not associate himself, in the bringing forward and accelerating of which he was not very largely concerned, and his ideas were always fresh and brought a new outlook even on technical aspects to the people concerned with carrying out the work of re-armament.

His remarkable capacity for absorbing the technical details and procedures of specialist work is, I think, the outstanding feature of his ability. He worked out a scheme of co-ordinated supply which has been undoubtedly responsible for the very large part Malta has been able to play in the Mediterranean warfare.[31]

Edward Jackson looked back on their association as a very happy one: 'Well, my dear Jacko, Malta is still a part of your cares, I'm glad to think, so we'll see you back again and if you dare to stay at any house but ours we shall be deeply offended. Audrey and I look on you as one of the family.'[32]

During the ten months following his departure very few supply ships reached the island. One small merchantman arrived on 18 December, another on 8 January and three more on 19 January. In early February convoy MW9 left Alexandria with three merchantmen. They were so severely bombed that none of them reached Malta.

Jackson was frustrated at being away from the action. Dobbie wrote: 'My dear Jacko, I can sympathise with you in your desire to get back to definite defence problems .... The non-arrival of MW9 was a great blow. ... Thank you very much for the cello strings; if you could help with shaving soap, tooth paste and safety razor blades I would be very grateful. ... God bless you, Jacko. He is working His purposes out, and I have no fear in the future. Yours ever WGS Dobbie.'[33]

Later in February a convoy of three merchantmen was forced to turn back. In March, of the four in convoy MW10 from Alexandria one was sunk at sea; one was sunk on the south coast of the island with her precious 5,000 tons of oil intact but unreachable and the other two were sunk in Grand Harbour before they were unloaded. Possibly the worst setback of all was a convoy from Alexandria – OPERATION VIGOROUS – eleven merchantmen escorted by eight cruisers and twenty-six destroyers – which was forced by the Italian Navy to turn back; one cruiser and five destroyers were lost, and no supplies were delivered. Shortly afterwards two out of six in a convoy from Gibraltar reached Grand Harbour; the supplies which they brought were only sufficient for two or three months. Meanwhile the island suffered intense bombing; the tonnage dropped on Malta during March and April was twice that dropped on London in the worst year of the blitz

The bread ration was now only seven ounces a day. A working man would eat from four to six times that quantity, and there was very little else; fresh fish was almost unobtainable. For a long time kerosene was the only means of lighting and cooking. The basic ration was about two thirds of a wine bottle a week, then it was reduced by half. The horses were kept for transport to save petrol, but the other animals were gradually killed off and their meat went to the communal Victory Kitchens. 'In spite of all this, however short the rationing got there was one complaint that no one ever made. No one ever asked why we didn't get more ships. They knew the cost of convoys.'[34]

When Jackson had stressed the importance of the role of the civilian population in defending the island he could not have realised the weight of the burden they would be expected to bear. Their courage was recognised by King George VI who, on 15 April, awarded the George Cross

TO THE ISLAND FORTRESS OF MALTA,
TO BEAR WITNESS TO A HEROISM AND DEVOTION
THAT WILL LONG BE FAMOUS IN HISTORY

By August the situation was desperate. The British Government knew that a supreme effort must be made to get supplies through and the Axis powers knew that they must be stopped at all costs. The Maltese people could only hope – and pray. The Feast of the Assumption – the *festa ta Santa Marija* – falls on 15 August; the Archbishop ordered a *novena* to be said in every parish – special prayers during the nine day period preceding the *festa* – asking that 'God the merciful may shorten the time of his scourge and grant us help'.

On 10 August a convoy passed through the Straits of Gibraltar. This was OPERATION PEDESTAL, by far the biggest Malta-bound convoy of the war: fourteen merchantmen – the largest and fastest that could be gathered together, including the American oil-tanker *Ohio* – with an escort of four aircraft carriers, two battleships, seven cruisers and twenty-four destroyers. On 11 August the aircraft-carrier *Eagle* was sunk by a submarine, taking with her a quarter of the convoy's air cover. Fierce air and sea battles raged for the next two days; one after another nine of the merchantmen were sunk. On the evening of 13 August the crowds waiting to cheer on the ramparts saw just three ships, scarred and torn, enter Grand Harbour; there was no sign of the oil tanker. During the afternoon of 14 August one more arrived. Meanwhile *Ohio*, severely damaged but miraculously still afloat and not expected to last more than 12 hours, was being nursed along by two destroyers lashed alongside, with a third at her stern to keep her pointing

Ohio at rest in Grand Harbour.   Imperial War Museum GM 1480

in the right direction. After taking 48 hours to travel 40 miles she reached Grand Harbour with her decks awash but her precious cargo still intact, and settled on the harbour floor even as she was being berthed. It was the *festa ta Santa Marija*.

> 'It was, indeed, by little short of a miracle of skill and endurance that the Ohio was finally got into the Grand Harbour of Valletta. The 10,000 tons of fuel oil and kerosene salved from her torn hull set the seal on Operation 'Pedestal', Malta was saved.'[35]

Macintyre, writing in 1964 was correct, but at the time it was far from certain that Malta was saved. At least Malta had not surrendered, and 44,000 tons of supplies had arrived, but this was only one fifth of what was needed and no-one knew when the next convoy would get through.

The outlook was still grim. At the present rate of consumption the stocks of flour and wheat would last until early January. Increasing the bread ration to 17.5 ounces a day for men between 16 and 60 would reduce the period by two weeks. If the numbers using the Victory Kitchens increased as expected another 1,000 tons of flour would be needed, reducing it by another twelve days. The island was entirely without potatoes – the spring crop had failed, and it was essential to obtain imported seed for the next year's spring crop.[36]

It was mid-November when the next convoy arrived from Alexandria – four merchantmen escorted by five cruisers and seventeen destroyers; all the supplies got through. A fast mine-layer brought 175 tons of seed-potatoes, but it was not until another convoy arrived on 5 December that Malta could really believe that she was saved.

Jackson never forgot that Malta's survival was achieved at the cost of many lives – of civilians, soldiers, airmen and sailors – not least the crews of the many merchant ships that never got through. Nevertheless, had it not been for his Defence Scheme and his organization of the defence preparations in those early months, the outcome could well have been very different and those lives lost in vain. It was a very close run thing, and on it 'depended, absolutely, the success or failure of the campaigns in North Africa and hence, it can be said, of the whole war.'[37]

Jackson's part in bringing it about was revealed on 11 January 1946 when THE TIMES OF MALTA reported the 'COSUP EPIC':

> A great story which lay behind the successful conclusion of the Siege of Malta is revealed in the factual account of the activities of COSUP which has just been laid on the table of the Council of Government.
>
> Paymaster Commander RGA Jackson was on the staff of Vice-Admiral Sir Wilbraham Ford when Italy entered the war. ... It was his drive and foresight, coupled with the cooperation he received at the Admiralty that brought assistance to the Civil Government of Malta, that enabled the island, namely the people and garrison of Malta, to survive on the vital food and supply front. ... COSUP stepped in to help Malta in the hour of need.

It is surely not too much to claim that Jackson was the man who saved Malta.

*

A memoir written in 1943 by a Mrs Norman (possibly the wife of a Lieut-Commander based on *St Angelo*) told of 'the brilliant organisation and untiring energy of a young Australian Paymaster-Lieutenant on Ford's staff'.[38] In 1970 Stewart Perowne, in THE SIEGE WITHIN THE WALLS, identified the young Australian 'who contributed so fruitfully to Malta's ability to survive' as Commander Sir Robert Jackson KCVO, CMG, OBE.[39] The OBE was for what he had done in Malta.

4 The Middle East Supply Centre (MESC)

WITH THE MEDITERRANEAN CLOSED to merchant shipping, all supplies for the British forces in the Middle East had to go by the long sea route round South Africa – about 17,000 miles. Non-essential civilian imports were taking up precious shipping space and clogging the ports; this had to be stopped without depriving the population of essentials and this was the purpose of the Middle East Supply Centre (MESC).

Its principal functions were:

(1) to develop local production of essential food and materials in the Middle East through the cooperation of individual Middle Eastern governments and to ensure that necessary imports were obtained from the nearest possible source;

(2) to ensure that demand for imports of civilian goods was restricted to essentials;

(3) to assist Middle Eastern governments in control and distribution so that imports were used to the best purpose;

(4) to provide a Centre for the exchange of information on problems of agricultural and industrial production and distribution and economics generally.[1]

Its activities and influence extended from North Africa to Persia, and from Turkey to central Africa, an area of over five million square miles with a population approaching 100 million. Its constitution had been drawn up by Max Nicholson, head of the Shipping Division of the Ministry of War Transport; since cooperation with local governments would be essential he had selected the innocuous title of Supply <u>Centre</u> so as not to suggest that it claimed any executive or over-riding authority. This was to be the secret of its success – not having direct executive power (which would have been difficult to exercise) and yet in practice having the whip hand.[2]

On 24 April 1941 Jackson had represented Malta at the first meeting of the Middle East Supply Council in Cairo, at which MESC was inaugurated. The other nations represented were Egypt, Palestine, Trans-Jordan, Cyprus, Sudan and East Africa. 'Victory in the Middle East' he said 'required strict licensing of imports everywhere in the area, ruthless schemes of cereal collection and distribution to eliminate hoarding and profiteering and promote the regional distribution of local surpluses, stimulation of local production and intensive forward planning of imports from overseas.[3]

Nevertheless he was determined that MESC should not become responsible for provisioning Malta and generally gave the impression of being uncooperative, so when Nicholson heard in November that Lyttelton wanted him as executive head of a revitalised MESC he objected. Once Jackson was in charge they got on famously together.[4]

Sheila Collins was one of the secretaries in the Minister of State's Office in Cairo, an elegant villa at No. 10 Sharia Tolumbat. On Sunday 9 November after going to Mass she called there to finish off some work. She was alone in the building when in mid-morning the front door flew open and a tall figure in 'navy whites' burst in, in a state of near desperation. 'You're the only person in the building. I'm from Malta – I must get this done by 12. I've got to get it down to the Blue Villa' (the house near the pyramids where Lyttelton was living). Collins said she would do it. 'I work at double speed' said the figure in white. She remained calm and took his dictation straight on to her typewriter – it was all about coal and bunkers. Greatly impressed, he rushed off to the Villa with his papers for the Minister. Collins, also greatly impressed, was left alone in the office wondering what had hit her.[5]

Sheila was no ordinary secretary; educated in convents in England and France, she spoke French, Italian and German fluently. After training at St James's Secretarial College in London she was snapped up by the Foreign Office in 1932 and sent to the League of Nations in Geneva, then to Italy, France and Palestine, where she learnt Arabic, and in 1941 to Egypt. She was a woman of taste and good judgment.

When Jackson started talking about marriage she pointed out that she was a Catholic and he was married already. 'All my friends are Catholics' he replied,

'I'll see the Pope – I'll get an annulment'. Sheila panicked and went off to Beirut to get engaged to her boy-friend, who insisted on keeping it secret until he got his promotion, so she returned to Cairo 'tied' but with no ring to show it. Jacko was furious, and told her she was a dishonest woman. Dishonest or not, she felt she could handle the situation. Some weeks later he asked her to find out what she could about the possibility of an annulment. The local Dominican friars told her that it was out of the question, but they were prepared to see him. He was convinced that his magic touch would do the trick, but they just laughed: 'All your evidence is in Australia, so you can't do anything about it until after the war and you'd better say goodbye to that young woman'. Sheila could see that he would set MESC on fire and that she could help him in his work as no-one else could. If she could work for him she would be able to find out what her real feelings were for him. She decided to stay.[6]

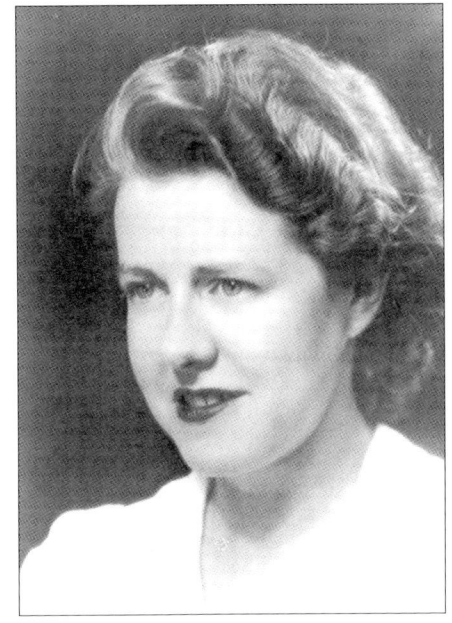

Sheila Collins.

Jackson hated being out of uniform, but he had been made a civil servant in the British Treasury (where he was on probation!) because if he was to run MESC he would be dealing with senior officers in the Army and Navy. Later he would be treated as a Lieutenant-General and addressed as Commander, but for the time being he was merely the Executive Officer of the Executive Committee. He felt he was wasting his time and longed to be back in Malta. When Japan attacked Pearl Harbour in December Wavell was Commander-in-Chief in India, with Durnford as his Chief of Staff. 'Both of them wanted me to join the new command. Lyttelton wouldn't listen, so I felt even more frustrated. I found a partner in frustration – a chap named Richard Kahn [an economist – a former pupil of JM Keynes who had been on Lyttelton's staff at the Bard of Trade, later Lord Kahn of Hampstead]. He was Keynes's white-haired boy, his intellectual successor. Richard and I were like two caged tigers.'[7]

The door of the cage was opened in January. The administration was completely reorganised; Jackson's title was changed to Director of MESC, then to Director-General. Lyttelton decided that the policy of MESC should be determined by the Supply and Transportation Sub-Committee of the Middle Eastern War Council, of which he was Chairman; the Executive Committee was suspended and Jackson was put in charge of the operations of the Centre with Kahn as his deputy. MESC's offices were moved into No 10, and Sheila reorganised the staff so that she could work for him.

Jackson moved out of his flat; he didn't need it, and felt guilty at being out of the services, so he had a camp bed put in his office, making a point of roughing it. He worked late at night and early in the morning; one of the secretaries would bring him coffee and rolls for breakfast. Evening visits to the cinema with Sheila helped to clear his mind; he would emerge having hit on the solution to some problem, and ready to dictate another letter. He could always mix serious business with laughter, and her occasional typing mistakes were greeted with hilarity. There was total trust between them, they knew where they stood and were utterly at ease; no demands were made on either side. She felt that such intimacy as there was between them reflected their mutual confidence and was a benefit to their work.

Because food was so short in Malta Bess decided that Roger would be better off with his master in Egypt, and sent a cable announcing his despatch by sea; the result was that his arrival was awaited by a group of intelligence officials. They had been expecting one of their agents, code-named Roger, and were bemused to find a cat skulking under the captain's bunk! Roger did not enjoy roughing it in the office with his master and soon moved into Sheila's flat.[8]

In February Lyttelton returned to London to become Minister of War Production; Churchill had recently met Richard Casey, the Australian Minister in Washington, and in March offered him the position of Minister of State in Cairo. 'Splenetic reaction' wrote Casey in his diary 'from Mr Curtin [the Prime Minister] and from Melbourne Herald about my accepting Mr Churchill's proposal'.[9] He did not arrive until 4 May, having come via Malta where he had the unhappy task of telling Dobbie that he was to be relieved as Commander-in-Chief.

During the two months between Lyttelton's departure and Casey's arrival Jackson had no hesitation in assuming the authority of the Minister. He had won the confidence of the military authorities, who were glad to be relieved of the burden of dealing with civilian affairs. He now needed to win the confidence of the rulers of the Middle Eastern territories.

He had to be constantly on the move. explaining the need for planning and control and winning their confidence by offering all possible help.[10] Depending on circumstances he would plead, cajole, persuade, or threaten, always making full use of Lyttelton's magic name and speaking as his emissary; but he did not merely demand: in exchange for cooperation he promised the full measure of his assistance to any legitimate demand for civilian goods and shipping space from overseas. The local rulers knew that their countries were in for a period of drastic austerity during which they could ill afford to lose the goodwill of the Minister of State and his lieutenants; moreover, the scheme proposed by Jackson seemed eminently sensible.[11] Its main elements were stricter licensing of imports by local authorities overseen by MESC, sharing of exportable surpluses, maximum local production of goods, and acceptance of the austerity inevitable at a time of war;

Director-General of MESC

if any country failed to cooperate MESC could effectively blockade it. All was as Nicholson had intended.

Casey found himself inundated with work. Though accustomed to dealing with people he was taken aback by the sheer number of military and civilian personnel involved.[12] He could see that Jackson knew what needed to be done and was content to let him get on with it, giving him a completely free hand and only concerned to help. Their mutual confidence was the foundation of a close friendship lasting for 35 years.

Casey provided the political backing MESC needed in its dealings with Middle East Governments and with the British Embassy in Cairo. Though highly regarded by the military men, he was unpopular with the British diplomats: he was a minister trespassing on their preserve and, moreover, a colonial – not a member of their club.[13] Jackson, another colonial, also found himself at odds with them: 'The British Embassy staff were very difficult at times, particularly the Ambassador, Sir Miles Lampson. He regarded himself as the King of Egypt. This was also very difficult for Alexander Kirk, the US Minister in Cairo, who could not have been more helpful to me. Very often I would ask him, as the American Minister, to speak to the British Ambassador who was being uncooperative. Sometimes I'd ask him to go to the Egyptian Government, to short-circuit the British. Most of our difficulties, I am sure, were because we always wanted to take a firmer line than the British Embassy in our dealings with the Egyptian Government.'[14]

This was a critical time in the battle in the North African desert; both armies were regrouping just west of Tobruk; Churchill was demanding a British offensive, but the Commanders-in-Chief were not ready and Rommel struck first, on 27 May. On 3 July 1942 the German army reached El Alamein, only 60 miles from Alexandria, to the shocked surprise of the people in Cairo. (The offices of MESC had already been moved to Jerusalem where they stayed until early October.) A second German attack in August was successfully resisted and at the end of October the battle of El Alamein began; the victories of the Eighth Army under Montgomery turned the tide of the war in North Africa, and MESC had played its part: civilian imports had been cut by nearly four-fifths to 1.25 million tons a year and military imports were running at a rate of over 5 million tons a year.[15]

By June 1942 the staff had grown to over 150, and Jackson needed more. A Treasury official sent out to inspect the Centre reported that London had not realised the complexity of its operations: different territories had different problems; MESC had to hold the balance and look after them all; differences in political status and relationship to the British Government made for much work; it was not possible to distinguish clearly between military and civil affairs; close cooperation with the military was vital; these problems called for a rare combination of diplomacy and expertise; MESC's range of activities should be enlarged to promote expansion of production and better mobilization of local resources; greater pressure would need to be applied to governments on matters which they would regard as domestic. London agreed to provide more staff including a Deputy Director-General, Dr E E Bailey (replacing Kahn), to assist Jackson and act in his absence. Five Directors of Divisions were appointed, including Keith Murray for Food and Agriculture (later Lord Murray of Newhaven).[16]

The United States had a significant interest in the Middle East through the Lend-Lease Act, which enabled it to provide arms and other supplies and services to countries whose defence was deemed vital to the USA. American military supplies to the British forces had contributed to their successes in North Africa in November 1941, but when the United States entered the war in December these could not be spared; sending civilian supplies, however, such as food and other essential goods, even to non-combatant countries, could be justified on the grounds that the maintenance of law and order and the prevention of famine and civil unrest were vital to the military success of the Allies. Strict control of distribution would be essential, and it was important not to interfere with MESC's own arrangements. Jackson realised at once that close cooperation with the Americans would be needed, but it was not until May 1942 that the State Department appointed Frederick Winant, (Chief of the US Export Control Office) as its senior representative, with William Rountree (of the Office of Lend-Lease Administration) as his assistant. The Board of Economic Warfare nominated Marshall MacDuffie to be Director for Materials, and the Department of Agriculture sent Ben Thibodeaux. Those four men were all that the United States could spare for MESC. After consultations in London in July Winant arrived in Cairo in August with Rountree. MacDuffie and Thibodeaux did not arrive until October, and Thibodeaux was soon replaced.

According to Wilmington (an American) the fact that the US could only provide four men 'augured badly for the success of Anglo-American cooperation within the Supply Centre. Without a thorough American impregnation of the Centre it was hard to visualize how its recommendations could be effective in Washington. Of course much depended on how respectfully the British would accept the 'American slant' which the Winant embassy of four was to implant in MESC policy.'[17]

What Jackson wanted was American co-operation, not American slant, and if the Americans were good they won his respect. The success of the Anglo-American partnership resulted almost entirely from his determination to make it work and the whole-hearted support which Winant was to give him.

On 14 August 1942 Jackson sent Nicholson the first of a series of letters intended to start a triangular correspondence between Washington, London and Cairo. He usually wrote twice a month. These are remarkable letters, often ten or more closely typed pages, covering all the on-going problems – grain control, import control, staff and Anglo-American co-operation – providing a detailed record of his activities and concerns for two years; they are the source of much of what follows in this chapter. They demonstrate his astonishing ability to carry a mass of detail in his head, to see it always as part of an overall picture and to present it all with precision and at great speed, often dictated against the clock, when an aircraft was about to leave. Nicholson rated his set 'a gold mine'. Of this first letter less than one third is quoted here:

> 14 August 1942: During the past six months we have known broadly what we have wanted to do, but ... we have been handicapped both by numbers of staff and the quality of men whom we have been able to obtain. There has been a natural reluctance to provide good people from England, whilst in the Middle East the only means of obtaining assistance is from the Army. All good civilians are already in key jobs (eg oil companies), or have joined up. Now, however, we are much better off (largely due to the Army helping us wherever possible) and the arrival of a few good Americans who are prepared to undertake specific jobs should let us get together a really good team of people.

We now feel that we should be devoting far more attention to the various economic problems which will arise as the result of our activities. Both the British and American Governments are spending large sums of money in this area on defence works, the construction of roads, etc., and the spending power of the area as a whole has been greatly increased. By restrictive action, however, we have greatly reduced the quantity of goods which is available for purchase. This is leading to all kinds of complications and in Palestine wages are already beginning to chase prices with consequent labour troubles.

Again, in determining quotas for the area we worked to the principle that the exportable surpluses of some territories could meet the import deficiencies of others. There are many practical difficulties to be overcome, however, – eg the cost of production in the exporting country may be far and away above the price which the importing country wishes to pay. It seems to us, too, that as the war becomes more intensive in this area, normal trade links are likely to break and we shall have to rely more and more on imports under government control. This will make lease-lend far more important to us than in the past and in this sense the Americans have arrived at a particularly good time.

Agricultural problems must be our main concern in view of the very great tonnages involved and because wheat is undoubtedly the dominant political factor in this area today. In Egypt the Government promised us that they would introduce a scheme of complete control and then, the next day, in typical Egyptian style, enacted a scheme of only partial control, so that speculators had a fine time. After much patient work we managed to get a scheme of complete control into operation, but I am still wondering how we managed to do so! Today we have nearly 500,000 tons of wheat under Government control out of the target figure of 700,000 at which we are aiming.

After visiting Persia last week I am most suspicious that the crisis in Teheran was engineered by pro-Axis elements of the Persian Government then in power with a view to causing us as much embarrassment as possible and by forcing us to supply wheat, and possibly interrupt supplies to Russia. It has been made very clear to the Persian Government that under no circumstances do we intend to see any interference with supplies for Russia. [Persia, suspected of harbouring German agents, was occupied in June 1941 by the British and Americans in the south and the Russians in the north; supplies were being sent to Russia via the Persian Gulf.] The Government and the administration generally is inefficient and is characterised by the graft and corruption which is part of the social order of that country. The Persian problem is, I think, the main difficulty with which MESC is concerned.

When people are thinking of the cereals problem in the Middle East, it might be worth while considering some of the minor difficulties with which we have to contend. Here are three examples. Firstly, we wanted more information about certain stocks in one part of Persia. The three government officials sent out were all murdered very effectively. That did not help us much. Secondly, the local people were endeavouring to stop smuggling in Syria. For once there were honest Syrian guards on the frontier. They blocked the lorries of a local large land-owner twice in one morning. They were all removed from the area the same afternoon. Then we wished the Government of Egypt to buy barley secretly, so as not to disturb the price. The Minister of Supplies wrote a secret letter to the Minister of Finance asking that the requisite money should be provided. The secret letter appeared in all the Arabic newspapers the next morning! I think that shook even the Egyptian Ministers. These instances arise almost daily. We appreciate the trials and tribulations which beset people in London and Washington. But we have our own as well!! ...

The next important general problem has been that of restricting imports into the area as a whole. A few months ago there were no import licensing systems in the majority of the territories. Import licensing has now been introduced in every territory throughout the Middle East except Turkey and Saudi Arabia. It has undoubtedly caused us more detailed worry than anything else. There is every reason to hope that things will become steadily better from now on.

As to coal our main opportunity lies with the conversion of the Egyptian State Railways to oil. The rate of conversion in April was two locos per month; we hope to achieve 40 a month by September or October. With luck ... all 500 should be converted by June 1943, when our coal imports for the railways will have been reduced from between 50 and 60 thousand tons a month to less than 10,000 – my only regret is that the job was not done two years ago.

Our next major job is in relation to transport, particularly trucks. Motor transport throughout the Middle East is in a very bad condition. Spare parts are a particular problem. At present the majority of lorries which are coming forward are being requisitioned by either the RAF or the Army. This is placing civil transport in a yet more difficult position and our main hope lies in receiving a steady supply of spares to keep existing vehicles on the road.

We are busy with schemes to get unessential passenger cars off the road. This is far from easy in neutral territories. Our best chance will come through petrol rationing (not easy when the area is overflowing with this oil) and through the denial of tyres to Governments unless they remove unessential transport. We aim to make our control of tyres absolute.

Now as to the Americans. Mr. Winant has arrived and our conversations during the past week have been most excellent. I feel that we have been given an ideal collaborator. We will regard him as our American Adviser in MESC and he will be brought into all our problems – not merely those concerning America and American supplies.

It seems clear that the Americans do not as yet realise all the complications of supplies for Persia where they are affected by the limited port capacity in the Persian Gulf on the one hand, whilst on the other we are doing everything possible to increase supplies to Russia and to build up base supplies for the Xth Army. However, I think Mr. Winant will soon learn all about this when he has been to Persia and Iraq.

I regret the length of these general notes, but from them it may be possible to select parts which will be of use to our people in America.

Nicholson replied that he fully appreciated the staffing problems Jackson had been up against. 'In fact the work the Centre has performed in the last year and a half with the staff at its disposal appears almost miraculous and surpasses anything which we hoped in our wildest dreams to see achieved within so short a period.'[18]

Two months later Jackson wrote

14 October: The territories are often faced with a great task in forecasting requirements to a few thousand tons. It would help us greatly if you could assure all those concerned with our cereals requirements that both MESC and the territories themselves consider actual requirements in the greatest possible detail. We are not only interested in the shipping aspect – locally, we have an even greater problem: area port capacity and internal transport

facilities are often less than the shipping available. ... Because of our internal transport problems London can remain assured that our demands will be cut to the minimum.

You refer to the development of the triangular relationship between London, Washington and Cairo. This is clearly going to require the most skilful handling

in the early stages. In Winant we have a first class man to help in building up this relationship. Already we are forming the basis of a solid friendship; our views on England and America are very much the same and we are very much at one in our general views about post-war conditions ...

There is no doubt about the care which will be necessary in developing this combined organization. What we need quickly is assistance at the top. ...

I am now off to a meeting. I will reply to your third letter as soon as I get back.......

Now it's my turn! It's 1930 and an air mail is closing at 2030 – leaving for England at 0200. I have about fifteen minutes left. This last part deals entirely with the Americans. On my side it is the most important part of our work at the moment. If we fail to develop an effective relationship at the very beginning, we may miss what I regard as a unique opportunity to show the outside world what Anglo-American co-operation really can mean. I have spoken of Winant already. We could not have a better man. It is a joy to me that we understand each other. Rountree is fitting in very well and from what you say it is clear that MacDuffie should be a similar success. Winant has just received the first reactions from the State Department to the work which he has carried out since he arrived. The SD is clearly behind him completely. That is more than satisfactory. If Washington is behind him, and London is behind us, we can't go far wrong.

In the practical sense we can show the Middle East the value of an effective Anglo-American supply organization by stimulating agricultural production with American machinery, and by guiding inter-territorial trade in such a way that assistance can be given, not only in the matter of supplies, but also in contributing to the solution of some of the political problems of the area.

Jackson was already looking to the future, but his hopes of solving the long-term political problems of the Middle East so simply would not be fulfilled.

Keith Murray reckoned that Anglo-American cooperation was Jackson's great achievement, although in practice he found it irksome and at times wasteful, given the shortage of staff. If he went on a visit, say to Saudi Arabia, he had to be accompanied by his American Assistant Director. 'If things have reached the stage', he thought, 'where it takes two people to do one man's job, perhaps it's time I left.' In his opinion the Americans at that level did not contribute much, but the important thing was that Anglo-American cooperation could be <u>seen</u> to be happening, and he knew Jackson was right.[19] For Jackson it was not only a means to an end, but an end in itself – a unique opportunity to show the outside world what Anglo-American cooperation really could mean – though Anglo was hardly the word, given that he was Australian, his deputy a New Zealander, and three Divisional Directors Scottish!

Jackson and others outside No 10 Sharia Tolumbat, Murray in white suit.

MacDuffie, attending his first meeting of the Licence Committee, was not a little bemused by its proceedings. They were vetting import licences which had already been scrutinised by the various specialised divisions – Food, Medicine, Materials and Transport – and graded in order of importance and urgency: The committee's job was to decide which licences were essential and which were not. 'The papers were picked up and quickly passed down the line of uniforms with barely audible comments in the clipped rapid-fire speech that is characteristic for person-to-person communications among the British military. The session ended without Macduffie having understood a word of what was going on. Yet in that short hour several hundred claims on Anglo-American resources, of vital importance to millions, had been processed, most with finality, a few with referral to further study.'[20] After a while he was able to play his part!

In November the British Government released information about MESC; articles in the British press described it as a brilliant example of British vision, efficiency and success, a pioneer lead in combining planning and freedom, a first wartime instalment of collaboration between all nations in the economic field, in striking contrast to the plunder by Germany on the other side of the Mediterranean. It was 'a novel and significant example of international economic cooperation'.[21]

But after the allied victories in North Africa in 1942 the territories were no longer under threat from the axis powers and resented import controls; severe inflation over the whole area was becoming a greater problem than supply. The original tasks of the Minister had been accomplished and Casey felt that his presence could only be justified if he were given new longer term responsibilities to consolidate what had been achieved.[22]

He wanted to explore, in partnership with the Americans, the possibilities of long term development in the Middle East, covering such matters as irrigation and flood control, measures to improve health and nutrition, development of transport and communications, all of which he thought should be considered in relation to the Middle East as a whole. Though the area included independent states, mandated territories, and those under French control, their problems were similar and planning for the future should treat the whole as a single economic unit. The problems which peace would bring also needed to be identified. These were undoubtedly Jackson's views too, and the two of them put this proposal to the Minister of War Transport, Lord Leathers, in London on 21 December.

Seven months later the War Cabinet agreed in principle that MESC should be developed by degrees into a Middle East Economic Council. But it would all depend on securing the cooperation of the Americans, and that depended on their recognising that the British Commonwealth's interest in the Middle East was greater than their own, otherwise they might set up their own rival organisation.[23] Which, as we shall see, is exactly what they did; Jackson and Winant, however, were still at one.

In the spring of 1943 the theme of post-war cooperation was taken up by THE ECONOMIST (a London weekly) in three articles describing the situation in the Middle East and the work of MESC. Given the detail they contain it is clear that the author – Barbara Ward, the Foreign Editor – must have met Jackson when he was in London.

> A revised MESC, representing the United Nations, [at that time the term denoted the Allies] could provide the capital, the machinery, the experts, the advisers, the educationalists without which there can be no speedy raising of Middle Eastern living standards, no end to the recurring crises of want, little genuine political co-operation and little hope of the area being withdrawn finally from the struggle for predominant influence between the Great Powers. The machinery, the personnel, the administration methods for such a transformation and expansion of the MESC exist. Cooperation between the great nations and between the local Governments is a fact. But it would be simply futile to suppose that the existence of the machinery in itself is enough to secure the survival of the experiment. Only if the United Nations are resolved on their policy will they be able to take up the implements the war has forged for their use. The MESC is one of the most outstanding – and one of the most precarious.[24]

In mid-March Jackson set off on another grand tour: to Syria and the Lebanon, Trans-Jordan and Palestine, south to Nairobi, north to Angora, east to Damascus for a Cereals Conference, to Persia with Casey and finally to Iraq, returning to Cairo on 19 April – 'a very much wiser man!'[25] He found relations between the authorities in the territories and MESC greatly improved, but officials were swamped with papers from MESC, the result of unceasing American demands for information. (In November Nicholson had told Jackson: 'they want to know how many typewriters would be needed in the Middle East by the end of 1943. We will give them the answer when they tell us how many questions Washington is going to ask us in the same period!')[26]

Since prospects for the coming harvests in most areas were good, it was all the more important to ensure that the local governments introduced effective measures of control. The need for more staff was as great as ever – 'in Turkey, to assist with the control and distribution of cereals ... In Syria to act as Economic Adviser to the Spears Mission (a British Military Mission in French Levant associated with MESC) ... In Persia ...to assist with the collection and distribution of cereals ... In Eritrea ...to take charge of supplies ... In Iraq one or two men are needed to assist in the Ministry of Finance. It is useless to believe that any of these can be found in civil occupations in the Middle East. ... The only sources of supply are England and America. ... I consider this problem to be vital and urgent.'[27]

Road transport continued to be a major problem, especially in Persia, where the lack of trucks had put up the cost of local fresh goods, and even resulted in smaller crops of vegetables and sugar beet being grown. It was particularly important that the wheat control scheme in Persia should succeed in the summer of 1943, since it was the biggest single factor which could influence the delivery of aid to Russia.[28] American supplies for the Russian Army were transported from the ports in the Persian Gulf to the rail and truck terminals further north, to be collected by the Russians. They included arms, food, clothing, medicines, trucks and planes, and required all the facilities for land transport that were available. Had the scheme failed, imported grain would have had priority in the ports and on the roads and railways, interrupting supplies to Stalingrad. By ensuring the scheme's success MESC played a crucial part in getting those supplies through.

Jackson could see that if MESC was to have a continuing role more staff would be needed; he told Nicholson of his concern at the way policy for MESC was being handled in London: he was becoming more and more doubtful whether responsibility for dealing with MESC matters was rightly located in a Section of the Ministry of War Transport. There was no-one of real calibre in London devoting his whole time to looking after their day-to-day problems and fighting MESC's battles at the level where policy was decided. He felt there was insufficient recognition of MESC's achievements to ensure that its potential for dealing with post-war problems was fully understood.[29]

Nicholson replied that MESC was but one of his many responsibilities. In any case he had always recognised MESC's independence and made a point of seeing that Jackson's authority and status as Director in complete charge in the field was properly recognised.[30]

Jackson's point was fair, but the fact was that future policy for MESC was the concern of the Foreign Office and the Colonial Office, and they doubted the wisdom of dealing with the area as a whole, reckoning that the common interest of the territories arose only from the shortage of shipping; when that ended they would want to go their own ways.

Jackson went to Washington in June for talks with the State Department; he also met Herbert Lehman, Governor of New York State, who was in charge of the Office of Foreign Relief and Rehabilitation Operations which Roosevelt had set up to prepare the way for an international relief effort at the end of the war. Lehman had heard about MESC and was very impressed by Jackson. Returning *via* London, he must have met Barbara Ward again, for on 4 September another article appeared in THE ECONOMIST:

> AN INTERNATIONAL EXAMPLE
>
> ... The Middle East is a microcosm of a much broader world problem – how, in an area which in order to achieve prosperity and security cries out for unification, to transcend a multitude of jealous national sovereignties. ... The question here is not the activities of the Centre during the hostilities, but whether as a piece of machinery it can serve a vital purpose after the war. ...
>
> Britain has not only the most urgent interest in using the methods exemplified in the MESC to further international co-operation. It also has the best practical experience of how they work. ... The pooling of sovereignty, the transfer of power to a world authority, is the ultimate problem of international society.[31]

But nations have never been too keen on pooling their sovereignty, and already even the British and American governments were less concerned with future cooperation than with protecting their respective post-war markets. Casey had already warned the War Cabinet that American actions in the Middle East often seemed to be prompted by some suspicion of the British position, or even by a spirit of opposition to British interests.[32]

Winant's poor health (the result of a wound during the first World War) had forced him to leave MESC in April. In September the US Government created a new diplomatic post for his successor: Director of American Economic Operations in the Middle East, with its Headquarters in a new American Economic Mission to the Middle East (AEMME). Its very title must have alerted Jackson to the possibility of storms ahead. That the man appointed, James Landis, a former professor of law and Dean of the Law School of Harvard University, had no experience of the Middle East, was hardly encouraging.

Jackson knew that they had been unbelievably fortunate to start off with a man like Fred Winant 'whose character, goodwill and desire to get the two sides together, were all outstanding features of his personality. If only his health had been better during the first four months of this year and there had not been a six month break they could have made great strides.'[33]

There had been a tendency for some of the Americans to work within the Legation on what they term 'non-MESC work'. That was all right so far as it went, but the main reason for American economic staff coming to the Middle East in the first place was to develop MESC into an Anglo-American agency. 'We very much hope that Mr Landis will physically spend most of his time in the MESC buildings rather than in the American Legation. Mr Kirk accepts this view, but realises that as American Director of Economic Operations Landis will have a whole heap of 'non-MESC jobs' to carry out from the American Legation. Fortunately I do not believe this.' He went on believing it, but for once he was wrong.

As soon as Landis arrived in Cairo in October he was called away to advise the American team in Teheran where a critical situation had arisen. 'In dealing with the Persia problem Mr Landis has shown himself to be extremely capable in every possible way. As to MESC, the conversation I had with him on 31 October was most useful from every point of view, and a general talk which he gave to the Officers of MESC last evening [3 November] dealing with his views of the Centre and of Anglo-American collaboration was extremely well received.'[34]

Meanwhile there was another enemy lying in wait, capable of launching an attack from the air which could have wrecked all MESC's efforts – locusts. They were known to recur in 16-year cycles, and a peak period was due in 1943-45. The main breeding grounds were in Sudan, Persia and Saudi-Arabia; clearly an invasion of locusts could devastate the harvests of the Middle East. They are most easily attacked before their wings develop while they are still 'hoppers' on the ground.

Early in 1942 Murray had set up an anti-locust unit to collect information, and in July 1943 MESC held an international conference to plan a campaign of attack. Governments from as far afield as Turkey, India and Russia agreed to exchange information about the appearance of swarms and the discovery of breeding grounds and to intensify their control methods. An operation to exterminate them in their breeding grounds in Saudi-Arabia was started in December 1943. The Army and Royal Air Force provided 24 officers, 800 other ranks and 329 vehicles. The Saudi-Arabian authorities were reluctant to allow uniformed troops to enter the country, so the men were issued with traditional Arab head-dress, which added a touch of glamour to the exercise. Local labour was also used with MESC providing the technical specialists and the poisoned bait; trenches were dug and filled with a mixture of bread, honey and arsenic, and after the locusts had died in the trenches they were filled in. By May 1944 the area was reported clear. In another operation in Persia swarms of locusts in the air and hoppers on the ground were sprayed from the air with poisonous dust. As a result of this campaign no severe loss of crops from locusts occurred during the peak years.[35] In the New Year Honours for 1944 Jackson was made Companion of the Order of St Michael and St George (CMG) in recognition of its success.

In December Casey was appointed Governor of Bengal. Jackson badly needed a month's leave, but too many of the staff were away sick. He had a large carbuncle on his right shoulder and a boil on his head, which he saw as a warning that he was overdoing things. For once he obeyed doctor's orders, sitting in the sun while his medication did its work. By the middle of January he was feeling extremely well, but agreed with the doctors that he should rest for a little longer. He knew he had a very lucky break for the last seven years, and did not want to crack up then.[36]

Jackson soon began to detect an attitude of unfriendliness, even aggression, on Landis's part; Sheila was also conscious of this 'but Jacko soldiered on, making him privy to all matters involving contact with Headquarters, the Embassy and so on.' Only later did Jackson reveal his misgivings to Nicholson, who considered Landis unsuited to his job, being too much of a politician whose main anxiety was the possibility of US aid helping to strengthen British post-war trade.[37] Indeed one of the prime tasks of the new American Mission was to see that wartime economic controls would not adversely affect American commercial enterprise after the war.[38]

With Winant's departure Anglo-American cooperation was nearly over. He continued to support MESC in Washington, but the British concept of MESC as a dispenser of valuable services was not shared there; it was seen as little more than a convenient mechanism for the control of exports and shipping.[39]

In May Jackson faced up to the situation: unless Landis was prepared to cooperate fully with MESC it would clearly be impossible to set up any long term Anglo-American agency in the area. 'If the Americans are not reasonably clear as to the role they wish to play in the Middle East in the near future, then any plan we may embark upon either on a British or an Anglo-American basis in Cairo, will be practically useless.'[40] In fact the Americans were very clear.

On 12 June Jackson went on leave, first to India, where Casey wanted his advice on dealing with the severe famine in Bengal; thence to Australia, where he saw his brother but not his wife, on to Washington for talks with the State Department and Landis; then to London, where the flying bombs were falling, down to Casablanca and across North Africa in short hops, arriving back in Cairo on 6 August. In early September he and Sheila spent a short holiday in Cyprus, staying with Edward and Audrey Jackson.

On his return to Cairo he concentrated on two things: trying to hold the organisation together on an Anglo-American basis, and preparing proposals for Stage II – decontrolling supplies. Landis had been away for three months and the Americans were dispirited and uncertain about the future; there was no senior man to take decisions on their side. There had been no friction between the British and the Americans, and if left to their own devices they should be able to work out most of their problems. For Stage II his aim was to limit control to the four bulkiest commodities and those still under combined allocation.

His main worry was about staff. Rountree, a staunch Anglo-American, was about to leave; Bailey had returned to England, Murray was far from well, the Americans were about to withdraw two or three key men; some of the staff had volunteered to go to UNRRA (see Chapter 5) and other military personnel had been repatriated under the Army scheme. 'The final straw which may break the camel's back is the fact that the Foreign Office have now telegraphed simply asking for Sheila Collins to return – without replacement – and saying 'Inform Jackson'! There is no suitable relief available for her out here and, if she were to go, I should lose what is practically my right hand. The Minister is intervening. If it were not for the urgency of the situation out here, I myself should probably have retired to hospital for penicillin treatment. My old enemies have attacked me again in force – seven big boils on my leg, a champion on one hand, and yet another beauty on the back of my head.'[41]

On 2 October he wrote what turned out to be his final letter to Nicholson:

> My main concern regarding Stage II is that Landis should not formulate a whole lot of American ideas on this subject and then try and force them down our throats without proper discussion. Anglo-American relations have continued peacefully while he has been away, and in a quiet way quite a lot of our problems have been dealt with. If Landis returns here shortly, determined to settle our various Anglo-American problems in his way and in a short time (thus enabling him to return to the States as the American Knight who broke down the British gates into the Middle East, opening this British domain to the Army of American Exporters) then I can see a singularly unpleasant time ahead of us. However, we shall see.
>
> The Americans have not, in fact, implemented their oft-repeated promises to provide top level staff in MESC. What has hurt the British most is that whilst failing to provide that staff, a separate Economic Mission has gone to Ethiopia, duplicating much of the work which we have already done.

A separate American Economic Mission in the Middle East has been set up, and now an Agricultural Mission for Saudi Arabia is being assembled. That too is bound to duplicate the work which MESC has been doing.

Looking back over our work during the last two or three years, one is conscious of the opportunities that have been missed in the Anglo-American field. It is fair to say, however, that it is the Americans who have mainly been responsible for missing them.

PS The Egyptian Police shot (by mistake, they say) my precious black Maltese cat, Roger, who had survived 1392 air raids in Malta.[42]

At the end of October Jackson was summoned to Athens to see Harold Macmillan, the Minister Resident in North Africa who was now also responsible for Greece. As a result of the German occupation Greece was almost starving, and Macmillan wanted him on a committee to advise General Scobie, whose task it was to expedite supplies of food and vital necessities to Greece. Murray went too: 'We had got shiploads of supplies to Greece, but there was no transport available. Eden, the Foreign Secretary, listened to what we had to say; we had prepared a programme and knew what tonnages of cereals were there in the harbour; the urgent job was to get them distributed. When Eden told Scobie he must produce a certain number of lorries the next day Scobie replied that unloading armaments was far more urgent than distributing grain, whereupon Jackson said that if this was not done at once there would be riots. He could be very forceful when he had to.'[43]

William Hasler from the Foreign Office was there too: 'Bill and I were together on that wonderful night when the Acropolis was illuminated for the first time in nearly four years. We went to the Athens Radio Station and found a record of Smetana's MA VLAST and broadcast it over and over again.'[44] That piece – MY COUNTRY – would always mean a lot to Jackson, and part of it was played at his funeral.

It was here that Jackson encountered Military Liaison, (ML) by which the Army would take over general responsibility for the civil population for up to a maximum of six months after conquering an area, whilst the relief organisation, UNRRA, mobilised itself as quickly as possible to take over, freeing the Army for its normal duties. On 18 January 1945 Macmillan summoned him again: 'A very late night, because I had to see Commander Jackson, of MESC, who is helping with economic problems in Greece: relief, the future of ML which is now responsible for relief, how to bring in UNRRA, how to make UNRRA reasonably efficient, etc. Finally I decided to send Jackson to Caserta with the FM [Alexander]. He can have talks there and then go on to London. I would like to detach Jackson from Cairo and make him my economic adviser. Jackson would like this.'[45] Jackson wrote a note about what he thought should be done to reduce the burden on the British Army in Greece and his advice was accepted.[46]

When he arrived in London at the end of January for discussions with Ministers about certain appointments in Greece he was asked to stay a couple of days longer. Richard Law, the Minister of State at the Foreign Office, had returned from Washington, where several Americans had expressed great concern at the condition of UNRRA. Lehman himself had asked him to say frankly whether the British Government had confidence in him as Director-General. Law tactfully replied that if the question was re-phrased – whether they had confidence in UNRRA as an Administration – the answer would be no, that Lehman had not got the staff he needed. Lehman pointed out that he had already been waiting nine months for the British to provide a new Senior Deputy Director-General. None was in sight and the man he wanted was Jackson.

On 29 January Law and the Chancellor of the Exchequer and their officials discussed how Jackson could best be used in that capacity – by helping Lehman in Washington or directing operations in Europe. Law preferred the latter, the Chancellor the former; this was the question which Jackson himself would later have to face. It was agreed that Sir James Grigg, the Minister for War, should be asked to release him.

Hasler had already sounded Jackson out and saw him that afternoon. Jackson was not keen to go to UNRRA, (he had already turned down two approaches from Lehman), but said he would do so if asked by HMG and would like to be free to leave after a year. He wanted to remain under the wing of the Treasury, which he regarded as his 'godfather', seconded to UNRRA.[47]

Shortly before Lehman learnt of the British Government's decision to appoint Jackson he had appointed Roy Hendrickson (his Deputy Director-General for Supply) to go to Athens with full power to put UNRRA's Greek office in order. He felt that he could not now deprive Hendrickson of that responsibility by giving it to Jackson, but at the same time he was anxious to have the benefit of Jackson's experience of Greece.

The Foreign Office cabled Jackson: 'Hendrickson will be leaving for Caserta on February 10th and Lehman is anxious that you should join him there. You will no doubt appreciate that Hendrickson will only just have learned of your appointment to position senior to him and he may be slightly sensitive.

'We hope while you are in Caserta you will be able to look at proposed UNRRA operations in Italy as well as in Greece since we feel that apparent inactivity of UNRRA in Italy, of which we have received several critical reports here, may lead to scandal unless checked. We regard the success of UNRRA's work in Italy as important both as test case and for general political reasons.'

To which Jackson replied: 'I will do my best to play a good innings with Hendrickson and I am quite content to leave the bowling to him at this stage.'[48] He also made sure that he could retain the services of Miss Collins.

MESC's days were numbered; hopes of a continuing Anglo-American partnership evaporated as the Americans' suspicion of British policy and influence in the Middle East grew. In August they were pressing for its dissolution as quickly as possible, proposing 1 October; the British wanted 31 December, and the two governments finally agreed that MESC would close down on 1 November.

In his Foreword to Wilmington's book (see [3]) Jackson wrote:
> As the tide of war started to recede from this most sensitive strategic area, a unique opportunity was presented to the British and American governments to formulate constructive policies for the postwar phase. A few individual officials in London and Washington saw this opportunity but at the highest levels, the necessary vision, imagination, and statesmanship were lacking and what could well have been a turning point in history was lost. It is not too much to say that had this opportunity been seized, the tragedy of the Middle East – which has already [1971] brought untold agony and suffering to millions of people for nearly a quarter of a century – might well have been averted.[49]

This remained a theme to which Jackson often returned – if only MESC had continued or been succeeded by a similar organisation much of the tragedy of the last 50 years in the Middle East might have been avoided. Nevertheless speculation as to what might have been must not let us lose sight of what MESC had achieved. Even the US State Department acknowledged that 'the success of the Supply Center was an indispensable condition both to achieving the necessary flow of supplies to Soviet Russia and to winning the battle of El Alamein.'[50]

Like Malta, the Middle East survived – its peoples did not starve or rebel and the armed forces were enabled to do their job of winning the war. The vital importance of the fourth leg of the stool had again been proved. And even if MESC had no future, it left a legacy, as Wilmington recognised:

> The Middle East Supply Centre had been a part of those developments which hastened the identification of the Middle East as a regional entity recognised as such on the inside and the outside. It had demonstrated to what an extent economic coordination among the territories of the region could be carried if the political environment was favorable. In doing so it had considerably expanded the horizon of problems held susceptible to regional cooperation. … This was the way in which the regional economic commissions of the United Nations were to conduct their deliberations.[51]

It is how they continue to do so.

Nicholson considered Jackson to be one of the most outstandingly able all-rounders holding a key post through 1941-44, and one of the very few who could put it down as it happened; his interests and abilities were amazingly broad, covering at a high level the strategic as well as the political, diplomatic, managerial and not least the human aspects, both detailed and day-to-day, and international, medium-term and long-term; to him goodwill and building up warm personal relationships was paramount; while demanding high performance he was most aware of people's character limitations and personal problems, in spite of which he did miracles in creating and running a happy ship. 'It must be borne in mind that he was then responsible for a realm greater than that of the Indian Civil Service and much less amenable, but, unlike it, he came through without any disaster like the Bengal Famine, on a much smaller and more scratch staff team. That is a measure of his greatness.'[52]

5 UNRRA – the first UN organisation

IT WAS LITTLE MORE THAN A YEAR since UNRRA, the United Nations Relief and Rehabilitation Administration, had been set up by 44 nations agreeing 'to co-operate in its work for the victims of German and Japanese barbarism, each nation according to its own resources.' UNRRA would operate in areas of food shortage until the return of peace enabled the liberated peoples of the occupied countries to support themselves.[1]

UNRRA's Council resolved that each unoccupied country should contribute roughly one per cent of its national income for the year ending 30 June 1943.[2] This one per cent was the main source of UNRRA's funds for its operations during its first two years.

Since the USA would be the largest contributor the Council appointed Herbert Lehman as Director-General, and since Britain would be the second largest Lehman appointed as Senior Deputy Director-General (SDDG) Sir Arthur Salter, formerly Head of the British Merchant Shipping Mission to the USA. Salter accepted the appointment temporarily, and kept the organisational structure flexible,[3] perhaps too flexible.

By the time of the Council's Second Session in September 1944 the liberation of France had begun and it was clear that effective action was urgently needed. Lehman appealed to members to reaffirm their faith in the collective effort by supplying goods, funds, expert personnel and advice; the members, however, were not greatly impressed by the achievements of the administration.[4] The lack of strong administrative control and drive was not entirely Lehman's fault; the British and American governments had undertaken to do what they could to provide good staff, and they had failed; such people were simply not to be found; they were either in the forces or doing essential government jobs. Salter resigned and Lehman's pleas grew louder, but to no avail. By the end of the year there was little doubt that if left to itself UNRRA would fail; the British Government was looking to Jackson to save the sinking ship.

Unlike Salter, he already had very clear ideas about how UNRRA should be organised. During 1943 a working party had been set up in Cairo in conjunction with MESC to consider post-war problems. One of its members, Lieutenant-Colonel JPB Ross, recalled how they were invited to a working lunch in the mess: 'our host was an extremely young-looking Naval Commander, the Director. During the meal he invited each of us in turn to give a very brief outline of the most urgent problems we foresaw from the point of view of our specialised knowledge. After this *tour d'horizon*, and over coffee, in a virtuoso performance of succinct analysis, he brilliantly summarised our presentations; he then went on to outline the likely pattern of obstacles to be cleared, by-passed or surmounted, with the initiation of emergency relief operations on a scale never previously attempted. He then revealed to us the early projected creation of an organisation to be called 'UNRRA', to coordinate all emergency relief operations. We wondered why, with such a genius around, there was any need for us and our clumsy working party at all. Indeed, the organisational chart he had outlined on the back of an envelope became the prototype document of UNRRA's foundation.'[5]

Jackson and Hendrickson spent most of March in the Balkans where relief work was being undertaken by the British and US armies; they inspected the training of UNRRA Missions and negotiated agreements with President Tito in Yugoslavia and Hoxha in Albania to receive them. In Cairo they expedited the return to Yugoslavia and Greece of the many thousands of refugees under military care in camps in the Middle East.

In April they visited the European Regional Office (ERO) in London. It was meant to control all of UNRRA's activities in Europe, but despite employing about 1,000 people it had never really come into operation. It was directed by an Administrative Council of three Deputy Directors-General, one British, one American and one Russian, all with equal powers and each able to suspend action if he disagreed with the other two. It was committed to work with Supreme Headquarters, Allied Expeditionary Force in Europe (SHAEF) in handling the displaced persons problems in Germany and was expected to produce about 6,000 staff by the beginning of July; of whom only 800 had been recruited.[6]

After spending ten days examining its various sections, housed in six separate buildings, Jackson and Hendrickson reached the same conclusion; they told Law that it suffered from lack of leadership and was built around personalities, it was pervaded by schisms and conflicts and seriously overstaffed in some sections. The Administrative Council of three must be abolished and one man must run the office.

Law asked whether Jackson, as Senior Deputy DG, might be appointed to take over the ERO for a period. He was the only man who would command everyone's confidence and who also had some experience of the job which the Missions in Europe would have to do. Jackson agreed reluctantly; the Washington HQ also needed reorganising and he knew that Hendrickson was more familiar with the business of procuring supplies.

They agreed that the three Deputy DGs should continue to run the three divisions (supplies, operations, finance and administration) but realised that the appointment of a new head of the ERO would put one of them – Sir Frederick Leith-Ross – in an impossible position. Leith-Ross was one of UNRRA's founding fathers, having helped to draft its original agreement; Jackson was anxious that some way could be found for UNRRA to continue to benefit from his advice and his unique contacts with the Allied governments. This would be possible if he were made Chairman of the European Regional Committee, but that could be difficult, as the present chairman, Ernest Brown, was a government minister. Hendrickson said that unless that were done he could not recommend the Director-General to delegate extensive authority to the ERO. Law said he would consult the Chancellor and the Prime Minister.[7]

Jackson and Hendrickson arrived in Washington on 23 April, and found things were as bad as in London. The Headquarters was large and cumbersome, over-centralised and over-staffed. Worst of all, there seemed to be no clear idea of what UNRRA's policy was.[8] They put their proposal to Lehman – that Jackson should be appointed to run the ERO as his Personal Representative. While Lehman saw the advantages of this he also saw two disadvantages: first he would be deprived of the additional administrative strength which he badly needed in Washington; secondly, and more important, he was being asked to delegate his full powers to a man half his age, whom he knew only slightly.[9]

Churchill proved reluctant to move Ernest Brown and on Wednesday 25 April Jackson phoned Law threatening to throw in his hand. Law immediately spoke to the PM: it was not merely a matter of making a place for Leith-Ross, they really wanted him as Chairman of the Committee, where his particular qualifications would be of great value; unless they could offer Leith-Ross the Chairmanship Lehman would almost certainly not proceed with Jackson's appointment to Europe, in which case Jackson would resign and that would be the end of UNRRA. Churchill agreed to see Brown, but he was out of London.[10]

The next day Churchill was coming round to the proposal, but still wanted two or three days to think it over. When Jackson heard this he was desperate and asked Lehman to telephone Law, who then sent a further minute to Churchill.[11]

On the Sunday evening, 29 April, Lehman and Jackson had a long talk. Mrs Lehman was also present. Lehman told him of the difficulties which the proposal created for him; Jackson said he understood, but the situation which he and Hendrickson had found in Europe had forced them to the conclusion that

Edith and Herbert Lehman

there was no alternative. 'Mrs Lehman saw very clearly the position in which her husband was being placed, and felt that very strong – and almost unfair – pressure was being put on him.' The next day Lehman told him that he had agreed to the plan.[12]

Jackson looked back on that meeting as the start of a very special friendship. Herbert and Edith Lehman treated him with great consideration in their official dealings and spoilt him with kindness in their personal relationship.[13]

On 3 May the appointments were announced. Lehman formally assigned Jackson to serve as his personal representative for a limited time in charge of the office of the Director General in London, and put Hendrickson in charge of the Office of the Senior Deputy Director General (SDDG) in Washington in Jackson's absence; and Leith-Ross chaired a meeting of the European Regional Committee.

On Monday 7 May (the day Germany surrendered) Jackson took charge. He held a meeting of senior staff at 9 every morning except Sunday. The meetings, like the minutes, were usually brief and to the point – to establish what needed to be done and who was to do it. Even on the Wednesday – VE Day, when the whole of Britain was celebrating victory in Europe – it was business as usual in the ERO. Sheila had now joined the office, fresh from a month's leave after clearing up the loose ends of MESC in Cairo.

On 15 May, having worked in UNRRA for three months, Jackson sent Law his promised report: briefly – UNRRA was in chaos. This prompted Hasler to write to Law asking if it was worth trying to inject life and sense into an organisation headed by Lehman, 'a man without common sense or guts – Mrs Lehman takes all the decisions', and advising that the Government's policy should be 'Lehman must Go'.[14] Hasler's suggestion was not pursued, nevertheless his note implies that Law shared his opinion, (as did Law's tactful reply when Lehman had asked if the Government had confidence in him). But this was never Jackson's opinion; Lehman became one of his great heroes – possibly the greatest.

On 30 May the Chancellor of the Exchequer, Sir John Anderson, called a meeting of Ministers to consider Jackson's report.

Meeting on the threatened collapse of UNRRA

Commander Jackson, the able and energetic Australian who has been appointed, at our insistence, Chief Deputy Director General of UNRRA, in the hope of saving it, gave an extremely disturbing report on the situation.

The present state of UNRRA is chaotic. The administration is in complete disorder, there is no system of authority or discipline, work is uncoordinated, there is a serious lack of good personnel in key positions, money is being uselessly squandered, there is no proper planning of major operations – in fact the leaking ship is rapidly heading for the rocks. Commander Jackson has done everything possible to patch the leaks but does not think he can save the ship without immediate and energetic help from HMG on a number of specific points.

A further serious development is the growing loss of American interest in UNRRA. Criticism is developing rapidly and may lead to a refusal to furnish future funds. There is, according to Commander Jackson, a possibility of the United States Government withdrawing from UNRRA any serious support. There are several signs that the Americans are thinking of transferring their money to more promising investments. Other countries would of course follow suit.

The Chancellor and the other Ministers present decided that it must be regarded as an important British interest to save UNRRA; but Commander Jackson made it clear to the meeting that, while he thinks he can hold UNRRA together for a few weeks longer, he can only hope to save it on the following conditions:

These were, briefly, that HMG must

(1) provide a few really first-class men who must be asked by their senior authorities to lend their services as a national duty,

(2) provide administrative help – eg make suitable accommodation available and secure generally better facilities,

(3) persuade the Americans to renew their support.[15]

Not a lot happened. The Foreign Secretary sent a telegram to the US Secretary of State, saying that the UK had recently produced Jackson 'at some sacrifice', he hoped the US Government could join with the UK by putting in a few first class people.[16] Office accommodation seems not to have been improved either then or later. As for providing staff – a list of suggestions for the nine posts had already been considered at the meeting and several people were approached, but for one reason or another none was appointed. Back in London two weeks later Jackson found that the War Office had made no attempt to select or approach officers; the immediate need was a first class man to take charge of displaced persons (DP) operations in the SHAEF area (mainly Germany) in which the army was also involved. He delayed his return to Washington in order to see a possible candidate, Lieutenant-General Sir Humfrey Gale, but Gale, having been the Chief Administrative Officer of SHAEF, was not prepared to take on that job. Jackson returned to Washington empty handed and despondent.[17]

In Washington the news was more cheering: the British Minister Resident cabled to Law that Jackson's effect on UNRRA had been electric. 'I would not have thought it possible for one man to do so much in so short a time. The effect on Lehman has also been remarkable, and although he is reacting a bit now it is none the less a fact that a most successful operation has been performed and the patient is now entering the convalescent state. How this convalescence goes in the next few weeks may well settle the future of UNRRA.'[18]

By the end of June most of the 6,000 staff for handling the DPs in Germany had been picked. They worked in teams in Assembly Centres where the DPs were collected, usually about 5,000 in each, with a Director, his Deputy, a doctor, a nurse and two welfare workers. The Army had been concentrating on getting them back to their homes and UNRRA found itself left with the hard core of the 'non-repatriables', the Poles, Czechs, Balts, and other nationalities, who – it was said – did not wish to return. It was probable that 850,000 of these would remain by the beginning of October when UNRRA was to take over maintenance of the Centres where they were living.

Bridges found a possible candidate for the most senior job – to succeed Jackson as the Director General's Personal Representative in London. Finding him unsuitable he offered this post to Gale, who agreed to take it. In September Lieutenant-General Sir Frederick Morgan, who as Deputy Chief of Staff in SHAEF had been senior to Gale, was appointed Head of Displaced Persons Operations in Germany, the post which Gale had declined.

He went to Rome to see how supplies for the Balkans were being handled; he was dismayed to find that they were not arriving fast enough and saw a danger that the efficient distribution organisation which UNRRA was providing in Europe might fail for lack of supplies. Coal for the railways to transport the food was needed as much as the food itself, and he saw that a stronger supply team in Washington was needed. Given the likelihood of a severe winter in Europe and the risk of starvation which could result, it was imperative that UNRRA should operate efficiently over the next few weeks. He was also worried that funds would run out at the end of the year; only a few months remained in which to demonstrate that UNRRA must have more resources. He wanted to shout out to the world that the democracies – especially the US and England – were throwing away priceless opportunities and even inviting disaster by refusing to provide a few good men for this operation.[19]

Alfred Katzin, whom Jackson knew from Military Liaison in the Balkans, was now Deputy DG of the Department of Finance and Administration in the ERO. His immediate job was to get the staffing arrangements in Europe under control: inevitably this had to be done at tremendous speed, firing and hiring with little time for careful attention to personal feelings. 'Katzin's surgical methods, though perhaps arbitrary, resolved the crisis quickly if not painlessly.'[20]

Jackson did his share of the firing, 'going very energetically about the task of cutting out dead wood, and finding plenty of it to cut'.[21] This nearly got him into trouble. He was puzzled to get a call from Gil Winant, the US Ambassador in London and brother of Fred, telling him that whatever else he was doing that afternoon the two of them were to have tea with Mrs Churchill. They went together to the underground offices of the Ministry of Defence.

> There were some rooms there for the Prime Minister, including a small sitting room where Mrs Churchill was, and tea was served. Mr Churchill was apparently suffering from a heavy cold, and he was down a corridor in the bedroom, but he could be heard. After we had tea, Gil said 'the reason why I asked you to come and talk with Mrs Churchill is, the Prime Minister intends to fire you immediately. Do you realise that <u>you</u> have fired between 25 and 30 of <u>his</u> friends during your recent activities in Cairo?' I said I was totally unaware of that fact. What I had done was without reference to any individual's friendships. All that I was concerned with was to make UNRRA efficient to do its job. Anyone who had seen the

destruction wrought by the war – as undoubtedly Mr Churchill had seen when he was in Greece – would want to see relief, rehabilitation and reconstruction started as soon as possible. I was quite blunt. I was Australian and if Churchill didn't want me there were plenty of other things to do. I said UNRRA only existed to help these people. I really weighed in to Mrs Churchill – perhaps the Prime Minister heard me. I ended 'if you've just been in Russia, you too realise what needs to be done, and that it is not a matter of friendship, it's a matter of getting the job done. And at least I did it in the Middle East and I did it in Malta.' It was bang, bang, bang!

So she said, 'Have another cup of tea.' I did. She walked down the passage to the PM's bedroom; then – you could hear growling, like a bulldog: 'urrgh, – urrgh, – urrgh.' Then a long pause and a very long 'Urr – rrgh', which meant that it was all right.[22]

By the time of the Third Session of the Governing Council (August 1945) the sceptical attitude of the member states had given place to a determination to make UNRRA succeed, and they finally agreed to contribute another one per cent, on the assumption that UNRRA's work would end in March 1947.

Though physically exhausted, Jackson did not slacken his pace, continuing to chair staff meetings throughout the period of the Session. When Katzin collapsed from overwork and was ordered to rest for six months William Hasler was seconded from the Foreign Office to take his place. Gale joined the staff on 10 September and went to Germany with Jackson later in the week. On the following Monday, 17 September, Jackson chaired his last ERO meeting and handed over to Gale. He remained Personal Representative of the DG until the end of October. It had been a gruelling nine months.

A Labour government had been elected in July, and Philip Noel-Baker was the new Minister of State. Shortly after taking over as SDDG in Washington on 11 November Jackson sent him a long and depressing report: the organisation at Headquarters needed changing, the top-level personnel were far from satisfactory and financial control had been disgracefully lax. Lehman had agreed to the appointment of Major- General Lowell Rooks of the US Army (formerly Deputy Chief of Staff in the Mediterranean) as Deputy DG and Chief Executive Officer, to relieve him of some of the day-to-day work and deputise for him when he was away. If another three or four men could be found the administrative structure of UNRRA should at last be well established; without them it would never be efficient and the capable men would be overworked until they broke – like Katzin. He thought seven senior officials should be removed, but for political and personal reasons Lehman would not agree; fortunately, except for one they were relatively harmless.

He had discovered that the financial situation was very serious: lack of senior staff and failure to coordinate the work of separate divisions had obscured the fact that the cash was running out. Back in March 1944 Congress had <u>authorised</u> a grant to UNRRA of $1350 million (the one per cent pledged at the First Council Session), but $550 million of this had still not been <u>appropriated</u> (that is to say handed over to UNRRA). Hearings in Congress had been going on for five weeks, but progress was slow and these funds would not be available until the end of the first week in December at the earliest. Already requisitions covering $50 millions' worth of agricultural machinery, seeds, medical requirements and other supplies, had been frozen so that food could be shipped in December and January. There was a great danger that a large part of UNRRA supplies would arrive too late to have the best effect in Europe. Oils and fats had just come off the ration in the USA and the Department of Agriculture had offered $12 million worth. They would have been worth their weight in gold, but the dollars were not available.

Equally urgent was to obtain Congress's authorisation for the second one per cent before the Christmas recess. Without that further funds would not be available before February and a break in supplies would be almost inevitable. 'We have no illusions as to the political difficulties facing us over the next few weeks. We intend to use every possible argument and political manoeuvre – we have little to lose and everything to gain. Basically it is a matter of dollars or death for many people in Europe.'[23]

Continuing financial support for UNRRA was now a party political issue in the USA and the republican opposition lost no opportunity to discredit UNRRA. Roosevelt had died, Truman was President and the personal link between Lehman and The White House was over. The US Government had at first been one of the great forces behind the establishment of UNRRA but its policy towards the USSR was shifting and difficulties were now emerging. Much of UNRRA's work was going on in Eastern Europe, Yugoslavia and Albania; requests for assistance from the Ukraine and Byelo-Russia had been received, and some US officials were now questioning the wisdom of putting American resources into the international organisation. UNRRA had not had a good press in the US – many of the criticisms were unjustified, but some were valid, such as that certain staff had been too highly paid. Congress was sensitive to all these influences, creating a situation which UNRRA could only neglect at its peril.[24]

The administration had given no thought to the importance of obtaining political support; it had no policy on what it wanted from Congress, and little had been done to impress on the President, the State Department, and Congress itself the vital need for additional funds. Jackson therefore did all he could to build up support for UNRRA from the public and the press: Lehman made a coast-to-coast broadcast, General Eisenhower testified to Congress on behalf of UNRRA, he also refused to allow the Army to assume responsibilities for relief work in Europe; and Pope Pius XII urged Catholics in the USA to press for support for UNRRA.

Hasler finished his stint in the ERO in mid-October when Major-General Richard Lewis (USA) was appointed DDG for Finance and Administration to succeed Katzin. Back in the Foreign Office he wrote:

> 'My dear Jacko, Report has it that you are finding a certain number of things to do in your spare time, and I have therefore refrained from deluging you with my usual witty correspondence. I think it can be said that ERO has survived the change-over [from Jackson to Gale] remarkably well and I have been greatly impressed by the improvements in the machinery which have been introduced over the last six weeks. I am glad to see from the recent telegrams that you seem to be getting along better over the 1%. It must have been a pretty grim mess to get back to. Love to Sheila. Yours ever, Bill.[25]

Jackson replied that he was too tired to tell him all the ins and outs of the situation; the whole campaign had been run from UNRRA's office. 'The President has not been prepared to come out completely and the State Department has not carried the ball.' At the end of January he would obey the instructions which the doctors had given him in August: he would go away, feeling that he had completed his initial task in UNRRA. 'Thank you for all you did during the period in which you transferred your affections from Whitehall to Portland Place. It was a decisive factor in ensuring that the turn-over was as successful as it has proved to be.'[26]

On 4 December Congress approved the appropriation of the remaining $550 of the first 1%; on 13 December the President signed the Bill; the following morning $435 million had been committed – a measure of the extent to which supplies had been held up during the previous seven weeks. Authorisation of the second 1% was no problem and was given on 6 December. Appropriation was another matter and required some astute tactical manoeuvres by Jackson, given the shortage of time before the Christmas recess. He tried to initiate simultaneous hearings, one before the Foreign Relations Committee in the Senate and the other before the House Appropriations Committee.

Then the difficulties began: Senators A and B, in the Foreign Relations Committee, did not want to be involved, and Congressman C, the Chairman of the Appropriations Committee, had gone off on a junket to Paris in the first TWA service. (We got him back in a special plane by 0100 hours on Sunday 9 December – a few hours before a big snow-storm closed down all the airfields on the East Coast).

> Monday 10 December was a Bad Day! There was no move on the morning of Tuesday 11th so we arranged for Lehman to see the President (at twenty minutes' notice) and fired every gun we had. The President responded well. The Senate leaders agreed to have Hearings in the Foreign Relations Committee on Wednesday 12 December, but did so reluctantly, and consequently gave our team a very rough handling before the Committee meetings on Wednesday and Thursday.
>
> In the House of Representatives Congressman McCormick kept telephoning the President until finally Mr Cannon agreed to get his Appropriations Committee together. I was called as the chief witness, with Lehman also present. The hearings were brief and concentrated almost entirely on the administrative efficiency of the organisation. The members gave no indication as to whether they would support the appropriation before the Recess. It was clear that politically it would be impossible to get the whole appropriation in one bite and we agreed among ourselves that we could settle at between six and seven hundred millions before the Recess, with reasonable safety.

At 10pm on the night of Thursday 13 December we heard that members of the Senate and Congress had agreed to tack on $400 million to another Bill and would defer further consideration until after the Recess. While this would theoretically cover the period of the Recess, in practice it would not be enough to save UNRRA because Congress would almost certainly not vote new money immediately they came back. We decided to carry on the fight.

The President helped most effectively; Acheson, (Secretary of State for Economic Affairs) was also most helpful. All the columnists, leader-writers and commentators backed us up with broadsides. It worked. Our strategy – that only pressure from the people would carry us through – had been correct. Senator Vandenburg remarked, just before the debate started: 'We do not really like this, but the pressure from the people makes it impossible for us to do anything else but go through with it.' Late on the Friday night the $400 million was increased to $750 million. I celebrated with four double orange juices![27]

At one point during the debate Jackson himself was held to be an obstacle to Congress approving the increase. Senator Langer from North Dakota was appalled at the prospect of all that money being handled by a foreigner: 'A few days ago I heard that if one wished to see Mr Lehman, he must first obtain the consent of a Britisher. I did not believe it at the time, but I hold in my hands the headquarters telephone directory, sure enough, I find that Mr Lehman's assistant, the man whom one must see if he wishes to see Mr Lehman, does not come from Tennessee or from the State of Montana or from Maine. He does not come from any one of our 48 States. He is a Britisher. Looking further, we find the Office of the Senior Deputy Director-General. Who is he? Not one of the veterans whom my distinguished friend from Illinois mentioned a few moments ago. He is Sir Robert Jackson, of England, who has an office here, and who will handle the $750,000,000 which we shall appropriate sooner or later. So I have prepared an amendment: Provided, That all of said money shall be administered and distributed by American veterans of World War I and World War II.' Senator Hayden came to the rescue: 'My information is that the second largest contributor to this fund is Great Britain. It seems to me therefore entirely appropriate that in an international organisation composed of 44 nations the deputy administrator should be a representative of the British. I am advised that the deputy administrator is not only a Britisher, but a Scotsman, and that he is very cautious about the expenditure of money. So there is a positive advantage in having a Scotsman looking after our expenditures, to see that the money is not wasted. Perhaps there is an asset rather than a liability in that respect.' Nothing daunted, Senator Langer tried again: 'I ask the distinguished Senator from Arizona if he does not believe that when Mr Lehman is called away, as he very frequently is, the man in charge of all this money should be an American citizen? I may suggest that many American citizens are of Scotch ancestry.'[28] No more was said about Jackson, and after a long debate the amendment was passed. UNRRA had survived.

Hasler wrote that everybody in London was delighted at his success with Congress; equally nobody had any illusions as to who was responsible for the great improvement in the standing of UNRRA in the USA.[29]

Jackson was informed that he had been given permanent status in the British Civil Service, on probation for a year, during which he would have to satisfy the Commissioners that he was in every way suitable! On that happy note 1945 came to an end.

1946 began badly. On 2 January Lieutenant-General Sir Frederick Morgan, Head of Displaced Persons Operations in Germany, gave a press conference in Frankfurt. After making his prepared statement he agreed to answer questions. One of his replies was seized upon by the British and American press. THE TIMES, for instance, reported on 3 January:

'WELL FED' JEWS FROM POLAND –
SIR F E MORGAN ON A 'NEW EXODUS'

Lieutenant-General Sir Frederick Morgan stated today that he believed European Jews had a 'positive plan for a second exodus' – this time from Europe. General Morgan said he had seen an exodus of Jews from Poland in Russian trains on a regular route from Lodz to Berlin. All of them were well dressed, well fed, healthy, and had 'pockets bulging with money'. As these Jews were not displaced persons, he added, they did not come under the jurisdiction of UNRRA.

Criticism in the USA mounted very quickly, particularly of Morgan and the British staff in UNRRA. The Lehmans were on their way to California for a brief holiday; after consulting Gale in London Jackson himself took the decision that Morgan could not continue to serve UNRRA.[30]

He informed Lehman when their train stopped at Albuquerque, New Mexico. To Jackson's surprise they both decided to fly back immediately; Mrs Lehman had never flown before.

When appointing Gale and Morgan Jackson had made it absolutely clear that they were never to make any public statement bearing on the general Zionist problem unless it had been authorised personally by Lehman.[31] Jackson accepted that Morgan might have felt that he was speaking objectively, 'but as a soldier he had disobeyed orders, and if he'd done that in the army he would have been court-martialled on the spot and out.'[32] Having just secured the appropriation of more funds, Jackson must have been appalled at the possibility of the remaining $650 million being put at risk by the Morgan furore, so it is understandable that he acted quickly to restore UNRRA's image by announcing that Morgan must resign. Possibly he also wanted to present Lehman with a *fait accompli*: the one matter about which they did not see eye to eye was the firing or down-grading of unsatisfactory staff. He had recently found that some were so overpaid and under-worked that he prevented publication of UNRRA's internal budget for fear of providing powerful ammunition for its critics; even so, Lehman had been reluctant to take any action which would precipitate personnel trouble at HQ.[33]

The next day the British Ambassador in Washington cabled the Foreign Office: the press was very bad; keeping Morgan in post would jeopardise the balance of the appropriation; given the strength of Jewish feelings he was satisfied that UNRRA had no alternative but to ask Morgan to resign.[34]

When Morgan received Gale's formal request to resign he refused, saying he would appeal to Lehman, as all UNRRA staff were entitled to do.[35] Perhaps there was a clash of personalities too: the ERO staff found Humfrey Gale – 'Grumf' – a bit pompous; Morgan, the more colourful character, had been senior to Gale in SHAEF and may have thought it a bit rich to be fired by him.

The Foreign office thought Morgan's appeal should be heard;[36] UNRRA staff in Germany all agreed that his words had been highly distorted by the press, and that, as the man who had really got the DP operations going, his services should at all costs be retained. Even representatives of Jewish Agencies attached to UNRRA said that he should not be asked to resign.[37] There was now a risk of losing Gale, which Hasler thought would be a greater calamity than mass resignations in Germany. Events had moved very fast, and his advice to Jackson was that they should all try to relax and take it more easily.[38]

Lieutenant-General Sir Humfrey Gale
Fred Hess & Son

Morgan sent a more conciliatory telegram to Gale, pointing out that it would be bad for UNRRA's image if it were known that a senior official could be dismissed at a moment's notice. Hasler hoped that Lehman and Jackson could send a sympathetic reply to Morgan and would not rush things. The matter was now for Lehman to decide. 'If Morgan went certain sections of Congress would regard it as a submission to Jewish influence; if he stayed anti-British elements would regard it as further proof that UNRRA was now virtually run by the British for their own interests and that Lehman had no real control.'[39]

After seeing Lehman in New York Morgan wrote a letter accepting responsibility for his remarks, saying that he realised that certain of his words were such as to lay him and the administration open to charges of political or racial bias and reiterated his regret at uttering them. He rejected any suggestion of being anti-semitic, assured Lehman of his loyalty and asked to be permitted to carry on working for UNRRA. On 28 January Lehman reinstated him.[40]

On 2 February THE ECONOMIST congratulated UNRRA on its director's sensible decision to retain Morgan's

Lieutenant-General Sir Frederick Morgan

services: 'No organisation can lightly dispense with the services of a first class man. UNRRA needs its good men, and General Morgan is one of the best.'

Jackson had met Barbara Ward again in London in October and November, but not since. Perhaps she thought she was giving him the credit for Morgan's reinstatement, unaware of his disagreement with Lehman. He wrote to her: he was not entering into the rights and wrongs of Morgan's actions, but sorting out the mess had cut straight across his work in January and he resented every moment spent on it.[41] Jackson accepted Lehman's decision with good grace, seeing it as 'an example of his exceptional generosity of spirit.'[42]

Morgan returned to Germany determined to get his own back; Jackson was equally determined to catch him out if the chance came, as it did in August, when LaGuardia 'released' him and the War Office recalled him to London.

Of the eight million DPs some two million were unwilling to be repatriated. The USSR had made it clear in 1944 that they did not want UNRRA's assistance in Soviet-occupied territories, and after the war ended they wanted to retrieve 'their' DPs from the other occupied zones of Germany and Austria; these included many (Ukrainians, for example) who had collaborated with the Germans, whom other member-nations of UNRRA did not want sent home to be killed. There was also a great difference of view between UNRRA and the military in charge of the prisoner-of-war and refugee camps.

According to Alfred Davidson, UNRRA's General Counsel who advised on policy matters, 'the British Generals weren't worrying much about what we thought in UNRRA, they wanted to turn those fellows out and let them get back where they belonged; some of them were sent back home, and God knows how many went to their deaths or into trouble. In the end we won the question of principle, that people should not be sent back where there was reason to believe that they would be subject to recriminations. So it was agreed that Russian military and other officials should interview people in the camps. It was essentially a face-saving arrangement for them.'[43]

Davidson had joined UNRRA in November 1945, shortly before Jackson arrived in Washington, and attended the daily staff meetings: 'Jacko had a real sense of organisation. In his staff meetings there was no question of a debate or discussion of policy, it was a means of communication by which the head of each division could report each day on what they had done yesterday and what they thought would happen on the next day and what they proposed to do about it. When something didn't happen he knew who to jump on to find out why not.

'He was regarded by some people as a paragon, but he was by no means a very popular figure. He had the mannerisms of a military commander, the way he spoke, the way he treated people, very formally; he could relax and have a drink with the people in the same echelons of command (and I was one of the lucky ones), but he wasn't a very popular fellow as such. Those who regarded him as a paragon were those who could see the enormous value of what he was doing; but he was taking over an organisation which was disorganised and there was great suspicion of people who had to make decisions. His real contribution was to make order in the flow of business by assigning responsibility for particular actions. The nature of the organisation was to deal with the emergency, the immediate needs. He wasn't inclined to bring in people from outside to pick their brains, looking to the people who held the job to do it. There were occasional exceptions: it was essential to have a proper accounting system and controls, so he brought in Harry Howell from the War Department as chief accountant. As an operator concerned to have a machine that worked efficiently Jacko was superb; I never saw a fellow who was so good at that.'[44] (Financial control was the last element in UNRRA to be reorganized; changes suggested by the Council's auditors had been resisted by Lehman.)

With Rooks now installed as a Deputy Director-General and Chief Executive Officer Jackson was free to go to London in February. He had three reasons: first he needed to see Gale, who was still disconcerted by the Morgan affair; secondly the first General Assembly of the United Nations Organisation was taking place in London and the Secretary-General, Trygve Lie, had asked Lehman for advice on recruiting staff. Jackson met Lie on 24 February and suggested he should talk to Bridges and look out for the young high-fliers.[45] Thirdly, he wanted to see how the UN might take over some of the UNRRA's functions. The ERO was pressing for a new organisation for refugees, and the UN General Assembly referred the matter to its Economic and Social Council (ECOSOC) for urgent action. This led to the establishment in 1947 of the International Refugee Organisation (IRO) to take over responsibility for the remaining DPs. The General Assembly also appointed a committee representing eleven nations to discuss with the Director-General and Jackson 'the means by which the utmost good to the whole UNRRA programme might be accomplished'.

UNRRA was now providing relief and rehabilitation in over twenty countries: in Europe (Eastern as well as Western), Byelo-Russia, the Ukraine, the Middle East, Ethiopia and China (Communist as well as Nationalist). Items supplied ranged from food, clothing, sewing machines, materials for shelter, seeds and medical supplies, dairy cattle and chickens, to tractors, trucks and railway engines, as well as horses and mules for distributing food in mountain areas.[46] But difficulties were increasing: in the short term strikes in the USA were preventing UNRRA from getting urgently needed grain; in the longer term the cold war had started, the iron curtain had descended and the USA was not prepared to give any further assistance to communist regimes. It was also clear to the Administration that the

LaGuardia addressing UNRRA Council at Atlantic City, March 1946   Fred Hess & Son

need for supplies would continue well into 1947 and that UNRRA would not have sufficient resources to provide them. The Fourth Session of the Council at Atlantic City during the second half of March was therefore of critical importance.

During the very harsh winter in Europe UNRRA's resources had been stretched to the limit in order to prevent starvation. Senior staff were convinced that the immediate task of providing relief and rehabilitation to Europe and the Far East could not be accomplished within the compass of the two 1% contributions from member Governments. The US now wanted to terminate all UNRRA's operations in Europe by 31 December 1946, and in the Far East by 31 March 1947. Its attitude was made clear when no senior member of the US Administration attended the opening ceremony.[47]

It was at this session that Lehman announced his resignation. (He wanted to seek selection as a candidate for the Senate.) Jackson had been warned by Mrs Lehman and found it hard to contemplate UNRRA without him. When the name of his successor was announced – Fiorello LaGuardia, former Mayor of New York City – she was appalled and collapsed weeping into his arms, crying 'how can they do this to my husband?'[48] When Lehman said farewell to UNRRA at a reception later Jackson was too moved to respond on behalf of the staff.[49]

Food shipments to Europe slumped badly in March and April as the full extent of the world food shortage became apparent. In India the monsoons had failed; and in North America large amounts of grain were being fed to animals. Hasler wrote suggesting that Britain might be able to reduce its stocks of grain in the short term to help UNRRA through a difficult period.[50] Attached to his letter was a manuscript note; Jacko had asked 'whether any supplies were needed *chez* Hasler?' He said his priorities were a nightgown for his wife, soap, a large comb and stockings size 9½. A few weeks later they were both drowned when on holiday in Devon. Jacko had lost a great supporter and friend.

The feeling was growing in the Administration that the UN was not moving fast enough to take over UNRRA's functions and that the whole question of the run-down of UNRRA would have to be faced at the Fifth Council Session in August. Jackson sent a strong *aide-memoire* to the member governments reminding them that if it were decided that UNRRA should continue, new resources must be provided; if a successor supply agency was to be created it must be up and running by 1 January 1947. Receiving countries likely to need help until the harvest of 1947 must therefore prove their case conclusively. The Council must then decide whether supplies should be furnished by bilateral, multinational or international arrangements. LaGuardia's contribution to the document was to insert a sentence saying that he personally did not recommend that UNRRA continue – hardly helpful in a document which was tacitly recommending UNRRA's continuance as the obvious solution to the problem.[51] LaGuardia assumed that he would serve until 31 December and many of the staff believed that he had been appointed by Truman to preside over the liquidation of UNRRA.

A two-hour wait for a delayed flight to Washington in May gave Jackson an opportunity to write to his brother: when they met in 1944 he had hoped 1945 would see him in a quieter job, with another chance of a private life and a second shot at married life; now he had worked to a point where everything, and all feeling, had gone. 'If I have made a mess of myself it is perhaps some consolation that the organisation has been saved – though we will <u>not</u> succeed this winter in saving all the lives entrusted to us, no matter how hard we work. I hope to get away by mid-June.'

His main purpose in writing was to see whether Alan could explain to Peggy that any idea of trying reconciliation before he could get fit again was hopeless. He had suggested she should get a divorce but she seemed to think a situation which existed nine years ago could be restored by a wishful thought. He admired greatly all she had done and took some responsibility for the situation. He was in love with no one in particular, he just wanted to get away.

'You will of course see it through different eyes. If you are prepared to extend your brotherly affection to seeing what you can do with Peggy I should be more than grateful to you for her sake, not my own. I do not know how this letter may change your feelings towards me, but I shall always remain your affectionate brother, Rob.'[52]

On 24 June he sailed from San Francisco to Sydney where he disembarked on 1 July. Peggy was there to greet him; so were the press. 'Hobart woman lionised by Sydney newspapers' proclaimed the HOBART MERCURY. Peggy, still unaware of his feelings towards her, said that she would shortly be sailing to London where she hoped to see him more often than once every two years as he flitted to and fro on his world missions. 'I'm thrilled and proud of his wonderful appointments, but I <u>should</u> like to be able to settle down to some real home life'.

Jackson asked the Prime Minister, Ben Chifley, if Australia would take some DPs. When Chifley asked 'how many?' he suggested a hundred thousand. 'Why?' – 'Because whoever gets the first 100,000 will get the cream of the crop'. 'We'll do it,' said Chifley. 'The boys won't like it, but it will be done'.[53] Once Australia had agreed Jackson was able to persuade other countries. New Zealand took 1000 Polish orphans, Brazil, Argentina, the United States and others followed. Thus the numbers in Europe were reduced to about a million and a half.[54] Years later Jackson occasionally met people who had been saved by UNRRA and given a chance to start a new life down under.

After seeing his brother in Melbourne he spent a week in New Zealand; it must have been eleven years since he had seen Relda. On his way back to London he met LaGuardia in Cairo to show him some UNRRA Missions; they flew to Athens, staying a night on the way with the Jacksons in Cyprus. Edward wrote to Sheila: 'It was grand seeing Jacko again, even for so short a time. We covered a lot of ground and I was helped a little by my brief glimpse of 'the Mayor'. We would both like to hear as much as your admirable discretion will allow you to tell us of what you are likely to be doing yourself when UNRRA closes down. Our love and best wishes to you and Jacko.'[55]

In Rome LaGuardia had an audience with Pope Pius XII. "The friend' has paid devout homage to 'the Father',' proclaimed the *Osservato Romana*. (LaGuardia had always begun his wartime broadcasts to Italy: 'This is your friend LaGuardia speaking'.) 'In these years of trial and anxieties, of privations and sacrifices, Fiorello LaGuardia has proved to be the inimitable champion of Christianity.'[56]

After three days touring Yugoslavia Jackson went to London while LaGuardia and his party visited Munich and Prague. They met again in Geneva for the Fifth Council Session (5-17 August) in the *Palais des Nations* – formerly the headquarters of the League of Nations.

The question now was whether or not UNRRA's supply programme would be continued. In fact the US had already made it clear that it would not; when agreeing to release the final instalment of its second one per cent William Clayton, the

Assistant Secretary of State, had said that he expected that to be the last hearing for an appropriation for UNRRA. As he later put it 'the gravy train was going round for the last time'.[57]

The receiving countries obviously wanted UNRRA to continue; Britain, as usual, would follow the US line; the others, including the British Dominions were undecided. The USSR said it would be prepared to contribute if other nations did.

> Once again the *Palais des Nations* was the setting for the knell of an international effort. The Director-General opened his report with the statement that UNRRA's activities were ending. No provision had been made for UNRRA for 1947. The emergency task was over. He admitted that neither the Administration nor the contributing countries thought that the needs were over. Ways would be found to meet those additional wants.[58]

Resolutions were passed providing for UNRRA's work to be continued by other organisations: the World Health Organisation (WHO), the International Refugee Organisation (IRO) and the Food and Agriculture Organisation (FAO); it also proposed setting up an International Children's Fund. The IRO later became the UN High Commission for Refugees (UNHCR) and the Children's Fund UNICEF.

Since there was no other body to organise supplies for 1947 the Council proposed that the UN General Assembly be asked to set up an agency to review the urgent requirements of the liberated countries for food and agricultural supplies which they could not pay for. (Resolution 100).

LaGuardia had admitted to Jackson and Davidson that part of his reason for wanting to hasten the end of UNRRA was that he, like Lehman, was seeking nomination for Senator from New York. Greatly depressed, they decided to go to Geneva to lobby all the delegates to vote to continue UNRRA. They got a lot of support, but in the end there was in effect a US veto – they were putting up the largest share of the funds and they voted against, and that settled the matter.

When Lehman won the nomination LaGuardia changed his colours; he told them to drop everything and go with him to New York. They were to lobby the General Assembly to overturn the decision that he had helped to make in Geneva![59]

But first they spent six days dashing round Russia, ending with an hour-long meeting with Stalin. LaGuardia asked him: if the UN were to decide that relief would still be needed in 1947 and were to designate a new agency to distribute it would the USSR contribute? (Jackson thought that if it were known that the USSR would contribute to a successor agency the United States might be brought back into the fold and ask Congress for more funds.) Stalin replied that the USSR would give its share to UNRRA if the US and UK did likewise. LaGuardia pointed out that UNRRA was ending and again raised the question of a USSR contribution to a successor agency. Stalin said that he had stated his position and had no more to add, though he did not explicitly refuse to contribute to a successor agency.[60]

LaGuardia then had an inconclusive meeting with Attlee, the British Prime Minister, and saw Truman, who made it clear that the US was not interested in international relief; the State Department intended to ask Congress for financial assistance to a number of European countries but had not yet decided which.[61] Meanwhile Jackson's friendship with Barbara Ward was deepening; they had met in London on 1 August.

> I had reached a milestone and I was uncertain as to my next step. I wanted to try and make myself clear to you, and guessed that I would be sent firmly on my way. Instead of which you said something to me which I value more than anything that has come into my life. And so you helped me pass my milestone and guided me to the future. For that, if you desire it, you have my complete devotion.
>
> You send me on my way very happy; I take away with me a perfect memory and happiness. I love you. J.[62]
>
> 1 September: And so the first month ends, I being left with the same sense of surprise that you find in me anything that was worthy of your attention. All happiness to you, my darling, and come back safely and quickly. My love is yours and make of me what you will. Robert – and I too have to get used to that!![63] (Barbara refused to call him Jacko.)

Sheila, back in the London office, knew they had been meeting and writing to each other. On 31 August her eyes were opened when she saw a letter from Barbara. She was horrified, not so much on her own account; she was not asking to marry him, but she was helping him to get on with his job and resented Barbara's influence. She felt that she could be of no use to him if he was being pulled from this other direction. The next day she cabled him, saying that for personal reasons she was asking the Foreign Office to re-post her. For once she had no reply. A few days later Harold Caustin (Assistant to the SDDG) told her that Jacko was upset by her cable and wanted to see her in Copenhagen (where he and LaGuardia were attending

UNRRA 1946

Cartoon by LOW, September 1946. Solo Syndication / Associated Newspapers

an FAO conference). When she said she would not go, he handed her an air ticket; on 6 September she went. Jacko said she'd got it all wrong. 'Have I?' she said. She wasn't arguing about it, she wasn't asking for any commitment, she never had, but she couldn't work for him in this situation. Her use to him depended on complete trust on both sides. That was all she demanded.

She saw that he was bewildered. The next morning she went on to Berlin with him; he was his old self, as charming as ever. As the plane taxied in after landing she saw a figure standing on the ground: 'Doesn't that look like Miss Ward out there?'

Barbara swept him off, leaving the official car for her. Later she said he must make up his mind. Her only concern had been to work with him, and she felt she couldn't do it in the present circumstances. They both went on to Prague. There was no sign of Barbara and Sheila returned to London with nothing settled.[64] He followed on Monday 10 September. Two days later he and Barbara saw *Tosca* at Covent Garden, then they spent the week-end in the country with her friends Humphrey and Elizabeth Neame (her former flat-mate). Peggy was in London and could only contact Jacko through Sheila, who knew where he was. Sheila telephoned: 'Oh, Mrs Neame, I'm so sorry to disturb you, this is Sheila Collins; is it possible that Commander Jackson is staying with you?' 'Oh yes,' came the reply, 'would you like to speak to him?' 'There is no need to trouble him,' said Sheila, 'but would you be kind enough to tell him that his wife is trying to get in touch with him'. Silence.[65]

The Neames would not have known that Barbara's friend was married; possibly even Barbara did not know. She did now. If Sheila enjoyed dropping that bombshell she should be forgiven; she had always done what she could to salvage his marriage to Peggy.

> 21 September, New York: Since I left you I have spent most of my time thinking about you and the complete change which you have brought into my life. I have told you of the few women who have come into my life – equally so I have said honestly that never before have I found contentment in its fullest and most perfect sense as I have already known it with you.

Peggy agreed to a divorce and he asked his brother to talk to her about grounds. 'I do not know whether there is any legal provision for a case such as this. I never thought life could work out like this. One wrong aeroplane ride could simplify matters for you all so much.'[66]

Sheila, knowing how much he depended on her, continued to work for him, but found it difficult. After they returned to Washington Barbara turned up. Jacko was embarrassed, so to clear the air Sheila arranged to meet her at her apartment. Her first words were 'When I marry Robert'[67] Whatever Jacko might say, there was never any doubt about how Barbara saw the situation. Confiding to a friend she made no bones about 'wanting to have Robert's child'[68], though for that she would have to wait nine years. She returned to London.

29 September: As to the real battle, relief needs in 1947. All nations except the US acknowledge the fact that relief will be needed next year, and that some countries will not have hard currencies. After their great and wonderful generosity the US has now swung away to an unrealistically hard attitude – they stand to lose all the good will and gratitude they have earned through UNRRA. Clayton is convinced that by ending direct relief these countries will be forced to 'free trade'. In our experience such a policy will have the very reverse effect, will increase distrust of US and the countries will try any alternative to getting into the clutches of the US economy.

The US position is the key to the whole situation: the USSR and the eastern countries are lined up, the British Dominions would play and the UK sits uneasily on the fence. This is an area where the East and West could be brought together, but during this last week I have wondered whether the West really does want this now.[69]

Rome, 19 October: You have brought to life in me a new person. I have come out of my cave. Thursday evening will remain for me the most perfect time in my life – and the evening star will be a guide and a companion to me at all times when we are separated. I pray that the path will be the one which means complete happiness for you – I will do all I can to make that path. But whatever happens, there will be within me always a love for you such as I have never before felt for any one in this world.

London, 27 October: These days of separation [Barbara was still in Rome] have only confirmed what I knew to be true – that you have come into my life as no other person and that you have brought from me a response which I did not know could exist. But if P XII cannot help there will be great sadness, and I do not like to think too much about that. If God is merciful and understanding – and forgiving, too – perhaps it will all work out: I pray that that may happen.

The question of what, if anything, the Vatican could do about his first marriage was always on his mind; he would speak to the Catholic authorities in New York at the first opportunity.

The UN General Assembly referred UNRRA's Resolution 100 to its Second (economic and financial) Committee which LaGuardia addressed on 11 November. He had already proposed in a draft resolution that the General Assembly should set up a UN Emergency Food Fund, and said that there should be no gap between the end of UNRRA and the start of the new organisation.

He departed from his brief several times, claiming (i) that Stalin had said that the USSR would like to see international relief action continued into 1947, and would contribute its share, (ii) that the UK would respond to a new call for aid, and (iii) that Truman considered that the US would have to continue to participate in the work of relief (which was half true).

There were, he said, three ways of meeting relief needs: national – 'the old imperialistic way', multinational – 'power politics', and international – 'meeting needs without regard to race, creed or political belief – Christ's way'.[70]

Having prepared a draft resolution providing for a survey of relief needs by an international committee of experts, the US delegation now tore it up.

On 18 November it was the turn of the United Kingdom delegate, Philip Noel-Baker, to speak. He had been instructed to support the US line. Davidson was friendly with him and knew that he was personally against it. Fifty years later he recalled the incident:

> 'He was an old League of Nations man and wanted to speak against the US; all of his thinking was in line with ours. He made a brilliant speech – he was a very able fellow. He made such a brilliant speech that you couldn't tell by the time he sat down whether he was backing UNRRA or wanting to close it. LaGuardia, who was very quick-witted, asked for an adjournment on the grounds that it was time for lunch, and then proceeded to give a quick press conference in which he congratulated Noel-Baker on his courage, and the courage of his country in seeing the importance of keeping UNRRA alive, which of course threw everybody in a stew, and the British Government had him on the plane to London the next day!'[71]

No vote was taken on LaGuardia's draft resolution and on 9 December another one was adopted unanimously, providing for a committee of ten experts to study the minimum import requirements of countries needing assistance and report to the Secretary-General on the financial assistance likely to be needed. The outcome was that in May Congress agreed to provide $350 million to be shared between Austria, Poland, Italy, Greece, Hungary and China.

> 16 November: My real concern is the knowledge that most of the good things which could have been salvaged from UNRRA will probably be lost; I think UNRRA will go out on a poor note, when it could have gone out well.
>
> Whether I was in love with you or not I'd be in a mood like this – seeing my UNRRA work ending, unhappy that the job hasn't been completed, knowing I'd have to make a complete stocktaking early next year – officially, physically, personally and most important of all, spiritually.

Somehow he found the time and energy to write almost daily, often long letters. It was his only way of letting off steam; he deplored the US attitude and that of the British even more; he was angry that LaGuardia had wrecked his plans to influence the Committee's decision, in particular by his account of the meeting with Stalin.

> 17 November: I believe we could have persuaded the Russians to lead if Butch had stuck to his text – but Molotov blew up (in my judgement rightly) when he publicly placed a wrong interpretation on Stalin's agreement. It's a tragedy – we had them so near collaboration in a matter of much importance – and now the chance is lost. We could have developed confidence and goodwill from the East – as it is we will only have destroyed much of what had been achieved.
>
> I've taken a licking all over the place. I'll go on fighting as hard as hell – so long as P XII doesn't hand out a licking too. If so I'll have quite a lot to think about. Until that day at least I can go on loving you completely, solidly and without reservation.

The Catholic authorities in New York could offer little encouragement and advised him to go to Rome to obtain a Canonist's opinion as to whether there was a sufficient ground for submitting an appeal to the Supreme Rota (the

Barbara Ward   Dorothy Wilding

highest ecclesiastical tribune). There was still a glimmer of hope.

The Sixth and final Session of the Council took place in Washington in December. After paeans of praise were sounded for LaGuardia and Lehman, Lowell Rooks was elected as the third Director-General, to be responsible for completing the current operations and liquidating UNRRA.

Bridges was aware that Jackson had been approached about running the new refugee organisation. 'I am sure you would do magnificently, but the time has come to call a halt and to tell the willing horse that he is not to go on carrying all the heaviest loads. In other words, when UNRRA comes to an end you are to take a rest and get thoroughly fit again; and so far as I am concerned this is a command and I greatly hope that you will take it as such. When you have had a rest, there will be plenty of things still for you to do! Yours ever, Edward Bridges.'[72]

He still had work to do in Australia, China, the Far East and Europe, but before setting off for Australia he had to come clean to his brother about Barbara. It took him seven hours to type the letter, 27 pages long.

After going over old ground about his condition, spiritual, personal and physical, he told him that for some years he had known one of the most brilliant women in England. She had remarkable administrative qualities, was a brilliant musician and Foreign Editor of one of the most influential papers in England. His own work in the Middle East and in UNRRA had matched the foreign policy of that paper. For the last three years he had assumed, like many others, that she would marry' a very brilliant chap in the Foreign Office', (which she might have done had his Quaker genes not been overwhelmed by her catholic vigour!

The chap was probably Richard Stokes, who at that time was the Minister of Works).

When he had told her about his personal problems some months ago she said that he had become the only man in her mind for over a year and had not known until later that he was married. Just when he thought life couldn't be worse this utterly unexpected development took place. If they had not talked that evening, he would not be writing this letter. Just to make things simpler, he said, the 'new development' (no name was mentioned) was one of the leading Catholics in England.

He would see Peggy in London before the end of the year, discuss the new development with her and find out from the Vatican whether or not a plea for annulment would be considered. If not, he would have to clarify his religious beliefs and re-marriage would be ruled out. He had discussed the whole problem with his closest friend and best adviser – Sir Edward Jackson – who agreed with the line he was proposing. Only then did he reveal to his brother the story behind his marriage nine years earlier and how he had been influenced by Mrs Dick (as told in Chapter 2).

He was humbly thankful that the new development had appeared so quietly and with such good effect on him; there was no wild emotion, but she had given him an inspiration and a strength which had carried him through a period of tragedy which could have broken his heart for all time in a way which even the misery of the last nine years could not have done.[73]

After a brief visit to Rome he flew to Australia to see his brother and Peggy's family. (Peggy was still in England.) Mrs Dick said that she now realised that she should never have forced him to marry her, but could not have faced the social prospect of them calling it all off at the last minute; Peggy's brother George and his wife understood his position. He told Alan: 'I now feel less stressed about my part in the whole sad episode and am satisfied that I am proceeding on the right lines.'[74] En route to China he added: 'I won't hesitate to ask for your help in relation to the Catholic Church if I reach a stage where I want honestly to be admitted. Whatever happens I'll go on trying to do my bit for the outside world – that may make up a bit for the sadness I've caused.'[75]

UNRRA's aid to China had been greater than that to any other nation; its policy was to help Chinese people living in areas which had been occupied by the Japanese during World War II, some even earlier. These comprised roughly the eastern one-third of China. UNRRA worked in partnership with CNRRA, the Chinese National Relief and Rehabilitation Administration set up by the Chinese Government under Generalissimo Chiang Kai-shek. The fact that much of the previously occupied area was now under Communist control made this very difficult. CNRRA was supposed to distribute UNRRA supplies to such areas, but since it considered them 'enemy territory' there was much foot-dragging. Though UNRRA was committed to the principle of non-discrimination, its effort to achieve this was on the whole unsuccessful.[76] Furthermore, there was corruption among UNRRA's own staff, among whom were former American troops, who, having survived the Pacific war, were not too keen to make sure UNRRA supplies reached the communists.

At that time China was in the throes of galloping inflation. Jackson and the Director of UNRRA's China Office, Major-General Glen Edgerton, realised that if the value of the Chinese dollar dropped heavily UNRRA would be unable to complete its work there, so they persuaded the Chinese Government to agree to a scheme by which UNRRA received its payments for the proceeds of sale not in cash but in cotton – a saleable commodity with a reasonably stable value. The cotton was sold as operating funds were required.[77] Edgerton then had to resign because of ill health; Jackson appointed Harlan Cleveland in his place, whom he had recently met in Rome, working for the Allied Commission in Italy. Having heard about the corruption among the staff in China Cleveland asked for authority to fire people without reference to Washington, which Jackson gladly gave.[78]

After meeting Chiang Kai-shek in Nanking, Jackson arrived on 12 February at Tsingtao (now Qingdao) near the mouth of the Yellow River. Not in the best of health himself, he spent a week in temperatures 20° below zero inspecting reclamation projects. UNRRA's tasks included repairing the dykes on the Yellow River, which had been deliberately broken by the Chinese in 1938 to stem the advance of the Japanese army. As a military tactic this had succeeded, but tens of thousands of peasants were drowned and over three million acres of agricultural land inundated. Here was an opportunity to reclaim farm lands on a scale large enough to increase the world's food supply significantly.[79] This work was jeopardised by continued fighting in the area, so one day Cleveland simply declared a local cease-fire. Everyone was so surprised that for a few days it actually worked and the fighting stopped. 'I called up Jacko to tell him what I'd done, and he saw that I never got into trouble. Two things I recall about him: he had enormous personal prestige, and when someone took an unauthorized action in the name of the organisation which he headed he did not complain, but gave his full support. He was that sort of person.'[80]

By 5 March Jackson was back in London, being treated in hospital for an infection he had picked up in China. Peggy now intended to seek an annulment, but was advised that this would fail, since a determination not to have children did not amount to non-consummation. She therefore entered a petition for divorce on grounds of desertion – the only course left to them; it would take three years. On 19 April he sailed to New York and spent a week with Barbara in Virginia before returning to Washington.

UNRRA still had its problems: the accounts were potentially a political hot potato. Harry Howell, had successfully established financial control, but had strongly antagonised the London firm of auditors, Deloitte, Plender, Griffiths and Company. They had produced a draft report covering UNRRA's first two years which, if published, would blow UNRRA sky high; the facts were correct but the tone was vicious, and clearly intended to lead to the professional ruin of Howell; it was suitably toned down. Howell, in his haste to complete the accounts, had split his own Bureau, the chief accountant had just left and others were getting offers. What with that and unjustified press attacks on DP operations, Rooks was on the verge of throwing in his hand. Jackson had hoped to leave UNRRA on 30 June but knew he must to stay until these problems were solved.[81]

Bridges was getting worried: before Christmas Jackson had promised to obey his command to stop. He repeated his command – to get free of UNRRA not later than 15 July. 'I am quite sure that this is right, and I expect you to act accordingly.'[82]

But Jackson had agreed to hold the fort for Rooks through July to enable him to take some leave before taking on the job of running down UNRRA; if Rooks cracked they would have a really bad situation on their hands. Once Rooks returned his own departure should soon follow. If Bridges would approve this plan, Jackson would see him as he proceeded on leave.[83]

When Bridges cabled reiterating his command[84] Rooks wrote to the British Ambassador: no-one was more anxious than he that Jackson should be free of UNRRA and go on leave, but given the political dangers associated with the accounts and problems concerning the start of the IRO he was anxious to keep Jackson until mid-August; Jackson was willing and he hoped HMG would consider his request sympathetically.[85] Jackson wrote to Bridges again: 'I feel certain that your sympathetic acceptance of our difficulties will give UNRRA a much better chance to atone for the sins of the past, and to be buried, if not with full military honours, then at least with decency. I am leaving for London on 13 August and much look forward to seeing you then.'[86]

Bridges replied: 'As this is probably the last letter I shall write to you before you leave UNRRA, may I say what you already know, namely how intensely grateful we are to you for the work which you have done for UNRRA which has been of incalculable benefit. But for what you have done, I do not believe that the UNRRA ship would ever have made port at all; and my only regret is that you were asked to carry a heavier burden than should be put upon the shoulders of any man.'[87]

On 5 June George C Marshall, the Secretary of State, had announced the United States' offer of $20 billion aid for Europe. Europe had no hard currency, and the US government thought something must be done for humanitarian reasons and also to prevent the spread of communism. There was a condition: the nations of Europe must together draw up a plan showing how the aid would be used. Jackson saw the Marshall Plan, later known as the European Recovery Plan (ERP), as the logical outcome of UNRRA's failure to obtain a third contribution. When he had once suggested that a sum of this order would be needed no-one believed him; 'a billion or two would suffice'.[88] He was deeply, passionately, concerned that this plan would succeed; it did: $13 billion of aid enabled Europe to stand on is own feet and General Marshall became his third hero.

During the next few weeks many tributes and letters of good wishes poured in from organisations ranging from the auditors to the Vatican; from Ministers and Ambassadors and from colleagues and staff at all levels. They usually began by thanking him for his letter of thanks and good wishes!

He was continuing to take instruction from the Roman Catholics, anxiously observed by Sheila. Her family and Alan's had already been in touch, so she wrote to him, saying that as a Catholic, born and bred, she could say that the Church in its wisdom and experience would only <u>offer</u> its knowledge, it would not coerce.[89] What she did not say was that she thought Barbara was pushing him much too hard; he needed more time. Indeed she felt so concerned for him on this account that when she was in London she had called on Father Heenan to express her misgivings, but with little or no effect. (Heenan was a Roman Catholic priest whom Barbara knew; he later married them. He was appointed Archbishop of Westminster in 1963 and Cardinal in 1965.) Alan replied that it was only during his last visit that they got back to their old footing after ten years apart. He was not enamoured of the path his brother was considering, but it was his life.

Back in London Jackson wrote his final report on 'The life and death of UNRRA' for Noel-Baker: The period from August 1945 to March 1946 was the most successful; the reorganisation of the staff had worked, the administrative machine was running smoothly, supply lines had been established and a steady stream of goods flowed to Europe and Asia, and surplus military supplies were becoming available.

For him personally the most satisfying single operation had been getting that two billion dollars out of Congress before the Christmas recess. It had succeeded mainly because the press, radio and public supported UNRRA's aims. UNRRA's name was lifted out of the mud for the one and only time in its life, and Lehman's prestige grew. The appointment and maladministration of LaGuardia had been a disaster: publicly criticised by its own Director-General, UNRRA's newly won reputation was soon lost.

'It is not for me to assess the success or failure of UNRRA. History will make that decision. I think it is true, however, that this international organization did, in fact, achieve the primary objectives for which it was created.'[90]

UNRRA had purchased, shipped and distributed among other things food, seeds, chickens and cattle, clothing, sewing machines, tractors and railway engines, all to the tune of $3½ billions (equivalent to about $25 billion in 2000). Over 25 million tons of goods had been provided, mostly to Europe (more than three times the amount distributed after World War I).[91] And two million displaced persons had been enabled to start new lives in far-off countries. Furthermore there were no serious epidemics in Europe during the winter of 1945/46; (in 1918/19 over 30 million people died from influenza alone.)[92]

It had successfully carried out what remains to this day the largest and most complex disaster-relief operation ever undertaken. It had also demonstrated two features of the international scene which have persisted to the present day: the reluctance of the USA to support international organizations, and Britain's willingness to follow the American line.

Jackson spent a week or so with Barbara and her family at Felixstowe; perhaps it was there that he was received into the Catholic Church. At the end of August he went to Geneva and Rome, and had an audience with the Pope at Castel Gandolfo.

On 20 September LaGuardia died of cancer; Jackson attended his funeral in New York, whence he wrote to Bridges: 'I shall finish with UNRRA officially on 11 October and then proceed on leave. As you know the doctors want me to get out and rest completely for six months if I am to recover my health. I should very much like to carry out their wishes, but realise that circumstances in the near future may not permit me to do so.'

Jackson at Castel Gandolfo, August 1947

Circumstances? If he and Bridges both thought that he should rest for six months it is hard to see what could have prevented him, but this was a time when opportunities to work in the international field were appearing; and perhaps he was afraid of missing the boat. He mentioned the possibility of being asked to advise the US Government about the Marshall Plan; he would therefore remain in the USA until early December, and then go away for eight to ten weeks and obey doctors' orders. 'As things stand it seems to me that a final decision about the future need not be taken until about March 1948, when I could have completed my refit. I should like you to know how much I have appreciated your great personal kindness and sympathy to me during the last few years. To have had your support and understanding has made my own work immeasurably easier.'[93]

It could be said, just, that Jackson did avoid taking a final decision until the following March, but by the end of December he would have virtually committed himself to a course of action that was to prove unfortunate.

On 6 October he bade farewell to his colleagues in the Washington office before going on leave. On 11 October his appointment was terminated and the post of SDDG abolished. He was already in New Hampshire, walking in the White Mountains. Alone.

6 Operation Cool-off

The mountains rise up from gentle slopes – all heavily wooded. The trees have a brilliance of colour which is breathtaking – they range from the crimson of the maples to the emerald green of some of the firs. In between reds, sunset browns, browns, honey, every tone of yellow and green make a sea of colour which sweeps across the hills and valleys until it merges into the dark blue of the mountains, which stand out clearly against the pure blue sky. The trails through the woods are like fairyland, the leaves make a pattern which no weaver of carpets in Bokhara could equal. The days are sunny and the air is sharp. All I do is walk and climb and take a book to read.[1]

HE WAS REBUILDING HIS STRENGTH, walking a bit further each day, aiming to reach 25-30 miles a day, when a cable for him arrived in Washington. It was from Richard Casey, advising him 'not to accept any other appointment until he heard from him'. He resumed his holiday, with Barbara now, only to get a message from Trygve Lie, who wanted to see him in New York as soon as possible.

On 4 November Lie told him that he was experiencing great difficulties and was dissatisfied with the organisation generally; it lacked effective co-ordination and executive direction, the division between economic and social affairs was unsatisfactory, and he wanted to remove two of the eight Assistant Secretaries-General.[2]

HMG's opinion of the UN secretariat was even lower: a report to the Cabinet in March by Gladwyn Jebb (Under-Secretary in the Foreign Office responsible for UN affairs) had concluded that the Secretary-General himself was indecisive and neither a good leader nor a good administrator; what was needed was a really good Deputy Secretary-General to take charge of administration generally and in particular to coordinate the work of the Economic and Social Departments. There were three able Assistant Secretaries-General: the American, Byron Price (Administration); the Russian, AA Sobolev (Political and Security) probably the most able, though of doubtful impartiality; and David Owen, British, (Economic Affairs). The others – Henri Laugier, Victor Hoo, Adrian Pelt, Benjamin Cohen and Ivan Kerno – were second rate; if they could be induced to leave, so much the better.[3]

Lie himself had wanted to appoint a Deputy, but this would require the approval of the General Assembly, and the USSR and later the USA were strongly opposed, uneasy at the idea of any one person having the ear of the Secretary-General, so the idea was not pursued.

Lie told Jackson that he would like him as head of his office with the rank of Assistant Secretary-General (ASG), from early in January 1948; he had already mentioned the matter informally to Hector McNeil (the British Minister of State) and Evatt, the Australian Minister of External Affairs.

Jackson said that if the British Government were to release him they would need some assurance that the conditions of service would offer a reasonable chance of more satisfactory results being obtained. Reporting the meeting to Bridges he remarked that Lie himself had been a compromise candidate lacking the very qualities of direction for which he was asking. Short of changing the Secretary-General the next best thing would be to appoint an effective Chief of Staff. He would be willing to help Lie wherever he could, but would prefer not to start until he had fully recuperated, some time in 1948.[4]

Two days later he saw Lord Bruce in Washington. Viscount Bruce of Melbourne was an old friend of Casey's; he had been Prime Minister of Australia after World War I, President of the Council of the League of Nations in 1936, and was currently Chairman of the World Food Council. He had played a major part in the creation of the Food and Agriculture Organisation – FAO.

Bruce pressed him strongly to agree to become Deputy to Sir John Boyd Orr, the Director-General of FAO, saying that if he did he would 'without a shadow of doubt' be selected as Orr's successor sometime the following year. Jackson's first reaction was that this would offer him a more effective field of activity than the UN; the prospect of building FAO into a permanent and effective organisation strongly appealed to him after the experience of temporary organisations like MESC and UNRRA. Nevertheless he would tackle the UN job if HMG thought that more in their interest.[5]

All his life Jackson had gone where he was told: the Navy, Malta, MESC, UNRRA.

Now, for the first time, he was given a choice: he preferred FAO, but told Bridges he would leave the decision to HMG. He could see that the UN job was made harder by the fact that its rank was only equal to that of the half-dozen or so ASGs who needed to be coordinated, but felt that that was where his duty lay.[6]

By 12 November he was in Florida, resuming OPERATION COOLOFF, staying at *Whispering Sands* – a hotel in Sarasota. The beach was about 250 yards away and there was a little bay running up to his window. 'It is a fishing paradise for herons, blue cranes, loons, pelicans and many others. The water is as clear as glass and one could spend all day watching them at work – they are like lightning under water, and most graceful.'[7]

He wrote almost daily to Sheila in Washington, not letters but brief 'SITREPs', light-hearted, occasionally serious, signed T (for Toad).

> 17 November: I have had an official invitation from Cornell to lecture there on 18 December. Would this wreck one of our theatre nights?
> 20 November: Sitting in the sun and enjoying it. Large boil on my shoulder – refuse to worry – probably too much food and exercise.
> 21 November: Could you ask FAO for a copy of Dr Fitzgerald's last report on the world food situation.
> 22 November: It's a beautiful morning here – my boil is beautiful too!!!

On 24 November he heard from Bridges: after long discussions the question of his posting had been referred to the Foreign Secretary, and Bevin had decided that on balance it was more in the public interest that Jackson should serve in the United Nations secretariat rather than in FAO. That was also Bridges's own view and he hoped Jackson would come round to it himself.[8]

The Foreign Office cabled McNeil telling him to impress upon Lie that HMG would release Jackson 'provided that Lie would arrange for him to have sufficient standing and authority vis-a-vis ASGs to enable him to do a thorough job'.[9]

Bruce stressed the same point: if it was to be the UN he must have unquestioned authority subject only to Trygve Lie. As to that, in his view the UN and Lie were both hopeless and the re-organisation needed more than the insertion of one man; it would be an impossible task; the UN was stiff with political difficulties. On the other hand FAO was free from politics and with forceful leadership could contribute to the current food crisis and promote international economic co-operation and the co-ordination of the specialised agencies.[10] (FAO, WHO etc; they are more fully described in Chapter 11).

On the eve of Thanksgiving Sheila flew down from Washington to join Jacko for part of her leave. For ten days they enjoyed the simple delights of the seaside as he got fitter and browner.

Jacko

Sheila

The paper table-mats at *Whispering Sands* depicted various sea creatures; a lobster, an oyster, a crab and several fish. One day at lunch with Sheila he gave them all names: Boyd Orr – still waiting for help, Lord Bruce – not beaten yet, Bridges – like the oyster, keeping quiet, Poor Toad, Bevin – blowing the Toad towards Lie, Lie – waiting for his meal, B.Ward – likely to turn up anywhere, and Hall-Patch (Deputy Under-Secretary at the Foreign Office) – clearly NOT pleased. D(udley) Ward had been UNRRA's General Counsel in London. Frivolous though this was, it showed that he had no illusions about his predicament. But why was Hall-Patch not pleased? A letter from Barbara to Sheila suggests that it was because of Bevin's decision: she was <u>quite</u> clear from what Hall-Patch had let fall that 'this Uno

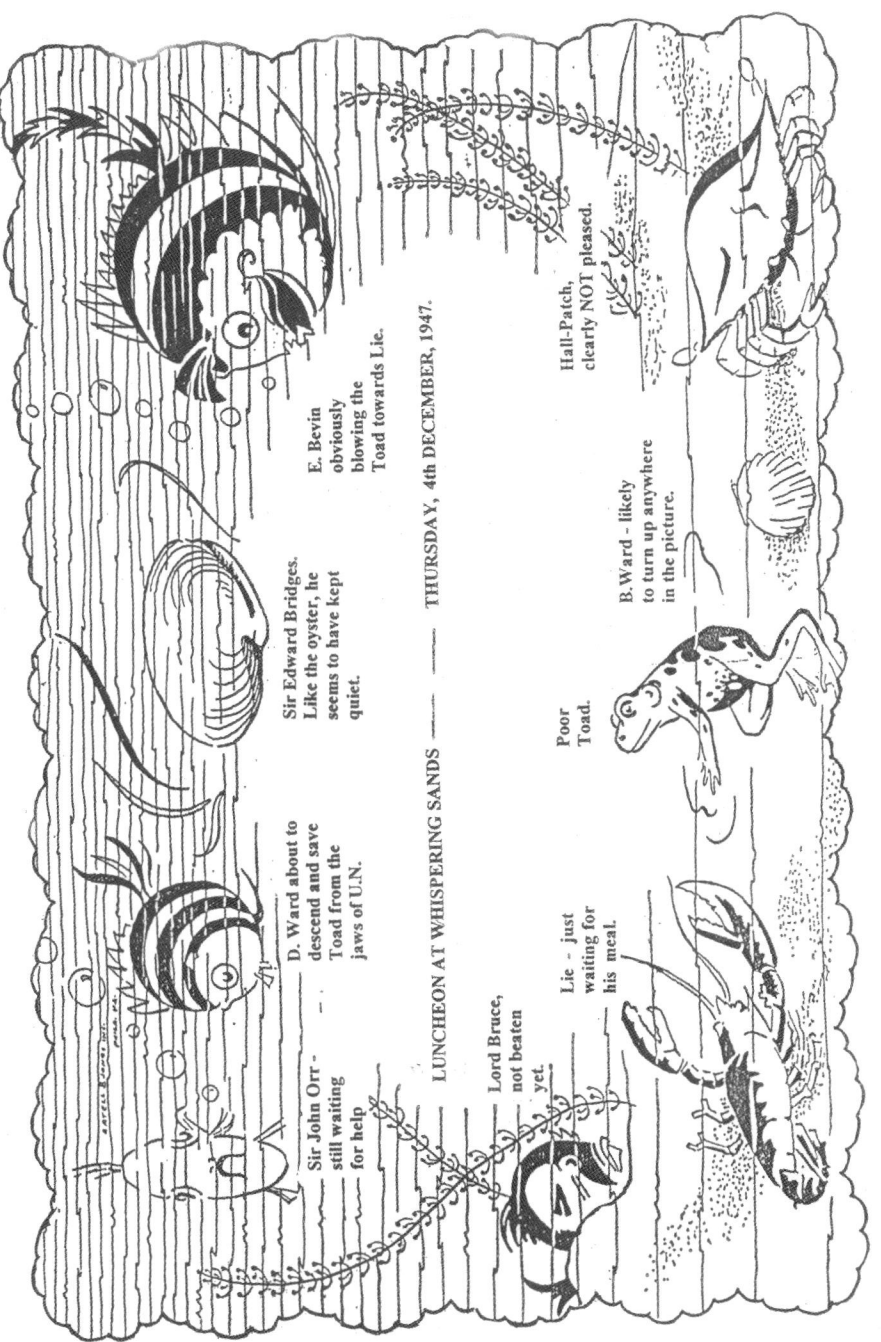

The table mat

thing' cut right across Bridges' ideas for Robert, which had been that his probable field would be planning in Whitehall; Hall-Patch preferred the Commonwealth, but both were jobs Robert wanted; he was missing the chance of getting them and being side-tracked into something 'which only pleased that silly old buffer, Bevin'. She had written to Robert urging him to disentangle himself from Uno at all costs, either by putting his terms too high for Lie, or telling him and Bridges that he was too tired even to think of the Uno job, and must be released from any commitment. 'Then he should get on his ship and there should not be another telegram from him until April!'[11]

Jacko did not discuss the matter with Sheila; he seems to have accepted that his future lay with 'the Uno job'.

On 8 December he developed two carbuncles on his face, one on his chin and one on his nose, painful, grotesque, and in those days dangerous; he blamed it on an infection picked up while swimming. He was taken to Sarasota Hospital, where they got a vaccine just in time; Sheila stayed on at *Whispering Sands* for the rest of her leave.

> What a poor ending to an invitation to come and have a few days rest and fun. It was a great joy to have you here and I felt that it was a very successful operation. I believe that the basic foundation has been found again, and that an effective relationship will remain always. The next move, I think, is to examine the next job (if any!) and see how we fit into it.
>
> It was a period of rest and mentally we were both at peace. Going to mass, collecting shells, watching the birds – they were all simple and good. Which is how I like to live. I shall miss you and Whispering Sands will not be the same.
>
> Thank you for your unending goodness and kindness again and again. The Perfect Partner – that is the most genuine tribute I can offer. God bless you in every way. My love to you S. J.[12]

A letter from Lie arrived, formally offering him the post of Assistant Secretary-General for the Office of the Secretary-General. Lie had discussed the proposal with the other ASGs, who welcomed it.

> I would like to say how much importance I attach to this appointment. I can think of no individual who could make a greater contribution than yourself

to the work of the Secretariat and of the United Nations as a whole in this post at this critical time.

With best wishes for your speedy recovery.
Yours sincerely, Trygve Lie.[13]

With the letter was a list of the ways in which he would assist the Secretary General:

a) By expediting the implementation of programme decisions.
b) Co-ordinating, formulating and proposing, in co-operation with Departments, programmes and policy decisions involving more than one Department or Service.
c) Assisting in the supervision of overseas offices and in establishing field missions.
d) Coordinating liaison with the Specialised Agencies.
e) Directing the Executive Office of the Secretary-General.
f) Undertaking special assignments.

More sitreps followed:

Saturday 20 December: HOT NEWS SITREP – MOST IMMEDIATE etc. At 2030 a Blessed Event occurred – my B....Y CHIN BURST!!! I am now receiving the congratulations of the entire nursing staff – anyone would think that they had done it!!!

Sunday 21 December: I think it is wiser to see Lie before he leaves [for London] – object – to get the UN proposal clear on both sides leaving me (a) an escape clause if I need it at 31 March or (b) the way to accept it finally at that time if HMG has nothing for me.

Monday 22 December: They released me today. Spoke for 45 minutes to David Owen, and put my points on UN to him clearly. He considered them reasonable. Lie agrees to defer any further action until the meeting on 2 Jan.

Sheila now wanted to know where she stood and wrote asking him 'if he was committed to marrying B. Ward' so that she could assess her own capacity to continue 'to play in his band'. For eighteen months she had tried to play Number Two Girl; on the official side she had succeeded but it had not been easy, and when all and sundry seemed to delight in teasing her about 'Jacko's girl-friend' she found it hard. She was not complaining; she simply wanted him to tell her frankly what the situation was before they embarked on another chapter in their official life. Perhaps the triangle would work – but 'it was time he was entirely frank about the situation.'[14]

She never got a straight answer.

> 24 December: We can talk the matter out, as convenient, during the coming meeting. It is not, however, to be permitted to spoil your enjoyment of theatres.
>
> 26 December: I hope that your Xmas has been happy. Midnight Mass was very calm and peaceful. David Owen arrives to spend Sunday night [28 Dec] and to tell me about 'difficulties – Boss'. You guess what that means. I've given my views – I will <u>not</u> negotiate over terms of reference. Either Lie can play square and give me a reasonable break from the beginning (in which case I'd do my best to help), or he can play a political game of appeasement, and leave me with an even worse wicket on which to bat. If that happened and HMG told me to go ahead I would do so (always subject to the 31 March clause) … but I do not like such a way of doing business. Summed up, I guess Lie realises that he needs someone like me, but neither wishes to admit publicly, and probably hasn't the moral guts to insist upon giving, the real terms of reference which would help so much to get the job done. We'll see.

Jackson saw Lie on Friday 2 January 1948, and reported to Sir Alexander Cadogan, British Ambassador to the UN, that the Secretary-General intended to operate this new appointment on the principle of a Commander in Chief and his Chief of Staff. He intended to work through his Chief of Staff to his Assistant Secretaries-General and ensure that they worked to him through the new Chief of Staff. He had emphasised this several times, and said it was essential for him to be free of day to day control of the Organisation as quickly as possible.[15]

With Cadogan's agreement Jackson wrote telling Lie that, providing the Foreign Secretary was agreeable, he was willing to accept his proposals on the understanding that (a) there were one or two points in the terms of reference which might require further consideration in the light of experience; (b) as ASG for the Office of the Secretary-General he had to serve in the capacity of a Chief of Staff; Cadogan understood that the character of the appointment would be made clear to the senior staff on Monday 5 January and hoped to give Lie a reply from the Foreign Secretary by Tuesday evening, 6 January.[16]

On the Monday evening Cadogan had a visit from David Owen and Brian Urquhart (Lie's Personal Assistant in his Private Office). They told him that Lie had failed to obtain the agreement of the other ASGs to Jackson being 'Chief of Staff'.

> Not very satisfactory, and it has all been made much more difficult. Agreed that Jackson must first be informed (he is at the moment in Washington) and then I shall have to consult the Foreign Office. If he will agree I think I shall recommend to the FO that the arrangement should be given a trial on the basis of the terms of reference given us by the Sec.Gen. on Dec 18th. But of course it is quite problematical whether these will now work out in the way intended – more especially now that the suspicions of the ASGs (and of their Governments) have been aroused.[17]

The next day Cadogan received a telegram (No 61, 6 January) from Hall-Patch, unaware that the other ASGs had refused to agree to Jackson being 'Chief of Staff':

> We agree to <u>secondment</u> of Commander Jackson ... on clear understanding that Secretary General will in fact make nature of appointment as 'Chief of Staff' entirely clear to the other ASGs and obtain their agreement to accept the new arrangement.[18]

Cadogan replied :

> Whilst there was no particular opposition to the general outline of Commander Jackson's proposed functions the expression 'Chief of Staff' raised objections on the part of all except David Owen, and the meeting was therefore inconclusive.
>
> We have managed to recall Jackson from Washington this morning and explain to him what happened.
>
> He tells me that, so far as he is concerned, he would still, if HMG wish, be prepared to take on the job on the basis of the proposed terms of reference on the understanding that those terms are 'fluid and flexible', and this description seems to have been accepted at yesterday's meeting. He is of course not blind to the fact that yesterday's meeting will make his

task no easier, as the objecting ASGs will be more on their guard against encroachments, but he does not think this would be fatal. Secretary-General proposes to add to his title 'in charge of general co-ordination'.

I have informed him of contents of your telegram and he has now left for Jamaica. I myself would still recommend that Commander Jackson should be allowed to make trial of the job, as he is ready to do.

David Owen, who has been in consultation with Jackson and myself, believes provisional terms of reference, plus Secretary-General's assurances, give Jackson a very good chance of doing effective job, and he earnestly hopes HMG will make it possible for Jackson to accept.[19]

That was a very messy situation, nevertheless the facts do not bear out Jackson's later claim that he was under orders – <u>sent</u> to Lake Success by HMG. On 6 January he knew that the other ASGs had not agreed to his status as Chief of Staff and he had seen Hall-Patch's telegram (No 61) agreeing to his secondment on condition that they had. That was the moment when he could have said no; HMG's conditions (as well as his own) had not been fulfilled, and there can be no doubt that HMG would have accepted such a decision. But he let the chance pass and told Cadogan that he was still prepared to take it on if HMG wished, and set off for Jamaica.

Several factors could have influenced him: Owen wanted him to take the job and Cadogan thought he should be given the chance, and he had missed the FAO boat; but the decision had been his.

The following day Cadogan received a cable from Jebb:

It seems clear that the abandonment of title of 'Chief of Staff' will to some extent diminish Jackson's status, whatever may be said to the contrary. However, if he and you still think that he will have sufficient scope to do an effective job we have no desire to stand in his way and therefore agree, though reluctantly, to his being engaged on the terms now suggested.[20]

Had he been aware of Jebb's telegram, which arrived after he had left, would he have decided otherwise? It is impossible to say, but his hasty departure itself suggests that his mind was made up. Urquhart had the impression at the time that he wanted the job very much.

Lie informed his senior staff that Commander Jackson's stipulations as to his title had been withdrawn 'and a perfect understanding of the nature and title of the post established.'[21] The appointment was announced immediately. Apart from the addition of the words 'and for general coordination' in his title, all was exactly as proposed in the original job description.

Jebb's telegram had a second paragraph:

> You should however make it quite clear to Mr Lie that we regard Jackson's appointment as an experiment and that if it should become clear after a few months that he cannot work satisfactorily owing to lack of sufficient authority or backing we reserve our right to withdraw him and provide him with alternative employment more suited to his very considerable talents.

This was unfortunate, for it gave Lie an opening to use later.

Lie told McNeil that he had carried Jackson's appointment against the hostility of Sobolev and the disgruntlement of Byron Price, though Price had now come round a little. Sobolev had for the first time become rather bad tempered towards Lie, probably because he was under instructions to oppose Jackson's appointment and had now lost caste in Moscow. Consequently, said Lie, initiation of Jackson would be difficult, but the British Government could depend upon him giving Jackson all his support. He meant to employ him primarily for the business of co-ordination, especially in relation to the specialised agencies and for courier and semi-political duties at the highest level.[22]

In Jamaica Montego Bay proved to be less than ideal – a main road separated the hotel from the beach and the other guests were a bit much. There was an Austrian prince married to a Colombian heiress, a Spanish prince up to no good, various Wall Street tycoons, wealthy British escaping the winter, sugar kings from Cuba, the Duke and Duchess of Sutherland, and the place read like a social register. Just to make matters worse the food was excellent and meat was permitted on Fridays![23] (He was allergic to fish.) Ocho Rios along the coast turned out to be too expensive so he returned to *Whispering Sands* for a fortnight.

On 15 February he saw Lie in New York when they agreed that no written acceptance of his appointment was necessary, he was still keeping his options open. Once again Hall-Patch was not pleased; he was well-known for his pessimism. It was said that when Bevin heard that a member of his staff was optimistic about finding the solution to a problem he snorted: 'Optimistic is 'e? Send for 'all-Patch, 'e'll chill 'is bones!'[24]

> I do not like an appointment of this importance to which we attach specific conditions, being handled in this loose way. If the conditions are not respected, and we wish to withdraw Jackson we may find ourselves in difficulties.[25]

Padre Pio

Jackson sailed to Cairo, where he found No 10 Sharia Tolumbat looking just the same; then it was Cyprus and Rome. A letter to Sheila in mid-March gives a hint of his continuing uncertainty about the UN job and also of an assumption that his status would somehow be a notch above that of the other ASGs. He thought it would be wiser to return to New York about the middle of April and use UN transport for two or three months. During that time 'having had an opportunity to decide whether there was a real job to be done he could lay the groundwork for a Cadillac for delivery after the General Assembly'.

The Vatican had been remarkably kind and were very keen that he should go as *chef de cabinet* and use that base as a strategic point from which to keep contact with all the boys – especially those in the East. They had offered to pay his expenses for any special journeys!!

> I saw P. XII yesterday; He gave His Blessing to you with great pleasure and insisted on blessing and sending one of the white rosaries to you. I had to smile at the way this was sandwiched in between the political situation in Italy and a request from me that He should intervene with Attlee and Truman (which He will do) to leave a special British force in Jerusalem to protect the Holy Places!

He had also spent a weekend with Padre Pio at Foggia in southern Italy, where it was proposed to build a hospital as a memorial to LaGuardia using surplus UNRRA funds. Padre Pio was the priest at *San Giovanni Rotondo*, and was said to bear Christ's scars on his hands; he was canonized by Pope John Paul II on 16 June 2002.

> He is a remarkable character, and a man of great happiness. There are five other elderly Franciscans there with him, and they all laugh from dawn until night. We talked in his cell for hours – and then the next morning when he celebrated mass (two hours and periods when he was clearly carried away by the exultation of his sacrifice) I was given the special privilege of holding his woollen mittens which normally cover the stigmata on his hands. All the time masses of small boys surrounded him, and at the altar he could hardly move. It is essential that the hospital should be built.
>
> My love to you as always, T.[26]

OPERATION COOLOFF concluded appropriately in the chillier climes of West Wales. He and Barbara and her parents spent the Easter weekend with other Ward relations in Aberystwyth. When they weren't at Mass they were walking in the hills. Back in London at the end of March he requested a meeting with the Foreign Secretary. On McNeil's advice Bevin agreed and all three met on 2 April. Philip Mason in the Foreign Service Department did his best to provide a convincing brief for Bevin:

> As Assistant Secretary-General in the Secretary-General's office Jackson would have powers at present somewhat undefined of coordination over the Secretariat's activities, but would not be entitled to interfere in the other Departments run by Assistant Secretaries-General of equal rank to his own. His task, it seemed, would be to act as the Secretary-General's eyes and ears so that he could intervene where things were going wrong.
>
> In that capacity a man of Commander Jackson's energy and initiative should have many opportunities of making suggestions and of pulling things together, and it is to be anticipated that his own authority in the general work of the Secretariat will become increasingly effective.
>
> The Secretary of State may remember that it was only agreed to second him on the assurance that he would have a really influential and important part to play there. The arrangements for appointing him were rather loosely drawn by the Secretary-General, to say the least of it.[27]

It was left to Hall-Patch to append a note of realism:

> With some experience of the working of international organisations from both within and without, and with some knowledge of Mr Lie and the other personalities involved, I do not think Commander Jackson will be able to do the job we (and Lie) want him to do unless he ranks above the other Assistant Secretaries-General.
>
> This we have been unable to secure. All we have is a promise from a notoriously weak Mr. Lie. Commander Jackson will therefore start this job under a great handicap. It will be surprising if he is able to do what is expected of him, in spite of all his qualities.
>
> Meanwhile, we are losing the services of one of the outstanding 'supply' officials thrown up by the war. There can be no doubt that MESC was a remarkable organisation. We are desperately short of this type of man and this shortage may become critical when ERP really gets going.
>
> If we had secured our terms I think the price of sending one of our best officials to UN might have been justified. I am not convinced that it is justified on the terms on which we are now proposing to release Commander Jackson.[28]

According to McNeil's record of the meeting Jackson told Bevin at the end that 'he wanted to make it plain that he was undertaking this job at the request of HMG and would do it with the utmost vigour'.[29]

Jackson's own account put it slightly differently: 'Commander Jackson said that, if it was the wish of the Foreign Secretary and of HMG that he should accept this appointment as an act of 'approved service', he would do so immediately. The Foreign Secretary confirmed that both he and the Government desired that Commander Jackson should assume the appointment.'[30]

Jackson had elicited the answer he wanted: Bevin and HMG <u>desired</u> him to assume the appointment; he could now say he was sent to the UN. Perhaps that was why he had asked for the meeting. He cabled Lie that the British Government had seconded him to the UN with effect from 18 March, signing himself Commander RGA Jackson[31]. (Lie had always addressed him as Mr).

Jackson had told Bevin that he might have difficulties with Sobolev and Price, so Bevin sent a message to Lovett, Under-Secretary at the State Department:

> I regard [Commander Jackson's] task as so important that I have agreed to second him for that purpose in spite of the fact that his services are urgently

needed in Whitehall. I am convinced that he can only hope to make a success of what is a difficult and even unpromising assignment if he can count upon the goodwill, not only of his colleagues in the UN Secretariat, but also of the Governments of Member States. I particularly count on Jackson having the closest and most cordial relations with the State department.[32]

Jackson was now raring to go: he held discussions in Geneva, Paris and London covering many subjects – the organisation of the UN's European Office, the relationship of the Director's office to Departments at Lake Success (UN Headquarters on Long Island) and to the Economic Committee for Europe (ECE); proposals for financing timber exports from Eastern Europe, public relations policy, the future of the WHO and various matters to do with the IRO. In Paris it was UNICEF and the need for closer coordination with UNAC (the UN Appeal for Children) and UNESCO; in London 'all aspects Unations relations with British Government and those of the Specialised Agencies', the relationship between ECE and continuing organisation of ERP, British contribution to UNICEF, outlets to British press, relations with BBC, and Palestine.

   He informed Lie of all this in a short but dense personal cable ending: 'Will amplify all this with you on arrival together with proposed action. Good to be at work again.'[33]

After further discussions in London he sent Lie another cable listing more things to discuss on his arrival.[34] *Point de zèle* perhaps? Talleyrand again? Lie may well have found these first manifestations of Jackson's way of working somewhat alarming.

On 15 April Robert and Barbara sailed for New York on the *Queen Mary*. A few days previously a paragraph had appeared in THE SPECTATOR, a London weekly:

> The best news I have heard of late about the United Nations – and good news about the United Nations is rather badly needed – is that Commander Robert Jackson has been appointed to a new office, second only to that of the Secretary-General, M. Trygve Lie, and is sailing to America to take up the work next week. The announcement will not mean much to those who know nothing of Commander Jackson. Those who have seen his vital and galvanic personality at work will realise how effective a driving-force is being put behind the United Nations' machinery. An Australian by birth, Commander Jackson,

who is 36, served for eight years in the Australian navy, was later a member of the Staff of the Minister of State in Cairo and Director-General of the Middle East Supply Centre, and then, as Senior Deputy Director-General, became the chief organiser of UNRRA. The administrative ability of which he has given conspicuous evidence in these posts should have great scope at UNO.[35]

That must surely have been Barbara's work, but THE ECONOMIST did not print that kind of chat. If it was done with Robert's connivance it showed an astonishing degree of self-confidence on his part. It did not go down well at Lake Success; Sheila and Alf Katzin were appalled when they saw it.

As for 'the driving force', that, in Urquhart's view, would turn out to be the problem: 'I soon began to see that we had installed a racing engine in a family automobile and could expect trouble.'[36]

Robert and Barbara on *Queen Mary*, 15 April 1948

7 Disaster at Lake Success

JACKSON WAS ENTERING A DIFFERENT WORLD. After six years of running his own show, where urgent action was usually the order of the day, hiring and firing to get good staff, he was now part of an organization that was not working very well, and expected to put it right without the necessary tools to do the job. For logistical skill, his supreme talent, there would be no call, and different qualities which he had so far had little need to practice – patience and tact – would be more appropriate.

Attending the Secretary-General's 113th Private Meeting with senior staff Commander Jackson said he was glad to be back again working in an international organisation. He felt that together the ASGs must work out with him the best way of handling the problems of the UN. In all his dealings he asked for three things: complete honesty; no mention of nationality in the work of the Secretariat; the whole Secretariat should be regarded as a team operating under the Secretary-General, to whom he pledged his complete support.[1]

That was the voice of the school captain, now addressing colleagues mostly twenty years his senior (he was 36), even if only three of them were there to hear it (Laugier, Pelt and Sobolev). He thought the two best were the two youngest: Owen (43) and Sobolev (45). The others were in their mid or late 60s and not of the calibre he had envisaged when advising Lie in 1946. Brian Urquhart thought them 'a pretty lack-lustre lot: Byron Price, the American ASG for Administration, formerly a senior executive in a big news agency (and himself a replacement for an inadequate predecessor) had no international experience and was out of his depth; Andrew Cordier, the Executive Assistant in charge of Lie's office, was a very decent Professor of History from Ohio, but had no experience as an administrator; the office was a shambles.'[2]

After discussing the staff situation with Price and Cordier Jackson drafted a top-secret memorandum to Lie expressing their agreed opinion that Sobolov,

Owen, Price and Hoo ran their Departments efficiently, and suggesting ways of dispensing with the services of the other four ASGs, recommending many changes of staff at lower levels and identifying some deserving promotion.³ He never sent it, but it shows what he and presumably they thought of their colleagues. When he saw Lie on 30 April they merely agreed that he should not formally sign on until September, when the General Assembly would consider establishing his new post. The intervening period, he said, 'would provide time to work out terms of reference which could be made acceptable to the staff',⁴ which he clearly thought were still negotiable. He even had an idea as to how to set about this, but it had to wait; the events of the next few weeks would keep him fully occupied.

Jackson and Trygve Lie, 23 April 1948 UN 10481

He spent three days in Washington, seeing among others the Vice-President of the World Bank, the Director of the IMF and the new Director-General of FAO. At the State Department he saw Averill Harriman (Ambassador at Large in Europe), Robert Lovett (Under-Secretary of State) Dean Rusk (the Assistant Secretary of State responsible for UN affairs) and Paul Hoffman, Head of the Economic Cooperation Administration and Managing Director of ERP (the Marshall Plan). The discussions concerned coordination of the policies of various bodies over a wide range of economic matters similar, it seems, to those he had held in Geneva, Paris and London.[5]

On 14 May the British Mandate in Palestine, established by the League of Nations in 1922, was due to end. Jewish immigration had already become an explosive issue and in the spring of 1947 Britain had placed 'the question of Palestine' in the hands of the UN. In November the General Assembly had passed a resolution proposing partition (into separate Jewish and Arab States), with Britain gradually handing over the administration to a UN Commission comprising representatives of Bolivia, Czechoslovakia, Denmark, Panama and the Philippines.[6] This Britain was not prepared to do. By March 1948 the Security Council accepted that the partition plan could not be implemented and recommended action by all available means to bring about the immediate cessation of violence and the restoration of peace and order in Palestine. The US Government then changed its mind, calling instead for temporary UN Trusteeship over Palestine. This might have worked six months earlier, but it was now too late. Lie, seeing this as a betrayal of the UN by the USA, nearly resigned.

On the day the Mandate ended the State of Israel declared its independence and was immediately recognised by the USA and the USSR. The General Assembly rejected a resolution setting up a special provisional regime for Jerusalem, and approved one to appoint a Mediator to 'promote a peaceful settlement of the future situation in Palestine'.[7]

The next day, Saturday 15 May, Arab armies from neighbouring states invaded Israel from three sides as their governments announced their intention of 'maintaining law and order and preserving the Arab character of Palestine'.[8] The Egyptian Government informed the President of the Security Council (who then happened to be Egyptian) that Egyptian armed forces had entered Palestine. The Council, being responsible under Article 24 of the UN Charter for the maintenance of peace and security, had to consider what to do 'in order to ensure prompt and effective action by the United Nations'. Given that two permanent members, Britain and the USA, had conflicting policies (Britain supporting the Arabs and the USA the Jews) the prospect of such action being taken was unlikely.

Deeply concerned lest the UN should fail, Lie called Cordier and Jackson to his home that evening to consider what he should do. It was decided that Lie should approach both governments to inform them of the difficulty of his position. The next day neither Marshall, the Secretary of State, nor Lovett the Under-Secretary, could be contacted, so it was agreed that a formal letter should be sent to each of the five permanent members of the Security Council making clear to them the Secretary-General's position in the matter.[9] The letter concluded: 'I most earnestly urge that your Government should take account of the extreme seriousness of the situation which now faces the United Nations and of the necessity for prompt action at this crucial moment.'[10]

Jackson delivered Cadogan's copy:

> Jackson came at 6.30 and stayed to dinner. He was the bearer of a message from the Sec.Gen. to the effect, roughly, that he couldn't sit down under what was going on in Palestine. His only practical suggestion was that the S.G. should enjoin a 'standstill'. After dinner I drafted a telegram to the Foreign Office reporting this and asking that I should be authorised to support a standstill if that were proposed. I got Jackson to take this back for despatch, authorising him to show it to Lie on the way.[11]

Lie decided that Cordier should go to Washington immediately to convey his views to the State Department and to try to find out where their difficulties lay with the British Government; it was essential to make personal contact with Marshall and Lovett to establish specific points of disagreement before anyone went to London.[12] Both were away, consequently that contact was not made. Cordier delivered Lie's letter to the State Department and discussed the situation with Dean Rusk (Assistant Secretary of State for UN Affairs) and various officials; he was left in no doubt about how <u>they</u> saw their difficulties with the British government, and reported to Lie that there was much emphasis upon the current differences between the US and the UK. These relations had been deteriorating rapidly and if the whole story were known by Congressmen and the public it would have a most serious effect upon the future of ERP.

> It is pointed out that it would be most unfortunate for both the US and Great Britain if British policy should <u>compromise the implementation of ERP or indeed if the US should find it necessary to use ERP as a leverage on Great Britain.</u> In this connection it was stated again and again that with the new initiative the US is prepared to take in the Security Council <u>the crux of the problem was to be found in London</u>. Department officials spoke quite

bluntly about their unhappiness over the British contribution to the wrecking of the plans for the truce. It is quite up to the British to modify their policy vis-a-vis the Arabs if any solution is to be found for the Palestine question.[13]

The underlining in that passage is in Lie's own copy of the note, and evidently in his own hand, but the word deserving emphasis was the thrice repeated 'if'. Cordier's note did not say that British policy <u>was</u> compromising ERP, it said that Rusk and the officials in the State Department thought it would be unfortunate <u>if it did</u>.

The Foreign Office replied to Cadogan that the proposed standstill was unfair; he should strongly support the idea of a mediator; HMG could not agree to any action by UN 'which would either in theory or in practice operate against one side or the other; in the last resort he should exercise the veto rather than acquiesce in passage of a resolution contrary to the above principles.'[14] 'Perfectly bloody-minded instructions' in Cadogan's view.[15]

The next day (May 16) Lie told Cadogan that he wanted to send Jackson to London to explain his misgivings and fears. 'I told him I had better prepare London for this, in the right way.' Later that evening a message from Lie confirmed that Jackson was leaving the next morning. 'So I drafted a telegram to F.O. explaining this antic.'[16]

Lie's immediate concern, he said, was the situation in Palestine, but he was also worried about what he saw as the progressive decline of the United Nations since its inception. Cadogan had reminded him that the UN was only a machine to be used wisely, if possible, by its members; faced with a fundamental rift between East and West, it could not be expected to work magic. A failure to restrain Arab members of the UN from defying a recommendation of the General Assembly would be an invitation to other nations, particularly the USSR, to follow this example. The UN's misfortune was to be loaded with problems with which it was not prepared to deal.

Cadogan had warned Lie that he did not think sending Jackson to London was a fruitful line of approach; he was now warning London of the purpose of his visit. His telegram concluded:

It seems to be intended that Jackson should also speak to you on ERP matters and on Anglo-American relations in this and other fields, but I did not ascertain with what particular aspects he would deal.[17]

The Foreign Office brief for Bevin gives some indication of the kind of reception Jackson was likely to get:

I am not sure that we need take too tragically this outburst by Mr Lie. He is notoriously temperamental, and is inclined to go from the extreme of optimism to the extreme of pessimism. I feel, in any case, that it is quite unnecessarily melodramatic of him to send Commander Jackson over. One can only hope that there may be something sufficiently important as regards the matters mentioned in the final paragraph of this telegram to justify his visit.' Marshall had recently made a powerful speech reaffirming the intention of the United States to make the fullest use of the UN as the mainspring of their policy. It was perhaps disappointing that this had not been followed up by something of the same kind in London.[18]

Jebb added:

I agree generally with Mr Mason's excellent minute. In particular I do not think that it was a particularly good move on the part of Mr Lie to send over Commander Jackson, though it seems possible that the Commander is acting as a salutary check on the Secretary-General, and is preventing him from major indiscretions such as a public statement under Article 99.

Article 99 enables the Secretary-General to bring to the attention of the Security Council any matter which in his opinion may threaten the maintenance of international peace and security.

Jackson arrived in London on the evening of Wednesday 19 May and saw Hall-Patch and Bridges the following morning. Bevin was away at the Labour Party Conference in Scarborough, but Sir Stafford Cripps, the Chancellor of the Exchequer, had not yet left London. Since the ERP was his concern, Bridges said Jackson should see him immediately. 'The Chancellor grasped the whole position very quickly, got in touch with the Prime Minister and urged that ministers should meet to discuss the problem as quickly as possible. It is clear that in the

Chancellor we have an understanding and willing ally. Sir Edmund Hall-Patch was present during our discussion.'[19]

That evening Jackson saw Sir Orme Sargent, the Permanent Under-Secretary at the Foreign Office, together with Gladwyn Jebb and Michael Wright, the Assistant Secretary for the Middle Eastern Section. They knew he had already seen Cripps. He told them of Lie's problems, stressing the need for speedy and effective action:

> Jebb clearly appreciated our position, but Sargent was very cautious and enquired whether you were, in fact, issuing a 'warning' to the British Government. Clearly he was sensitive that the United States might be using you as a means of exerting pressure on the British Government to modify their present position. I quietly but emphatically denied that. Wright said nothing. I was left with the impression that Jebb alone appreciated the true position and that Sargent and Wright were seeking to find some extraneous reason for my intervention as your representative.[20]

When Sargent asked Jackson to put Lie's views on paper he said he would 'record some broad headings'.

Afterwards Sargent added to the file his own comment on Cadogan's cable:
> This telegram gives a misleading picture of Commander Jackson's mission – paragraph 8 mentions incidentally that Commander Jackson may speak about ERP and Anglo-American relations. As a matter of fact this is the main burden of his message, and it is this linking of ERP (which is no concern of Mr Lie as Secretary-General) with Palestine which gives the whole thing such an unpleasant character.[21]

That evening Jackson saw Sir Roger Makins, another Assistant Under-Secretary at the Foreign Office, who made the same point: ERP was a red herring and irrelevant to the problem of Palestine.[22]

The following morning (Friday 21 May) Jackson drafted his general headings for Bevin, undaunted by the warnings of the Foreign Office. Perhaps his resolve was strengthened by the arrival the previous day of a telegram from Urquhart summarising the latest reports in the US press, which were highly critical of British pro-Arab policy.[23] For example THE NEW YORK POST under the headline 'GREAT BRITAIN BEWARE' called on Congress to 'reverse its authorisation of financial assistance to Britain [through ERP] unless it returned to the rule of law.'

Only one of Jackson's headings need concern us:

> 6 The Secretary-General shares the view of the Secretary of State for Foreign Affairs and the United States Secretary of State that the future of the United Nations is primarily dependent on ERP. (His views coincide exactly with those expressed by Mr Bevin at the meeting with Commander Jackson on 2nd April.) If the United States and the sixteen European countries under the leadership of the United Kingdom can make a success of ERP, the Secretary-General believes the United Nations can be kept afloat, on the assumption that positive results will lead to an improvement in East-West relations. On the other hand, the Secretary-General believes that any threat at the present time to whole-hearted United States – United Kingdom co-operation must reduce the chances of ERP succeeding and thus immediately and directly affect the existence of the United Nations itself.[24]

In fact Bevin had not claimed on 2 April that 'the future of the UN was primarily dependent on ERP'; according to Jackson's own note he had merely 'referred to the ERP and his hope that eventually western Europe … would stand as a major world force independent of the USA and the USSR'.[25]

Jackson saw the Foreign Secretary on the Saturday morning; Jebb and Wright were also present. Bevin hit the roof. For a start he was very jealous of Cripps and furious that Jackson had seen him first. Pounding his desk with a large silver inkstand[26] he said that he considered that Lie's move had been made under pressure from the US Government and as a means of indicating that if British policy on Palestine was not modified, then ERP would be used to exercise pressure. He would never yield to such a move; he spoke of mistakes made by the US in handling this problem, and difficulties caused by its recognition of Israel. He would never have British forces used in Palestine in a way which could in effect lead to the establishment of Israel.[27]

Jackson said repeatedly that the Secretary-General was not allocating responsibility for the situation to any government, or suggesting to any government that it should modify its policies; the situation threatened the future of the UN and he was expressing his concern to the two governments which could do something about it. The Secretary-General had made this clear in Washington more emphatically than he, Jackson, was doing in London.[28]

Wright accused Jackson of reading a lecture in Anglo-American relations – the place for that, he said, was Washington not London. Jackson was unaware that the previous day Wright had seen the American Ambassador, Lewis Douglas, who had flatly contradicted any suggestion that the Palestine question was affecting Washington's attitude to ERP.[29] He said yet again that Lie was not allocating responsibilities nor suggesting that any government should modify its policies.

Bevin said that all Anglo-American discussions were proceeding most favourably and that there was complete agreement on ERP, but there were elements trying to drive a wedge between the US and Britain. If the Secretary-General would read the British resolution he should feel that it would produce satisfactory results. (Resolution 49 called on all Governments to issue a cease-fire order.)

When Jackson asked whether he thought that such a cease-fire order (similar to one made a month previously) could check the Jews and Arabs from fighting Bevin replied that if Washington and New York could control the Jews, he thought the Arabs could be restrained. When Jackson finally asked if there was any further guidance he could give to the Secretary-General Bevin said there was not.[30]

To ensure that Lie's position would not be misrepresented at the Cabinet meeting on Monday Jackson had further discussions on the Sunday with Bridges (who told him that his visit might well have been the turning point in a new approach to the problem on the part of the government), and on the Monday with Hall-Patch, who did everything possible to ensure that Bevin understood Lie's position clearly. Hall-Patch felt that he had made some progress but that much would need to be done to overcome Bevin's sensitivity and suspicion about everything and everyone remotely connected with the problem of Palestine.[31]

After the Cabinet meeting Jackson learnt that two different reports had been given, one by the Foreign Secretary, one by other ministers.

> From this I had reasonable confidence that your own position was now well understood but that we were still lacking any clear-cut understanding of possible future developments. It seems to me that we must be guided by developments over the next day or two in deciding what our next approach to this problem should be.[32]

He arrived back in Washington on Tuesday 25 May and immediately telephoned Urquhart with a report for Lie: Bevin was suspicious and resentful of the recent developments over Palestine, had no real understanding of the SG's problems, did not appreciate Marshall's difficulties either, and was obsessed by a fear of ERP pressure being put on him to change the British policy in the Middle East. He was not at all helpful. Cripps, on the other hand, was clear about the issues and extremely sympathetic to the SG's difficulties. Attlee (the Prime Minister) understood the true position but knew that Bevin was very influential. The situation was exceedingly delicate and must be handled with care and discretion.[33]

Jebb was afraid that Jackson, given his mood when departing, might not exactly act as a sedative with Mr Lie. Feeling that 'a little soft soap might not come amiss' he drafted a telegram for Bevin to send to Cadogan:

> I found it difficult to understand Mr Lie's trend of thought in linking Palestine with ERP, and made it quite clear that we were not deviating from our policy for a moment as a result of any such considerations.
>
> I fear that Commander Jackson, who is, I rather think, a newcomer to high politics, may be returning to Lake Success in a disgruntled frame of mind. It is therefore important that you should, in conversation with Mr Lie and if you get the opportunity, say that I fully realise the difficulties and apprehensions of the Secretary-General and sympathise with them very much. He must not think that I in any way resented his approaching me beyond the fact that the coupling of ERP with our Palestine policy gave rise to an impression (which I am sure that he himself had not really thought of conveying) that pressure was about to be placed on us with the object of inducing us to do something which we knew to be wrong.[34]

Jebb's comment that Jackson was a newcomer to high politics was fair. His involvement with top politicians in MESC and UNRRA had been in the sphere of logistics in situations of emergency where he was a master operator and in a position of authority, but he had not been schooled in the diplomacy of what to say and what not to say in delicate political situations.

Cadogan replied to Jebb:

> I had gathered from your telegram that he had been a bit knocked about in London. He was a little bit chastened, but not repentant. I am sure that he had felt it to be his duty, at Lie's request, to put, as well as he could, the latter's misgivings as to the future of the United Nations – which of course depends – if it had any future at all, on continued Anglo-US cooperation.

I told Jackson that we accepted that Lie was acting honestly, according to his own lights, and was only concerned for the future of the United Nations. But I added that the coupling of ERP with our Palestine policy had been ill-advised. No harm done, I hope.[35]

On 1 June Bridges sent Jackson a personal note: 'As you say, the position moves too quickly for written comment to be of much use. But I would like to say that I think your visit almost certainly had much more effect than you could possibly have imagined at the time.'[36]

His reason for this could have been that on 25 May Douglas had met not only Bevin, but also Attlee and other Ministers and the British Chiefs of Staff. After some tough talking on both sides a measure of agreement was reached on the need to secure Arab acceptance of a Jewish state. Douglas considered this as a milestone in British thinking about Palestine. Two days later Britain proposed to the Security Council that there should be a four week truce and an embargo on the supply of arms to Arabs and Jews alike. After some amendment the British resolution (No. 50) was carried on 29 May.[37] If Bridges's comment was not merely more soft soap it can only have meant that Jackson had some influence on Ministers other than Bevin. It would also explain the resentment towards Jackson which Bevin would later display.

So Jackson's first special assignment – 'this antic', as Cadogan had called it – evidently had a satisfactory ending.

Shortly after his return from London he resumed his quest for 'suitable terms of reference'. When he had first arrived at Lake Success an information note (No 441) had been circulated to the staff announcing his duties, which Lie had agreed with the other ASGs. One of them was 'In cooperation with Departments, to coordinate the internal work of the UN and the execution of agreed policy'. There was no mention of 'programmes and policy decisions **involving more than one Department**', which Lie had specified in his letter of 16 December offering Jackson the post. This discrepancy was the slender thread on which Jackson's little scheme depended.

In presenting his proposal to Lie he surrounded that particular point with a mass of unexceptionable general points in a ten page memorandum[38] which he had very probably prepared before going to London. His covering note made it clear that he did not consider himself committed to his appointment on its existing terms:

> I have now had an opportunity to survey the appointment which it has been proposed I should assume, and I have also had the advantage of personal discussions with the Assistant Secretaries-General. Before taking any more formal steps to take up the duties connected with this appointment it seems to me wise that we should review the job generally and consider how best it can be carried out.
>
> The memorandum which follows has been written quite objectively, and without any reference to my personal position. I know you will agree that it is wiser that we should obtain a clear understanding of this appointment, have it approved by you and accepted by the senior staff, before attempting to commence work. I feel that it would be unfair to you, the senior staff, and the organization, if we started on a false basis, and that we would do more harm than good if we approached the appointment in that way. ...
>
> After agreement with you I suggest that informal talks are held with the Assistant Secretaries-General and that you should then convene a general meeting to discuss the paper.

The memorandum was in two parts:

Part I – Policy – said in effect: let us forget about your letter of 16 December and look instead at the terms of reference agreed with the ASGs and stated in Information Note 441: 'In co-operation with Departments, to co-ordinate the internal work of the UN and the execution of agreed policy.' He had already established contact with the other ASGs and thought that if discussed with them fully, there was reason to assume that agreement could be reached concerning the three matters (reducing the Secretary-General's work-load, co-ordinating the internal work of the UN and co-ordinating the specialised agencies.)

Part II – Implementation – had three sections: (A) definition of the appointment in general terms with a list of 17 specific tasks, (B) consideration of the manner in which these tasks could best be carried out; (C) timing of certain tasks.

What this boiled down to was that as ASG for the Executive Office he would be the channel through which the other ASGs would communicate with the Secretary-General on all policy matters (as he would have been as Chief of Staff).

After discussing the memorandum with Lie on 2 June he wrote a note for the record:

> After discussion it was agreed that a letter would be written to the Advisory Committee on Administrative and Budgetary Affairs stating that since your letter of 16 December it has been possible to consider the appointment from the standpoint of practical experience.[39]

Lie's copy has the word 'agreed' underlined and his comment in the margin: 'On what assumptions? Agreement and understanding between the ASGs!'[40] Precisely!

Jackson then sent copies of his memorandum to the other eight ASGs with a covering note saying that he hoped to discuss it personally before the Secretary-General's meeting on 4 June (in two days' time):

> I believe that the proposed appointment can be made to work if an effective relationship is developed between all those concerned. Without that no arrangement on paper will ever make the appointment succeed.[41]

On the morning of 4 June the meeting took place; two ASGs were absent: Sobolev and Owen (the one who would surely have supported Jackson).

> <u>The Secretary-General</u> referred to the working paper which had been circulated to all Assistant Secretaries-General concerning Commander Jackson's appointment. He said that since the meeting was agreed on the three general objectives there would be no need for detailed discussion on the paper, which had already been discussed individually with the Assistant Secretaries-General. ... [42]

Four ASGs made brief general comments and that was that. Lie wrote on his copy: '6/4 ASG's meeting OK'ed the general lines. TL.'[43]

It was game, set and match to the ASGs. 'I sat there like a tethered goat with six tigers looking at me' was how he later described it.[44] But it was no joke. Not only had he lost his battle over five words and any hope of gaining the authority he was seeking, he had also lost face with the other ASGs and any chance of winning their confidence, which, given time, he might have done. Most serious of all, there was no possibility now of him doing the 'big job' for which HMG had released him; He could hardly ask to be recalled on the grounds of 'lack of authority or backing' having been fully aware of this when he decided to take the job. Hall-Patch had been right. What is surprising is not that his ruse failed, but that he should ever have expected it to succeed, but Jackson was sometimes over-confident of his ability to persuade other people to see things his way (the Dominican Friars in Cairo, for example!). Perhaps he would have been wiser to address the problem for which he already had specific authority: 'coordinating programmes and policy decisions involving more than one Department'. The need to coordinate the work of the Economic and Social Departments was recognized by Lie (see page 6/1); working with Owen (his friend and supporter) and Laugier (whose ability he soon came to respect) would have given him a chance to show what he could do for the organization, and possibly have won the respect of all his colleagues, but that was not his way. No letters to Barbara revealing his feelings at this time have come to light; we only know that he soldiered on. There were still things for him to do: coordinating the specialised agencies, directing the SG's office and undertaking special assignments, but those were not the reasons why HMG had wanted him to go to Lake Success.

Owen and Urquhart had been keen for Jackson to be brought into the Secretariat. The younger members of the staff who had joined the UN in a mood of enthusiasm and optimism in 1946 were becoming increasingly disillusioned. Jackson had made a name for himself in the Middle East and UNRRA, and they thought he was the man to get.[45] But things had not turned out as they expected; According to Urquhart 'Jacko and Lie took an instant dislike to each other – it was hate at first sight' and he soon found himself in the position of being Jacko's personal assistant as well as Lie's, obliged to listen to each of them privately cursing the other and to observe their sickeningly friendly relationship when together. He found Jacko's behaviour overbearing and tactless; his insistence on being called Commander was not well received at a time when most people had put aside their former military ranks, and his military manner was out of place in an essentially civilian organisation. He could only operate at one speed – full speed ahead – 'since it is my habit to work every waking minute I shall require a dictaphone in my car'. While Urquhart quite admired this, others did not.

'Lie, right from the beginning, found Jacko simply too much and probably resented his name-dropping and his contacts in high places. It did not help that he understood very little of what Jacko was saying, particularly when he resorted to cricketing metaphors or arcane allusions, as was frequently the case. 'We've got to play a little slower on the bowling this morning, Secretary-General'. 'Vot does he say?" Urquhart believes Lie realised very early on that he had made a great mistake in taking him on.

'Jacko for his part probably quite rightly regarded Lie as devious and tricky and often compared him to Fiorello LaGuardia, for whom he now expressed a passionate hatred. He was also in a state of high emotional excitement almost certainly on account of his anxiety to get his first marriage annulled in order to marry Barbara; he was obsessed with the Vatican. During the short time that she was in New York the pair of them had presented an unusual picture of an engaged couple; it was as if they were embarking on a crusade to put the world to rights, rather than a marriage.'[46]

Jackson's involvement with Palestine continued. The Security Council had appointed Count Folke Bernadotte, President of the Swedish Red Cross, as Mediator in Palestine.[47] Ralph Bunche was his principal UN assistant and Jackson was the link between the truce team and Headquarters.

Bernadotte was in Cairo trying to get the Israelis and Arabs to observe the truce and needed their agreement to his interpretation of Resolution 50, which referred to the Council's desire 'to bring about a cessation of hostilities without prejudice to the rights, claims, and position of either Arabs or Jews'. He wanted the Secretary-General to confirm his own view that the intention was that no military advantage should accrue to either side during the period of the truce. Jackson's abortive meeting with Lie was barely over when a cable from Bunche arrived asking for clarification.

The Security Council had already ruled that the Mediator should interpret the resolution on the spot and only turn to the Council if challenged, but a message informing Bernadotte had not yet arrived. When told, Bunche asked Jackson if the President of the Council could confirm Bernadotte's interpretation; Jackson asked the President who agreed.[48] Jackson kept meticulous records of every conversation, even reading them to the President to make sure that they were correct. Perhaps the meeting that morning had left him bruised and anxious not to put a foot wrong.

Bernadotte secured the two sides' agreement on 9 June, and the truce came into effect on 11 June. It held well, except for the activities of the Jewish terrorist organisations (Irgun Zvai Leumi and the Stern Gang). With the fighting ended he needed to reach a longer term agreement with the two sides which he could present to the Security Council. He moved his Headquarters to Rhodes and held meetings with representatives of the Arabs and Jews, though always separately. He had little success. With the State of Israel recognised the Jews were at least prepared to consider some compromise, but the Arabs were not: the various nations involved, Palestine, Syria, Trans-Jordan, Iraq and Egypt, were hopelessly divided by their own rivalries. By the end of the month Bernadotte knew he needed to get the truce extended to give him more time.

On 22 June Jackson was in Rome, awaiting instructions to proceed to Rhodes, when a letter from Urquhart arrived telling him that Bevin, evidently still smarting from his encounter with Jackson, had played a dirty trick to get his own back by asking Douglas (the US Ambassador) to write to the State Department saying that Jackson had turned up in London with messages purporting to be from the State Department to the British Government, and that this did not seem a suitable method of diplomacy. The State Department had spoken to Byron Price, who in turn spoke to Lie. Price had recounted this story to Owen 'with somewhat ill-disguised glee' and Urquhart was worried that Price might thereby have interfered with Jackson's relations with Lie.[49]

After a phone call from Jackson Urquhart asked Lie if he felt Jackson should withdraw. Lie was emphatic that he should not. 'He takes it as a compliment to you and to your success in your dealings with the Foreign Office that they should take the trouble to try to do you down. The Secretary-General spoke in the highest terms of your efforts in London and with a very real sympathy for this difficulty. As far as he is concerned you can dismiss the matter from your mind.'[50]

His wait in Rome gave him an opportunity to call in at the Vatican with some good news: the Italian Government had approved the assignment of 250 million lire from its UNRRA lire fund for building a hospital in memory of Fiorello LaGuardia at San Giovanni Rotondo near Foggia (where Padre Pio was the priest). The money had been raised by selling off UNRRA equipment which had served its purpose. Jackson was strongly in favour of this proposal and he and Barbara helped it along whenever they could.

Bernadotte was glad of Jackson's visit:

> He said that if I succeeded in my task, that would mean a tremendous amount for the prestige and future of the UN; if I failed there was a risk that a dangerous split might develop in the UN. The next thing might then easily be to have the US supporting the Jews and Great Britain the Arabs, which in its turn might lead to complications between the leading Western powers. It was reassuring to know the importance attached in the UN to a solution of the Palestine question. Jackson's visit was certainly of great importance both to him and to me. It gave him a clear idea of the way we were tackling our problems. And I was able to feel sure that he, on his return to Lake Success, would speak favourably on my behalf.[51]

The visit was important to Jackson because he genuinely believed that he had something to contribute to the peace process, on the grounds that he was acceptable to the Arabs because of what he had done in MESC and acceptable to the Jews because of what he had done in UNRRA.[52]

He returned to London via Nicosia, doubtless visiting Edward and Audrey. Bernadotte was irked to find that while UN couldn't let him hire some man he needed, high officers in the UN could spend money as they wished, citing 'Jackson's junket to Cyprus' as an example.[53]

On 3 July Robert and Barbara gave a midday cocktail party at the Crillon Hotel in Paris. A guest noted in his diary that he 'met BW and her fiancé'.[54] Not only were they not engaged, her fiancé was still married!

Wanting to clear the air with Bevin, he consulted Jebb, telling him that Bevin's report was exaggerated and gave the impression that he had behaved either like a knave or like a fool; though he may have been a fool, he was not a knave! He wanted 'to get back to April 2nd' when, as he understood it, he had received the backing of the Secretary of State. Jebb's advice to Bevin was to 'treat him gently and accept his assurance of good intentions'.[55]

Though nothing of importance passed, his meeting with Bevin was civil; McNeil noted that Jackson was well satisfied with the conversation and no longer felt he was *persona non grata* with Bevin; he had been 'taken back into favour'.[56]

What with that and Urquhart's letter conveying Lie's praises and the cocktail party at the Crillon he must have felt that things were looking up.

Jackson's next task was 'coordinating liaison with the specialised agencies'. He was rapporteur to the Administrative Committee on Coordination and chairman of its Preparatory Committee. On the agenda for the mid-July meetings was 'Comparative Review of Reports of the Specialized Agencies', which had evidently not got very far. The UN representative on the Preparatory Committee said that the review was not an account of what had been done to implement various policies, but merely a dry enumeration, unrelated to a clear general objective of overall policy. Jackson pointed out that the great difficulty was the lack of an agreed point where policy should originate and priorities be decided. If it were not the Economic and Social Council (ECOSOC), where else would it be? The Comparative Review, he said, could be one of the most important aspects of the work of the Co-ordination Committee in assisting ECOSOC. The adoption of unrelated resolutions in the same fields by various committees, conferences, and other bodies could create a growing array of uncoordinated decisions.[57] The problem was that ECOSOC was supposed to coordinate the activities of the specialised agencies but had no power to do so. This was a fundamental weakness of the UN system, one which Jackson would address twenty years later. How much better the system would have developed if he had been able to address the problem then.

Jackson probably knew several members of the Preparatory Committee from the days when he was organising the transfer of UNRRA's functions to the agencies. 'Now chaps,' he said 'we're all in the same boat, and we've just got to get together, and row, row, row!'[58] His exhortation was enthusiastically received. Although he asked them not to mention the incident to Lie lest his nose should be put out of joint, evidently they did. (Though, as Urquhart has pointed out, anyone who got the specialised agencies together would have been extremely welcome to do so.[59]) This trivial event would not be worth mentioning but for the significance which Jackson later gave it as one of the ways in which he fell out of favour with Lie.

On his return to New York he had found 'evidence of unauthorised intruders' in his office. The Director of the Department of Conference and General Services, David Vaughan, had worked for him in UNRRA and they had not hit it off too well; Jackson saw a chance for a little light-hearted needling. In any case there was something missing from his life.

15 July: The work of the Executive Office of the Secretary-General has suffered considerably as a result of an invasion in the office which houses the Correspondence Unit. The invasion has taken the shape of either (1) a mouse, or possibly (2) mice. Does your Department provide facilities for dealing with this problem? If not, who does?

Personally I should be most satisfied for Cats, Black, one, Secretaries-General for the use of, to be provided for this Office. You may wish to consider the budgetary implications of this proposal.[60]

Vaughan responded in similar vein, pointing out that the cost might be high considering that provision would have to be made for the cat in respect of maternity leave, food, keeper, replacement during periods of absence etc. A week later Jackson sent him a reminder, ending: 'where the hell is the Large Black Cat which was promised to me?' But the real trouble was that the cat had been away for a whole month. He was the cat and the mice were at play. Sheila had been uneasy about his long absence from the office and cabled him to return, but he never replied.

The truce in Palestine expired, the Security Council adopted a resolution extending it and ordering a cease-fire in Jerusalem[61] and Bernadotte asked for 250 armed guards to monitor the truce, to be provided from the regular armies of member states. Some members were reluctant, saying that the UN itself should provide them. Even if that were agreed in principle, organising and training such a force it would take at least 60 days. Lie was in Paris, so Jackson issued a Memorandum suggesting that the governments most involved should lend their forces until they could be relieved by a UN force. 'The preservation of peace in Palestine' he said 'was of the highest political importance; the future usefulness of the UN could well depend on its success in handling this problem.'[62] It had some effect, but not enough. By the end of July Bernadotte was so desperate that he cabled Jackson personally: 'urgently request immediate action from secretariat … impossible maintain present situation Jerusalem if UN unable to meet as moderate a request as 40 armed guards. UN prestige and my position Palestine impossible to maintain if this lack of quick action from UN will continue. I blame this fact entirely repeat entirely on UN organization not on me or members of my staff. You notice without doubt that I am mad and I believe I have the right to be. Most sincerely Bernadotte.'[63]

After spending a weekend at Felixstowe with Barbara and her family Jackson saw Lie and Bunche in London on 3 August. According to Bunche Lie was willing to recruit a small force of armed guards but Jackson (and he says every senior man at Lake Success) was opposed. 'Jackson too much imbued with experience of British and fear of what Irgun will do. Result is a negative approach. Lie wants to do something, on his own if necessary.'[64]

The following day Jackson went to Geneva to attend ECOSOC meetings. On the Saturday he and Barbara had lunch at the Lion d'Or at Cologny, beside the lake. Not a cloud was in the sky. He flew to Rhodes to explain to Bernadotte the difficulties encountered by the secretariat in its negotiations with Washington.[65] Bernadotte acknowledged that his quarrel was more with the United States than the UN. 'They had proposed the resolution and declared that they would do everything they could to facilitate his work, but fourteen days later only 30 American officers had been placed at his disposal as against a promised 125.'[66]

When Bernadotte said that he intended to go to Jerusalem Jackson tried very hard to dissuade him, reminding him that Lord Moyne (Casey's successor as Minister in the Middle East) had been assassinated and pointing out that Bernadotte would be an obvious target for those who did not want the UN intervention to succeed. When Jackson urged him to invite representatives of the two sides to see him in Rhodes Bernadotte referred to their earlier conversation in which Jackson had said how important it was that the UN should not fail at this time; 'compared to that his own life was insignificant.'[67] Jackson's fears would be proved right; six weeks later Bernadotte was assassinated in Jerusalem.

Aid for children was an issue that Jackson cared about deeply, having assisted at the birth of UNICEF. There was now a second organisation – UNAC, the UN Appeal for Children, the brain-child of Aake Ording, formerly Norway's delegate to UNRRA's Council. Believing that UNRRA had failed the children of Europe, he had the idea of asking salaried people the world over to give up one day's pay in support of aid for children. Though aimed at individuals, the project needed the support of governments. Lie had agreed that this appeal could be made in the name of the UN and undertook to provide the administrative machinery. At least half the proceeds would go to UNICEF, with the rest being used for children's programmes run by national voluntary organisations. Lie had launched the appeal in February, designating Ording as coordinator,[68] and Jackson had publicly supported it when he arrived in New York in April: 'There is before us this one opportunity to help the children of the new generation – to give them the health, the happiness, the conditions of life which may give them in their generation the peace for which we have sought so vainly in our time.'[69]

The existence of the two organisations inevitably muddied the waters; the British Government, for example, would not decide how much to contribute to UNICEF until it knew the total of the public response to UNAC's appeal.[70] By the summer Lie was uncertain whether UNAC should continue, but saw this as a matter for governments to decide; if, however, UNAC were to be continued he would not be willing for the UN Secretariat to assume any responsibility for handling any further appeals.

Jackson wrote to Ording, conveying the Secretary-General's request that while in Geneva (at the ECOSOC meeting) he should, at his discretion, inform representatives of UNICEF and any governments interested in the general question of UNICEF and UNAC of his views about any further appeals. The Secretary-General thought UNICEF the most suitable organisation, but would not oppose some other arrangement agreed by governments so long as his reservations on the facilities provided by the Secretariat were observed.[71]

As far as Jackson was concerned that was an order, but perhaps the courteous tone of his letter and the words 'at your discretion' led Ording to take it less seriously; he was in any case an old colleague of Lie's, having served under him in the Norwegian Government in Exile, and may have felt he could always rely on his support; perhaps his view that UNRRA had failed the children of Europe had produced some lingering resentment towards Jackson, and UNAC was his idea. For whatever reason, he disregarded the order, as Jackson discovered when he returned to Geneva from Rhodes.

The telephones were out of order so he cabled Cordier: 'On my return here yesterday I was informed that Ording had obviously disobeyed the instructions I gave him last Friday [7 August], ie to adhere to the Sec-Gen's policy which was given to him in writing before departure from New York.' Ording, he said, had worked up various delegates, particularly Evatt of Australia, to a point where they were going to press a resolution in ECOSOC on lines opposed to the Secretary-General's own wishes. Never before had he been associated with a staff which failed to obey the orders of the head (he seems to have forgotten General Morgan!). Either the Secretary-General would have another large scale appeal on his hands or he, Jackson, would have to approach delegates to ECOSOC such as Evatt in a way which would cause embarrassment to the UN, the Secretary-General and himself.

He asked Cordier to discuss this with the Secretary-General and telegraph instructions immediately: should he exercise his authority in the Secretary-General's name, try to persuade Evatt to take a different line, and tell Ording to return to Lake Success with a view to his services coming to an end?[72]

Lie's response did not arrive for several hours and was not much help:

As stated on previous occasions I cannot personally approve existence of two separate administrations on relief for children, am anxious no sources of support for relief of children be cut off but numerous problems arising from coexistence of two administrations should be avoided.[73]

Jackson replied:

Regret that seriousness of situation reported yesterday does not seem to be appreciated. I endeavoured to do this again by telephone in the middle of the night. Critical plenary session [of ECOSOC] will start at 1000 hours your time today Thursday [12 August] I have explained to Cordier what I am trying to do in order to save you, as Secretary-General, from the embarrassment which you must inevitably suffer if no-one here intervenes on your

Robert and Barbara in London, 16 August 1948.

behalf. This situation is being caused solely by Ording and without your authority to handle it I cannot do more to rectify the situation than I have in the past. I believe I could be more help to you if I could have answers to the three questions about this problem contained in my telegram to Cordier yesterday.[74]

Evidently he had no further response from Lie. He had handled the matter impeccably but possibly irritated Lie in the process. Had it been anyone other than Ording he might well have dealt with the matter himself, but Ording was a friend of Lie's, and Lie did nothing to help. (Four weeks later ECOSOC voted narrowly not to support any future UNAC appeal.)

After having a tooth out in London he flew back to New York on Wednesday, 18 August, and had a long discussion with Lie about the ECOSOC meeting and various problems affecting Headquarters. The atmosphere was normal and friendly.

The following day he saw Lie again several times about routine matters and again at 4 pm to arrange their movements in relation to the forthcoming General Assembly in Paris. These meetings also proceeded normally.[75]

At 7.0 pm Lie summoned him again, saying that he had expected him to refer to matters on which they had disagreed while Jackson was in Geneva. Jackson said that this was because the points of disagreement had subsequently been cleared up and he regarded the matter as closed (though clearly the Ording affair was not). Lie finally steeled himself to say what he had to say. Jackson described what followed in a long memorandum to Cadogan:

> Mr Lie then asked me whether I could make arrangements to 'leave' this appointment. ... He said he thought the present arrangement would not work and then very quickly said that I was 'too strong', and 'too big' for the appointment. He then added that he had 'never been shown such consideration' in his work by any official in his previous career. I found the discussion at this point somewhat bewildering ...
>
> Further confused discussion followed during which he complained that the present organisation of the Secretariat was all wrong, that there should not be nine Assistant Secretaries-General but three Deputies. He

then asked whether His Majesty's Government would withdraw me and 'give me a big job'. I suggested again that he should discuss the matter with the Government and not with me.

I find it very difficult to suggest the real reason for Mr Lie's present attitude. Some factors which may bear on it ... may be (i) I believe his mind has been set against me during my absence in Geneva and Rhodes as a result of misrepresentations about me from senior officials who could see their own departments ultimately being affected by my work, e.g. Cohen is well aware that his Public Relations Department is unjustifiably large and extravagant ... Price has probably become aware of the <u>American</u> proposal that the budget work now done in his department should be transferred under my control ... I am clearly quite defenceless if Lie accepts statements made about me ... and will not at least ascertain from me whether they are true. (ii) My position has inevitably been affected when I have at Lie's request cleaned up dirty messes between departments and individuals. (iii) Lie probably has some fear of his own position as the result of his own small 'Palace clique' playing on his vanity and plugging the line that I may become too strong. (iv) Lie demonstrated considerable irritation when the Specialised Agencies recently unanimously expressed appreciation at the progress made in co-ordinating their work with the United Nations. (They did this despite my personal request to them not to do so). ...

Mr Lie saw me again this morning and asked me what I now thought of the situation. I replied that my views had not changed – that I desired to help the United Nations and him in accordance with the understanding on which I originally came to the organisation and that I felt it premature to come to any decision at this time. I took this attitude despite my personal desire to speak more strongly as I did not wish to prejudice any future action which His Majesty's Government might wish to take. Mr Lie then said our personal relations were 'excellent', but that the concept of the appointment was wrong. He said he wanted some time to think about the problem and said that we should talk again later today.

As to my personal position in this matter, it is known that I was never anxious for this appointment. I realise however ... that there is a major job to be done to improve the Secretariat internally ... and there is also a major job to be done in co-ordinating the activities of the Specialised Agencies ... I have not shown any personal feeling in these discussions with Mr Lie and have simply left the matter open.[76]

Jackson delivered the memorandum to Cadogan, who was about to leave for London.

> Jackson wanted to see me urgently at 12.30, so I asked him to lunch with me at the Pierre. He told me he had been given sudden warning by Lie the night before. Lie himself came to see me at 3.30. He evidently won't keep Jackson a day longer, but his account of what has led up to this is notably different from that of Jackson. One of them is lying.[77]

That afternoon Lie suggested that Jackson should fly to London to be available when Cadogan was there. 'He emphasised again that the reason for making his decision was that the 'concept' was wrong and said, with emotion, 'you have been a victim of my own bad judgment' and 'I have hit you below the belt'. He ended the discussion by re-affirming his friendship for me and expressed his fear that 'I may have greatly damaged your future'.[78]

Jackson spent the weekend alone at the Pierre Hotel in the depths of despair; this must have been the worst week-end of his life, bar one. (The other, quite different and much worse, came many years later.) On the Monday morning Lie saw him again. 'The atmosphere was very cordial. Having yet again expressed his appreciation of the work which I had done for him, he proceeded with some petulance to complain about the eight 'barons' whom he felt he could not control. He said that he did not blame himself for this lack of control, but regarded it as an inevitable result of the organisational plan which had been forced on him at the beginning. Once more he said that it was only the 'concept' of the appointment which was wrong, and that what he really wanted was three good deputies, adding, as previously, that I should take charge of them for him.[79]

On the Wednesday Lie gave him a copy of the draft of a letter which he proposed to send him.[80] Who had drafted it is not clear, but the first paragraph suggests that Jackson may have had a hand in it; the trial period had been entirely his idea.

> My dear Commander Jackson
>
> In the conversations which you and I held in January with regard to your appointment we reached the understanding that the appointment was to be subject to a trial period. We both realised that the new post which you were being offered involved a considerable innovation in the organisation of the United Nations Secretariat, and that we would need to review most carefully the suitability of such a position to that organisation.

During the past months you have applied yourself without stint to the service of the United Nations, and I have had ample confirmation of my original regard for your outstanding abilities and your high qualities of mind and character.

I have at the same time been giving detailed and thoughtful consideration to the advisability of placing your appointment on a permanent basis. After such consideration I have been forced to come to the conclusion that a position such as the one you hold cannot be suitably fitted into the administrative and organisational structure of the Secretariat. There are, of course, still many problems of coordination within the Secretariat and with the Specialised Agencies. I am now convinced, however, that a different organisational arrangement for dealing with these problems would be preferable to the arrangement which you and I had ventured upon.

It is therefore with the deepest feeling of personal regret that I have decided not to extend my arrangement with you and to take steps for the abolition of the post as of 1 September.

As you leave this Organisation, I can assure you that you have my sincere gratitude for the devotion with which you have assisted me and served the interests of the United Nations. I extend to you my best wishes for your future happiness.

With warm personal regards,

Sincerely yours, Trygve Lie.[81]

Strangest of all, perhaps, is a hand-written note which Jackson sent Lie the next day – still hoping:

My dear S.G.,

This is simply a parting note to say that, on experience so far, I think our partnership can help UN. There is more than enough work, and it looks as if we are all agreed on where I can help. As I said at the beginning, I don't know what results may be achieved, but we will certainly have some laughter!!

This note is simply to say 'thank you very much' for your kindness and understanding to me. Our agreement was complete honesty between us, and I'm sure that that is our strongest asset.

I can get back at 12 hours' notice.

I hope very much that Mrs Lie improves, give her my kindest regards.

Yours sincerely Jacko.[82]

In London Jackson and Cadogan discussed the situation with McNeil, Jebb and Mason:

> The impression which we have gained from these discussions as well as the earlier talks in New York as recorded in Jackson's memorandum of 23 August, is that Mr Lie has been subjected to strong pressure from some of the other ASGs, who have been coming to him in Jackson's absence from Lake Success on missions from the Secretary-General, to represent to him that the creation of Jackson's post and of the powers of co-ordination which that post carried, created great difficulties from their own point of view. How far personal rivalries came into the matter must be largely a matter of surmise. It seems, however, that Mr Lie has yielded to this pressure and it is to be gathered ... that Mr Lie would have liked the situation to be eased from his point of view by our withdrawal of Jackson for other duties.

McNeil thought that the important thing was to try to avoid dealing in personalities and to concentrate on the importance of the post itself not being abolished. With Bevin's agreement[83] he wrote to Lie: The creation of the post had been under discussion for a long time and was shortly due to come before the General Assembly; if the Assembly decided to have it established, HMG would be in an awkward situation. He urged Lie not to take any final decision until they had a chance to discuss the matter, but since he (McNeil) was going on two weeks holiday, that would not be possible until 14 September.[84]

Lie replied that he did not think such discussion would have any practical value and in any case the delay was unacceptable. He remained convinced that the conception of the post was wrong.[85] In any case he had already sent Jackson the letter terminating his appointment.

The UN issued a press statement that the post was abolished: it had represented a novel departure in the organizational structure of the Secretariat and had therefore been regarded as experimental. The Secretary-General was now considering other means of attaining the same objectives within the existing organizational structure.[86]

The NEW YORK TIMES reported that Lie had 'settled the long-brewing dispute within the UN high command', the HERALD that 'Jackson, the United Nations trouble-shooter, met the fate of many another man assigned to such duties today'. The JOURNAL DE GENÈVE had its ear closer to the ground: 'He fell, victim of the weakness of Mr Lie and the silence of two of his colleagues, the American Byron Price and the Russian Arkady Sobolev'.

Back from his holiday McNeil weighed in again with an unhelpful letter to Lie: 'I would be less than friendly and honest towards you if I did not say that both from the point of view of your advantage and ours it still does not seem to be a particularly good decision and it certainly seemed to me not the most tactful way of ending the situation… This of course is a personal letter so don't bother replying.'[87]

Lie didn't. Having previously decided to give Jackson one year's salary in compensation, he now reduced it by half.[88]

> Jacko's partnership with Sheila was ended, but not their friendship:
>> You have given me something far beyond service and loyalty over these seven years. I appreciate it to the limit of my understanding. Where I have failed is to repay what you have given – and I don't know how I ever can do so. I shall always acknowledge that whatever good I have helped to achieve has been primarily through your guidance and help. I shan't forget it ever. God bless you – give you peace, happiness and understanding. I just try to say 'thank you' – and for what it is worth, that strange thing once known as my love goes to you. I shall remember. Always J.[89]

Urquhart had been on leave and only heard about Jackson's dismissal when he met Lie in Paris on 16 September. He told Lie he thought it was outrageous; and was shocked that he had not been consulted. Lie was furious and their cordial relationship came to an end.

David Owen told the Foreign Office that he thought that the prime reason for Jackson's dismissal was the conflict of personality between him and the Secretary-General. Jackson had hustled him more energetically than his somewhat sluggish temperament could stand. Lie therefore decided that the only way out was to make a quick break. Owen was convinced that Lie's claim that it had been an experiment was merely an excuse. He thought that Jackson had done an adequate job in the short time he was there. His relations with colleagues were correct if not cordial; there had inevitably been some ruffled feelings due to the very nature of Jackson's work and partly because of his somewhat masterful personality. He said that there was no suggestion that either Price or Sobolev had pressed for his removal.⁹⁰

There is an apocryphal story that Lie was faced with the resignation of all eight ASGs and told Jackson 'I have to decide whether to lose them and keep you, or let you go and keep the others', at which point Jackson resigned. Those who tell it insist that they heard it from Jacko himself; possibly they did. Some credence is given to it by an entry in Casey's diary three years later: 'I called on Trygve Lie to say goodbye to him. He spoke in a very kindly way of RGA Jackson and said that he had a great appreciation of him but that he had clashed hard with one ASG after another and that, in order to keep UNO as a reasonably smooth working machine, he'd had to part company with him.'⁹¹

From one point of view the whole episode could be seen as no more than a minor setback to a career. He had taken on a job without securing the necessary conditions. It didn't work out because the post was misconceived and after four months it was terminated. That was all, he must find another job.

But Jackson had not only lost a job, he had lost a career. The brilliant future which should have been his had vanished into thin air, and he knew that the decision to go to Lake Success had ultimately been his. This was something he could never bring himself to admit. 'I went there against my better judgement' was the closest he ever came. The wound which he had suffered would never completely heal.

The reason for his dismissal which Jackson later gave was disagreement with Lie about Palestine.⁹² Though understandable, this was never convincing, but it persisted until his dying day. He also put it about that he had been *Chef de Cabinet* or even *de facto* Deputy Secretary-General. This is strange, since it was the very fact that he was not which was the reason for it all ending in tears. These claims would even be repeated in some of his obituaries.

If Lake Success was a tragedy for Jackson so it was too for the UN. He could have contributed so much in those early days; only someone with his qualities of leadership could have brought the specialized agencies to heel. He would be back, though not for fourteen years.

Part Two – What Next?

8 Odd job man

HAVING BEEN 'DOUBLE-CROSSED BY LIE', on his return to England in October he was double-crossed by Bridges who told him that no 'big job', such as he had been led to expect, was available. He spent the next three months unwinding in Cyprus with Edward and Audrey.

'I hope you are being philosophical and being thoroughly lazy and enjoying your holiday' wrote Bridges. 'In the long run, knowing how terribly hard you work yourself, it may be no bad thing that you should get a longer holiday than you bargained for'.[1] He replied that he thought his most useful field of operation in future would be one involving direct executive and administrative responsibility. He had felt most at home in MESC and UNRRA, particularly in organising the wide range of development and reconstruction which they had involved.[2]

He returned to England in mid-February; 1949 it would be an unhappy year for Barbara as well as for him; her 'black period' she called it.

In March Bridges came up with a suggestion which he hoped Jackson would find pleasing. 'Myself, I think it has got great possibilities.'[3] A new Director of the Department of Scientific and Industrial Research (DSIR) was soon to take over with a brief to undertake a comprehensive review of the work and organisation of the Department in the light of the more important role it was now expected to play. This called for some preparatory work: Jackson would chair three Government Commissions, to examine (i) the application of science in the UK, (ii) the organisation of scientific research in the Commonwealth and (iii) the problem of unemployment in Northern Ireland. Max Nicholson was head of the Department and saw the importance of giving Jackson sufficient authority and status: it was not important to assign specific responsibilities to him, or to give him a title; it <u>was</u> important to announce publicly that he was going as a Treasury Official with full authority to propose reorganisation of DSIR and with a rank clearly higher than the existing administrative officers.[4] A new post at the level of Deputy Secretary was created to which he was appointed on 22 June. For Jackson these jobs were pretty small beer, but they kept him occupied and justified his salary.

The application of science in the UK took him to the Midlands and Scotland, visiting scientific institutions and universities. His only encounter of any interest was meeting Alan Turing, the mathematical genius who had succeeded in breaking the German Enigma code when U-boats were decimating the Allies' convoys to Britain. The purpose of his wartime work, like that of Jackson's, had been to get essential supplies through to where they were needed; they both had made major contributions to the final victory. Turing was now working on computer science at Manchester Univesity; Jackson reckoned that he was the most brilliant man he had ever met.

Scientific research in the Commonwealth took him to South Africa to attend a conference in Pretoria at which an Organisation for Scientific Cooperation South of the Sahara was formed. By mid-November he was back in London.

His petition for annulment of his marriage had been rejected by the Tribunal at Rome in July. The case was not proven; more precisely 'the sentence was negative'. The grounds claimed for nullity were *contra bonum sacramenti et prolis'* – that is to say one or other or both had married with the express intention of excluding the permanence of marriage and of excluding children. Whose the intention was had not been established.[5] (It was undoubtedly his). He appealed to the Tribunal.

In December Sheila wrote telling him that she was going to marry the man she had once been engaged to in Cairo. For Jacko that meant writing a new volume, not just a chapter, into his own life. 'So I rejoice ... and hope, that as time mellows the colours of our lives, the memories you keep will be the good ones ... keep them in the volume which has now gone on the shelf. Look at it now and again – but only occasionally – your real purpose, your real happiness will come from the volumes you write now and in the future. I send you all my good wishes – from a heart and mind filled with gratitude and admiration for you. And, too, that strange thing – my love. J.'[6] Sheila's marriage was a happy one and Jacko's love for her continued until he died.

9 Casey to the rescue

HE NEVER GOT TO NORTHERN IRELAND. In January 1950 Richard Casey, now Minister for Supply and Development in a new coalition government, invited him to Australia to set up a new Ministry of National Development. The Commonwealth was passing through a critical stage: the rapid growth of population resulting from immigration was not balanced by the increased industrial and rural production needed to sustain it. Casey saw this new Ministry as a small high-grade specialist department, and wanted at its head 'a man of vision and drive, as well as intelligence and judgment, not tied to red tape, but of rather an adventurous habit of mind.'[1]

Of twenty names suggested none fitted the bill, so he approached Jackson, who flew out to meet Robert Menzies, the Prime Minister, spent the week-end with the Caseys in Melbourne and set off back to London. A short stop in Rome gave him time to call in at the Vatican, where he learnt that the Tribunal had referred his appeal to the Holy Office which had granted him not an annulment but a dispensation enabling him to re-marry on the grounds of non-consummation of his first marriage; as a spokesman at the Westminster Tribunal in London remarked to me, 'Someone must have known someone'.

Once again he could see a future. He had a decent job and he was free to marry the woman he loved. But there was a problem: how to combine the two? In those days divorce was considered shocking and could severely damage a man's career; moreover Peggy – 'the injured party' – was Australian. This was not the moment to spread the good news; his marriage would have to wait.

He asked Casey if the Government would agree to send him back to England for four or five weeks towards the end of the year, to deal with personal commitments which he was previously unaware of and which he could not settle immediately.[2] He may even have welcomed this delay, for now that all obstacles to his marriage had been removed he was beginning to have doubts.

On his way back to Australia he spent three days with Edward and Audrey. Although Barbara had not yet met Edward the two of them had formed a strong friendship through their correspondence and by now he was her confidant as well as Jacko's. Letters were flying in all directions; on 14/15 March she wrote to Robert:

> You'll have left Edward. How I hope you were able to sort the situation out and also that Edward was helpful as he always is for 'us'.
>
> 20 March: Dearest love, <u>two</u> letters from you this morning – from Cyprus and Cairo and with them a very long one from Edward faithfully and affectionately recording your long talk together. There is so much to say that I hardly know where to begin ... of course, you have the essentials on page 7 of your letter from Cairo. We are working on the assumption that all will be well ... I agree wholeheartedly with Edward that mind is much more important than body. The devils <u>can</u> be cast out. [Edward believed that Jacko's 'devils' were his fears that Barbara was worried that his way of life might not suit her.] The chief thing now is that the external devils of Vatican, divorce, UNO, joblessness, Whitehall are overcome. ... I have set up practically a mortar service and am lobbying my prayers on to the target hour by hour. I really can't have any doubts about the final result because <u>how</u> can God refuse the grace of peace, since He is lord of it? To know that our partnership was successful and happy I would cheerfully put a stick of dynamite under THE ECONOMIST, the BBC, the OLD VIC [she was a governor of both] and all the occupations which are supposed to represent such a hold on my life. ... To attempt a quieter and deeper life is salvation to <u>me</u>, quite apart from 'us'.
>
> 21 March: Dearest love, ... I am with Edward in his confidence and his belief that we shall 'run beautifully together'. I sometimes wonder if I am grateful enough to God for having someone I can love so wholeheartedly and unreservedly. ... You will be settling in Melbourne, I suppose, by the time this reaches you. Now you are at sea, shedding a devil with every sea mile and a trail of prayers streaming out behind you over the Indian Ocean.
>
> 25 March: I wrote a long letter to Edward this morning. Poor Edward! Did he realise what obligations he was taking on when he first began a letter with "Dear Miss Ward"? – I can hardly wait to meet him.

Edward sent the long letter to Jacko because he thought he should know exactly what she was thinking; he also sent him a one-and-a-half page summary of his long reply to her, believing that 'it should help him to get rid of the king of all his devils'.

His message to Jacko was, briefly, that despite his love for her and need of her, he had a fear of love, not of loving but of being loved, because he felt that it would somehow dismember his personality. This fear showed itself most clearly now that all the barriers were down; hence her suspicion that he might want to escape. If she could convince him that he need not fear dismemberment, his devils would go, 'pacification' would enter in and his health would return. He might think he could walk alone but he couldn't. She had recognised the 'underlying drag' in him – 'off to caves and over mountains' for relief by escape; she hoped he might find that kind of peace in love and companionship, but that was the one thing he couldn't do. 'Self-centred people, like the two of us, have deep inside them an inner citadel which they can surrender to nobody, least of all to the person they love best. To that citadel they must retire. Even if what they find there is not peace but devils, they must go there and wrestle with them <u>alone</u>. At such times she would want most to help; she <u>could</u>, but only by sitting quietly, she must never try to follow. Audrey had had to learn this – the hard way. Do you think this was the right line? If not, God help us all!'[3]

Barbara's daily letters to Robert continued:

> April 1: It certainly is easy to love you, my sweetest love, and it grows easier year by year. In spite of the pain and the grief of the last 18 months, it <u>is</u> a remarkable fact that we have a good chance of combining the friendship of a long-standing marriage with the ecstasy and experiment of a honeymoon! I don't recommend the recipe and would have been perfectly ready to try a simpler one – but since it has happened in this way, I do thank God for the very peculiar concentrated and exquisite delights it makes possible – don't you feel so yourself, my darling one?
>
> April 4: I know exactly what you feel about children – I have the same misgivings ... but I believe that I would be a more loving person if I had children. Yet they would always be absolutely secondary compared with <u>our</u> relationship. Anyway it's in the Lord's hands. ... I'm not marrying you for children or even for sex – I simply want to spend the rest of my life with you in the circumstances that make us tick.

April 10: Yes I agree that our assumption must be that all will be well.

April 18: I have on the bed an immense letter from Edward ... By now you will have had his letter to you ...   I wonder if Edward is right.

Years later with the benefit of hindsight Jacko would say that Edward's advice that he should marry Barbara was the one bad piece that he ever gave him.

The new Ministry would be responsible for planning the essential development of the Commonwealth in conjunction with the six State Governments and other Commonwealth Departments. Its long term objectives included development of rural industries, water conservation and its use for power and irrigation, development of mineral and other natural resources, transport, manufacturing and housing. Many of its projects called for collaboration with State Governments and agreement on sharing costs; a sum of £250 million was to be made available for approved projects.[4]

After consulting senior Commonwealth officials and about 400 in the States Jackson's conclusions were that:

(a) The whole economy was badly out of balance; primary industries were short of materials, manpower and essential services – power, transport and water. Too many resources were employed in secondary industries;

(b) The Government should encourage essential development in primary industries and discourage it in unnecessary and undesirable secondary industries.

(c) The idea of a £250 million loan for 'development works' should be dropped. Forget about individual projects, the Government should concentrate on analysing the economy as a whole.

(d) Immigration, especially of qualified tradesmen, should be maintained, and capital equipment such as steel and timber purchased abroad, where it was immediately available; dollars were urgently needed for purchasing essential imports.

(e) More must be done to develop forests for timber, and to assist universities – there was a shortage of engineers and scientists.

(f) Productivity was not taken seriously as a national objective.

(g) The financial pattern between the Commonwealth and States was a crazy patch-work.

(h) The administrative structure was too large; there was no effort to use State administrative machinery as agencies for the Commonwealth.

(i) General relations between the Commonwealth and the States were bad.

It was this situation that was the main cause of inflation, not, as some thought, the communists.

During May and June he expounded his views at several meetings, but he found ministers and officials reluctant to grasp the nettle of inflation. Hardly anyone was willing to apply the tough measures which were needed.[5]

The pace of work was already beginning to tell and he felt he lacked the strength to do all that was asked of him; a gall-stone was removed, but for his continual head pains the doctors offered no remedy beyond telling him he should not work so hard.

In the light of his analysis Menzies and Casey decided to seek a dollar loan from the United States. Menzies therefore flew to London in July to get HMG's agreement, taking Jackson with him. For Barbara this was 'an oasis – a wonderful shot in the arm' but the effect soon wore off.[6] His head pains continued and his London doctors merely confirmed what he had been told in Australia, telling him he should stop work for two months as soon as possible. He decided to carry on until October, when he would return to England as planned. He was prepared to give Australia the whole of 1951, but he desperately needed a Deputy; he had been promised one from the start, but no-one suitable had yet been found. It is an indication of how ill he felt that he had even said he was prepared to have someone else take over his job and stay on himself to assist him[7] – which is in fact what happened.

In Washington Menzies and Jackson negotiated a loan of $100 million, but the Commonwealth machine took its time to set up an agency to handle it; meanwhile prices rose in the USA. It was not until February 1951 that all the dollars were committed for purchasing essential equipment (diesel-electric locomotives, heavy earth-moving equipment, agricultural tractors, generating sets etc).[8]

Before going to Washington he had been drafting a paper for Casey to put to Cabinet on the future work of the Ministry. Its starting point was the lack of awareness in Australia of the immense political and economic forces at work in the wider world and the need for national development to relate to national security and the general strategy of the Western powers. (The Korean war had begun in June.) The paper covered a lot of ground and drew important conclusions, but it was discursive and very long. He left a copy for William Dunk, the Chairman of the Commonwealth Public Service Board, whom he knew from UNRRA days, inviting his comments.

Dunk put them in a very tactful letter, accompanied by a page and a half of notes. These are worth quoting, being the only example we have of criticism of Jackson's drafting by a more practised civil servant who knew better how to present issues concisely, (something which university might have taught him):

> I appreciate that it was an early draft and that you had just been getting all your thoughts down with the idea of sorting them into a clearer structure later. Nevertheless my notes may help. I hope you do not think they are over-critical.
>
> The paper is too long and I do not think it will be read by the people who should read it in its present form – even conceding considerable pruning. It requires a fairly comprehensive covering memorandum. I think the first objective of security should be linked with the second one of national well-being. Obviously we must achieve the first before we give any undue weight to the second. The prime problem is however, not only manpower as is emphasised in the paper, but horse-power – the latter divided into its two primary sections of static power (for machines) and mobile power (for transport).
>
> As to content, I think there are too many opinions on such matters as the international situation, the political side of national development, US Treaty of Friendship, Tax Agreement etc. These questions are important, but they need to be dealt with by people in that particular field. Obviously all the facets of overall development and of the problems and necessities which will arise from it cannot be dealt with in an initial basic paper – in short, cut out all the trimmings.
>
> There is reference to a five year plan. This I think should be given a more prominent place if for no other reason than it forces a target. Politics may not like it for that very reason.[9]

Jackson took Dunk's advice to heart, and Casey sent his redrafted paper to Cabinet in September: its main theme was that development of resources should lead to increased national security and strategic strength; efforts to increase available manpower in essential sectors should continue; development policy and immigration policy were dependent on broad economic policy; individual projects were not the answer.[10]

At the beginning of September Robert in Australia and Barbara in England were preparing the announcement of their engagement and revising his entry in 'WHO'S WHO'. The reference to his earlier 'marriage' (as Barbara called it) would be deleted. They planned to start their honeymoon with a visit to Rome. 'Will you', she wrote, 'ask Montini about a papal blessing for our marriage? I would like P. XII to give us a special start.' (Monsignor Montini was then in the Vatican Secretariat; in 1963 he became Pope Paul VI.) Their engagement was announced in London on 30 September.

A suitable relief for Jackson had been found in Major-General JES Stevens who was appointed, not as his deputy, but as his successor, starting on 1 October. Casey wrote to Bridges: Jackson had not had an easy time, as he had had to absorb an entirely new situation in which economics and politics were inextricably mixed; his health had not been good, ending in his having his quite bad tonsils out. 'In spite of all this he has made an extremely valuable contribution and I am most grateful to you for having spared him to come out here.'[11]

Bridges must have mentioned this letter when Jackson saw him in London, for Jackson immediately wrote to Casey: 'Perhaps I should add that your recent letter to Bridges was a little too compressed for him, and I think he may feel some doubt as to whether, in fact, I have given you the help you expected in Australia. I leave it to you whether you want to set his mind at rest on that subject.'[12]

Casey took the hint and wrote to Bridges again: 'There was a line or two in his last letter to me [from London] that made me wonder whether I had properly expressed to you my appreciation of what Jackson has already done for us – and which I hope he will amplify in 1951. I hope you are not in any doubt as to my feelings on this subject. He has been of very great use to us – and he will be of great use again when he comes back here. I hope this short break – and his marriage – will have been a help to him. He has been going too hard for too long.[13]

Bridges replied that he could not think of anything he had said to Jackson which could have suggested that Casey was not fully appreciative of all that Jackson had done for him. 'So please put anything of that kind out of your mind.'[14]

Evidently it was Jackson's mind rather than Bridges's which needed to be set at rest, but perhaps he was not over-sensitive in finding Casey's praise somewhat faint, for Casey's biographer also got the same impression from his letter to Bridges. Quoting only one sentence he implied that Jackson had been a failure:

> The Press liked him, but he did not stay long, and whether he contributed much besides headlines before he returned to Britain late in 1950 to recover from illness and marry economist Barbara Ward is open to question. Casey was inclined almost to apologise for him to his English masters: 'He had not had an easy time here, as he has had to absorb an entirely new situation in which economics and politics have been inextricably mixed'. Fortunately Casey recruited a good man as Jackson's deputy and successor, Major-General JES Stevens.[15]

The Nuptial Mass, St Felix Church, Felixstowe, 16 November 1950, celebrated by the Very Reverend JC Heenan.

The importance of Jackson's work during 1950 was established in December when the Cabinet approved the paper he had written for Casey. It recommended a complete change in the Commonwealth Government's approach to development. Previously seen in terms of big individual projects financed by Government loans, it was now accepted that development was best secured by bringing the economy into balance and concentrating efforts in those sectors of the economy which could do most to strengthen national security. In bringing about that shift in government policy Jackson made a significant contribution to his country's future.

On 16 November Robert and Barbara were married in the tiny church of St Felix in Felixstowe. The bride wore white and her brother-in-law played Bach on the harmonium as the rain hammered on the roof. The Nuptial Mass was celebrated by their friend the Very Reverend Dr JC ('Jackie') Heenan, They started their honeymoon in Rome and went down to Foggia to inspect progress at the hospital in memory of LaGuardia. *La Casa Sollievo delle Sofferenza* was partly built and already in use; in the chapel was a stained glass window of the Madonna, bearing a striking resemblance to Barbara. She had visited the hospital before, was virtually part of the establishment and known as *La Madrina* – 'the godmother'. The news of her engagement (seen there as 'a manifestation of the love of Divine Providence' – was the Papal Dispensation another?) had produced a flood of letters of congratulation addressed to her there.[16]

After an audience with the Pope they spent a week with Edward and Audrey in Cyprus and another in Cairo before setting sail for Australia, arriving in Melbourne on 2 January 1951.

They set themselves up in Cliveden Mansions, a smart apartment block in Melbourne with its own restaurant, where the Hilton Hotel now stands. They bought a car, a 3½ litre Jaguar, mainly to visit his family in

La Madrina

Cheltenham – Alan (Bill), Bett his wife and Andrew (Tam), now eleven years old. There were tensions; the divorce business was still fresh in their minds. Bett's sympathies had always been with Peggy and she had declined to give the investigating catholic priests the kind of information they were looking for. Robert spoilt Tam outrageously which made Barbara jealous, and Tam consistently beat her at Chinese Checkers which didn't help. Nevertheless they had good times together – Bett fed them well and Alan dispensed *Mateus Rose* liberally, and the family were often invited to Cliveden Mansions.[17]

Owen Dixon was a friend from Jackson's time in New York and now one of Australia's leading judges. When the Jacksons weren't having Sunday lunch with the family they were usually with the Dixons or the Caseys, and would spend the afternoons discussing the politics of Australia, the Empire, the USA and the problems of the world in general.[18] This kind of intellectual conversation was food and drink to Barbara. 'Barbara has taken to Australia like a duck to water' observed Robert; possibly, but unfortunately there were not too many ponds in Australia where ducks of her kind could swim. The family never met the Dixons or the Caseys; they got the impression that Rob thought them not quite good enough, which they resented, though Alan maintained that he would rather get on with his gardening.

At the end of March Jackson had a letter from Hector McNeil, now Secretary of State for Scotland, offering him nothing less than the Chairmanship of the Herring Industry Board: 'There are many overseas markets for herring – the American and Canadian markets offer possibilities for luxury kippers'.[19] Luxury kippers! Had things really come to this? He declined the offer in typically courteous terms: he was committed to the Australian Government until the end of the year.

In April he and Barbara visited the Snowy Mountain Scheme, where work was progressing rapidly. This was an enormous hydro-electric scheme which also increased the irrigation of the plains of Victoria and South Australia by diverting the Snowy River from the east to the west. Large lakes were being created high in the mountains, connected by miles of tunnels. The Scheme would take 25 years to complete, and would provide power at times of peak demand by releasing stored water to generate electricity, pumping it back up again at times of low demand; it is thus the ideal complement to thermal power stations which can generate power round the clock.

It was arousing considerable opposition, chiefly on the grounds that it made excessive demands on men and materials. Since most of the labour was provided by immigrants (thanks largely to UNRRA) and most of the machinery was imported, these criticisms were unjustified; nevertheless the case for the Scheme had to be made repeatedly, and its importance for defence purposes stressed. (This part of Australia was designated a 'Main Support Area' in the event of war.) Barbara wrote articles for the New York and London press, drumming up support and deploring the continuing opposition of some Australians:

> One might reasonably assume that a project of such magnitude, concerned with so many vital aspects of the Australian economy, would have already captured the imagination of the Australian people. Yet the Scheme, though it has warm supporters, has also had to survive a surprising amount of hostile and uninformed criticism. It has become the victim of the present diversion of workers and material into less essential industry. There are also confusions arising from the fact that the Snowy Scheme, though managed by a separate Commission, is Government financed and in these days of inflation the cry goes up again and again to 'cut Government expenditure' irrespective of the project upon which the money is being spent. The manufacture of colloidal dolls is exempt from attack because it is 'private'. Vital power and water projects such as the Snowy are attacked because they are 'public'.[20]

While Robert was glad of Barbara's support for his own work, she had a way of taking it over which he resented. 'She can win on the centre court at Wimbledon – why can't she let me win my own little tournaments?' His fear of being overshadowed by her would grow over the years; Barbara was blissfully unaware of the effect she was having.[21]

Jackson found himself running the Ministry once again, as Stevens had been sent to England and Canada for advice on how to do the job! Following an election on 28 April Casey was made Minister of External Affairs and William Spooner succeeded him as Minister of National Development. .

Casey told Bridges that he and Jackson had worked happily together; it was largely due to his skill and enthusiasm that their approach to the development problem had evolved on sound lines. They had also managed to overcome the traditional rivalry between Commonwealth and State Governments, and Jackson was now on term of confidence with his opposite numbers in all the State

Governments – a great feat. 'So far as I am personally concerned it has been a great satisfaction and comfort to me to have had him with me here in the not very easy last 12 months – and when the time comes I shall say *au revoir* to him with the greatest reluctance.'[22]

On 1 August Robert and Barbara set off on leave in the Jaguar, driving north to Sydney and on to Queensland and the Pacific coast, arriving twelve days later at a tiny village called Surfers' Paradise, where they stayed for ten weeks in a little house – KITAWAH. As his leave ended he wrote to tell Bridges the main conclusions which he had reached during his appointment. There were three problems:

(a) a lack of national unity and national purpose; that was where England could do an immense amount to help in 'the missionary job' which he'd mentioned before.

(b) a political malaise in every corner of society; the human material in Australia was magnificent, but wrongly used and consequently frustrated.

(c) an unbalanced use of resources: all seven Governments realised what should be done; each State had a good programme to make good the major defects in basic development (power, fuel, water, transport, forests etc) but some had suffered badly as a result of political bargaining. In Victoria, for example, the Commonwealth had deliberately wrecked the development programme as a political manoeuvre designed to unseat the present Premier; that kind of small town politics was rather disheartening in a world threatened by Moscow.

> Can I now tell you a little about our personal life? Our back lawn runs out onto the beach, which is about twenty miles long and a hundred yards wide; the sand looks like snow in the sun and like silver in the moonlight. The sea is never-ending in its beauty and fascination. The surf rolls in endlessly and the colours change again and again; blues of every shade – sometimes dark green, then the strong sun brings out a bottle green – on rare occasions a storm turns everything to indigo, the horizon is filled with lightning and sometimes the scene is completed by a rainbow of wonderful intensity. Our lives are filled with colour, and the final contributions come from the semi-tropical flowers and the birds – gaily coloured parrots, cockatoos, and kingfishers.

Here for some weeks we have lived in complete peace, surrounded by beauty on all sides. This is a very wonderful oasis after the strains and vicissitudes of the past decade and more. Fortunately there is a small church close by where we can endeavour to express our gratitude.

Yet we have not been altogether lazy: Barbara has written steadily (mainly for America) and the local Post Office has taken a new lease of life as a result of the cables! In keeping with the times, I assist her productivity by operating a bonus system which produces a bottle of local champagne each time an article is written. Most of the developmental authorities throughout the Commonwealth have kept me (nicely) busy with their problems, and soon these days will end. We shall never forget them. The result is that neither of us has been so well for years, and we are both agreed that we have never known such happiness.[23]

They toured Queensland for a fortnight as part of his fact-finding mission, spent a few days in Sydney with the Dixons, and reached Melbourne on 20 November. He visited his old school at Mentone, sold the Jaguar to Alan and set off with Barbara on his final tour of Western and South Australia. There he found the picture more reassuring; people in the country were much more sensible and hard working than those in the industrial areas, but the ineffectiveness of the Federal government remained deplorable.[24]

When Casey was in London in November he discussed with Bridges how best Jackson might be employed on his return to England. He had in mind 'a missionary job in which Jackson's particular and peculiar abilities would find their best scope' – some high-level liaison task linking the various members of the British Commonwealth, the USA and possibly other countries. Despite the existing framework of High Commissioners there was too little personal contact between all the governments. He also mentioned how the UK could help India and Pakistan in their development plans by allowing Jackson to visit New Delhi and Karachi soon after his return to London in February. Bridges thought this a good idea.[25]

Hall-Patch, as usual, could see the snag: while he agreed that this was a task crying out to be done and would do all he could to promote the idea, to be effective Jackson must have a secure and unassailable base in London, be recognised as belonging to a Department and able to represent its views at high level meetings. Without that he would lack the weight to discharge the task. With full authority he would do it admirably and it might make a great change in Commonwealth relationships. If he were to be offered the job he should insist on a secure base in Whitehall with appropriate status.[26]

On 10 January 1952 Robert and Barbara sailed from Sydney; Barbara stayed in the USA for a few weeks to carry out speaking engagements. Back in London he saw his doctor about his head pains; after giving him a thorough going-over Dr Bodley Scott pronounced him organically as right as rain; he thought it very unlikely that they indicated a tumour.[27]

Casey's plan to send Jackson to Pakistan and India now came into operation: the Australian Government would pay him as part of their contribution to the Colombo Plan. (This provided a forum for discussing cooperative economic development in South-East Asia.) After the usual week in Cyprus Jackson arrived in Karachi on 29 March. He and Barbara were already finding this separation difficult; for her there was 'the tedium of ending each day without the exchange of news, the summing up, the endless conversations. Please God this is the last jaunt. We have I know gained from it in consolidating financially and it was absolutely right, but it's quite a cost all the same.'[28]

He landed at Karachi at 5.30 am on 30 March and went straight to Mass; the cathedral was packed and he was deeply moved by the scene inside – 'people of several races, several colours, and several tongues all kneeling down together with a common purpose and a common belief' – and as deeply shocked by what he saw outside: 'the dirt, the squalor, the lack of drainage, the pathetic humps under cheap pieces of cloth which were starting to stir and reveal themselves as many more of God's children. So much is to be done; the inequalities of this world are so great and so cruel.'[29]

His first meeting was with the Indian Minister of Finance, Sir Chintaman Deshmukh, whom he thought first class; the second with the Pakistan Permanent Under-Secretary of the Ministry of Economic Affairs, Said Hassan, who seemed very much on the defensive to start with, though clearly very able. The following day he let his hair down completely: 'What we want you to give us, Commander

Jackson, is a <u>completely integrated</u> development plan for Pakistan'. I naturally put my hand in my pocket and handed him one!'[30]

> 8 April: Today has been the best day I've had with my head in a long time. I jotted down some general notes and impressions for the local boys. I've written them very simply, dealt with the pattern of the economy they should seek to develop, the means of doing it, where the emphasis should be placed; given them some dope on the perils and frustrations of Constitutions, notes on the machinery of government, and then a few general hints on science and so on. I think it will make them feel that I haven't wasted my time here!!

For his last few days he stayed with the Australian High Commissioner. His house turned out to be near to the main railway line, with an encampment of refugees close by with no water or sanitary facilities; at times the stench was overwhelming. One way and another he reckoned that his two weeks in Karachi were among the most unpleasant in his life.[31]

New Delhi was more to his liking:

> 16 April: Deshmukh's house is large and comfortable – in the old days it was that of the Private Secretary to the Viceroy. They have worked out a very full plan of discussions for me until Saturday, but I neatly sidestepped a four-hour trip leaving at 8 am tomorrow. These chaps are years ahead of the Pakistanis – they really have done a great deal of work and thinking.
>
> 18 April: Today has been another long series of talks – thank goodness they're now nearly over! I've <u>had</u> India and Pakistan in a big way!! But we've achieved – at fearful expense – our Income Tax Operation; never again, I trust. 11 pm: I've just finished another four hours with Deshmukh – all very useful, but golly I <u>have</u> had a bellyful of talking.

He reported to Casey that Pakistan had no development plan, only a Six Year Development Programme, consisting of a few uncoordinated projects hurriedly assembled when the Colombo Plan was first suggested. Discussions had concentrated on how to draw up a plan for the integrated development of the economy and the machinery of government which it required, rather than on the Six Year Programmme. Little thought had been given to the administrative machinery needed for providing reliable information on which to base decisions, or for ensuring that decisions were executed effectively. He had suggested that the Government should stop inviting foreign experts to advise on individual aspects of the economy; any necessary advisers should form part of a planning group with clear terms of reference for the preparation of a national plan.[32] This was a theme he would return to later. (See Chapter 12).

India's development planning was three to five years ahead of Pakistan's, thanks to some extent to its having inherited (from the days of the Raj) a government machine and some very capable civil servants. Its draft Five-Year Plan was soundly conceived, with its emphasis on agricultural production, the development and better use of water, increased production of electric power and an improved transport system. His discussions had covered a lot of ground; the enthusiasm and intelligence of the members of the Planning Commission and the Secretariat made it possible to devote plenty of time to each subject. The Commission needed to obtain better information about available resources before facing its main task of deciding how best they could be developed; then it would be possible to produce a more detailed plan for India as a whole.[33]

With that task done he was once again wondering about his uncertain future and the 'missionary job'. He told Casey that his recent experience had confirmed his view that there was a gap to be filled between the countries of the Commonwealth in exchanging information; for example, a new depreciation allowance scheme recently introduced in Canada would suit Australia ideally; Australian schemes for assimilating immigrants could help Canada; Canada's and Australia's experience of development within a rigid constitution could help Pakistan. 'Do you feel like returning to the attack with Bridges?' he asked. 'This is, of course, far more important than any personal consideration.' Should Casey decide to mention him it would also be appropriate to suggest that 'the other half of the family could contribute by her writing and speaking.'[34] Casey's next letter to Bridges once again pointed out how well-suited Jackson would be for the job, but made no mention of the other half![35] Anyhow nothing came of it.

In September he was approached by the Treasury about a job in the Gold Coast – soon to become Ghana. It was proposed to build a dam on the River Volta to generate electricity to be used mainly to smelt local bauxite to produce aluminium, which Britain badly needed. The consulting engineers, Sir William Halcrow and Partners, had identified two possible sites for the dam; they saw the smelter, the main consumer of power, as essential to the scheme; without it there could be no dam. Given its cost the dam should be publicly financed, but since smelting was a specialized process the smelter should be constructed and operated by a commercial company. Two had expressed interest – The British Aluminium Company Ltd and Aluminium Ltd of Canada (ALCAN) – but were cautious on account of the political uncertainties at the time. HMG too was cautious; having recently burnt its fingers over the Ground-nuts Scheme in Tanganyika, written off at a cost of £35 million. The dam would create the world's largest man-made lake, submerging thousands of homes. Since the logistical, social, political and financial questions it raised were so great Halcrow's recommended that a Special Commissioner be appointed to handle what they called 'The Volta River Project'.[36]

This was not a job which Jackson fancied, nor did the prospect of living in West Africa appeal to Barbara. His pent-up resentment came pouring out in a letter to Bridges:

> I have now for over four years been much distressed in mind as a result of the dishonest treatment and double-crossing which I received in the United Nations from Lie; followed by the failure of HMG to honour its undertaking to provide me with 'suitable alternative employment if the UN appointment blows up'. That undertaking was not fulfilled and I have never had a chance to re-establish myself after a bitter and damaging experience. In 1949 – after seven months unemployment following the UN episode – you said you feared I would feel HMG had given me a raw deal. I confess I have not been able to get rid of that feeling.[37]

He had, he continued, gone to Lake Success against his personal wish; his temporary job with DSIR had been a stage in his service to the Crown when he took a major blow from which he never had a chance to recover. He had hoped that Australia would give him a chance to repair the damage done to his reputation at UN, but the political and economic scene there was so confused that the best he could do was proceed as tactfully as possible and endeavour to guide opinion quietly.

Now, six months after his return to England, no permanent job had been offered to him and he was beginning to doubt whether HMG had any real use for his services. Other people were not slow to draw inferences and if HMG had no use for his services his chances of doing anything outside Government service would be greatly reduced. The work in Africa would preclude any prospect of doing the kind of work he had most hoped for, and he could not decide about it until he knew that there was nowhere else for him to go.[38]

He and Barbara had been invited by Deshmukh to visit India in December, and when they saw which way the wind was blowing they decided to get away to Cyprus as soon as possible. The day before they left Bridges told him that he accepted his letter as fair, found it difficult to say how much he sympathised in the very raw deal which he had had, and accepted personal responsibility; he had hoped again and again that the right appointment would emerge, but it had not and Jackson had paid the price.[39]

The weather in Cyprus was superb and they were able to relax as they never could have done in England. 'The days have passed away in real peace', he told Alan: 'plenty of time for sleep, reading, walks among the groves at the foot of the wonderful Kyrenian hills. B has been able to swim and sunbathe and is miles better for it. We have had time to think and try and readjust ourselves to what the future may hold.'

They were both coming round to the idea of Africa. 'The proposal has naturally caused us much heart-searching for it is quite foreign to anything which we had ever thought about, nevertheless it has two very important aspects for us: it could be a real moral challenge; we've both talked and written a lot about how the blacks and the whites _should_ get on together – well, here's a chance to do something about it.' They still had one more week before going on to Delhi. 'Here we are, still bobbing about on our sea of uncertainty; we paddle along, and that's all that matters. We get three meals each day, a decent bed, and the Old Girl manages to obtain a decent ration of drink – so we might be much worse off.'[40]

They decided to stay in Cyprus for the fourth week. 'Baba didn't want to leave here a day earlier than she had to,' he told her father, 'she is ten times the woman she was – she now has only 27 diseases and complaints as opposed to the 394 she had the day we left England.' (Who was he to talk?) 'Some of the diseases I do not expect ever to leave her ... one is the Dry Tongue whenever within One Hundred Miles of Booze, beautiful Booze.'[41]

In New Delhi they were Deshmukh's guests. Also staying was the Cabinet Secretary, Sir Raghavan Pillau. 'Our hosts could not be more pleasant. There is no lack of talk in this house, and round about 7.30 you are apt to find the four of us drinking at a rate acceptable to your daughter (heaven help the other three of us!) and finally tottering off to dinner between 9.30 and 10.'[42]

After ten days they set off on a series of tours: a week in the north west to see the Bakra-Nangal scheme and Simla; a fortnight in Lucknow and Darjeeling (not work – having come so far they had to see the Himalayas) – on to Calcutta and the big multi-purpose schemes in the Damodar Valley and at Hirakud; then Madras, Bangalore, Hyderabad, Travancore, Bombay on Christmas Day, and finally back to Delhi for a week with the Planning Commission. 'I've long lost any desire to travel, but I admit that the Indian Government is doing us proud in this programme.'[43] After the inevitable week in Cyprus they arrived back in London on 12 January 1953.

Meanwhile Casey had been exploring yet another avenue: Trygve Lie was once again contemplating a reorganisation of the higher posts in the UN by creating three posts of Deputy Secretary-General. Casey must have written to Anthony Eden, the British Foreign Secretary, mentioning Jackson's name, for Eden replied to him saying that although he had the highest regard for Jackson's great gifts of drive, zeal and organising ability, the prospects of Lie's plan were at present 'pretty nebulous'. He also thought that Lie intended to fill these posts with outstanding personalities from smaller countries; furthermore Lie's own future was uncertain at the time. 'If some other appointment of a scope commensurate with Jackson's abilities is likely to be available in the near future (as, I understand, is the fact) we might be the losers if we advised him to refrain from taking it for fear of missing what is at present a rather hypothetical opening in the higher ranks of the Secretariat.'[44]

Jackson would surely never have considered working for Lie again; he was more interested in the question of who would succeed him. Could he have been thinking of himself? Bridges wrote telling him that since the choice of Lie's successor had to be acceptable to all the members of the Security Council that person was likely to be chosen from one of the much less important countries. In any case, he said, the Colonial Secretary (Oliver Lyttelton, who had snatched Jackson from Malta to run MESC) had passed his name, in strict confidence, to the Gold Coast Government, which had agreed that he should be offered the appointment.[45]

The Volta River Project

10 The Volta River Project

THE GOLD COAST HAD LONG BEEN SEEN as the model British colony, with its traditional culture of chiefs and people advancing steadily towards independence. In 1948 this image was shattered by outbreaks of rioting with some loss of life; a state of emergency was declared and a new constitution drawn up, providing for parliamentary elections. Kwame Nkrumah, a leading political activist with degrees from American universities, formed the Convention People's Party (CPP). When it started campaigning for 'direct action' to challenge the Government he and his associates were imprisoned. In a general election in February 1951 the CPP swept the board and Nkrumah himself won a seat. The Governor, Sir Charles Arden-Clarke, released him and appointed him 'Leader of Government Business' on the understanding that if the CPP would give up their demand for 'self-government now' they could expect it before very long. The Governor retained substantial reserve powers and the British civil servants still ran the departments of defence, finance and justice, but a large measure of power passed to Nkrumah. The rapid change in the political atmosphere was striking; Nkrumah and his ministers were first taken aback and then won over by the willingness of the Colonial Service to work for the new regime.[1]

In November 1952 HMG published its proposals for a VOLTA RIVER ALUMINIUM SCHEME,[2] by which the two Governments and the Canadian and British aluminium producers would produce 210,000 tons of aluminium a year. The total capital cost, to be shared between the parties involved, would be about £100 million initially, rising to £144 million. It would guarantee the UK industry much needed aluminium supplies from the Sterling Area, and would enable the Gold Coast to develop its mineral wealth and create a new source of power of great potential benefit to its future social and economic progress. The dam would be sited at Ajena, the smelter at Kpong and a new harbour constructed at Tema. HMG was keen to participate, but given the size of the scheme set up a Preparatory

Commission to examine the problems that would have to be overcome. In the Gold Coast the Scheme was seen as a symbol of the British Government's good intentions.

It was against this background of mutual trust and hope that Jackson entered the scene in 1953 as Special Commissioner in charge of the Preparatory Commission. His salary would be £5,000 a year (higher than the Governor's) plus allowances and a furnished house for an annual rent of £150. His appointment was expected to last for less than two years. He saw that it could lead to a much longer commitment if the scheme were adopted, but could not assume that he would be appointed to see it through.

When he met Nkrumah in February the two of them 'clicked'. He made himself known to British Aluminium in London and ALCAN in Montreal, took his Civil Service leave, including a week with Barbara in Taormina. They arrived in Accra at the beginning of May, when he formally took up his appointment, and stayed at the Governor's Residence at Christiansborg Castle while Barbara saw to furnishing their house; she returned to London to attend the Queen's coronation in June, leaving Robert in Accra to wave the flag in any local celebrations, then they moved into their house in Switchback Road. This was one of several originally intended for Ministers but used instead by Ambassadors and other high-powered people; it was suitable for the heavy entertaining which was *de rigueur* in such circles. They called it NOAH'S ARK.

He lost little time in securing a plot of land on the beach where he built a hut. '£2 to the Chief, £5 for the village elders, and after that six bottles of good gin for the Chief again!' Surfing, gentler here than in Australia, would be his chief relaxation. It was also a joy to have the church so close; they attended Mass every Saturday and some Fridays.[3]

He spent much of the next few months touring the country. There were the immediate technical and logistical issues to be addressed: the need for new railways and roads, supplies of materials and manpower, the building of new townships at Ajena and Kpong. In the longer term there were the effects of creating a lake of 3,500 square miles, its implications for health and sanitation (including the risks of river blindness and other water-borne diseases), the rate of evaporation, the provision of inland water transport and lake ports, financial compensation and relocation in new townships for the 80,000 people whose homes would be flooded, as well as the effects of the dam on the area downstream – its agriculture, irrigation, fisheries and forests. Knowing that he needed the best technical advice available Jackson brought in international experts on all these matters. The accountants, Cooper Brothers and Co., were asked to adopt a new approach, working with the consulting engineers <u>after</u> their first estimates had been prepared, analysing the costs of other comparable projects, in order to produce more reliable estimates (a procedure subsequently adopted by the World Bank).

The Commission went to great lengths to explain the scheme to the people, mounting an exhibition with models, relief maps, and details of the proposed new townships to replace those to be flooded. 'This travelling circus – for this is what it resembled, with its marquees and lorries and mobile generators, its loudspeakers and cinema vans, its bunting and its atmosphere of jaunty excitement – proved to be a great success, and in the two years that it operated probably did more to attune the people of the Gold Coast to the purposes of the Volta River Project than any other form of publicity. Commander Jackson himself kept in close touch with public feeling and recognised people's particular concern about matters of land ownership and inheritance.'[4]

Jackson described the scene to his and Barbara's friend Elisabeth Murdoch (wife of Melbourne newspaper magnate Sir Keith, mother of Rupert, later a Dame of the British Empire):

> Our report from this part of the world is a good one. The political experiment, as you know, is one of great importance to the rest of the continent, and as we look to the north, east and south of Africa we can see little reason for hope. Whatever chance there may be of developing that racial understanding which we believe to be of crucial importance, both to the white man and his darker brother, seems to rest only in this part of the continent. We are asking these people – whose main contacts with the white man have brought war, slavery and exploitation – to accept our advice and guidance, and to come into economic partnership with us at the very moment when we are removing our political control and – as they see it – restoring independence and freedom to them. All of this demands a quite exceptional test in human relations, and my own guess is that both the political development and the

Volta Scheme will be ultimately determined by the personal relationships between relatively few men. The African experience has so far turned out far more successful and with far more happiness than we ever thought was possible. Most of all, we feel the work has a certain importance in a moral sense, and there is little doubt that that gives us an additional satisfaction. The local people are clearly in great need of disinterested help and assistance, and we are only too happy to do what we can to help them.[5]

The technical investigation of the scheme has proceeded steadily and efficiently, and most important of all, a political and personal relationship has been built up with the African Ministers which seems to demonstrate that we have secured their confidence: that is vital.[6]

He went to see the dams of the Tennessee Valley Authority (a multi-purpose hydro-electric scheme extending over seven states) and several others in various parts of the USA and Canada, spent most of June in London, and returned to Accra for his 'second innings'. Seeing that his immediate task was likely to occupy him for more than two years he asked Nkrumah to increase the period of notice in his contract from three months to six.

Life in Accra was not so bad after all. He was working hard at a worth-while job; they had a garden and two Siamese kittens, Smith and Webster; he went big-game fishing with the Governor and caught a tarpon weighing 200 pounds. People were passing through NOAH'S ARK at the rate of half a dozen a day and there were frequent dinner parties to which they invited a much wider range of guests than was customary, enabling the large influx of Afro-American diplomats and advisers to meet the more laid back colonial administrators and the occasional minister at the dinner table, to their mutual advantage. A frequent guest was Erica Powell, who had first come to Accra as Arden-Clarke's secretary, been obliged to leave on account of her friendship with Nkrumah, and returned later to work for him. Though the white establishment viewed her askance the Jacksons always gave her a warm welcome, not as the Prime Minister's secretary, but as a friend.

The food provided on these occasions was less important than the intellectual fare: 'The chief attraction was the conversation that crackled backwards and forwards between Jackson, at one end of the table, and his wife at the other, with the guests in between snapping their heads from side to side like spectators at Wimbledon.'[7]

After visits to other parts of Africa, presumably to see more dams, and a fortnight's non-stop work in London he took Barbara to Taormina for a twelve-day holiday, and slept solidly for the first five! She had not enjoyed the high humidity of the early months of the year so went back to England while he returned to Accra to work on reports for the Governments and the aluminium companies. March 1955 took him to London and Montreal; he collected Barbara from New York and they returned together to Accra in April.

After he finished the technical parts of his report they set off in mid-July for London, Montreal, and Vancouver, thence by sea to Australia for a month, part work, part holiday, visiting Alan and his family. He did a short stint in India continuing what he had done in 1952 and returned to London in October for three weeks' discussions of the financial aspects of the Project. There was no point in his hurrying to complete his report since the two governments could not enter into an agreement to proceed until the country was independent, which was unlikely to be before 1957; he used the time to work out detailed resettlement plans for the

Barbara, Alan (Bill) and Bett

80,000 people whose homes would be inundated by the lake.

On 31 December Jackson delivered his report to Nkrumah; it was not published until July 1956.[8] He had reached six general conclusions:

(1) the Volta River Project was technically sound, and could be constructed successfully,

(2) on the evidence available the Project was not capable of significant improvement from an economic point of view,

(3) the greatest return would be derived by achieving maximum production of aluminium as soon as possible

(4) it should be competitive provided that ... the aluminium companies were satisfied that the internal cost of operating the smelter would be acceptable

(5) the local effects of the dam and the lake [resettlement and health] could be dealt with satisfactorily

(6) the Commission considered that other factors which might influence the Project should not affect it adversely provided that ... the climate for investment in the Gold Coast was attractive.

As envisaged by HMG in 1952, the Project would comprise a partnership between the two governments and the two aluminium companies. The Gold Coast Government would establish a Volta River Authority to build the dam and power station at Ajena, for which the British Government would lend the capital; the Gold Coast Government would also build the railway links between the bauxite mines, the smelter at Kpong and the new port at Tema. The companies would finance and build the smelter and develop the mines. By making maximum use of mechanised methods of construction the Commission had reduced the original estimate of manpower from 25,000 to 15,000, but the final cost was estimated at £230 million compared with £144 million in the White Paper. The construction of the dam was expected to take seven years.

Nkrumah had given an assurance that no-one would be worse off as a result of the creation of the new lake; the Commission therefore proposed a programme of 'aided self-help' in which people would be fully compensated for loss of their property and so enabled to buy new land, with the Government providing building materials and technical assistance enabling them to re-establish their communities.

Jackson's two provisos (in paragraphs (4) and (6)) were extremely important. The price the aluminium companies paid the Gold Coast Government for electricity would be a crucial factor on which the future of the scheme would depend. In March their negotiations with the two governments – the so-called 'Rubicon talks' – began. Coopers had estimated that the price per unit of electricity would be slightly less than 0.4d initially, falling to 0.2d finally ('d' denoting a British penny). ALCAN, which had far the greater financial interest of the two companies, could see better opportunities for expanding in Canada, and was not prepared to pay more than about 0.25d initially and considerably less later.

Furthermore HMG, though still ready to participate in the scheme, was not in a position to support it on the scale formerly envisaged and acknowledged that financial support from outside the sterling area might be necessary; and since independence would increase the risk of political instability the climate for investment in the Gold Coast was not attractive. So neither of Jackson's provisos was satisfied.

Nkrumah remained confident that the scheme would ultimately come about, though he said that the final decision would be for the people of the Gold Coast. But without a guaranteed purchaser of a large share of the power to be generated there could be no dam. Jackson was dismayed; three years' work had come to nothing. His own future was as uncertain as ever; being appointed Knight Bachelor was little consolation.

On the family front the news was better: during the summer of 1955 Barbara became pregnant, somewhat to the surprise of their friends, who had never imagined that two such god-like creatures could descend to the mundane business of procreation. Their surprise was not entirely misplaced. It was nine years since Barbara had remarked that 'she longed to have Robert's child', and over four years since they had married. At last her wish was to be granted. She planned to spend February at Felixstowe and go to London in March for the birth. On 22 February she showed signs of blood poisoning and was admitted to the London Clinic. She became seriously ill and on 25 February a son was delivered by Caesarian operation. He weighed 3 pounds 10 ounces and was put into an oxygen tent; for Barbara too it was touch and go for the next two weeks.

Working at the Clinic as an agency nurse was Joanna English, filling in time before taking up a senior nursing appointment in Canada. She found herself looking after this elderly first-time mother (Barbara was 42) and her tiny baby 'who looked like a skinned rabbit'. When they left hospital a month later Barbara was advised to engage a midwife to look after the baby, and English was prevailed upon stay with them for three weeks over Easter at the Hyde Park Hotel.

Robert and the baby's godmother (a close friend of Barbara's) took Joanna out to an expensive lunch and had little difficulty in persuading her to stay longer, as she was undecided about going to Canada. Knowing that her future employer was a Catholic she was surprised to see him eating steak on a Friday, but given to understand that he had obtained a papal dispensation on the grounds that he was unable to eat fish.[9] She would have plenty of time to get used to this; having agreed to look after the baby for three weeks, then for six months, she would continue to do so for seventeen years. Anna, as they now called her, would become his surrogate mother. After Easter she went to Felixstowe with Barbara and 'MacDuff' for a few weeks, until they moved to a house in Jersey which Robert had rented. The baby had been christened Robert Ward and was usually called Robin. His nickname, though appropriate – 'from his mother's womb untimely ripp'd' – seems a trifle lacking in tenderness.

The Gold Coast Government, assuming that the project would go ahead, wanted to appoint Jackson Chairman of the proposed Volta River Authority; HMG, not so sure, would not let them give him a contract. In June both governments agreed to maintain the Preparatory Commission for another nine months and review the future in the light of the study which the World Bank was proposing to make. He told Bridges that it was only because of the way he felt about race relations that he was willing to stay longer in the Gold Coast.[10]

Following a second election in 1954 an entirely African cabinet was formed and Nkrumah became Prime Minister. Nevertheless there was a substantial opposition party demanding a federal constitution, and since HMG needed to be certain which party it would hand over power to it insisted on holding a third election in July 1956. The CPP were returned again, but changes within the Government gave Jackson a few headaches. The officials were at sixes and sevens, and in three key positions where the Volta was concerned and where the heads should be in agreement they were at each other's throats.[11]

> We've now had 10 years experience of each other. Like all such partnerships there are credits and debits. The best analysis is the simple one that we are still in partnership – despite some great strains. We have MacDuff for whom we can work as our own parents worked for us. The main snag is that I've lost the field of work I love and any cool assessment indicates that there is virtually no chance of my getting back into it. I'll talk more to you about this in September – by early next year (preferably before you leave for USA) I'd like to have an idea of where we're headed. The main theme in all this now is MacDuff, and that's as it should be.[12]

When Britain announced that the Gold Coast would be given independence on 6 March 1957 Nkrumah was carried shoulder high through the streets. The Volta River Project was seen as the symbol of the new nation's development and Jackson's hopes rose, but he knew that this would take a long time to come to pass.

The next few months were tough; uncertainty about his own future unsettled his relationship with Barbara. This link between his professional moods and his personal feelings would persist throughout his life – work and love would always go hand-in-hand.

> I know that I'm not much good when I'm going through a period of mental strain. This is such a period and I'm running true to form. I do not think I can ever be very demonstrative with you, Ba, for several reasons. One is my own nature – another is a fear that because your own emotional RPM are unusually high it is all too easy for both of us to get 'spinning' and then judgement goes to hell. The only way I can express love and affection is to do things for others. I have tried to show my love by doing things for you. I can go on doing that very happily – I think I can do it better when, please God, we are a little more settled. Nevertheless, as we are both agreed, a base would be more desirable – and, as far as MacDuff is concerned, will at some stage become essential.
>
> As I see it now, it may be a choice between a goodish Government job and a well paid and reasonably interesting industrial appointment. I would not find the switch easy, but it might be the best compromise

answer. So let us play along through these next six months – I'm positive that if we do as well as during the last eight we'll come out with the right answer. Let this, too, be one way of showing you that you have my love.[13]

They spent a few days together in Jersey before he sailed to New York. 'The lunch on Thursday, the two films, and the perfect day on the Wednesday with the walk on the beach – those are things for which we must be profoundly grateful.'[14]

He endured 53 boring and frustrating days in the USA, sometimes walking miles simply to fill in time. He hated the meetings, but they were mostly with the Bank and he knew they were vital to the eventual adoption of the scheme.

At the beginning of 1957 he had some tentative approaches from business concerns in the City of London but he was beginning to think that the Gold Coast was more important than his own future.[15] His mind was made up when Nkrumah asked him to stay on as Chairman of the new Development Commission.

This was John Duthie's idea. Duthie was head of the Ministry of Development, and Jackson's regular contact with the Government. He and his wife had become good friends of the Jacksons and were frequent guests at Noah's Ark, sometimes staying there to look after Smith and Webster when their owners were abroad. Duthie knew that the Cabinet was in disarray, with several ministers at odds with their officials. With independence imminent, Nkrumah was on edge and anxious not to put a foot wrong. Duthie was planning to leave the Colonial Service immediately after independence and was not convinced that the VRP would come to pass. He thought it all the more important, therefore, that the next Development Plan should be held in safer hands than appeared likely as more and more expatriate advisers left the country. Knowing that Jackson's term with the Preparatory Commission was ending and that the Ministers had a very high opinion of his abilities, he suggested that they should invite him to direct the proposed Development Commission in a quasi-ministerial role.[16]

This time HMG agreed; they also agreed, albeit reluctantly, to extend the life of the Preparatory Commission by a further three months, until the end of June, to enable discussions with the World Bank to be resumed after the interruption of the independence celebrations which would occupy most of March.

Bridges had now retired; his successor at the Treasury was John Winnifrith, to whom Jackson wrote explaining why he'd felt he had no choice but to remain: the fall in the price of cocoa had convinced the African ministers that the Volta project was their best hope of diversifying the economy and providing the additional source of revenue essential for maintaining political and social development; the Development Secretariat had become steadily weaker over the last two years and the Ministry of Finance also needed reinforcement. Some members of the Preparatory Commission would still be needed, not least the person heading it. He had 'suggested modifications' to his contract which would give the Government a saving of about £2,000 per year.[17]

But was that his idea? As an employee of Ghana he would be paid in accordance with Ghana's salary scale, not HMG's. This meant taking a cut in salary of £1500, providing his own car, and paying higher rent for his house. Winnifrith advised him not to let his conscience carry him to quixotic limits. 'I shall be very cross if you make a preposterously inadequate bargain.'[18] Inadequate or not, he agreed to it and became Chairman of the Development Commission.

In March Barbara finished a series of lectures at Harvard, where she was Carnegie Fellow, and returned to Jersey to join Robin and Anna; in August they all went out to Accra, which became their base for nearly four years. As Barbara's commitments in the United States steadily grew Anna took over the role of mother. The inevitable gossip about her relationship with Robert was wide of the mark.

He was now working on the Second Development Plan, arranging for its financing and staffing, dealing with national security, setting up new organisations for research and the promotion of industrial development, overseeing work on the new port at Tema, simplifying government procedures, setting up an Electricity Corporation and always looking out for some means of bringing the VRP back to life. When Nkrumah attended the British Commonwealth Prime Ministers Conference in London in June he was left in no doubt that money for it was not to be found in Britain. Jackson saw that Ghana must now look to the United States.

It happened that in October the Minister of Finance, K A Gbedemah, was visiting the USA after attending a meeting of Commonwealth Finance Ministers in Ottawa.

Calling at a roadside restaurant in Delaware for a glass of orange juice he was told that because of his colour he could not be served. The press reported this and when President Eisenhower heard about it he invited Gbedemah to breakfast at the White House. When Gbedemah mentioned the Volta Scheme the President's ears pricked up and he asked for more information about it. Considering that the United States had more than enough capacity to produce its own aluminium it may seem surprising that Eisenhower should have been interested in Ghana's hopes of doing the same, but the affair of the Aswan Dam had left painful memories. Two years previously the USA had offered to finance the construction of this dam on the Nile, but when the Egyptian President, Colonel Nasser, decided to recognise Communist China the offer was withdrawn. Nasser promptly nationalised the Suez Canal and turned to Russia for help with the dam. The thought of Russia muscling in on the Volta was not to be borne.

Nkrumah sent a copy of the Preparatory Commission's Report to Eisenhower, who offered to help in two ways: first by trying to bring together companies which might be interested in financing the smelter operation and secondly by considering making a loan towards the project.

In February 1958 ALCAN agreed to surrender its mining and smelting rights. The International Co-operation Agency then proposed that the US Government should lend Ghana capital towards the cost of constructing the dam and power station, and that the smelter should be built and operated commercially, with Ghana repaying the loan from the sale of power to the smelter (just as had been proposed in 1952).

In July Nkrumah made a state visit to the USA, taking Jackson. The two governments agreed to carry out a re-appraisal of the engineering reports, re-examining in particular the need for a seven-

Jackson and Nkrumah in Delhi, October 1958.

year period of construction – the main reason for the high cost of the project. Among the firms considered for this was the Henry J Kaiser Company, whose work for the Snowy Mountain Scheme had impressed Jackson. At his suggestion Nkrumah met Edgar Kaiser, President of the Company, on 28 July 1958; they took to each other at once.

In October Jackson went on leave, taking Barbara, Robin and Anna to Surfers' Paradise where they stayed at KITAWAH for nine weeks. The others then moved to Victoria to be nearer to Alan and Bett, while he went to India, where Nkrumah was paying a state visit to President Nehru. Why he went is not clear; perhaps he thought that with his experience of India and its Ministers he ought to be on hand, but Nkrumah's officials thought his presence something of a joke. He seemed on edge, and told Nkrumah that he had to return to Australia for an interview about a job.[19] One of Jackson's private passions was preserving white tigers, so perhaps his real reason was to avoid going on a tiger-shooting expedition!

Anna and Robin at sea, January 1959.

In January 1959 they all sailed to San Francisco, where he discussed with Kaiser the draft of his report on the Volta, and after a week in London he returned to Accra. He wrote to Sheila: 'And so I have come back to the 'land of never a dull moment'! After two dormant years the Volta Project is stirring again. In addition the Queen is coming here about the end of the year, and that is also squarely on my plate.'[20]

Kaiser's report proposed three major changes to the scheme. Firstly the dam would be built at Akosombo, ten miles further downstream, where the river was narrower and deeper than at Ajena. A dam at Akosombo could be built in four years not seven, and would have a greater generating capacity. Secondly the smelter would be built at Tema, not at Kpong (thus avoiding the cost of building a third new township). Thirdly alumina powder for the smelter would not be obtained from bauxite mined in Ghana, but imported, at least initially. The development of new mines, the construction of an alumina factory and the railway to link them were postponed; Kaiser's strategy was to keep down the initial cost in order to get the scheme started, and expand it later. The decision to import alumina was a bitter pill for Ghana to swallow, for the mining of local bauxite had always been seen as an important part of the scheme, nevertheless the cost reduction of 30 per cent made this a more realistic proposition.

Jackson could see that Kaiser would be keen to build the dam, as would many other firms. The problem would be to get someone to buy the power — and Kaiser was also President of the Kaiser Chemical and Aluminium Company. Jackson suggested to Nkrumah that after Kaiser formally presented his report he should invite him to 'take off his engineering coat and put on his aluminium coat'. Nkrumah was delighted with the idea and the following morning, after thanking Kaiser, put the suggestion to him in those very words.[21]

Kaiser knew that he was depriving his engineering firm of any chance of constructing the dam and power installation, but he responded without hesitation. His decision at that time was a critical factor in bringing the scheme to life, but nearly three years of uncertain — and towards the end dangerously rough — political weather lay ahead before the Volta ship could be navigated into port.[22]

Preparations for the Queen's visit were well under way when Jackson had a message from Buckingham Palace that her Assistant Private Secretary, Sir Martin Charteris, was flying to Accra that night and was to be collected from the airport runway as discreetly as possible. Jackson took him to NOAH'S ARK for a bath and thence to meet Nkrumah in his office at the Castle where he revealed that the Queen was expecting a child. Nkrumah turned grey at the news — it was the worst he had ever heard. He calmed down when Charteris told him that the visit was not cancelled, merely postponed. Meanwhile preparations must continue until an official announcement was made. In the meantime only Nkrumah and Jackson knew the secret. It was planned that an announcement on the BBC would be followed by a statement by Nkrumah, to be recorded about an hour beforehand. This took place on 29 June:

> The PM sat at his desk with a microphone in front of him, and the technician and I retired out of his sight. He was reading clearly and well, when his large Alsatian in the next room started to bark frantically ... Once more all was going well, but we had forgotten the grandfather clock in the PM's study. Twelve loud chimes finished that recording. Third time lucky? Once again the PM was going splendidly, but we had not allowed for the musical tastes of his wife, Fathia. There was a great burst of loud jazz and so the third effort hit the dust. By this time we were both conscious of the passage of time, so security staff were ordered to empty all rooms near the study of any form of life, and in peace and tranquillity the fourth attempt succeeded – with ten minutes to spare!![23]

Kaiser formed a new company – the Volta Aluminium Company (VALCO) – to draw up proposals in cooperation with the Ghanain Government for the development of an aluminium smelter in Ghana, and undertook to complete the design of the dam and power installation by 1 September 1960. Preparatory work on the dam site and access roads had already been started and orders placed for two special suction dredgers which would take nine months to make. Since the necessary financing had not yet been secured these decisions represented a considerable act of faith on the parts of Kaiser and Nkrumah, saving a year in the time needed to complete the project. Meanwhile in January 1960 the World Bank sent a team to Ghana to assess its credit-worthiness for loans for the VRP and other development proposals.

Since Nkrumah intended to declare Ghana a Republic in the summer and wanted Jackson to be there during its early stages he agreed to defer his leave until September.[24] In any case Barbara's doctors were advising her to take a long rest.

As talks between the Government, the World Bank and VALCO proceeded he became increasingly alarmed at the rate at which Ministers were planning to spend the country's dwindling resources. He tried to bring home to them that there were limits to the country's financial resources, but this was not a popular message. He kept discovering substantial expenditures on items never authorised by the Cabinet. His objective was simply to try and keep things in modest shape, avoiding all new major commitments and anything except essential expenditure until Nkrumah's own report could be considered.[25]

He warned Nkrumah that the Government had entered into commitments costing £60m and that the funds available were £81m. This left £21m to cover the completion of Tema Harbour (£8m), to provide a reserve for the Cocoa Marketing Board, to provide Ghana's own contribution to the VRP and to pay £7m for an assortment of unessential items.[26]

Nkrumah thought Jackson's resistance to some of the Government's proposals over-cautious. Anxious to dispel any idea that he was at odds with Nkrumah, or seeming to criticise him, Jackson explained his approach to development as simply as he could in a long and repetitive note, emphasising that Ghana should not invest its own money if it could borrow from another source. This approach – borrow, borrow, borrow – had been one of the reasons for Australia's tremendous growth in the last ten years. This should be Ghana's policy too, going beyond the 'calculated risk', taking every possible risk in order to develop Ghana. He had not, for example, opposed buying more ships and aircraft for Ghana, he had opposed using Ghana's money when he knew they could have got somebody else's. He explained that by borrowing, two plus two could be made to equal to six or eight or even ten. He was confident that with the better organisation within the Government which he expected in the first year of the Republic results could be dramatic, listing 18 examples of possible development including increased cocoa production, the start of the VRP, the completion of the port at Tema, new ships, new aircraft, a new airport, hotels, hospitals and a medical school. The strength of the defence and police forces would also be increased. This was, he submitted, a remarkable programme for a country the size of Ghana.[27]

In May the World Bank said it was willing to make a loan of £30 million (its largest to date) subject to certain conditions, one of which was a satisfactory agreement between Ghana and VALCO on the price of electricity.

When the Republic was inaugurated on 1 July 1960 Nkrumah assumed absolute powers as President. He styled himself 'Osagyefo', which usually meant 'warrior' or 'victorious one' but in his case came to mean 'saviour' or 'redeemer'. Jackson too had a new title; his three year stint as Chairman of the Development Commission had finished and he was now 'Adviser to the President on Development and the Volta River Project'.

On the same day the Belgian Congo was granted independence. No attempt had been made to prepare the Congolese to take on the task of governing their vast nation; indeed the exercise was largely a sham, since the Belgians expected to remain in effective control. The army rebelled, Belgian paratroopers were sent in, Katanga, the largest province, broke away. 'In ten days the Congo, technically the most advanced of all African colonies, had crumbled into anarchy and chaos'.[28] UN troops were sent in, including some from Ghana.

Seeing that the UN operation might go on for several years, Jackson warned Nkrumah of the possible costs of maintaining Ghanaian troops in the Congo: urgent action was needed to ensure that Ghana was not expected to pay an unfair share of the bill.

> Osagyefo: My personal experience in the United Nations indicated that it takes an immense amount of effort for that organisation to get member governments quickly to cough up the cash for operations such as these. They are quite ready to support resolutions but are very slow in providing the money to implement them.[29]

On 27 August he gave Nkrumah a summary of the position on all outstanding matters: the Government had agreed to re-phase its Second Development Plan where possible so that the financing of the Volta River Project could be better undertaken; nevertheless they were committed to projects costing about £20m more than their existing resources; this was a calculated political risk.

Kaiser had promised to cable Nkrumah very soon about developments relating to the agreement with VALCO about the price of electricity. 'I believe that all the progress which has been made up to date', wrote Jackson, 'should not be lost through trying to drive a bargain which VALCO will not be able to accept. On the other hand I believe that the Government of Ghana can make relatively few further concessions.'[30]

Those were his final words of advice to Nkrumah before going on leave to Australia; he offered to return if necessary but was not asked to.

Tenders were invited at what turned out to be a fortunate time for Ghana; the bids were mostly lower than expected and the contract for the dam was awarded to the Italian firm of Impregilo whose work on the Kariba dam was nearing completion.

The World Bank was now advising Ghana to negotiate for 1/2d per unit of electricity, but was prepared to agree 1/3d as the minimum rate on which they would provide a loan (d denoting an old penny). The highest rate that VALCO would consider was 1/4d per unit. Talks in Washington in August had some success in eliciting undertakings from the World Bank, the United States and the British Governments to provide substantial loans, but failed to close the gap over the price of electricity. Kaiser still hoped to convince the Bank that his figures were realistic; during his visit in October he had got the impression that the Ghanaian Government thought he was trying to drive too hard a bargain; his intention had been to negotiate terms which would be beneficial both to Ghana and to VALCO. He wrote telling Nkrumah that he was disappointed that the discussions had turned sour and suggested that the first aim of their proposed meeting in November should be to restore a healthy climate for their negotiations.

Kaiser's letter and his pressure on the World Bank did the trick, and when all three met the Bank and Ghana agreed to VALCO's price of 1/4d per unit. On 17 November Edgar Kaiser and Ghana's Minister of Finance initialled a Master Agreement. Jackson later wrote: 'From my personal experience, I know that these negotiations were conducted in a spirit of reasonableness and goodwill, and that there was always the common objective of creating a Master Agreement which would be fair to all concerned. Nevertheless if past history is a guide, that Master Agreement is bound to be attacked at some stage or another in the future; but nothing can now change the fact that Ghana has developed most successfully one of its most precious natural resources, the waters of the Volta, and that from now on it will have at its disposal some of the cheapest power in the world.'[31]

True, and VALCO too would have at its disposal the cheapest power in the world. Nevertheless it would have been virtually impossible for Nkrumah to have obtained better terms. Being politically committed to the dam he was in a very weak bargaining position. His hopes for Ghana's future rested entirely on the Volta River Project; he had no other programme. On the day of the crucial negotiations Kaiser had asked for the meeting to be adjourned so that he could explain personally to Nkrumah that his shareholders would not support the project if Ghana asked for a higher price of power than his. Nkrumah told his team to agree; he needed the Project whatever the cost.[32] The Rubicon was crossed, but at a heavy cost, and there was still one more river – getting the loans.

In January 1961 the Ghanaian Parliament unanimously approved the Project and authorised the Government to conclude the remaining financial negotiations. Nkrumah, determined to demonstrate Ghana's non-alignment with either the Western or Eastern blocs, immediately announced that an agreement had been reached with the Soviet Government for the design and construction of another hydro-electric project at Bui in the far north-west!

John F Kennedy, the new President of the United States, was well disposed towards Ghana; as a Senator he had been instrumental in agreeing a US loan of £10¾ million. Nkrumah by contrast was becoming increasingly hostile towards him, largely on account of events in Zaire, the former Belgian Congo. Patrice Lumumba, the Prime Minister and to some extent Nkrumah's protégé, had been captured by Belgian troops. Nkrumah had expected that the USA and the UN would make some attempt to rescue him; Kennedy had refused to do so and Lumumba was murdered.

Nkrumah was shattered and wrote to Kennedy accusing him of bad faith. Taken aback by the fierceness of Nkrumah's attack Kennedy consulted Barbara, whom he had known since the 1940s, when his father was US Ambassador in London. During Ghana's early years of independence she had kept him informed of Nkrumah's achievements;[33] she described him now as 'temperamental, mercurial, and caught in the shifting sands of the Cold War', and urged Kennedy to meet him as soon as possible.[34] While she did her best to cool Kennedy's anger at Ghana's criticisms of America Jackson tried to persuade Nkrumah to curb the excesses of the Ghanaian press.

Kennedy invited Nkrumah to Washington in March, going to great lengths to suit Nkrumah's convenience and, at Barbara's suggestion, arranging for him to address the UN General Assembly. Jackson wrote him a note pointing out tactfully that 'other nations, especially the USA had formed a wrong impression of Ghana as being anti-America and pro-East' and suggesting that he should make it clear that Ghana's foreign policy was unchanged since Independence;

and that Ghana was attached to neither of the great power blocs and wished to have good relationships with all countries willing to work with and assist it, while fully recognising Ghana's absolute independence.[35]

Press reports described their talks as 'most fruitful', but according to Moxon 'Nkrumah got a 'balling' from Kennedy in the garden. It seems that the new President pointed out that he was already under considerable pressure not to ratify the financial agreements entered into by his predecessor. In a sense this had been the whole purpose of this eleventh hour invitation, for Kennedy had been receiving more and more reports of Nkrumah's growing fascination with the Eastern bloc, together with accusations that Ghana was only paying lip-service to her declared policy of political non-alignment.'[36] Barbara persuaded Kennedy to continue his support, 'otherwise Nkrumah may not be able to resist, after <u>ten</u> years deferred, the open cheque book waved under his nose in the Kremlin. Must we have two Aswans?'[37]

On Nkrumah's return to Accra in April Jackson gave him a memorandum, Secret and Personal, which as usual he had typed himself so that no-one else would see it. His message was the same:

Ghana's political image was seen as having shifted to the left. This was apparent from its strong criticism of the West and lack of criticism of Russia or China, Ministerial statements slanted strongly towards the left, and the editorial policy of state-owned daily papers and RADIO GHANA, which were held to reflect the Government's policies and views. This image was hurting Ghana's chances of obtaining capital from both West and East. The policy needed adjustment if capital was to be obtained from abroad and Ghana's political independence maintained at the same time.[38]

A month later he was still worried:

> For months past, Government channels of information have maintained a consistently anti-American and non-neutral attitude. I know from Barbara that all of this has been presented to President Kennedy, who is distressed and somewhat bewildered since he paid you the compliment, paid to no other Head of State since he took power, of meeting you at the Airport and believing that he had reached an understanding with you.
>
> On Monday 3 April President Kennedy was singled out by RADIO GHANA for a personal attack. The next day it accused Kennedy of 'nearly plunging

the world into war', likened him to 'a small-boy' and referred to his official visit to de Gaulle at the end of this month as 'a holiday'.

I do not know whether these attacks really represent the Foreign Policy of Ghana, but if they do I cannot believe that the outside world can see Ghana as independent and non-aligned.[39]

Ghana's financial situation was going from bad to worse. By 24 April proposed expenditure for the next financial year (to June 1962) was exceeding available resources by £23.6 million. By early May the estimated shortfall had risen to over £35 million. On top of that Ghana would have to start paying its share of the Volta River Project, and £7 million would have to be found to top up expenditure which could not be entirely financed by overseas loans.[40] Each month revealed another £10 million spent as Ministers thought that it was only necessary to have an idea for the money to be provided.

Preparing papers for Nkrumah for a meeting of the Standing Development Committee he wrote: 'In this folder there is hardly 10% of revenue-producing projects; the great bulk is for Government buildings – your primary objective of industrialisation does not appear to have been thought of.'

Nkrumah had called in the Cambridge economist Professor Nicholas Kaldor for advice on Ghana's financial and economic policy. He would be back in Accra very soon and could give an impartial opinion. 'The proposals in this folder are nearly all contrary to the recommendations made in his preliminary report.'[41]

Jackson discussed this with Nkrumah the same day (18 June), repeating his warnings: the Government was being asked to authorise expenditure at a rate five times that of the Five Year Plan; this could only end in disaster.

The following day Nkrumah directed that all papers relating to the committee meeting were to be deferred for consideration until after the Budget was announced in July. Jackson must have been desperate at the thought of expenditure running unchecked for even a few more weeks, but Nkrumah was facing growing political opposition (hence the secrecy of Jackson's notes). Ministers wanted to spend on their pet projects and Nkrumah was unable or unwilling to stop them.

During May and June officials from Ghana were in Washington for the last lap of negotiations with the World Bank over its proposed loan. Among the documents was a draft of a side-letter imposing limits on Ghana's debt and annual development expenditure – a normal requirement of the World Bank. Nkrumah did not like the limits proposed and instructed that the wording should be modified. When Kaldor returned he said there should be no limits at all and an amended side-letter drafted by him was sent to Washington.

On 29 June Kennedy announced that the US Government was prepared to participate in the Volta Scheme, subject to Ghana resolving any outstanding problems with the World Bank. On 3 July Gbedemah, who was leading the Ghana team, cabled that complete agreement had been reached. The next day Nkrumah made an upbeat statement about the VRP in Parliament; two days later he and Kaiser's company agreed that the contract for Akosombo could be signed.

When Nkrumah, Gbedemah and Kaldor met the next day they realised that Kaldor's amended side-letter was not the one to which Gbedemah had obtained the Bank's agreement. There followed an almighty row between Kaldor and Gbedemah; Nkrumah was furious, realising that he had misled Parliament and Jackson did his best to calm them down. All parties agreed that it would be premature to sign the contract and Kaisers extended their letter of intent for 60 days. Attempts to draft a suitable letter led to further acrimony between Kaldor and Gbedemah. Nkrumah set off on a visit to Moscow, Peking and Eastern Europe and it was left to Jackson to give a diplomatically worded account of all this to the American Ambassador and the UK High Commissioner, who undertook to do their best to soften up the Bank on the outstanding points.[42]

For the next five weeks Jackson's plate was full. Since the Volta River Authority (VRA) had not yet been established it was up to him to ensure that work was proceeding and arrange for the signing of documents and the formal start of work at Akosombo. He was also keeping an eye on water supply, electricity, telecommunications, and works at Government House.[43]

As Nkrumah toured the Eastern bloc countries, where he was fêted and flattered as he attacked British colonialism, Ghana was engulfed by strikes provoked by the draconian budget prescribed by Kaldor and a state of emergency was proclaimed. On his return on 16 September Nkrumah revoked the order and appealed for a return to work. It was not until he dismissed four cabinet members and all the British service chiefs that the strike ended.

The Minister for Presidential Affairs wrote telling Jackson that he was free to leave Ghana by the end of October, and conveying Osagyefo the President's gratitude for his valuable services etc., etc.[44] In fact Jackson would be deeply involved with the arrangements for the Queen's visit in November, as Osagyefo must have known.

Nkrumah's tour of the east had been his way of demonstrating Ghana's non-alignment, but his courtship of the communist bloc and the offers he received there caused Kennedy so much heart-searching that he told Nkrumah that the USA was reconsidering its participation in the VRP. Greatly dismayed, Nkrumah wrote Kennedy a personal letter which did something to repair the damage.[45] Kennedy himself was still well disposed towards the scheme and sent a mission to Ghana with instructions to review the situation, if possible favourably. The mission's report was not favourable, but the British luckily got wind of it before it was released.

The Queen was due to arrive in ten days time, against the advice of Her Government, which was understandably concerned for her safety at a time of such political unrest. The British Prime Minister, Harold MacMillan, therefore asked Kennedy to hold back from making any negative announcement about the Volta. The British Ambassador to Washington went so far as to say that a leak of the mission's report 'would place the Queen in a dangerous position'. Kennedy took the point.[46]

The royal visit went without a hitch. As HMS *Britannia* put to sea The Queen's Private Secretary, Sir Michael Adeane, wrote:

Dear Robert,

If it had not been for you and Robert Milton [of the Ghana Civil Service] this visit would not have come off. One cannot often say that about one or two people in connection with anything but one can in relation to this. So you may have the satisfaction of having contributed something very substantial and important to The Queen's reign, and I do not have to remind you how very real and deep her gratitude is.

During the weeks immediately preceding the visit when there was pressure in the British Press and in the House of Commons to abandon it, some of us who were, like you, concerned with the arrangements felt strongly that whatever the results of a cancellation might be for Britain,

Ghana and the Commonwealth, they would certainly be serious for The Queen. At the time, of course, everyone would have been ready to put the responsibility elsewhere – on Ghana, or the Commonwealth and mainly on the British Government – but in the long run it would have come back on The Queen and it might no doubt have been said that in the first crisis within the Commonwealth in which the Head of the Commonwealth could play a constructive part, she had cast aside that responsibility. This would have been particularly unfair in view of Her Majesty's own very firm views on the subject (which played a considerable part in the final decision) but I have not the least doubt that it would have been the verdict of history.

Happily the right decision was taken and I am sure it will be of real and long term benefit to Her Majesty and the Monarchy. But if you had not been there to help and if you had not created the circumstances in which a thoroughly trouble-free visit could almost be guaranteed, I think it might well have been, and possibly even should have been otherwise.

That it has been trouble free goes without saying. I do not think I ever remember being on one of these visits which, after it had once started, went so smoothly and stuck so closely to the programme. It has also been most enjoyable for all concerned and not least for the writer of this letter who, like all the rest of the party, owes so much to Barbara and to you for your kindness to us all.[47]

Had the pineapples helped? Anna had been despatched by Jacko to deliver a load to *Britannia*. She had certainly enjoyed her glass of sherry on board, chatting to the officers; whether The Queen enjoyed the pineapples is not recorded!

Nkrumah asked Jackson to stay until he knew Kennedy's decision.[48] Macmillan wrote to Kennedy again, reminding him of the Aswan Dam fiasco, and on 16 December the United States formally announced its participation in the Volta River Project. Kennedy wrote to Barbara: 'We have put quite a few chips on a very dark horse but I believe the gamble is worth while.'[49]

The agreements were formally signed on 22 January 1962. The USA would lend £47 million, the World Bank £17 million and the British Government a mere £5 million.

The following day at Akosombo, before a vast crowd, President Nkrumah released a powerful blast which mushroomed above the dam site to signify the formal start of work on the dam.[50]

Nkrumah wrote thanking Jackson for all the help he had given and asking him to continue his association with the Project as a Consultant to the Volta River Authority. He would serve on the Board for the next fifteen years.

On 20 February 1962 he was appointed Knight Commander of the Royal Victorian Order (KCVO) for services to the Monarch. 'What, twice a knight?' cabled Barbara.

Jackson, Kaiser, Lodigiani and Nkrumah, January 1962

Four years later, on 22 January 1966, the inauguration ceremony took place. Everyone was there – people from Halcrow's, from consultants to the Preparatory Commission, the Kaiser team in strength, Impregilo, the bankers, Ministers and Judges, the Akwamo Paramount Chief and hereditary landlord of Akosombo, and a Roman Catholic Archbishop bearing greetings from the Pope, but not Barbara, who was busy as usual in America. The United States and Italian Governments were represented, but not the British, owing to a break in diplomatic relations following Rhodesia's Unilateral Declaration of Independence. By the time Nkrumah spoke it was getting dark and when he turned the switch the dam was bathed in soft green light which blended with the fading colours of the sunset. There were fireworks and the revelry continued through the night.

'After the dinner, which was attended by several hundred people, I went over to Dr Nkrumah to take my leave of him. He drew me to one side and clasped my hands very firmly in his own and then said: 'Thank you for everything. I shall not forget what you have done for Ghana and for me. I hope this is not goodbye, but I have a strong premonition that something very wrong is going to happen to me.'

'I could see that he was greatly disturbed. Knowing that he was just about to leave for Peking and Hanoi I said that I was also due to go to Bangkok at the same time and asked whether he would like me to fly first with him to Peking. He paused for a minute or two and then said, slowly and deliberately: 'Thank you, but I think it best that I should be by myself'. So we put our arms around each other and I said goodbye.'[51]

They never met again. On 24 February, as Nkrumah arrived in Peking, he was deposed by a coup d'état in Accra. The new Government soon discovered that it was faced with foreign debts of some £300 million. But at least the dam was built and Ghana had its hydro-electric power.

As the price of electricity soared throughout the world during the 1970s VALCO agreed to some small increases. In 1979, after the seventh military coup since Nkrumah had been deposed, a new government led by Flight-Lieutenant Jerry Rawlings came to power. Rawlings was determined to reduce Ghana's crippling debt, and one way of doing this would be by getting more income from the smelter. Talks with Kaiser in 1983 aimed at renegotiating the Agreement ground to a halt, but the scales were now tilted in Ghana's favour; the dam was there and no-one could take it away, and the water level was low. The turbines were shut and Ghana would decide when to open them and restore power for the smelter. In January 1985 a new agreement was signed in which the price of electricity was increased almost three-fold.[52]

The Mekong River Basin

Part Three – Back to The UN

11 Not forgotten

THE VOLTA HAD TAKEN NINE YEARS OF HIS LIFE – happy years on the whole. He had gained a son, but his marriage was beginning to fall apart; once again he had no job and no immediate prospect of one; he was fifty. He had a year's salary to see him through and another trip to Australia with his family to keep him occupied, but first he made a quick visit to Bangkok and Phnom Penh for a meeting of the Mekong Committee. Back in October he had been invited to join its advisory board but his commitments in Ghana had ruled out a visit then.

The committee's purpose was to promote the integrated development of the lower basin of the river Mekong on behalf of its four member-nations which had neither the resources nor the expertise to do this themselves. Thailand needed water for irrigation in the northeast, Vietnam wanted increased river flow in the dry season to raise food production in the delta, Laos needed hydro-electric power to develop its agriculture, and Cambodia needed more water for irrigation. The committee was the first example of direct UN involvement in developing an international river basin; it had an advisory board of three engineers and a representative of the World Bank.

When Jackson joined in 1962 the significance of economic and social aspects of development was becoming apparent. 'Behind the shift in emphasis was the growing realisation that the beneficiaries of the development process had ultimately to be able to live with the changes that had been made; but this often involved deep-seated and in some cases disturbing and difficult administrative, social and political adaptations that developing countries had to be assisted, if they so wished, to make.'[1] Who better qualified to advise than Jackson?

During the next eight years the Mekong Committee made numerous feasibility studies; small-scale developments were carried out on the tributaries, each within a single nation, and by the late 1960s several multi-purpose schemes were operating in Thailand, Laos and Cambodia. But the main river remained 'a sleeping giant – a source of tremendous potentialities ... but a source virtually unutilized.'[2]

Jackson usually attended two meetings each year and the Mekong became one of his lasting interests, but the political convulsions that were to come – the Vietnam war and the tragedy of Cambodia – ensured that the sleeping giant was not aroused, at least in his lifetime. (Nor has it been since.)

On 31 January he sailed from London with Robin and Anna, arriving in Melbourne on 1 March. Barbara joined them from the USA on 1 May. He was approached about the chairmanship of the Victoria Hydro-Electric Board and was now seriously considering settling permanently in Australia; he thought of buying a farm which his brother and nephew could run, leaving himself free to pursue his own interests. Although Alan and Andrew quite fancied the idea of becoming farmers they were not attracted by that particular arrangement! In any case Barbara refused to consider living in Australia. It was at this point that he finally realised that his marriage was finished, and decided to rent a house in Jersey again as a base for Robin and Anna which he and Barbara could visit as they chose.

Jackson was not entirely forgotten in UN circles and at the end of June he was approached by Paul Hoffman, the Managing Director of the UN special fund (the latest component of the UN development system), who was looking for a high-level consultant to keep an eye on some of the fund's large-scale projects in developing countries, particularly those concerning multi-purpose river development, and sort out problems on the spot. Jackson was obviously well-qualified so he invited him to New York and offered him the job; Jackson asked for time to consider it.

Also visiting Hoffman's office that day was Joan Anstee, the fund's resident representative in Bolivia (and the only woman in such a post), in New York with a delegation of ministers to seek financial support for Bolivia's development plan. As 'resrep' it was part of her job to liaise between the government and headquarters. Just as the office was closing she was introduced to Jackson by Myer Cohen, who had once worked for him in UNRRA and was now one of

Hoffman's senior assistants. Having spent ten years working for the UN in the Philippines, Colombia, Uruguay, Argentina and now Bolivia Anstee had her own views on how the development system worked and how it could be improved; going down in the lift together they began to talk. Jackson, always on the look-out for young people of ability, especially women, soon realised that Anstee was special. They went on talking as they walked up First Avenue together; deep in conversation in the evening sun they must have made a striking pair, he tall and slim and looking younger than his 51 years; she a mere 36, very attractive and well turned-out. He invited her to join him for

Joan Anstee

dinner, but she was not free to accept. It would be three years before their paths crossed again, but he never forgot that meeting. It was then, he would say, that he fell in love with her.

His new rôle of consultant to the Volta River Authority (VRA) took him to Accra in July; he went on to Monrovia, the capital of Liberia, at the request of President Tubman. Tubman had met him in Accra at the first meeting of the Heads of African States in 1958; he now had financial problems and wanted Jackson as his permanent confidential adviser. Jackson would not commit himself; he thought that short regular visits would be better.[3]

On his way to rejoin his family in Melbourne he visited Relda in New Zealand, as he would whenever he could. A hernia operation at the end of August kept him in hospital until mid-September, when the four of them sailed for Southampton.

Dear Bill, we proceed on our way; B proceeds on her own way. On a day to day basis she continues to get everything she wants – but in the process has lost the thing that matters most. Her Carnegie work may go on for another four years. As long as the Bomb is protected and Anna has a reasonable life I don't care much. I have no doubt at all that B will evolve a way of life which will give her much more satisfaction and comfort than most people get, even if she (and thus I) have missed the main chance. When the Bomb is properly organised at school I'll decide how I can best play out the rest of my innings. Despite the mess in my own family, it was a great joy to see you both again: March and April were good months.[4]

In October Tubman offered him a three-year appointment, starting in January, as 'Adviser to the President of Liberia' spending about three weeks there every three months; he would be paid a handsome fee: $10,000 a year plus expenses.[5] Knowing that he could no longer rely on HMG to find him a job he decided to sever his formal connection with his 'godfather', the Treasury, telling Tubman: 'From the moment I work for you my loyalty and responsibility will be to you and the Government of Liberia alone.'[6] This did not preclude his accepting Hoffman's offer, and on his return to the US his appointment was confirmed, also starting on 1 January 1963. His remit was 'to undertake specific assignments as directed, designed to facilitate the Fund's operations with particular reference to its future work.'[7] This marked the beginning of an association with the UN which would last for 25 years, though always on a yearly contract under which he would be paid for days worked. He welcomed the freedom that this arrangement gave him to spend more time with Robin.

Once again he was on the move, visiting Africa, the Middle East and Asia, inspecting projects which were not going well and helping to put them right; he was meeting old friends again, among them Sheila and her husband who was now working in Iran. Once again he knew he was doing a worth-while job and was reasonably pleased with life.

When inspecting a special fund project he would first discuss any problems with the resrep and consider possible solutions to suggest to the agency representative and the government; with his authority he could sometimes put things more strongly than the resrep. Having got their agreement he would draft a letter for the resrep to send to headquarters suggesting what should be done.

After discussing it there he would write back to the resrep telling him – in one instance her – that the proposal had been agreed, replying to his own letter!

Occasionally he found himself at odds with headquarters: in February 1964 he cabled from Singapore saying that he had promised the government $5 million of special fund money. He was told 'You can't do that! What are the projects?' Jackson stuck to his guns: 'Give them the money first and let them decide the projects'.[8] This fundamental difference of approach would come to a head in 1969 when he carried out his study of the UN development system, the subject of the next chapter.

In October 1965, after a visit to Christchurch, he was suddenly taken ill in Brisbane; he cabled Anna to come out at once, saying that he was in hospital with sinus trouble. She saw immediately that there was more to it than that; in fact he was being treated for serious depression; his heart was also playing up. They went to Surfers' Paradise for a month, during which he succeeded in reducing her to the same state of depression as his own.[9] For the next year he took things more gently and his travels were by his standards quite modest.

He next met Anstee at a meeting of resreps in Mexico in 1965 and again in Turin in June 1966, when he succeeded in taking her out to dinner. When she was in hospital in England in August for an operation he sent flowers and wrote every day. She was flattered by his attentions and enjoyed his company from time to time and their animated discussions about the UN, but her feelings did not go beyond friendship. In October she met another man; for both of them it was love at first sight, but he was married. A year later she was in Geneva giving a talk about the work of a resrep; she had been expecting to meet the other man there. When he failed to turn up she was devastated; Jackson picked up the pieces and took her out to dinner again.

As resrep in Ethiopia one of Anstee's main concerns was a multi-purpose river development in the Awash Valley, which was running into difficulties. In October Jackson went there to advise, and for a week they worked closely together. Whatever his feelings for her, hers for him were still simply warm affection and friendship, as well as great admiration for his professional capacity and integrity.

In November 1967 she took a year's leave from UNDP in order to be near her mother who was seriously ill with some mysterious sickness. She was given a temporary appointment as Senior Economic Adviser in the Office of the Prime Minister (Harold Wilson) and frequently met Jacko in London. They dined together, went to plays and films, and he helped her to get medical advice for her mother. Their friendship grew closer.

Nine years had elapsed since the special fund had started and it was now part of UNDP (the United Nations Development Programme). This was a period when donor governments were prepared to respond generously, and annual contributions to the development system had already trebled, but questions were being asked about how much further the system could grow, not least because Hoffman was looking forward to the day when UNDP's resources would be doubled again. The major donors, particularly the US as the largest, were not prepared to consider doubling their contributions without first establishing that UNDP would be able to handle projects on that scale satisfactorily. As someone who welcomed constructive criticism, Hoffman was keen to have a study of UNDP carried out which would lead to improvements in its operations and increase its capacity

In the spring of 1968 he asked Jackson if he would do a study of UNDP 'from the inside'. Jackson declined; he knew what that would involve and could see that he would find himself 'the captive of the system'.[10] When the suggestion was repeated at a meeting in May he again declined – at first. 'And then various people nobbled me after lunch and I said that I would do it, but only if I was asked to by governments'[11] (i.e. by the governing council of UNDP).

*

Readers unfamiliar with the UN development system may find a brief account of its evolution helpful in understanding the situation that Jackson would have to address. Its beginnings contained elements of impotence, compromise, opportunism, greed, and a forced marriage – as well as idealism.

It began with **technical assistance** – advice for developing countries about economic development: facilities for training their own people and obtaining up-to-date information. The obvious sources were the 'specialised agencies', particularly the Food and Agriculture Organisation (FAO), the World Health Organisation (WHO), the UN Educational, Scientific and Cultural Organisation (UNESCO), and the International Labour Office (ILO), as well as the relevant part of the UN secretariat. The agencies' original purposes were to collect information, set international standards, and become centres of excellence, providing facilities for the exchange of technical information; they had no operational rôles. Although they form part of the so-called 'UN development system' they are autonomous bodies with their own governing councils. The UN's Economic and Social Council (ECOSOC) was and still is supposed to coordinate their activities but has little power to do so. That was the problem then and it is one which repeated attempts to reform the UN system have so far failed to resolve satisfactorily.

In 1946 the General Assembly allocated funds for providing expert advice on a small scale; in 1949 a larger system was set up, funded by voluntary contributions from member states. The immediate problem was not so much raising the money, as deciding how it should be shared between the agencies. The UN secretariat favoured a single fund, to be allocated by ECOSOC; the agencies each wanted their own fund. The result – **EPTA, the Expanded Programme of Technical Assistance** – was a compromise, as such matters inevitably are in the UN. Funds for the first year were allocated by ECOSOC, but the agencies, having established their positions, made sure that their 'agency shares' remained much the same for the next twenty years. To some extent this negated the principle that services provided by EPTA to each country, and the form they took, should be decided by its government.

EPTA provided assistance over a very wide range of subjects including economic planning, public administration, education and training, agriculture, health, communications, statistics – almost everything, but its assistance was limited to advice given by international experts and fellowships for training nationals. In 1952 David Owen (who as ASG for Economic Affairs had played a large part in setting up EPTA) was appointed as its Executive Chairman. As a means of coordinating its activities in the field he sent out **resident representatives** to developing countries to liaise with governments and coordinate the work of the agencies' experts. Although they had little formally delegated authority 'resreps' with initiative had considerable freedom to act, particularly in the early days.

During 1957 a novel suggestion was made – that the UN should set up a fund to finance surveys of mineral, water and soil resources which would high-light opportunities for productive investment. This was Paul Hoffman's idea. Hoffman was a businessman who had spent most of his life working for the Studebaker-Packard Corporation; in 1948 he had been appointed by President Truman as Managing Director of the ERP (the Marshall Plan). The US government was prepared to support such a fund, provided that there were **no agency shares**, and projects were considered on their merits rather than as part of any country programme.

The General Assembly decided to establish this **special fund,** whose projects should advance development by facilitating new capital investment. This was known as **pre-investment**. It came into operation in January 1959, with Paul Hoffman as managing director. He was advised by a small board, and the agencies had no say in the allocation of funds for projects. Hoffman saw his role as one of fund-raising and public relations, in which he was extremely effective – and generous too, often entertaining delegates of donor governments at his own expense.

He left day-to-day management to his two assistant administrators, Myer Cohen and Paul-Marc Henry, who ran the 'bureau of operations'. Cohen handled overall administration; Henry examined the projects submitted, often visiting the countries concerned. Together they decided which projects to recommend to Hoffman for submission to the governing council for approval. The bureau was regarded, certainly in its early days, as efficient and positive in its approach. For all three men the principle that money should only be allocated by the council for first-class projects was paramount. Resreps now had a second rôle as directors of special fund programmes.

Since the mid-1950s the agencies had been executing their own EPTA projects. Executing special fund projects was a more demanding task, and long delays in their implementation soon became common. To improve their performance Hoffman held regular discussions with them and appointed consultants, including Jackson, to work with recipient governments to improve the preparation and execution of projects.

For the agencies the stakes in the special fund were high; projects meant prestige and expansion of staff (financed by the overheads they earned on each project) and they used all possible means to retain and increase their shares. Inexperienced governments of some developing countries were persuaded by their salesmanship, sometimes aggressive, to submit projects which did not reflect their priorities; they were understandably reluctant to refuse an opportunity and risk offending the agency. Resreps could see that agency representatives in the field, though expert in their particular subject, had very little concern for what a country most needed as part of its development plan. Agency heads also had a say in the appointment of resreps and in assessing their performance, occasionally threatening those they thought uncooperative.

From time to time the idea of merging the special fund and EPTA was considered; their functions were different – pre-investment and technical assistance – and their aims diverged: the special fund was not concerned with country programmes, whereas EPTA was, even if there was little formal procedure for promoting it. Owen, Cohen and Henry saw scope for conflict, and Owen also saw EPTA becoming the junior partner, but Hoffman saw a merger as a means of attracting bigger contributions, and in 1966 they were amalgamated as the **United Nations Development Programme (UNDP),** with Hoffman as administrator, Owen co-administrator, and Cohen and Henry continuing as assistant administrators. Jackson was made senior consultant. A new Inter-Agency Consultative Board (IACB) was formed, but had little success in improving coordination.

As contributions increased, so did overheads, and the weaknesses of both programmes remained. Before long the conflicts arose and Hoffman, who saw the special fund as a cut above EPTA, turned to Cohen for advice more than to Owen. In the governing council complaints about administrative costs continued and the excessive influence of the agencies on the selection of projects was deplored.[12]

That was the situation in May 1968 when Jackson told the IACB that he would undertake the Capacity Study if invited to do so by the governing council. He had already discussed this with Anstee, who encouraged him to do it. She had until then worked exclusively in the field and written extensively about the need for better administration of international aid; she believed that the system would collapse unless there was a complete overhaul. It was not responding to the needs of developing countries because it was unable to. The special fund was making most of the running, as Owen had feared, and the principle that EPTA programmes should reflect a country's own development plan had been lost sight of. The bureau of operations run by Cohen and Henry was severely overloaded and had become something of a law unto itself, and the power of the agencies in determining programmes was unacceptable. The remedies would have to be drastic: what was needed above all was country programming; doubling UNDP's resources, as Hoffman wanted, was not by itself the answer. Anstee's and Jackson's views coincided and she felt that he was the only person with the stature, experience and courage to undertake the exhaustive study that was required. He was reluctant, being more aware than she was of the political machinations at headquarters – the competing personalities and the in-fighting with the agencies – which she had not experienced. When he said that he would only do the study if she would be his chief assistant she was faced with a double dilemma: she had been offered the post of resrep in Morocco and wanted to get back to the field; she was also becoming aware of his feelings for her which she could not reciprocate; she still cared for the man who had failed to turn up in Geneva, though they had agreed not to meet again. Jacko recognised this. 'From your side, I hope that Geneva for about eight months could be bearable, assuming that I was not padding around like a bear with a sore head. If I could forecast the future in Geneva, I'd guess that your personal life would be full to overflowing without much of me, and that my own personal life will tend to become more of a retreat into my shell.'[13] She agreed to help him and he came out of his shell.

12 The Capacity Study[1]

WHEN THE INTER-AGENCY CONSULTATIVE BOARD met in May the agency heads whole-heartedly supported Hoffman's proposal for a study of UNDP.[2] Since its purpose was to show that UNDP's capacity could be doubled (bringing them more business as executing agents) they could hardly have done otherwise. They widened its terms of reference: it should 'make recommendations for the further development of an efficient and economical system of formulating and delivering a Programme composed of projects truly responsive to the ascertained needs and priorities of the developing countries, as requested by them, and also reflecting the policies of the agencies'. Since the latter were at odds with the former that was expecting too much.

In June the governing council widened the terms still further to include consideration of the most efficient arrangements for the 'appraisal and processing' of projects (choosing the right ones), the most effective utilization of the resources and finances of UNDP, and general principles concerning administration, staffing and financial implications; furthermore the original text of the report was to be submitted to the Council, with comments of the IACB annexed.[3]

It would now be a study of the whole system, not just of UNDP, and the report, unexpurgated, would go direct to the governing council. Some representatives expressed the hope that the Commissioner (Jackson) would pull no punches, be bold and imaginative, and above all independent, and that his report should be hard-hitting and written in 'non-UN language'.[4] They need not have worried. 'Consideration of the most effective utilization of resources and of general principles' unlocked a door which Jackson would throw wide open; clearly UNDP failed to see the significance of this.

This was not the first time Jackson had addressed the subject: ten years earlier he had given three lectures at Syracuse University making the case for an International Development Agency. His third lecture had concluded with the question 'am I my brother's keeper?' That challenge, he said, might have been accepted in principle, but the practical remedies were not proving very effective. Now was his chance to suggest better ones.

> 28 June: Dear Bill, I'm landed with this new UN job which I don't want and everyone else wants me to have. ... It means a review of the entire UN system wherever it's concerned with development. I'm pretty sure governments have created a Frankenstein that they cannot control. So I'm [not] too enthusiastic about the chances of anyone now solving this one.[5]

Hoffman asked Owen to consult Jackson about the other members of his team, and between them they chose Léonce Bloch and Sixten Heppling, both of whom, like Anstee, had been resreps for EPTA and subsequently directors of special fund projects. There were two others: Karol Kraczkiewicz, a Pole taken on by UNDP as an Assistant Administrator for finance and administration (to ensure representation of the eastern bloc) who had not proved effective, whom Jackson agreed to include at their request, and Marc Nerfin, a young high-flyer previously working for the UN, brought in to assist Anstee, researching and producing charts and maps.

Jackson set up two advisory groups, one from within the system, comprising senior officials from the organisations concerned (UN, UNDP, IBRD, WHO, ILO, FAO, UNESCO and UNIDO) to ensure that they were closely associated with the study from the outset; the other a panel of consultants from outside, chosen for their personal qualifications and experience of the system. They came from developed and developing countries – the USA, Sweden, the USSR, Thailand, Libya, Mali, Venezuela, Chile, and Hungary. They included ministers and former ministers, not as representatives of their countries, but as individuals with independent views. He also engaged McKinsey & Co to advise on information systems.

In July he sent a questionnaire to UNDP and the agencies asking for basic information. The senior staff of UNDP were too busy to respond, being under great pressure of work at the time; in any case they were convinced that the study would concentrate on improving the efficiency of the agencies in executing their projects, rather than on UNDP itself. When Jackson asked for direct access to the resreps on a personal basis Hoffman readily agreed, and they too were sent the questionnaire. Their responses were exceedingly frank, both in their criticisms and suggestions for improvement. Great care was taken to protect the confidentiality of all views expressed, and when Jackson refused to pass on to Hoffman those of <u>his</u> resreps he was very angry,[6] nevertheless information was forthcoming which otherwise might not have been.

Anstee's London assignment finished at the end of October, and in beautiful autumn weather she drove Jacko to Geneva, pausing at Rheims to raise a glass to the success of the task ahead. On 1 November the team got down to work, using offices provided by WHO. Different aspects of the study were shared among them, and their ideas were discussed by the team. Marc Nerfin contributed his share, Kraczkiewicz little more than clouds of cigarette smoke and great charm. Anstee's task was to transform the papers and the notes of their discussions into a draft chapter for further discussion, and ultimately to weld the chapters into an integrated report.

On 1 December Jackson sent Hoffman a hand-written personal letter describing two long telephone calls he had recently had with Myer Cohen and Paul-Marc Henry.

> Both had felt we were assembling a case for the prosecution against UNDP. They seemed surprised to learn that the agencies felt that we might be defending UNDP and attacking them! In fact we are, of course, assembling no cases for the prosecution, and we will not attack anyone. The 'System' is continuously trying to strengthen itself (illustrated by this Study) and we intend to try and help that process. ...
>
> They were concerned that I would exceed my terms of reference and thus propose unrealistic recommendations which could damage the machine you and they have done so much to create. I think that I have relieved their minds on this score.
>
> I have reminded them of the major changes made by the governing council in Vienna to the original terms of reference agreed by the IACB. We are bound to look at the wider issues – governments want this, and those to whom I have spoken have emphasised that this is essential. So too with

the panel of consultants – all of them have indicated that they will raise these issues at our meetings. ...

As you were the first to recognise, this present job is not an enviable one. It has to be done, however, and I will do it to the best of my ability. Yet I will inevitably come under attack for many reasons – whether valid or not. It is thus fortunate that I am expendable. Whatever happens, all I hope is two things.

First that the system will have been strengthened by the Study – my own position being unimportant; and second that our personal friendship will remain.

I am well aware of the pressures to which I shall be subjected to the extent that the powers of parts of the system and the powers of individuals are affected by our work. I can survive this if our understanding of each other remains complete.

Yours ever, Jacko.[7]

Attached to the letter was a note suggesting that it should be destroyed after he had read it.

This is an important letter because it demonstrates precisely Jackson's dilemma: he knew that his study was going far beyond what Hoffman had originally wanted, and that Hoffman did not realise the full implications of this – that it would mean the end of the special fund. There were two reasons why Jackson could not come clean: first, the governing council's decision that the report should go unexpurgated direct to them virtually imposed a vow of silence on him, and second, to have done so would have given the game away; it was absolutely out of the question. But Cohen and Henry had sensed danger, and he had done his best to relieve their minds. For once he had been 'economical with the truth' – but what else could he have done? Jackson realised that it might all end in tears, and this letter was a warning to Hoffman, not to be revealed to the other two. The machine was the special fund, the powers of its parts were the powers of the bureau of operations and the individuals whose powers would be affected were Cohen and Henry. Jackson could hardly have given Hoffman a broader hint than that.

Jackson and Anstee saw the study as 'the big opportunity to try to right the mess caused by the piecemeal development of the UN'[8], which undoubtedly it was; they hoped, with good reason, that the system would be strengthened by it; they also hoped that Hoffman's reputation would be enhanced by it, that he would be able to retire on a high note as the man who had initiated a major reform of the UN development system. That was an admirable intention but was it a realistic hope? Jackson realised that their friendship was at risk. At some stage the reasoning behind the report would have to be explained to Hoffman very carefully, and objections from Cohen and Henry forestalled.

Hoffman's reply gives no indication that he took the hint. He said he had read the letter with deepest interest; ten years ago he had arrived in New York to fulfil his promise to Dag Hammerskjöld, Secretary-General at the time, to spend no more than two years getting the special fund off the ground. In 1958 the total 'peace building' operations of the UN had, he said, cost about $60 million; in 1969 they would cost $500 million.

> These figures, essentially guesses, underscore first the fact that we have been growing at a rather rapid rate and second, the need for strengthening the entire UN development system so that it can both carry out its present programme more efficiently, and second, get ready for a further doubling of the programme in the next five years.
>
> I have agreed to stay on for two years because I want to do whatever I can do to make more effective the Commission's work. You already have contributed much to strengthening our organisation and you are going to contribute more.
>
> Sincerely, Paul.[9]

14 December 1968, *en route* to Monrovia and Accra: Dear Bill, I do not think that I have worked so hard since the end of the war – in the last month I have been in The Hague, Paris, Bonn, North America, Moscow and heaven knows where, averaging 18 to 19 hours a day; I hope the effort is worth it – personally I believe it is, or I would not have undertaken the job.'[10]

Barbara saw his task as poetic justice: 'He had been thrown out of the UN twenty years ago for suggesting that such an enquiry was necessary; she was delighted to see the mills of God grinding sure and not so slowly'.[11] That was not why he had been thrown out, but he was doing now what he had hoped to do then, back in the days before EPTA; poetic justice there certainly was. In his

Foreword to the study Jackson wrote:
> I wouldn't be human if I did not feel I had come full circle. I was at the centre of things at Lake Success about twenty years ago, and the roots of many of today's problems were apparent even then, but governments were not prepared to deal with them effectively.

In January 1969 he and Anstee went to New York for the first meeting of the panel of consultants and on to Montreal to make contact with the Pearson Commission on International Development, which was taking place at the same time. Lester Pearson, a former Prime Minister of Canada and an old friend of Jacko's, was examining the effects of development aid generally during the last 20 years in order to identify the scope for improving its quality and increasing its quantity. Commissioned by the World Bank, his study was a response to a perceived crisis in aid when the gap between the developed and developing countries was growing. The two studies were complementary: Pearson was looking at what the developing world needed, Jackson at how best to provide it. They were both due to report in the autumn of 1969 and kept in close touch.

In New York Jackson explained to the governing council how he was approaching the various issues involved. As to what needed to be done, in his opinion a UN development system needed clear definitions of objectives and functions at all levels, agreed policies and procedures, and consequently a logical framework of organization. While expansion of the programme would need money, he saw the availability of qualified staff at all levels as the crucial limiting factor. Would the UN be able to attract and retain sufficient highly qualified personnel to make the best use of available resources?

Finally, he asked, could the agencies surrender enough of their independence to make it possible to operate an integrated system? Could governments overcome their own failures to act consistently when dealing with the different agencies? When acting collectively could they control or even influence the agencies? If not, the present multilateral system would have reached its limit, providing one more example of political failure to develop national and international institutions reflecting recent technical advances. 'I find this a sobering thought – but it will only serve to make us try and prepare a realistic report for you.'[12]

At the end of January David Owen announced his intention to resign as Co-Administrator of UNDP in mid-year. His relationship with Hoffman had not been easy after the merger and he felt he had little influence in UNDP; Hoffman now looked upon Myer Cohen as his number two, so Owen had found himself another job.

Jackson was worried about who would be appointed to succeed him, afraid that political considerations might take precedence over managerial; after some hesitation he wrote to Hoffman pointing out the relevance of the Capacity Study to this appointment. Given the rapid growth of UNDP, thanks largely to Hoffman's success in raising funds, a very high level of management would be needed, especially at the top. 'A premature appointment or one of someone without exceptional qualifications would pre-empt the Study's proposals and defeat its main object.' He ventured to suggest deferring any appointment until governments had considered its recommendations.[13]

Hoffman did not take kindly to this, indeed he was 'somewhat amazed' by it. He replied that when proposing the Capacity Study he had had two objectives: firstly that it would lead to self-examination by the agencies and UNDP and hopefully to their strengthening, and secondly to further strengthening of the UN system as a whole as a result of its down-to-earth recommendations. (In other words he wasn't expecting anything far-reaching. The penny had still not dropped.)

In saying that UNDP's growth had been due to his successful money-raising, he wrote, Jackson had mistaken effect for cause. UNDP's growth was due to the success of its programme. Credit for that was due to his associates, including Jackson. The decision about whom to appoint and when rested with himself, in consultation with the Secretary-General. 'We will do our best to act with wisdom'.[14]

Unabashed, Jackson replied: 'I am sad that a genuine attempt to give you assistance in dealing with the very real and unexpected dilemma over David's successor – and one on which the Capacity Study must have a direct bearing – should have been misinterpreted.'[15]

Not so much misinterpreted as summarily rejected; but Jackson was right to worry. When Owen left in June CV Narasimhan was appointed as Deputy Administrator, combining this with his existing position as *Chef de Cabinet* to the Secretary-General.

Jackson and Anstee were dismayed; 'CV' had a known track-record as a consummate wheeler-dealer, a good manager, practised in preserving the *status quo* but not familiar with development issues; and combining two such important posts was not a good idea.[16]

At the end of February Jackson's team and the fourteen members of the Advisory Group – the key men in UN, UNDP (Cohen and Henry) and the agencies – retreated to a hotel in Divonne just across the French border where they remained incommunicado for over a week, exploring all kinds of new ideas, discussing all suggestions, however unorthodox, all in complete confidence. Jackson revealed no details of what his proposals would be; for one thing he was still developing his ideas and for another to have disclosed them would inevitably have led to premature comment.

One of the possibilities considered was the use of 'Indicative Planning Figures' (IPFs). Agency shares, for all their disadvantages, performed a useful function: they were a method of dividing the cake, sharing out the available resources in any one year. If they were abolished some other method would be needed; IPFs could be the answer. Unlike agency shares IPFs were not actual allocations, but notional allocations to developing countries enabling them to plan ahead. Cohen and Henry advised strongly against this on the grounds that even though IPFs were not commitments they would be seen as such, with the result that developing countries would no longer be motivated to put forward excellent projects.[17] (This was the very point on which Jackson and Henry had disagreed when he cabled from Singapore in 1964.)

In February Anstee found herself a small house near Trélex, a village at the foot of the hills near Nyon, with views across Lake Léman to the Alps, and where the only sound at night was the gentle clonking of cowbells in the meadows. Not only was this much more to her liking, she succeeded in persuading Jacko to take over the lease of her flat in Geneva, where he was able to enjoy a more domestic existence than in the hotels he usually frequented at the time.

At Easter Joan invited Maria and me to Trélex for the week-end. Jacko was there too and that was when we really got to know him – we 'clicked'. The weather was crisp and sunny, and the four of us walked in the woods picking primroses. Jacko drove us round the lakes, and we had a picnic on the Sunday which he organised with his usual attention to logistic detail. Having put 'oranges' on the shopping list he amended it to 'blood oranges'. When I asked if he was particular about the blood group he was for once lost for words! On the Monday we enjoyed the first of many of his barbecues, using as always the best fillet steak. We ate and drank on the terrace in the sun with Mont Blanc just visible across the water and afterwards fell contentedly asleep on the grass. The next day they took us to lunch in the WHO building with its splendid view across Lake Léman, and we flew home, leaving them to resume their punishing schedule of work.

When not travelling to meetings Joan was busy from dawn till dusk drafting and redrafting the report. Papers were taken back and forth to Jacko's office in Geneva; each day a driver collected her latest piece and delivered his comments on her previous day's work; food was supplied regularly so that she never had to waste precious minutes going to the shops, and Jacko went to Trélex each weekend. During the first half of June Joan stayed with us at Petersham to be near her mother who was in hospital, working on the report every day and visiting her mother in the evenings.

Joan, James and Maria at Trélex

Later that month Jackson reported to the governing council in Geneva that the phase of consultation was over, it was time to start drawing conclusions and to make recommendations, but still he gave little indication of what they might be. (Some members had friends at court in UNDP and the agencies, and comments would soon have started flying.)

He did say that modifications were already being introduced – a wind of change was blowing through the whole system, to some extent as a result of the study. 'When assessing the value and impact of the final report I am sure that the Council will bear in mind the catalytic effect that the Capacity Study has had throughout the system from the beginning. This might make some of its findings seem anti-climactic, particularly against the aura of expectation which now surrounds the study.'[18] There was little likelihood of that!

Hoffman thought that the recommendations, concerned as they were with UNDP Headquarters, could usefully be discussed with himself, Cohen and Henry before final conclusions were reached.[19] To this end he invited Jackson, Anstee, Cohen and Henry to dinner in Geneva on 2 June, and Jackson and Anstee to lunch on 22 June. One important point lying at the heart of their recommendations needed further explanation: country programming and the proposed method of financing it through Indicative Planning Figures (IPFs). They knew that Cohen and Henry were opposed to IPFs on the grounds that developing countries would see them as commitments and they knew that for Hoffman approval of projects was the paramount consideration. It was clearly a point which called for very careful handling.

On 2 July Anstee and Jackson invited Hoffman to Trélex for supper in order to explain this crucial point. Their intention was 'to accompany intellectual indoctrination with blandishments of agreeable food and drink'.[20] Joan laid in stocks of his favourite tipple, and Jacko was all set to do great things with the barbecue. Unfortunately rain stopped play; it began soon after Hoffman arrived and went on all evening. Jacko did his best with the barbecue, running in and out of the house with a mac over his head, but the results were more of a sodden apology than a blandishment, and he was far too busy trying to salvage it to contribute much by way of intellectual indoctrination. Joan did the explaining and Hoffman appeared content or at least not discontent with what he was told; but, as subsequent events were to show, he had failed to grasp its full significance. He was after all one of those high-flying American businessmen who liked to look at the big picture and left tedious details (such as IPFs) to his staff. Anstee has often wondered 'whether the Capacity Study would have met a kinder fate had the weather been kinder on that critical evening'.[21]

At the end of July they went to New York to discuss their final proposals with Cohen and Henry; having participated in the consultative meetings they must have had some idea of what to expect, and it would have been pointless for them to go over the arguments again at this stage. However much of the report they now knew it seems that they did not reveal the full picture to Hoffman – that it meant the end of the special fund – his special fund. Myer and his wife invited Jacko and Joan to dinner, and they spent a civilized evening together.

On 1 September the panel of consultants met in Geneva for the final time. The main text of the report went to press at the end of the month and work on the Appendices continued through October. Then Jacko and Joan took a brief holiday together in Zermatt, walking miles; they spent a day on one of the paddle steamers on Lake Léman. Then it was time for Joan to leave to take up her appointment as resrep in Morocco. It had been a very special year for them both; the Capacity Study had been a joint endeavour which had brought together the two lonely travellers, who now had to go their separate ways; it was the start of a personal as well as a professional partnership, and for him, as always, the two strands were intertwined.

THE CAPACITY STUDY

Jackson introduced his report with a Foreword in the form of a long letter addressed to an unnamed head of state in a developing country: 'We have diagnosed the patient's sickness and written a prescription. It remains to be seen whether he will take the medicine.'

He had formed two strong impressions: firstly that technical co-operation and pre-investment were the most effective ways of assisting developing countries and that the UN, despite its limitations, was the ideal instrument for the job. (The terms **technical co-operation** above and **development co-operation** below had superseded **technical assistance**, reflecting the principle that development should be home-grown rather than determined by UNDP or the agencies.) This, he said, was an unprecedented opportunity to revitalize the development system, but could the governments of the world grasp it? His second impression was that, given their record of the last twenty years, probably not. The great inertia of the existing administrative structure seemed to render it immovable, yet change was now imperative, and only heads of state and governments could bring it about.

Governments had created this vast machine comprising the UN and many of its parts (UNDP, UNICEF, UNIDO, UNCTAD etc) and about a dozen specialised agencies. In theory it was under the control of about thirty separate governing bodies, but it had no central co-ordinating organisation to control it. It had become literally unmanageable, and was becoming slower and unwieldy, 'like some prehistoric monster'.

Complete control would require consolidation of all the component parts into a single organisation. This was out of the question, but the Study showed what could be done by introducing systematic management procedures, and re-structuring UNDP. The effects would be substantial, and resisted by those with a vested interest in maintaining the *status quo*, and by the agencies, which had 'become the equivalent of principalities'.

Governments themselves were sometimes part of the problem; a minister of agriculture talking to FAO might advocate a policy at odds with his government's overall policy; they too must get their acts together.

The best that could be hoped was for governments to transform UNDP into a strong and effective organisation and for UNDP, using enlightened managerial and financial procedures, to secure the co-operation of the agencies in bringing the machine under reasonable control and thus facilitating improved co-operation with the Third World.

Tragically too many people – including leaders in the affluent states – now appeared to believe that the plight of two thirds of mankind could be safely swept under the political rug and left there. However, the sheer force of political circumstances would compel governments to act sooner or later. The sooner they responded, the greater would be the prospects for a better world. The longer they delayed, the greater would be the dangers.

'We still have time to do the most constructive job in the history of the world.'

The Study was published in two volumes: Volume I (69 pages) comprised the Commissioner's Report, summarising his proposals; Volume II (500 pages) contained the details.

The report looked at the past, present and future. The growing pains of the last 25 years, said Jackson, had been sharpened by the introduction of 'a new dynamic' – **development co-operation** – into a structure not designed for it; the autonomy of the agencies made collective action difficult; the argument between the centralisers and decentralisers remained unsolved, and at present the former were winning. UNDP had achieved much, it was an active programme operating in 100 countries, but it was getting slower all the time and there was about 20% of 'dead-wood' – projects not essential for development. Current procedures did not address the real needs of the developing countries; too often projects were the result of agencies' salesmanship and the project-by-project approach of UNDP; they were also too big for the agencies to execute. There was no central administrative machinery devoted to co-operation with developing countries.

The system had tried for many years to wage a war on want with very little organised 'brain' to guide it. This lack might well be the greatest constraint on capacity. Without it the future evolution of the system could easily repeat the history of the dinosaur.

Now they were at the crossroads. They could stick to the well-beaten track – the *ad hoc* 'tinkering' methods of the past – but it was time for a change. That called for political decisions, which governments had so far failed to make; the agencies too had resisted change.

In Jackson's opinion the present system had reached its limit and could not effectively handle more. If governments were willing to provide more funds but unwilling to re-organise the system, then the money should flow through other channels.

UNDP performed a dual service: technical cooperation, whose value was out of all proportion to its cost, and pre-investment which was also of special interest to the World Bank. Lending by the Bank for capital investment was increasing rapidly; if UNDP did not take the lead in programming pre-investment the Bank would have to do so itself and UNDP would become the junior partner. This would be the negation of the purpose for which the special fund had been created: to fill the pre-investment gap.

UNDP needed to be transformed into an effective operational organisation. As to how this should be done, Jackson proposed ten precepts, of which three were fundamental:

1 The introduction of country programming – a method which would enable all inputs from the system to be combined into a programme consistent with a country's own priorities and its development plan, if any.
2 Effective and prompt execution of projects.
3 Organisational reform at all levels to integrate the components of the system; these should combine greater control at the centre with maximum

decentralisation to the field, where the authority of the resrep should be greatly strengthened.

Without doubt all this would be difficult, but if governments shirked the issues the system would become increasingly inefficient; its own development would have been stalled at the very moment when it could have been strengthened, and the ones to suffer would be the developing countries.

Country programming would operate within a development co-operation cycle of five phases: Phase 1 concerned the programme; it would be prepared by the government and resrep together, to reflect the country's development plan and match its duration; it would consist of a slate of projects drawn up within an 'Indicative Planning Figure' of cost (IPF) which would be provided by the administrator. The programme would be submitted to the governing council for approval, and reviewed annually.

The other four phases concerned the selection and handling of projects in the programme:

2. Formulation and appraisal of projects in the programme, again at country level, for their relevance, feasibility, costs and benefits and, if satisfactory, approval by the administrator (or, in the case of small projects, by the resrep.).
3. Implementation of the approved project by the executing agent appointed by the administrator.
4. Evaluation by qualified officials (to maintain the financial accountability of the administrator).
5. Follow-up to demonstrate the project's success or failure.

After the five phases were completed a new cycle would start.

In short, the governing council would in future approve <u>programmes</u> and the administrator would approve <u>projects</u> within an approved programme. The Indicative Planning Figure (IPF) was necessary in order to give each country a guide for planning purposes. UNDP would prepare its five-year budget, indicating the scale of support it would need (from donor governments), and allocate a sum for IPFs. Countries could then plan in the expectation of getting the same share of that amount as before. IPFs were not commitments, they covered the whole period of the programme, and they would be rolled over annually – that was essential, since the total of IPFs in any one year would depend on the funds available to UNDP in that year. Only when a project was approved and an executing agent appointed would funds be allocated.

The report also embraced the whole range of issues affecting development co-operation and made many other recommendations, including splitting up the bureau of operations into four regional bureaux, providing an up-to-date information system, appointing a Director-General for Development and establishing a staff college. The central recommendations, and by far the most important, were country programming and rolling IPFs. They were what the capacity study was really about.

The concept was simple enough but it turned the system over on its head, and the complex practical arrangements for operating it were spelt out in detail.

Despite the governing council's instruction that the study should be shown to no-one before the official presentation, out of respect for Hoffman Jackson gave him a copy on Friday 21 November, three days before the presentation. He and Anstee took the opportunity to explain to him once again the general thrust of the report and to stress that it was meant to support his efforts. Hoffman accepted their assurances and received the report very affably.

By the following Monday when the presentation took place his manner had changed dramatically. He was very angry.

What had happened during that week-end – who or what had turned him against the report – we cannot be sure. Jackson and Anstee thought Narasimhan was responsible. My own belief is that IPFs had a lot to do with it and that Cohen and Henry were involved. If they had not already made their views on IPFs clear to Hoffman they certainly would now. The funding of good projects which would lead to increased capital investment was the *raison d'être* of Hoffman's special fund. If he thought that IPFs would undermine that process he would not be happy. This view was confirmed by Narasimhan, though it has to be said that his recollection 25 years later of the point at issue suggests that he did not fully understand it! 'Hoffman, influenced to a very considerable extent by Cohen and Henry, was totally unsympathetic to the proposal which gives precedence to the country as the decision maker in regard to the resources allocated to it under the indicative planning figure and the country programme'.[22]

Jackson and Anstee were severely shaken, but was Hoffman's reaction so surprising? Expecting a report showing how the system's capacity could be doubled, he had been told that it had reached its limit and could not effectively handle more, and that the project-by-project approach of the special fund was part of the problem; the fears Jackson had expressed in his letter a year ago had been borne out.

If they had not guessed it already Cohen and Henry now knew that Jackson's proposals would bring to an end the work of their little empire, the bureau of

Hoffman puts on a brave face as Jackson presents his report, observed by Agha Shahi and CV Narasimhan, 24 November 1969   UN 111,418 Chen/RE

operations, but was this the only reason for their warnings to Hoffman? They genuinely believed, as he did too, that the special fund was the right way to go about things, that excellent projects were what mattered most, and that IPFs would remove the motivation for excellence. They could hardly be expected not to say so. Only people convinced that Jackson was right could have persuaded Hoffman to see it his way. Perhaps the outcome was inevitable. Jackson once said that Hoffman's remarks to him about the study were expressed in viler language than anything he had ever experienced.[23]

But if the old guard were offended, the young turks at HQ and the resreps in the field, who knew far more about what worked well on the ground than any of them, were delighted by Jackson's outspoken comments and bold remedies.

Hoffman knew, of course, that it would be for the governing council to decide the outcome, and two weeks later he sent Jackson a civil and rather sad letter:

> Dear Jacko, As you and I anticipated, the press's reaction to the capacity study has stressed the criticisms of the system and the need for revolutionary restructuring of UN activities in the economic and social field. There has been almost no mention of any progress that may have been made.
>
> Despite the bleak image the press has presented of the UN development system, I continue to believe that the capacity study can help to produce a strengthened UN system. It depends on how successful we are in persuading governments that enough has been accomplished to date by the system to justify our hopes for its future.
>
> May I repeat that I both recognise and fully appreciate the hard and conscientious work and thought which you gave to the capacity study. We are all looking forward to further discussion with you in mid-January. In the meantime I hope you will find time to take the holiday which you have so well earned.
>
> With all good wishes, sincerely, Paul.[24]

But a week later, presumably prompted by Narasimhan, he gave a hint of what was to come:

> The proposals ... must of course be considered with due regard to proposals in other studies which are being made, notably those of Pearson and [others]. We are very busy at the present time in just such an undertaking.

What I hope will come out of this is a programme for tentative discussion with the agency heads being scheduled for early February, and following this, recommendations for the governing council meeting scheduled for March 16, on steps which can be taken immediately to strengthen the system and others which may follow. It is going to take very careful handling, but I continue hopeful that during 1970 we can take a long step forward in strengthening the UN system.

With all good wishes for the New Year, sincerely yours, Paul.

The New Year was unlikely to be a happy one for either of them. The lines of battle were becoming clear.

13 The Consensus

UNDP'S GOVERNING COUNCIL comprised 37 member-nations, just under half of which were potential donors, the rest recipients. Its session in January confined itself to the exchange of preliminary impressions: the USA and UK were strong supporters of the study; the majority of developing countries were in favour of country programming and IPFs; a few thought the study did less than justice to what UNDP and the agencies had achieved. At the council's request Jackson attended all sessions 'to provide assistance and advice'[1], with Anstee, released from Morocco, sitting behind him producing arguments and references for him to use in replying to questions and correcting misunderstandings. The five days proposed for the special session in March were increased to nine. Members would then have three more documents to consider: the comments of the IACB (the agencies), those of the panel of consultants and a basic action programme proposed by the administration.

The IACB held a three-day session in February; their comments were not entirely unhelpful: the agencies found the issues so far-reaching and complex as to require further study and even reference to their own governing bodies. In their view the strength of the system was the outcome of continuing dialogue within the international community; concrete and lasting results could only emerge from the Capacity Study if its principal recommendations were subjected to the same process of adjustment of different views. That said, they were in principle in favour of country programming and welcomed a stronger role for resreps. They acknowledged the need for improvements in procedures, management and performance, and would use the study as a stimulant to drawing up their own recommendations in the light of the administrator's report and the deliberations of the forthcoming special session.[2]

That the panel of consultants welcomed the study unreservedly was hardly surprising.[3]

The administrator's report – A basic action programme for UNDP[4] – was another matter. It was what he thought the governing council would expect: a statement of his conclusions and recommendations about the future of the programme after a careful review of <u>all</u> the elements of advice and experience available to him. He saw the Capacity Study as one such element, and an extremely important one.

He had also to take into account the reactions of his senior officials (Narasimhan, Cohen and Henry), the IACB and the resreps; he had to view his responsibilities in the wider perspective of the whole UN family and the even wider one of world development outside the UN framework. He set out the changes which he believed should be brought about and the evolutionary means by which he believed the whole UN family would want to see them made (as if evolution was not what had brought the system to its present pass).

His proposed action to strengthen and expand the programme was based on general principles: increased resources (which surely begged the question), greater flexibility in using them, greater operational efficiency, and better coordination with all other inputs from the UN system. Measures already taken should be vigorously pursued, and further innovations required in terms of procedures, administrative practices, managerial techniques and organisational changes should be progressively introduced (all of which boiled down to 'we must try and do better').

He accepted the principle of country programming, but the programme would be presented to the council merely for information and projects would still require its approval. (This struck at the root of Jackson's proposals – that the council should approve programmes not projects.)

The special session of the council was to take place in New York between Monday 16 and Thursday 26 March, to consider those three papers and the Capacity Study itself. In the meantime senior staff of UNDP had not been lax in lobbying some key delegates. The first six meetings (occupying three days) were devoted to yet more general discussion. The first – not a very long one – was virtually monopolised by the delegate from Chile. Back in 1949 he had chaired the sixteen meetings of the committee of the General Assembly which had approved EPTA; he had barely a good word to say for the study. He had his own reasons for not antagonising Cohen and Henry and said he did not think that the council's role should be confined to policy making to the exclusion of participation in project approval.

Romania was in favour of joint programming; Cuba believed that only through revolutionary changes could under-development be eradicated, but in the meantime liked the idea of country programming. Italy thought the IACB was dragging its feet – 'resentment was altogether out of place'. It favoured country programming, but like Chile, thought the council should approve projects. The Congo welcomed the stronger role for resreps and favoured the country approach. Switzerland said that the contents of the Study, like those of Pandora's box, were surprising and perhaps alarming, but at the bottom of Pandora's box there had also been hope.

And so it went on; by the end of the third day 33 members had had their say. It was agreed that the rest of the session (six working days) should be devoted to detailed discussion of two topics: country programming and its implementation; not, one would think, an over-ambitious target.

The following morning Hoffman said that he was convinced of the value of the country programming system, and was prepared to follow the guidelines which the council gave him. Sweden commented that the general debate had shown that the council unanimously recognised the value of the country approach, but was divided as to whether it should approve programmes rather than individual projects.

Replying to the comments Jackson said he welcomed the general endorsement of the proposed development cooperation cycle; the five-year cycle was not proposed for every country, the period should relate to the national plan cycle; projects would be secondary to the objectives of the national plan; he emphasised the importance of project formulation as the second phase of the cycle, to ensure that before projects were approved they were thoroughly vetted on technical, financial, economic and social grounds and conformed to the country programme already approved by the council. From this followed the proposal that the council should approve country programmes and delegate authority for approving projects to the administrator. This was not intended to curtail the council's powers but to enhance its authority by widening its perspective and responsibilities. It would speed up the system.

Meanwhile at headquarters Alexander Rotival was beavering away appraising projects. He worked for Paul-Marc Henry, advising him on which ones to approve and why. Henry had a photographic memory so Rotival needed to have a thorough knowledge of all the projects in the pipeline. The walls of his tiny office were covered with files and more were lined up on the front of his desk 'keeping all intruders at bay like a kind of Great Wall of China. One particularly bad day I heard a voice in the doorway: 'Sandy, you are the reason why we are undertaking the Capacity Study!' It is superfluous to identify the author of that remark. I was privileged to be a close, albeit somewhat traumatised, witness to those days. We were fortunate to work in close relationships with strong and highly dedicated personalities, who, while not opinionated, had well-defined views, principles and positions. Jacko was one of those.'[5]

The last two days of the session were spent in trying to establish a consensus. On the Wednesday morning the council's president produced a working paper on country programming. After a whole day spent redrafting the first four paragraphs a drafting group was set up to finish the job.

The final outcome of nine days work by the council (recounted in over 300 pages of summary records[6]) was a progress report containing a draft consensus of views on country programming (three and a half pages) of which only the first four paragraphs had been formally agreed by the council, and a working paper on implementation (three pages) prepared by the president which the council had not even considered.[7]

This draft consensus[8] followed fairly closely the recommendations in the Capacity Study, and thus represented a major step forward, at least by the drafting group, if not the full council; it would be for the council to consider at its regular session in June; Jackson knew that the fight was not yet over.

> Dear Bill, I remain immersed in this battle about the future of the UN Development System. We have just finished two weeks of intensive meetings in New York where the majority of governments came out solidly behind our recommendations, with the natural result that the system has reacted just as strongly, if not more so. This business has been (and remains) pretty good hell for me. One's personal reputation, motives, everything, is ripped to pieces; no holds barred. Homosexuality is the only thing (so far) of which I haven't been accused.'[9]

By mid-April he was back in Geneva, unsure of his future and dissatisfied with much of his past. He wrote to Joan: 'In retrospect so much of my life has been wasted; I don't think I've really lived except Malta, MESC, UNRRA and above all, you.'[10] He had just left Jersey for the last time after nearly eight years, largely wasted except for what they had done for Robin. He was remembering Trélex where he had known deeper happiness than ever before, and she was far away in Morocco; 'Capacity' had brought them together and given him the happiest period of his life, but they both had to pay for it. Now, without any real work and with little prospect of any, he was trying to discipline himself and not retreat into his old shell. The news that Barbara had a recurrence of breast cancer did not help.

His skin was playing up, and with a nasty rash on his neck and jaw he spent three days at the beginning of May in Moscow. It was very hot, he hadn't got the right ointment and he couldn't sleep. He never had a moment to himself; when not at meetings he was taken sightseeing, and in the evenings it was the Bolshoi ballet. Back again in Geneva he was plunged into even deeper despair when he saw the Administrator's report – Strengthening the Capacity of UNDP.[11]

The draft consensus had contained no input from the administration and this new report was the Administrator's attempt to hold back the tide. It set out his proposals for action and claimed to take full account of the discussions so far held: 'he had borne in mind, however, that the draft consensus on programming did not necessarily constitute the final conclusions of the council, and had therefore felt it appropriate to regard the draft conclusions as a set of general and flexible guidelines.' Now the gloves were off.

Jackson was getting worried that council members, the USA in particular, would not have the guts to stand up to the administration. Then he heard by a roundabout route that Hoffman had been told by the US delegate that his report was unacceptable, and that unless he changed his policy 'he would be challenged at the next council meeting, when fireworks could be expected'.[12] This was indeed the case: the US representative on ECOSOC, Ambassador Glenn Olds, had told Narasimhan privately 'that he would have no choice but to propose that Paul Hoffman be asked to resign in order that the proposal might go forward under a more sympathetic Head' – a view which Narasimhan communicated to Hoffman with some difficulty.[13]

As for the fireworks, Jackson later described the council meetings as horrible – 'that's the only word – with Mr Hoffman sitting on a platform in the WHO conference room in Geneva with Mr Narasimhan, Mr Cohen and Mr Paul-Marc Henry; on every single issue the Secretariat of UNDP tragically was in opposition and on every issue they were voted down by governments and people later on said "well done, you've had a triumph".'[14] Cohen found the meetings the most painful he had ever attended. He thought it improper that a member of Jackson's staff should lobby delegations on points being discussed, but admitted that it was sanctioned by the council.[15]

The dead-pan summary records[16] do not describe the proceedings in quite those terms, but make it very clear that the draft consensus undoubtedly represented the views of the governing council, and that the corresponding part of the Administrator's Report did not.

The argument as to whether the council should approve programmes or projects continued. The draft consensus specified programmes, which UNDP continued to resist. The administrator's report said the programme should be for information only; projects would continue to be approved by the council, though in the case of those costing not more than $300,000 the council could authorise the administrator to approve them.

For once Jackson suggested a compromise: the administrator should approve projects up to a certain limit; in the case of larger projects council members would be given details with a deadline for raising objections.[17]

The council finally settled for a different compromise: the council would approve <u>programmes</u>; it alone would have the power to approve projects but would delegate that authority to the Administrator for three years. No cost limit was proposed but the council reserved the right to call in any project of whatever size. (This arrangement was renewed by the council every three years.)

The session was extended for a few more days to enable the council to finalise the consensus and agree a resolution for submission to ECOSOC and the General Assembly. They worked into the evenings and on the Saturday, finishing on Tuesday afternoon, 30 June, when the text of the Consensus and its accompanying resolution for ECOSOC were formally adopted.

Jackson had to leave for Accra before the end, so Anstee thanked the council on his behalf for its kind words; she said that naturally his team had never expected all of its conclusions to receive unqualified acceptance. She refrained from repeating what the delegate from Jordan had just said – that he had not thought to see the study mauled as it had been.[18]

The consensus incorporated many of the recommendations of the Study and to that extent represented a triumph for Jackson, but in several respects it failed to match up to his and Anstee's vision of a revitalised system. In their view its most serious shortcoming concerned the way in which IPFs were to be handled. The intention had been that both the IPF and the programme should reflect the timing and duration of a country's national development plan and that IPFs should be determined on a rolling basis. The Consensus did not provide for this, consequently an important element of flexibility in the original proposals was lost and the council, faced with an enormous peak load of work in year five, was unable to give each programme the attention it merited.

In July the Consensus was endorsed by ECOSOC after an anxious moment caused by Ghana: 'Eight out of ten members went out of their way to express personal appreciation and Marc (Nerfin) and I wished you had been there to share in it. Several called the Study 'monumental' – 'memorable' – 'a lasting landmark' – 'a sweeping and thought-provoking report which shows the way to the future'. Many people came after Marc and me and said we must be very satisfied – things have turned out much, much better than we could have anticipated. At the very end Ghana tried to block the governing council's draft resolution, so that ECOSOC would merely 'note it', not endorse it. Fortunately India, Italy, and the USSR took over and that was that. And so on to the General Assembly. Officially, Kate, we've done far more than we could ever have hoped. It is obvious that things now can never be the same for UN – we HAVE created the 'Wind of Change' and the future could be very much better for UN and the Third World.'[19]

Maurice Strong (President of the Canadian International Development Agency) wrote:

Despite all of the difficulties and the intransigence of the management, I think in perspective you must agree that the [ECOSOC] meeting represented a real triumph for you and the Capacity Study. It is a great shame that Paul and his colleagues could not have risen above their emotional prejudices and resentments. In the final analysis they have had to accept, however grudgingly, the verdict of the council although no one really expects that there will be many fundamental changes until the basic problem of management is resolved. The entire system owes you a great debt of gratitude which I hope they will find some more tangible form of demonstrating before long.[20]

The Consensus was approved by the General Assembly on 11 December and came into operation on 1 January 1971. UNDP duly set up the four Regional Bureaux, but by making political appointments for the Regional Directors failed to bring into being the integrated organisation which Jackson had intended. The proposal for a staff college got as far as the General Assembly where it was defeated by two votes.

One of the last acts resulting from the study was the appointment in 1977 of a Director-General for Development and International Cooperation, intended to strengthen the coordination of the operational activities of the UN system from the centre.[21] It had little practical effect on the agencies, partly because the post was not given the status envisaged, and partly because they were still reluctant to accept the authority of resident coordinators, as they were then called.[22] The post was abolished in 1992.

One more character in the drama remains to be mentioned – Thomas – the cat who arrived unannounced at the house in Trélex and settled down happily amongst the papers. He did his best to prevent the report from being written by firmly sitting on it. Jackson hoped it was not a precedent for governments.[23]

Thomas sitting on the Capacity Study.

In some ways it was. Certain donor governments which had supported the principle that UNDP should be the sole medium for technical assistance and pre-investment later went their own way, independently funding programmes put forward by the agencies, thereby kicking the ground from under the feet of both UNDP (as sole provider with the power of the purse) and of developing nations, whose own priorities ceased to be the paramount consideration. Also, as Jackson had feared, the World Bank increasingly took over UNDP's role of funding pre-investment and, even worse, technical assistance.

In 1975, at the end of the first five-year cycle, UNDP ran into severe financial difficulties which nearly caused its collapse. Its failure to adopt rolling IPFs resulted in all pending financial commitments coming home to roost simultaneously. The then administrator, Bradford Morse, set up a special unit to sort the matter out, headed – of course – by Anstee!

The Capacity Study, usually referred to as 'the Jackson report' is still seen as a seminal work. It has been the starting point for all subsequent attempts to reform the system, none of which have succeeded in fully resolving its basic flaws. Its analysis of the problem remains valid, even if its proposals did not quite succeed in bringing off 'the most constructive job in the history of the world'.

The problem remains: governments keep clamouring for overall reform to the system and undermine any proposals as soon as their own interests are affected. *Plus ça change* ....

The Fountain

14 The Fountain

ONCE THE CONSENSUS WAS APPROVED by ECOSOC Jacko was at a loose end. The next 18 months would bring little comfort, except during the brief times when he and Joan could be together, and even those were overshadowed by the uncertainties ahead. They wrote long letters to each other every day.

From his office in the *Palais des Nations* and from his room in the Richemond Hotel he could see the fountain – that water-spout 140 metres high which never stops. For him it was a symbol of time running out; wherever he was in the world he was conscious of it – it became an obsession.

He was worrying about what changes would be made at the top of UNDP, how long Hoffman and Co would last and the difficulty of finding people of calibre to succeed them. He expected Hoffman to stay until the end of 1971; the Secretary-General, U Thant, wanted no change during his final year.[1] Paul-Marc Henry soon left; Myer Cohen stayed.

In July he set off for his usual ports of call: Monrovia and Accra, London and Sussex; he spent a week with Joan in Taormina, and after a two year absence returned to the Mekong. In October he and Joan looked at a house in Tangiers which he thought of renting as a base where he could write, within easy reach of Rabat; after months of dithering he decided not to take it. They made a brief visit to Provence before he went back to New York, San Francisco and finally London, where he had a prostate operation in December. On New Year's Eve he returned to Geneva; it was bitterly cold, he was still sore, the whole place was shut down for the week-end and all his warm clothes were in his office. 'First and foremost, I miss you. I hate these separations, and I hate the bloody fountain. You questioned me last week whether I still loved you. This morning I discovered that one Post Office would be open from 1600 to 1900. I stood in a queue for just on 40 minutes to Air Express the letter to you – so I hope that the question is answered!![2]

He was packing up some of their personal possessions 'in case anything happened to him'. (He had a slight irregularity in his heart-beat which might one day require a tricky operation, possibly fatal. This was one more of his constant worries.) Barbara had now bought The Pound House at Lodsworth in Sussex, where he found Anna in a fury. 'B has not paid any of the money she owes to Anna (nor to me, for that matter, but let that pass) and yet, again just before she left, went out and paid £325 for colour TV. It's all beyond me.'³

Back in his office he found over 40 letters to sign and another 20 to answer; the fact that his contract as senior consultant to Hoffman had another year to run was little consolation.

> 13 January: Took Marc and Strong to lunch. Latter talked freely. He lunched with PGH [Hoffman] two or three weeks ago and told him that his successor was now an open question. PGH furious – no intention of leaving – the one year's extension was simply to synchronise with U Thant's term of office. 'I'll see the President to get this clear'. Asked for an appointment in the White House. Rebuffed. Guess his reaction? I am responsible for the White House doors being closed. Cohen admitted to Strong last week – 'Jacko was right – money is not the problem, it is the question of getting properly qualified people'. Marc said later that Strong had talked very freely to him in Paris about UNDP, and he [Marc] had found himself in a meeting about the present governing council in the Canadian Embassy in Paris, where the language was much stronger than Strong had used to me at lunch – a really unpleasant anti-Hoffman attitude now exists and one reason for it is his unrelenting attitude towards me, and his invariable attitude of blaming me for all that has gone wrong.⁴

At the end of the month he went to Bangkok for a meeting of the Interim Mekong Committee (Vietnam was not participating at this time). It had recently produced an Indicative Basin Plan providing a framework for development over the next three decades, which included four main-stream projects. The social problems of resettlement which he had pointed out in 1962 were still insufficiently recognised and the committee seemed not be facing financial realities.

> 31 January: I worry about the Mekong: it has been oversold by UN/UNDP; I disagree with General Black (he's on the Advisory Board) that the right project will always attract capital. Even by today's prices one can see $5-8

billion of investment and I do not believe that any source in the world would put up that kind of money for this kind of project today. Yet they go on with their publicity, their drum-banging and so on. By all means <u>survey</u> the whole river most carefully — define the best tributary projects but go easy on the main stem giants. Who will play the unpopular role of pointing out that the Emperor has no clothes? You've guessed, but I'll have to proceed carefully for obvious reasons.

I have tried to earn my keep — I've talked to all the key people — in one sense they are like sheep — they all agree once you give them a line of action. The Mekong, I'll bet, will never come to life solely underwritten by western capital. If it is ever developed, Japanese, Russian and Chinese investment will be involved — 10 to 50 years from now. That fact of life is of immediate significance to the role of the IBRD [the World Bank] — the same old story — refusal to cooperate — only willing to proceed their way and by themselves. What a tragedy that the immediate situation depends on McNamara [President of the World Bank and no friend of Jackson's], Hoffman et al. I've deliberately reminded people of the Bank's record of political ineptitude — Aswan High Dam, TanZam railway, loans to Greek Colonels (have they forgotten the democratic elements in gaol for 18 years?). I'll fight this one — either in September or January. Better to blow it all up and start again, than have the Bank prejudicing the political freedom of these small countries.[5]

1 February: 'Mekong Committee meeting is finished. I've achieved my main purpose — talking. Hanoi would participate after a real armistice is signed. Peking is also interested. All I want to see is that nothing is done now which may complicate possible sources of investment later. Which brings us back to the Bank. All signs indicate the usual 'going it alone' which is the reverse of co-operation. If they would only accept the political principle that independence means just that. And they fail to realise that 'agreements' virtually imposed by them on a government in 1971 on a 'take it or leave it' basis are bound to be thrown out sooner or later by a more nationalistic/revolutionary government. I keep at it — but I get bored. None of this would arise if Hoffman and McNamara were doing their jobs properly. Now, to all intents and purposes, I hole up here [in Bangkok] largely by myself for ten days. How the fountain must laugh. I can't think of one useful thing I've done since the Capacity Study was published.'[6]

He went on to Delhi for the third global meeting of resreps, the first since the Consensus had been adopted. His presence on this occasion, as well as Anstee's, was particularly important, for its purpose was for UNDP headquarters staff to explain to resreps how to implement it. In doing so they attacked the Capacity Study, much to the anger of the resreps who had welcomed it. It was a bizarre situation with the top brass doing their best to undermine it and the resreps constantly consulting Jackson, to whom nearly all were fiercely loyal.

After listening for a week they set up a small committee to prepare a paper setting out their own views to be given during the second week. Written contributions, to be treated in strict confidence, were slipped under the bedroom door of their secretary, Garth Ap Rees (the resrep in Botswana). The senior management got wind of this and on the Sunday morning Vaidyanathan, UNDP's Director of Administration (who had no experience in the field) appeared with a two page document for inclusion in the resreps' paper, explaining how he and HQ had devoted themselves to understanding how things worked in the field. Ap Rees pointed out that he was writing a paper on behalf of the resreps, not the management, and the following morning the committee decided to tear up Vaid's two pages. As soon as the resreps' paper was distributed Ap Rees was confronted in the bar by John McDiarmid, the resrep for India, who ripped off the front page and insisted that the paper be withdrawn; (he had his own reasons for not offending his New York bosses). 'Garth, you did a great job, but we don't want to push all that stuff about the Capacity Study down Hoffman's throat.' An anodyne paper was substituted, but when it was discussed Curtis Campaigne (the resrep for Liberia) bravely said all the things that had been on that front page. Other senior resreps, including the Canadian William Harding (Philippines) and American David Blickenstaff (Tunisia) staunchly defended the study. Hoffman, who was now showing his age, made no comment and Vaidyanathan responded by saying his piece in defence of HQ. The exercise was not a total waste of time, for a two-man commission was set up at HQ to take on board the concerns of the resreps, but it would be nine years before the next global meeting![7]

The likelihood that Joan's next posting would be to Chile added to Jacko's unhappiness; he knew it would be important for her, but hard for him.

In Monrovia he found his relationship with President Tubman as good as ever – their mutual trust had grown into personal friendship. In Ghana things were not so good, thanks, it seemed, to the Capacity Study: it was alleged that he was insisting that all country programmes were submitted to him personally, and that when asked in Delhi to help Ghana with its debt problem with the IMF he had refused. 'Laugh that off. Naturally I'm sad – 18 years with the Volta. I will almost certainly not be on the new Board and just as likely my last link as Consultant to the Authority will also be broken. So I'll be left with Liberia; at least I'm sure of my friend there. Well, I came here in February '53 feeling that Bridges and HMG had completed their final double-cross. Perhaps it's appropriate that I should go out on another.'[8]

> 26 March: Marc isn't impressed with UNDP's document on programming. UNDP seems to be out to kill the concept of a cycle. Hell! How one could rip to pieces their futile, senile actions in blocking action, maintaining business as usual and failing totally to comprehend what the CS said.
>
> 29 March: Jan Huyser [a friend in FAO who admired the Capacity Study] told me FAO would like me to get into the guts of the Aswan High Dam next month, but daren't say so, for the Bank want 'Jackson kept out at all costs'!!! On the whole I can take that as a compliment.[9]

Nevertheless as senior consultant to Hoffman he visited the dam at the end of April, spending six days in Egypt, meeting ministers and assessing progress on regional planning in connection with Lake Nasser, the new lake which would flood a 250 mile stretch of the Nile valley following the construction of the dam. UNDP and FAO were involved and he was not impressed. He was shocked to find what meagre resources each was devoting to this enormous project.

> At the end of the first day's meeting one of the FAO staff said 'But Jacko, now I realise what you were getting at in Rome [FAO's headquarters]. This is UN's chance of a lifetime!' Dear God! One of over 400 projects for FAO, one of over 1500 for UNDP. All the talent in the system could be directed to this one project and it wouldn't be too much.[10]

Despite the long uncomfortable train journeys between Cairo and Aswan he enjoyed being in the Middle East again; it was still as beautiful as ever.

> As always, my thoughts remain concentrated on you – always wanting to

> share beauty when I find it, and work when it's interesting. All my love goes with this from a slightly battered but completely devoted J.[11]

After a week with Joan in Morocco he went back to Accra and thence to Monrovia, for what turned out to be his last meeting with President Tubman.

In July he saw Robin at The Pound House and bowled to give him some batting practice, but stayed at a nearby hotel. They met Sheila and her husband, who lived nearby; she was now on good terms with Barbara and had become an honorary aunt to Robin. Anna was very stressed; no longer required to look after him she was expected to satisfy Barbara's demands to get the house into order before her return from America, making and hanging curtains and such-like. She made excessive demands on herself: gardening was one thing; making large quantities of strawberry jam was another.

> 11 July: When I look at Anna and Robin I realise what a mess has been created – to you and you only I would say – primarily as a result of a brilliant and talented woman's stupidity and utter selfishness. I now know that Robin is expected to join his godmother on the afternoon of Wednesday 21st and then join B immediately on her return to England, after which they will go together to Glyndebourne. One day less [for me]. Why should I care? To this day B, for all her protestations of being a dying woman, adheres to smash-and-grab – her own description.[12]

He wanted to start legal proceedings for a separation, but her illness ruled this out. Soon he would see Bodley-Scott (her doctor as well as his, and a personal friend of both), whose prognosis would be crucial. For the present all he could do was to establish his own position by never staying at The Pound House.

When he tried to contact Tubman in London he was shocked to learn that he was in the London Clinic, so ill that only his wife was allowed to see him. Jackson was allowed a brief visit a few days later and found him very frail; he died the next day.

> It is very nearly impossible for me to write. Instinctively I had the feeling when I parted from him last night that I might not see him again. Increasingly I had come to realise that I loved him – I venture to think that the feeling was reciprocated. <u>Complete</u> trust between two human beings – I have lost something that cannot be replaced. I must think. Do I want to go on trying

to help Liberia? Does Liberia want me to? Apart from you, my darling, I have an idea that I have lost my best friend in this world.[13]

Tubman's successor, President Tolbert, assured him that Liberia still wanted his help. The Volta River Authority did not; they thanked him for his services on the Board, which would no longer be required.

Bodley-Scott advised him that no further legal moves should be taken for the time being. 'Barbara is not well and is writing her book against a deadline; to move now would alienate every friend you have and my guess is, knowing Barbara, that she would endeavour to alienate Robin's feelings for you'.[14]

> 3 September: My constant reflection is that I've sent you bad news and that we are separated and cannot console each other with the 'touch of the hand'. It will be much better on Monday week – sharing is the key, whether it's good news or bad news, beauty or trouble.[15]

In what was possibly an inspired leak, on 31 August the UN revealed the name of Hoffman's intended successor. Rudolph Peterson, retired President of the Bank of America, was said to be President Nixon's choice. The Secretary-General had yet to consult the governing council before a formal appointment could be made, but the leak obliged Hoffman to retire from UNDP against his will.[16] A few days later Hoffman told Jackson to his face that he held him personally responsible for all his difficulties during the last 22 months and, consequently, for his enforced retirement. Jackson's contract, due for renewal at the end of the year, would be terminated, and there would be no possibility of that decision being changed by his successor.[17]

> 25 October, London: 'I wish there was not fourteen and a half years difference in our ages, but I rejoice in the companionship and beauty that we've shared; I rejoice in the love that you've given me. Despite all the adversities the last four years have been the richest in my personal life.'
>
> 14 November, Geneva: 'I'm confused about myself. I <u>talk</u> and <u>write</u> about what should be done about the Third World and development but I have not <u>acted</u> since the CS was published. Officially it has been a lousy year for me – pathetic response to CS – thrown out of VRA and now out of UNDP; Tubman's death hit me; B's health and my inability to move legally;

the surgery has hurt me physically and psychologically. The Fountain must have broken ribs from laughing!'

In Monrovia in addition to the usual meetings there was a lunch with President Tolbert and a reception with Mrs Tubman, so he had to sit up half the night reading long reports. The President agreed with him about what needed to be done.

> 19 November: I'm reasonably confident I can make the diagnosis and write the prescription (shades of CS) but very worried about the patient. He's in for a rough year or two, I'm afraid, and will need all the capable disinterested help he can get. Tolbert knows he needs it and welcomes it. If today's meeting goes reasonably well with the President I reckon that I'll have three to four very intensive days' work – then FREEDOM – and on my way to you.

Ten days later he was in Morocco, sitting by the fire writing his usual note of love, gratitude and farewell to Joan, with Toujours, the cat, curled up beside him.

> As the Fountain continues to smile to himself I do not find the partings any easier. I know that you realise this as well as I do and we do not need to traverse that ground again. Some things are easy to say – my love and gratitude for your own love and companionship, for the sense of 'oneness' and belonging to each other, for the 'touch of the hand'. These represent forms of beauty and joy, beyond the reach of the fountain.[18]
>
> 4 December, Geneva: As I walked back to the hotel I was suddenly aware – as never before – of the complete futility of this kind of existence. Day after day I'm wasting what remains of my life. Waiting – waiting for Bodley-Scott or Barbara / for U Thant / for doctors / for you – to decide where your future lies. It would be better for me not to be alive than going around like a gramophone record caught in a groove. I <u>must</u> break out or quit; to stick in a hotel room – to fiddle with third rate papers, and then to eat like one of those battery hens – no, no, no, this is the way to madness. … Even if one does the wrong thing, better to have <u>lived</u> than played safe and done damn all. Don't let's kid ourselves that it <u>all</u> arises out of B's health. We're at a crossroads, and I must not influence your objective decisions.
>
> But at some point the calculating – on both our sides – has to stop. The die – for both of us – may well be cast this month.

At the end of the year they spent a few days together at PIPPINS, Joan's house in Somerset, before going their separate ways, she back to Morocco, he to New York, Bangkok and Monrovia. He spent most of February on his travels: he saw Relda in Christchurch and his family in Melbourne; he looked over the Snowy Mountain Scheme and returned to London via Bangkok. Joan had been due to go to Chile in February, but her father's recent death and her mother's illness kept her in England until April. Jacko was at PIPPINS when Roberto Guyer, the Under Secretary-General for Special Political Affairs, phoned on 16 March asking him to see the Secretary-General – Kurt Waldheim – as soon as possible, with a view to taking over responsibility for UNROD, the UN relief operation in Dacca in East Pakistan.

The prospect of work of real substance and importance revived his spirits greatly. Perhaps it was as well that he had no idea of the size of the load he was taking on.

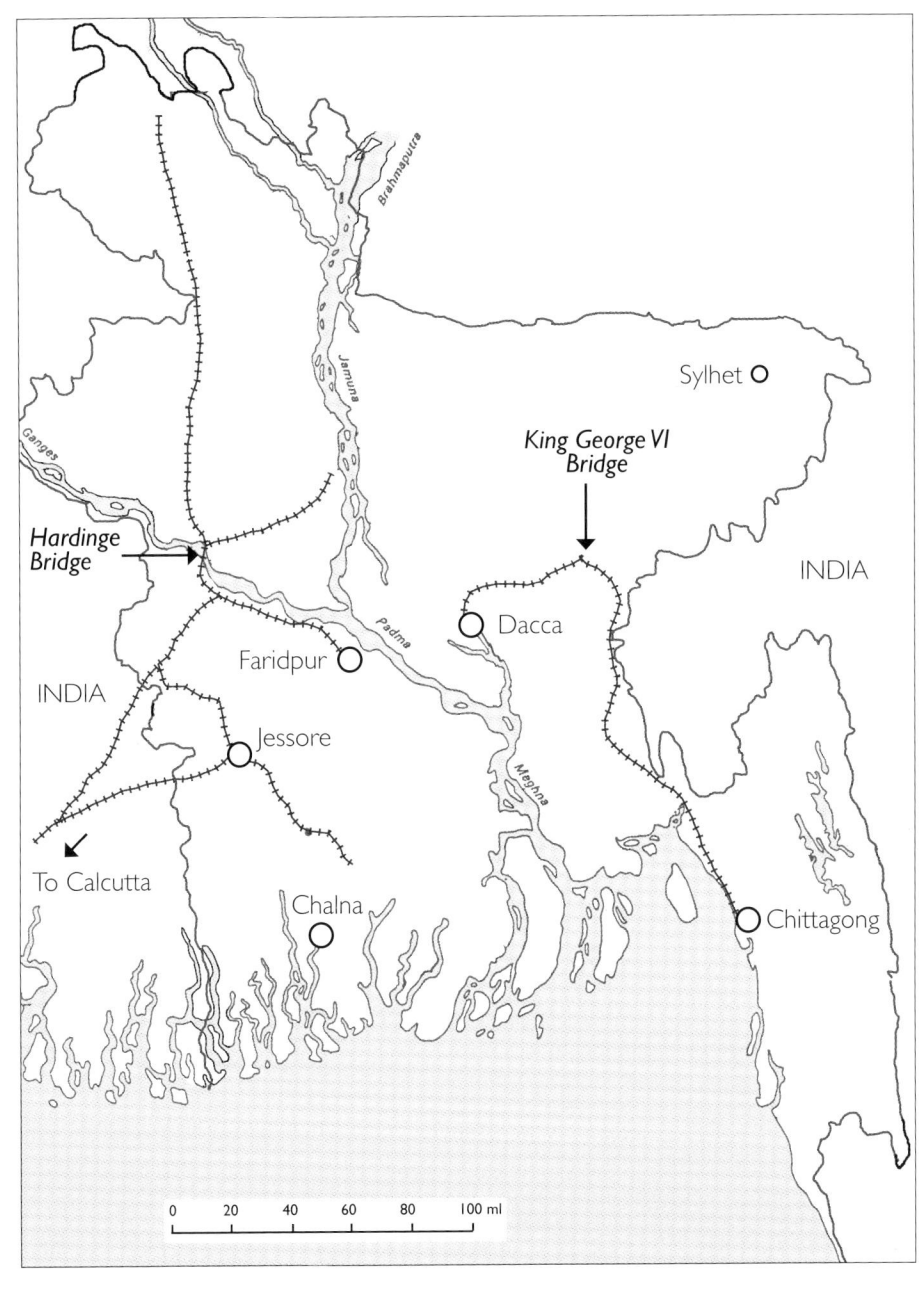

Bangladesh: Main Railway Supply Routes

Part Four – The Greatest of Operators

15 Bangladesh

TWENTY-SIX YEARS HAD PASSED since Jackson had been asked to take charge of UNRRA – to save a sinking ship. Once again he would be taking over a relief operation which, if not on the point of collapse, was certainly not doing too well; once again he would pull the chestnuts out of the fire. The UN relief operation in Dacca (UNROD) would be the largest and most successful since UNRRA and a model of how such things should be done.

East Pakistan, as it then was, had been doubly stricken. It was a mainly rural community, with tiny farms on the great plain of the Ganges delta; its few roads were regularly flooded during the monsoon and most freight was brought by rail to the capital, Dacca, from the main port, Chittagong, and from Calcutta. The smaller port, Chalna, had no rail connection; goods were conveyed inland in the thousands of small boats which also served as homes via the myriad waterways criss-crossing the delta. In October 1970 the worst cyclone in living memory created a tidal wave of destruction in which countless homes were wrecked and much of the agriculture ruined; the numbers of dead were in the hundreds of thousands.[1]

After natural disaster came man-made disaster. Pakistan was a military dictatorship; the Awami League was a political party in East Pakistan led by Sheikh Mujibur Rahman, whose aim was to resist domination by the larger West Pakistan. When national elections were held in December the League swept the board, winning 167 of the 300 seats in the new Assembly. The Pakistan People's Party in the West, led by Zulfikar Ali Bhutto, won only 83. Mujibur now demanded full independence for the East, which Bhutto refused; the result was political deadlock: Two days before the Assembly was due to meet in March President Yahya Khan suspended it, whereupon

Mujibur ordered a boycott and a general strike in the East. After failing to negotiate a compromise Yahya Khan denounced Mujibur as a traitor and sent in government troops. Mujibur and many of his followers were arrested; others escaped to India, having first proclaimed the People's Republic of Bangladesh as an independent state. Civil war began in earnest and refugees streamed across the border to India.

The Secretary-General, U Thant, was much concerned, but could do little about what was seen as an internal dispute. Furthermore the great powers were divided, with the USA and China supporting Pakistan, and Britain and Russia Bangladesh. Nevertheless in August his proposals for a UN relief operation received sufficient support for him to announce the appointment of Paul-Marc Henry as Assistant Secretary-General in charge of the East Pakistan relief operation (UNEPRO).

Henry found the situation in Dacca worse than expected: Chittagong was choked with supplies which could not be moved because so many trucks and boats had been taken to India by their owners, and the railways were frequently cut by rebels. By October there were signs of progress: trucks and 'mini-bulkers' were arriving. These were small versions of ocean-going carriers holding up to 1800 tons of grain, with no keels, ideal for use in shallow waters; they would prove to be the mainstay of the relief operation.

Hostility between Pakistan and India grew as India demanded that Pakistan should release Mujibur and his followers and return them to the East, which Bhutto refused. By the end of November it was clear that the assumption on which UNEPRO was based – that its humanitarian purpose would be recognised by all parties – was no longer valid.

On 3 December India invaded the East, and on 16 December the Pakistani forces surrendered to the joint Bangladeshi and Indian command. Within a week UNROD (the UN Relief Operation in Dacca) was established to carry on from where UNEPRO had left off. Released from prison, Mujibur returned to a hero's welcome on 12 January 1972 and was made Prime Minister.

The destruction wrought by the war had added vastly to the problems facing the new government: agriculture was crippled, irrigation equipment destroyed, few trucks and buses were available, nearly 300 railway bridges (including the Hardinge and the King George VI) were destroyed, the telephone network was useless, inland water-craft were sunk or damaged, channels to the two ports had been mined and blocked with sunken vessels by the Indian Navy and Air Force. As the thousands of refugees began to return from India the risk of mass starvation grew; the relief needs were formidable (for a start, 200,000 tons of food a month). In February the new Secretary-General, Kurt Waldheim, launched an appeal to donors: 'Never in the history of the United Nations' he said, 'has international assistance been needed so urgently and in such great amounts'.[2] While undoubtedly true, this statement made the situation worse by encouraging food hoarding by speculators and increasing prices.

Some progress had been made: mini-bulkers were distributing grain, tugs and barges were arriving, but UNROD was grappling with emergencies as they arose, without any clear plan of action or order of priorities. Food was getting through, but not enough. The approaches to the two harbours needed to be cleared quickly, but the administrative wheels at UN HQ turned so slowly that by the time tenders for the work were opened in New York Mujibur had already accepted an offer from Moscow to clear both.

The Indian Government was well disposed towards the people of East Bengal, and on 19 March the Prime Minister – Mrs Ghandi – and Sheikh Mujibur signed a 25 year defence pact; but neither India nor Pakistan would return any prisoners of war at that stage. Mujibur refused to have any dealings with Bhutto until Pakistan formally recognised Bangladesh.

In March Waldheim sent out a survey team led by Dr Erna Sailer (the Austrian Ambassador to India) to establish Bangladesh's essential needs for the next year. Even before they set out from Dacca Sailer cabled that the situation was clearly very serious; aid to the tune of $100 million, half of it for food, was urgently needed.

The immediate shortage was being met by deliveries from India; army engineers from Britain and India were repairing bridges and reopening culverts to traffic. Given the circumstances and the resources available much had been achieved, but the government's high hopes had not been fulfilled and the impression was growing that UNROD was not doing its job.

Henry was due to return to France to take up another appointment. Brian Urquhart (now an Assistant Secretary-General) had previously tried without success to persuade U Thant to put Jackson in charge of the operation; with

Waldheim he succeeded. 'At long last in Bangladesh we switched from quixotic amateurism to large-scale professionalism.'³

Jackson flew to New York the day after Guyer's call, told Waldheim he would take over the operation, and spent two days at UN headquarters discussing how it could be improved. His first recommendation was that all the organisations and agencies involved should work together and speak with one voice. Ten days later Waldheim personally appealed to his colleagues on the ACC to support the one-voice principle in all their activities in Bangladesh, whether field operations, setting priorities or appealing for funds. They agreed immediately. This was the first time such a procedure was adopted for a UN relief operation and it would prove essential to its ultimate success.

It was clear that a new Chief of Mission to run the operation in Dacca was needed; the current one, Toni Hagen, had made too many public criticisms of UNROD, though some were justified; in any case his secondment from UNDP would end on 31 May. A quick visit to Monrovia gave Jackson time to think, and on his return to Geneva he approached Dr Victor Umbricht. A Swiss of great energy with extensive managerial experience, Umbricht was a member of several UN panels on development and of the International Committee of the Red Cross (ICRC).

Jackson arrived in Dacca on 1 April; met Sheikh Mujibur, members of the government and UNROD staff and gave them what encouragement he could: pledges of assistance already received following the Secretary-General's February appeal had met some of the emergency requirements identified by Sailer, but the urgent need in his view was to improve internal transportation and organise the distribution of supplies; donor governments must not be asked to send more than could be efficiently handled through the ports or within the country. Back in Geneva four days later he heard from Umbricht that he would be willing to assume the appointment of Chief of Mission in Dacca.

Already he was feeling the strain, and worried that he might not last the course. Joan would soon be leaving for Chile so he wrote a note to welcome her on arrival. It wasn't very cheerful: he said he had never been so exhausted and torn to pieces since the worst days of UNRRA – when he was 28 years younger. The situation in Bangladesh was very bad, the job was beyond the government's capability, and what with internal unrest, lack of food and 12 million unemployed, the political outlook was black. He knew what needed to be done but neither the government nor the UN had the capacity to do it. His mind never relaxed, he had had virtually no sleep since Waldheim had summoned him to New York and he felt lousy; but he knew he must give all he had, whatever the cost. If he did pack up she would know that at least he hadn't jibbed and that he loved her always.[4] Before she left they both spent a week-end at Petersham. 'When you read this we shall have started our longest separation – in terms of time and distance. We have had our beautiful walk in Richmond Park and there are good memories of this morning. For these tiny oases I am very grateful.'[5]

Once Umbricht's appointment was approved by the ACC Jackson set off to get Mujibur's agreement. In Calcutta he was told that no UN planes were available, but that the pilot of one of their contractors was flying down to pick him up. There were heavy storms to the north and west. Dacca was 150 miles to the north-east; flight control said they might be able to edge round them.

He never forgot Captain Kit Blewitt and his Piper Cub, BRAVO DELTA:

> At one moment we had long jagged shards of intense gold, at another great chains virtually surrounding us and then the whole sky was suddenly turned into daylight, as it were, by sheets of energy released everywhere. Towering black clouds were on all sides of us – I felt that the Himalayas had come south and were pressing against our tiny craft, which picked its way through the valleys illuminated every minute or two by the sheet lightning. Every now and again we'd be swept several hundred feet at a time up the side of one of those mountainous clouds, the succeeding 'dump' invariably being converted into a long slide thanks to Blewitt's art and anticipation. We had just over one and a half hours of it; that Piper must be indestructible. We landed in a horrible cross wind – yet a perfect landing. As we pulled up his first comment was 'The beer's on you, Sir Robert'. What a boy![6]

After a late night he was at his desk at 5 a.m. and in the UNROD office at 7.45, keeping three secretaries busy. After getting Mujibur's agreement to Umbricht's appointment he made himself known to the US *Chargé d'Affaires* who said he was keen to help, although 'the White House wouldn't be easy'.

Meanwhile Hagen was speaking to the Russian Ambassador, Popov. Their divers working at Chittagong could hardly see in the 'black water' and Popov was worried that they would be unable to clear the ports in time to receive the grain which was on its way. Jackson told the Indians that he hoped that if the harbours choked they would send grain and rice across the border which UNROD would replace via Indian ports.

Pakistan was not helpful.

> Bhutto is Playing Pakistan Politics – that boy is on my list! He's offered Bangladesh 100,000 tons of rice <u>if</u> Mujibur Rahman will say the right words. No cheese. Can UNROD produce a formula? We'll see.
>
> Have the PM and I started to click? 'Tell me what you want done, Sir Robert, and it will be done. Anything you approve, I approve'. So far, so good. Kit Blewitt got me to Calcutta in 75 minutes – rough, but peanuts compared to last night.
>
> As far as I can judge all went well. I left convinced that given the circumstances I was about the only person who could do that job. In short, this journey <u>was</u> necessary. I <u>could</u> feel sad that I've lost over twenty years of 'operational' life that could have possibly helped UN, for it's probably true that this is my metier – Malta / MESC / UNRRA etc. But I'm NOT. I've no quarrel with the way the cards have dropped for me; I'm lucky, damned lucky, to have this chance to sing a swan song – but I wonder if my voice will last!! And how will the song end?[7]

Arriving back in New York late at night he was not cheered to learn that Peter Cargill, the Director of the IBRD office in Dacca, was trying to take over UNROD's work. For some years the World Bank had been financing development projects in East Pakistan. Though it had not so far been concerned with relief Cargill evidently now saw the Bank as having a special status and was trying to muscle in, contradicting an undertaking given to Waldheim by its president, Robert McNamara.

He took a sleeping pill, woke at 5 and worked at the UN from 7.45 a.m. till 9 p.m. Cargill phoned to say he would proceed in a way consistent with McNamara's stated policies; Jackson was not convinced.

> 16 April: 30 minutes on the phone with Mac the Croc [McNamara]. I managed to keep my temper and play it cool. That was 1100 to 1130. At 1200 he was back to me – all sweetness and light – he'd checked the situation and found he was wrong on all four points raised. He did as much

as he could to apologise and had the sense to realise I'd actually defended his personal position when Cargill had been on his take-over bid.

The report of the Sailer mission in mid-April said little that was new, but as an independent and authoritative report it provided a framework for UNROD's work. Jackson was now reasonably sure of sufficient supplies of food arriving to last through May, June and July, but less so about the means for distributing it. Recruiting staff was still proving difficult and he was putting pressure on the US, the Dutch, the British, the Canadians and the Russians; he found some for Umbricht, but none for his own office in New York; he was disgusted at UNDP's refusal to release anyone to help him. His assistant Pierre Sales – 'his right arm' – was very willing but 'not big enough' and finding the pace too tough.

He went to see Robin during his school holiday, but spent so long studying Sailer on the way that by the time he got to Sussex he was feeling pretty low. HMG had promised to provide the twelve sea-trucks he needed, but he was uneasy that it was superficially backing the UN while actually playing the IRBD game.[8] He still had the feeling that the Bank wanted to steal the show.

> 26 April, midnight: The main meeting with Waldheim was successful as far as he and the Croc etc were concerned – unpleasant and revealing in relation to UNDP. Peterson [Hoffman's successor] and Cohen put on a pitiful, self-centered performance. I may have parted brass rags with UNDP – but UNDP is at an all time low with Waldheim and UN etc. Absolute refusal to second personnel. A stinking performance.

> 28 April, midnight: Much resentment against Peterson's and Cohen's crude refusal to help – many sensing a continuation of the vendetta against me. Waldheim not amused – because he sees his reputation is at stake. We'll see. Seven and a half hours of meeting on Sailer, 45 reps from the system, said to have gone well. Sixteen to lunch left me $200 poorer; two thanked me. UNDP's latest – calm announcement they intend to appoint a resrep in Dacca in July. For Heaven's sake – what is Victor thought to represent? Another stupid battle to fight.

Jackson won the battle when the resrep, Marcel d'Astugues, was appointed as Umbricht's deputy.

Jackson likened the operation to a trio of umbrellas: the UN system itself, including the specialised agencies; the voluntary agencies, and governments providing aid on a bi-lateral basis, all of which were cooperating fully. He knew that he must convince donors that their further support was justified and that what they provided would be handled efficiently and reach its destination quickly. Since the sole aim of the programme was to alleviate suffering it would be limited to providing supplies and equipment necessary to preserve life: food, shelter, medicine, and transport; also seeds and fertilizers to produce food later in the year. Measures of reconstruction would be limited to those essential for carrying out the relief operation; some of Sailer's proposals for rehabilitation would have to wait. It was to be 'a sympathetic and hard-headed relief operation with no trimmings'.

Jackson met Umbricht in Delhi to give him a final briefing, but did not accompany him to Dacca, sensing that he wanted to take charge of the UNROD Mission in his own way – as would soon become very clear; he had no idea that Umbricht was armed with a letter from the Secretary-General setting out his responsibilities. When Sales went to Dacca to help him for a few weeks Jackson was assisted by Subhas Dhar, a very capable economist lent by the UN, until he in turn went to help Umbricht and Sales returned.

> Thoughts of his future – and Joan's – were no help.
>> 13 May: If we go on for much longer under present circumstances then I'm virtually sure there'll be nothing left of me, and maybe the same will go for you too. The June/July period [when they would both be on leave] is obviously a Rubicon whether we like it or not. In a few weeks you'll have to choose which of the two cards – Chile or Clot – represents the greater fulfilment in your life. If I get out and you quit UNDP what will you get? A burnt-out man. We will have to make a clear-cut positive or negative decision in June. Time is now closing in on us fast.

On the same day Joan found herself having tea with Barbara in Santiago. Chile was hosting one of the periodic conferences of UNCTAD (the UN conference on trade and development) in which Joan was heavily involved, and Barbara was there to give a lecture sponsored by the Roman Catholic Church. Joan had already been invited by a colleague (unaware of their situation) to meet her at lunch, and had found it convenient to visit a geo-thermal project far off in the Andes. When she returned Barbara was still there, bombarding her office with such insistent requests to meet her for tea at her hotel that she could not refuse. Barbara was affable and charming; they spoke about UNCTAD and Joan's work with Robert on the Capacity Study. Together they rained down curses on Hoffman, and Barbara said she admired Robert's commitment to Bangladesh. She also mentioned that she had a secondary cancer and was used to living 'from six months to six months'. It was all very civilised, but Joan, unsure of how much Barbara knew, assumed she was being given the once-over.[9] Barbara later remarked to Sheila 'if he marries Anstee it will be just like marrying me all over again'.

On 15 May Jackson cabled Umbricht asking if UNROD could last until the Secretary-General launched a new appeal in late August, after the monsoon. If not, how much did he think they should now seek from donor governments, and how could a new short-term appeal be justified? It would be better to avoid any new request just then.

> 19 May: Twelve days to the monsoon. Four Indian ships in Chittagong and ten outside; USSR 110,000 tons carrier inside; US ship 48,000 tons arrived today. The supplies are pressing against the frontiers. It's now a question of pushing them in. Victor seems to be doing very well.
>
> 21 May: Three days bad weather at Chittagong; bad luck. Cargill is still straining against the One Voice concept, mainly I think because he has run India and Pakistan for the Bank unchecked for nearly 20 years. Letters and cables from Victor suggest we're on the same wavelength. I hope that is correct. The CRUNCH is approaching.
>
> 25 May: The bloody monsoon is just about ten days _early_. How unlucky can one be? I fear that I am burnt out or nearly so. I ache and ache all day with tiredness. I don't know where I stand in the future; I don't know how to retreat from B'desh. The whole bloody thing has just been dumped in my lap. Whatever happens, I've loved you steadily for many years now – but I never foresaw a situation like this.

As he was preparing what he expected to be a moderately reassuring report for the Secretary-General to present to donor governments at the end of May Umbricht's reply arrived. Things were far worse than he expected: Bangladesh needed an additional one million tons of grain before the end of November, plus a cash contribution of 20% of its value to meet transport and operational costs, and in addition a further $425 million for priority relief and rehabilitation.[10]

Jackson had to explain to Umbricht just what would be involved in making an urgent appeal for aid on this scale: on 31 May the Secretary-General would, he hoped, preside over a meeting of representatives of all governments willing to help Bangladesh, and issue a clarion call for the extra one million tons of grain plus 20% costs, but given the state of international relations there wasn't a hope in hell of mobilizing overnight an extra $425million; that would require listing each item in detail, justifying it, and proposing likely sources of financing, which would take weeks. Any appeal for new non-food requirements must wait until the effects of the monsoon were known and everyone in Bangladesh had done their homework.[11]

The donors' meeting was less than a week away. How could he get commitments in six days for one million extra tons of grain and shipping? He knew who had the grain, but who would pay for the shipping? As for the politics … !!! He must have broken all UN records for telephoning and cabling all over the world. It was no consolation to be told on the 38th floor [where the Secretary-General and senior staff had their offices] that he had an impossible political and logistical jigsaw, but that none of them could help him; they were in his hands. [12]

> Sunday 28 May: From 0600 to 1245 I have been drafting KW's appeal. It's a political jigsaw and damned delicate. If he has the guts to say what I've written we should stand a good chance of success.

His letter to Anstee gave some idea of what he had written: Mrs Gandhi had said India would never let the people of Bangladesh starve; OK, she was next door. There was 100,000 tons of 'political' rice between Bhutto and Mujibur, if only he could find a way of getting rid of the politics. The tom-tiddlers nearby – Burma / Thailand / Indonesia / Philippines – say 50,000 to 100,000 tons. As for the parsimonious Japs, they were his chief target: 50,000 tons, plus the cost of shipping the rice from the others. He wanted KW to hit them hard. Australia was good for at least 150,000 tons. Canada perhaps 200,000; they were easy on supplies but trying to avoid shipping costs. That left 400,000 tons; the USSR and Argentina had had bad harvests but were worth trying; Uncle Sam could always be relied on; he would leave them till last.

Jackson was working under intense pressure, desperately tired, unhappy and uncertain about his future – and lonely. He had no-one to confide in, and his letters to her were his only means of letting off steam. However luridly he described events to her she knew that in his dealings with the 38th floor he always maintained a calm and dignified demeanour.[13]

> Tuesday 30 May 0230: This is Monday's note. The ordinary people in UN are extraordinarily kind to me – realise something big is afoot – and try to do things to help. The Big Shots – USGs, ASGs, Ambassadors, Diplomatic Bums find it expedient to smother me with praise and do damn all to help.
>
> I was back at UN by 0730. A pile of cables, the key to which is: has KW the guts to make a tough political appeal in which he'd (a) tell specific governments what to do and (b) tell them to keep 'relief' out of 'politics'? I'll know the answer in 48 hours or less. (Politely) ripped the Pakistan Ambassador to shreds; told him to tell Bhutto (who also wants $167.2 million for repairs etc) they were headed for mutual destruction. No discussions. Straight from the shoulder. McDiarmid [resrep for India] sold out to Mrs Gandhi. Told him to go and stand on his head and quoted the lady against her own arguments. I've got them over a barrel, I think. Japanese are mean selfish bastards – but if KW will do it we can put them on a limb. Can the 38th floor compete with this? I wonder.
>
> 30 May: Today has been bloody, bloody, bloody. I was at UN by 0730. The key people on the 38th floor were not present until 0920 (after three days holiday). They received all the documents as soon as they arrived. As I was leaving for a Mekong lunch where I <u>wanted</u> to talk to key people some fellow came over with the draft of KW's speech torn to shreds / dirty pencil / biro / red pencil. The bloody fool saying he brought the collective wisdom of the 38th floor spoke like a professor and obviously hadn't a clue. For once I let my temper go. They'd all gone off to a Security Council lunch. I ripped him to pieces / gave him messages for Guyer, Urquhart and Co and said my present intention was to resign at 1800. I was trembling with rage and emotion – and my heart wasn't funny. I won't describe the following hours. Each of them coming to my office, grovelling and what have you. At 1800 they all had <u>read</u> the speech – <u>understood</u> what I had written – and were singing halleluia. It ended up as I'd written it. Oh bugger it all – I hate hate hate this bloody existence. I know I'm indispensable at present and although I've got the guts to quit and clear out for all time – MORALLY I cannot do

this. Rarely have I been so distraught – not even when I was thrown out in '48. NOT repeat NOT upset by the stupidity of the speech thing, but all that that implied. KW all smiles and smarms at a Mekong Party at 1830. It ALL stinks. Your letter kept me afloat. I love you Kate, but I'm just about through. Your Clot.

31 May 2030: Early this morning I wrote you an angry and resentful letter. It was justified. When I went up to the 38th floor to collect KW (to make the appeal for 1m tons of grain) loving sounds on all sides. I was NOT moved. Well, you go on learning. Listen.

In the elevator going down (just the two of us) he said 'the speech is much too long'. (It wasn't). 'I'll give part of it and leave the rest to you.' Politicians! He stuck to all the general principles and left every hot issue to me – the appeals to individual countries, so I'd collect the brickbats. However, I didn't let him off Scot-free. I followed him immediately and in paying him a compliment underlined the responsibility and honour (ha ha!) I felt in accepting his invitation to continue speaking on his behalf.

The display chaps had done a beautiful job [with their maps], so after making the appeal in detail – delicate, for I was specifying to fourteen countries what the SG expected of them – it was easy to describe to all present what the actual situation now is. Comment: 'Why have we never had this kind of presentation before?' The whole show took about two hours and the general reaction seems to be favourable. We'll see.

This was one of Jackson's great days: not only had he persuaded donors to provide everything that was needed, he had demonstrated his complete mastery of the logistical situation, won their trust and established a reputation which would stand him in good stead for years to come. But it wasn't over yet.

But then dear God, it's all so futile; 38th floor: 'We must have a General Assembly document tomorrow, we must photograph your map, you must give a press conference tomorrow etc etc.' Not an inkling of what had to be done with 14 Ambassadors + UK + EEC etc. Told them to produce their own draft for the GA. It came down five hours later. Pathetic amateur stuff. They just can't WRITE. My priceless Subhas Dhar salvaged it (as far as anyone could) by 1900. A gem. God only knows what it will be like when he goes to Dacca. I remain bloody-minded. I want to get out. How do I do it decently?

2 June, 0040: I am so tired I can hardly write. ... I have averaged nearly 20 hours a day for 74 days. The system has let me down completely – but at least the UNROD operation is more or less under control. ... I do not doubt your love, it is what keeps me going.

2 June midnight: Waldheim has dumped this tragedy in my lap. I don't doubt the motives of Roberto Guyer and Brian Urquhart, but the result remains the same. I can't get the staff. No-one will provide them – Waldheim will give no directions. It's an impasse. Stalemate for one human being.

3 June, 2215: Three hours this morning with Roberto and Brian. The first two were all love and kisses and agreement and 'brilliant performance'. The last hour was the crunch. They <u>hated</u> my statement that I'd been 'exploited' – that word got under their skins. But they couldn't refute the facts. I was not accusing them directly – but they know they could have done more to put the basic issue to KW. Either he should free me from responsibility or <u>direct</u> people (eg Peterson) to give me help.

Subhas Dhar – 'my fireman!'

It was not many days since Urquhart, genuinely concerned about Jacko's health, had said 'For God's sake, can't you slow down?' to which he had replied 'Sure – get me a good number two'[14] (meaning Anstee). He seemed not to realise that Urquhart had other even more important matters on his plate – peace-keeping operations and such-like; his nights were probably even more disturbed than Jacko's.

What kept him going was the prospect of some leave with Joan; they planned to meet at Petersham on Saturday 17 June. On the Friday there was a minor crisis in Bangladesh, and airline pilots were proposing to strike on the Monday; Waldheim said he must get there while he could[15], so when Joan arrived from Chile there was no Jacko and Maria had to explain why; the flowers he had sent her were little consolation. It was not until the end of the month that they met at Petersham before spending a week at PIPPINS.

Evidently the crisis was in the north-east near Sylhet, where flash floods caused by the early monsoon had caused many deaths and left thousands marooned. Food and emergency supplies could only be got to the stricken area by air; three Hercules aircraft were chartered by USAID (the US Agency for International Development), the Swiss government provided a DC-6, and the ICRC's small planes were used to ferry relief agency staff to where they were needed. UNROD's own Skyvan delivered boats and pumping equipment.[16] The crisis had been handled very well and Jackson's journey was unnecessary – he only stayed for one day.

During July he and Joan were able to relax in Taormina for a fortnight. The Rubicon (one of his many) was faced but not crossed; they agreed that she would stay with UNDP and get herself comfortably installed in Santiago and he would carry on with Bangladesh and deal as best he could with the legal hurdle which he was now facing – separation from Barbara.

In August Jackson had two long meetings with Umbricht in Geneva at which there was some pretty plain speaking.

> Essentially he sees himself running the operation in Bangladesh with Headquarters simply playing a rôle to respond to his wishes and his decisions. Clearly the sun rises and sets in Dacca. Very confident of the success of the operation as directed by UNROD in Dacca; many criticisms of Headquarters and not one expression of appreciation.
>
> [He was] left in no doubt as to who is controlling the operation and where the final authority rests. Apparently quite blind to the wider political issues which the Secretary-General must take into account, not only in relation to Bangladesh, but also in relation to other Member States.
>
> He is clearly far superior to most people we could have obtained for this operation, but fails to understand very real problems facing Headquarters in delegating financial authority and that we have stretched the legal interpretation of delegated authority to the limit. I believe that the situation can be controlled until 31 March 1973 as long as reasonably frequent personal contact is maintained, but this assumes that there is no limit to the reserves of patience in New York.[17]

It was only later that Jackson discovered that at the time of his appointment Umbricht had received a letter from the Secretary-General which could be interpreted as giving him full control of the operation, with Jackson's role at headquarters being merely to get the necessary financial support. Who had drafted the letter was a mystery, but it could, he realised, have led Umbricht to misunderstand his responsibilities and would explain his sensitivity when Jackson exercised his authority.

Umbricht thought Jackson's cables unnecessarily long and did not conceal his irritation from his staff. He considered, reasonably enough, that the UN regulations on the delegation of financial authority were not conceived for emergency relief operations.[18] The tensions between the two would continue and Jackson's patience would be sorely tried, nevertheless he knew that he was lucky to have him in Dacca.

When Jackson next saw Sheikh Mujibur he was in a London hotel recuperating from a major operation.

> The Sheikh reminds me more and more of Nkrumah in the good days. No fool – realises the relative position and the relationship between Victor and me. Could not have been nicer about UNROD and my own activities. We then moved to the political side of life where I was acting for Waldheim. While remaining as relaxed and as pleasant as before, the highly professional politician appeared – another man.

Jackson had a message to convey from the Secretary-General concerning Bangladesh's application for admission to the UN. During a recent visit to China Waldheim had done his best to explain Bangladesh's problems to the Prime Minister, Chou en-Lai, hoping that he would consider the application sympathetically, but Chou was angry at India's continued detention of 93,000 Pakistani prisoners of war. Consequently, said Jackson, he (Mujibur) might feel that it would be in the best interests of Bangladesh not to force the matter to a vote. Jackson emphasised that he was merely conveying information and that the Secretary-General was not trying to influence the Prime Minister. Knowing that Mujib could get very emotional about the subject he probably wanted to avoid risking a repeat of his encounter with Bevin; he certainly went to great lengths to keep this part of the discussion separate from UNROD matters, even suggesting that they imagine themselves going into another room!

Mujib was not persuaded. He saw the application for admission as a matter of principle; the debate in the Security Council should follow normal procedure. Either way the result must be to the advantage of Bangladesh: admission would achieve his objective; a veto would increase the sympathy of countries wishing to help Bangladesh.[19] Four days later China vetoed Bangladesh's application.

The Russian team clearing Chittagong harbour was making slow progress because the water was only clear when there was little tide; they were unlikely to finish there before 1973 and reluctant to tackle Chalna. Jackson didn't wait: by the time they announced their decision he had already contacted General Wheeler, (the American who had organised the UN clearance of the Suez Canal in 1956-7) and Wheeler, now 86, had spoken to William Searle, (a retired US Navy officer and highly respected salvage expert who had once retrieved an atom bomb from the sea) giving him one simple order: 'just do whatever Jacko asks you and make sure that you do it well'.[20]

By 8 September Searle and his diver had surveyed the harbour approaches and he had made his report: there were nine hazardous wrecks, most of which were now submerged and full of mud, with only their masts showing. Five days later the Government formally asked the UN to undertake the operation; the next day Jackson sought the agreement of donor governments in New York. This was not a foregone conclusion since some saw the salvage operation as rehabilitation rather than relief, possibly diverting funds from UNROD's main task. Whichever it was, it was urgent, and when Jackson pointed out that no government had as much information as the UN had on what needed to be done the donors agreed.

Specifications were prepared, twenty-two salvage firms were approached, and six responded. After four weeks of intensive negotiations a contract to clear six ships (drawn up by Searle and Dr Nicky Beredjick, a UN lawyer) was signed with a consortium of four firms (from Holland, Germany, Japan and Singapore) and in mid-November the first salvage equipment arrived,[21] – all very different from the UN's efforts in January (when Searle had offered his services).

Jackson was still desperate for a capable number two. Subhas Dhar was now on his way to Dacca to join Umbricht, leaving only Pierre Sales, Joan Clark, his very efficient and dependable secretary, and a young Egyptian, Tardes, lent by IBRD).

Beredjick was very helpful, not only with the Chalna clearance: his expertise enabled him to weave his way through UN procedural rules and regulations, getting things done expeditiously; if he occasionally sailed rather close to the wind that was unavoidable in a UN emergency operation; he made a significant contribution to the success of UNROD.[22] The team in the Map Room on the 38th floor always made a special effort to prepare visuals to support his appeals to donors. What he lacked was high-level administrative assistance; he was still angry at UNDP's refusal to release anyone.

The second half of 1972 was not a happy time for him; the combination of Chile and Bangladesh was tough. He understood Joan's decision to go there but could not help regretting it, not that he had suggested any alternative; life would have been so different if they could have been working together, but they both knew that there was no chance of UNDP helping to make that possible. In letter after letter he railed against 'circumstances, bloody circumstances' which held both their lives in their grasp. On top of this he was inconsiderable pain and sleeping badly; the pain-killers prescribed by the UN doctor were not very effective. A check-up in London at the end of August revealed no serious damage, and as usual the advice was to take things more easily. Bodley-Scott's pills at least eased the pain, but he felt that they also dulled his mind.

Then there was his separation from Barbara. He saw her in London on 5 September, when she had discussed the matter calmly, 'all sweetness and light and objectivity – combined with an utter lack of generosity.' As to her reaction to legal action, he was left guessing and his guess was that she would contest divorce and accept legal separation.[23] He was in a weak position legally on account of his domicile – or rather lack of one – and he knew that Barbara was aware of this: Australia was asserting that he had by now surrendered his domicile there and it was far from clear that he had assumed a new one in Britain. His lawyers had always said that they would not proceed with an action for divorce if it would be contested by Barbara's side on grounds of domicile, since the court would refuse to hear it. He therefore had to consider the alternative of an action for judicial separation, which, if not contested, the court probably would agree to hear. Though very much a second best, it would at least free him of responsibility for Barbara's debts and thus protect Robin.

After his return to New York in early September he spent a 'non-weekend' seeing no-one and eating his cold suppers alone. He brooded over what he saw as his own weakness in running away from reality ever since he realised that 'B was not the woman for him'. To his list of those who had double-crossed him over the years – Lie, Bridges, Hoffman etc. – he now added her name at the top on the grounds that what he had told her in London about MESC had been in confidence and on condition that she never wrote about it in THE ECONOMIST. He was not complaining, he wrote, merely recording.[24]

The night of Tuesday 12 September was one of his worst – the sleeping pills bounced off like ping-pong balls as thoughts of recent rioting in Santiago, where Joan was based, went round and round. He was in the UN office by 7 a.m., worked for twelve and a half hours on papers for the next day's meeting with Governments, leaving behind six exhausted secretaries. He poured the stuff out in a kind of desperation against his feeling of futility, and returned to his hotel exhausted and alone. He felt he was living in a world of his own, one person to the public, another to himself – and that was the real one.[25]

The staff in Dacca expected that UNROD would complete its task by the end of 1972, when it should be possible to switch from emergency relief to reconstruction, for which Bangladesh would turn to the usual providers of aid. It was right that Bangladesh should be encouraged to become more self-reliant as soon as this was a realistic possibility, but the fact was that UNROD was still responsible for everything – managing the ports, the lightering, the trucks and vessels delivering supplies to where they were needed, and Jackson was not convinced that the task would be finished by the end of the year. Knowing that there could be no question of setting a date for its winding-up until the results of the *aman* harvest were established he engaged Professor Robert Chandler, a former director of the International Rice Research Institute in Manila, to carry out a survey of the harvest later in the year. Even before Chandler arrived Mujibur had formally asked the Secretary-General to extend UNROD until the end of 1973.

At the end of September Jackson went to Ghana for three days; on to Bangkok for a meeting of the Mekong Committee, and thence to Bangladesh on 3 October, when he dropped in – literally, by helicopter – on the *Manhattan*.

The largest vessel of the US Merchant Marine, she had arrived at Chittagong in August with 66,000 tons of wheat and was moored 56 miles outside the harbour where she would remain until late November as a floating warehouse. She was less than ideal for the job because having formerly been used in the Northwest Passage she had an outer ring of steel to ward off ice, which made it difficult for lightering vessels to get alongside. When the suggestion of sending the *Manhattan* was first made Umbricht had recommended using smaller vessels, but Jackson saw the importance of welcoming this offer by the USA, which had not so far been too keen to help Bangladesh. He cabled Umbricht that it was essential that she should be used successfully – 'we must all break our backs to ensure that this happens for political as well as practical reasons'. There were indeed difficulties in securing incoming ships alongside her to transfer their loads in the heavy swell; on the other hand the mini-bulkers off-loading the grain had few problems, and the operation was considered a great success; altogether nearly 110,000 tons of wheat passed through *Manhattan's* holds.

Back in New York he had to start drafting the Secretary General's report on UNROD for the General Assembly; what it would boil down to was '1972 was OK (just) but 1973's going to be a stinker. What do you want me to do about it?'[26] He was also faced with the prospect of eating eleven cold meals on his own before setting off again for Dacca. For all his dissatisfaction he knew that work was the only thing that kept him going.

> 19 October: Very full day yesterday – amiable meeting with KW etc for about an hour. I fear it won't be so amiable when I return if I don't accomplish something, although he says he recognises that I haven't more than three chances in a hundred.

This was another diplomatic mission: Waldheim wanted to see if a way could be found of breaking the deadlock between Bangladesh and Pakistan. Mujibur was still insisting that Pakistan must first recognise Bangladesh, which Bhutto refused. Could a face-saving formula be found which would enable the two of them to meet as a first step? He was sending Jackson to sound out Mujibur.

After two meetings with the Prime Minister alone Jackson was clear that although he would welcome a settlement of the impasse, he would not make any <u>independent</u> gesture because he believed it could cost him votes in the March elections. He would, however co-operate with the Secretary-General in a simultaneous move to improve relations between Bangladesh and Pakistan and proposed that the Secretary-General should 'send an emissary to the President of Pakistan', proposing that the two leaders should make simultaneous statements, each formally recognising the other's nation, expressing a desire to meet soon and inviting the Secretary-General to arrange this in a neutral country, having already agreed certain matters in advance (though the idea that they could agree anything in advance rather begged the question). Jackson reported to Waldheim:

It is the Prime Minister himself who is now stressing that time is not on the side of Bangladesh, and it is for that reason that he appears so sensitive to the willingness of the Secretary-General to make an approach to the President of Pakistan immediately.[27]

The question now was should an approach be made to Bhutto? If so by whom and when? He did not have to wait long for an answer. Two days later he set off to Lahore, where he had a long and cordial meeting with President Bhutto, who began by telling him that as a friend of Pakistan since its beginning he would always be welcome.

Jackson said that there was a strong consensus of opinion in the General Assembly that the present political deadlock was militating against everyone's interest, and the Secretary General wanted to ensure that both leaders were aware of his willingness to do anything he could to help break it. He then described his meeting with Mujibur.

Bhutto said that he would welcome an early meeting with the Prime Minister and any initiative the Secretary General could take to bring it about, but there could be no preconditions publicly announced. He accepted that a meeting would be a logical first step, but the PM must understand that he could not go to one having made concessions publicly beforehand. He was the leader of a defeated nation, his political and personal position would be undermined, and it would be an open invitation to certain Army elements to discredit him. If the Prime Minister would agree to meet without preconditions publicly announced he could be assured by the Secretary-General that the President of Pakistan would immediately do everything necessary both outside and inside parliament to secure the recognition of Bangladesh.

Jackson believed that both leaders wanted a meeting if a mutually acceptable formula could be devised, and were looking to the Secretary-General to maintain his initiative, but the deadlock remained: Mujib insisted on mutual recognition as a precondition, which Bhutto refused. Jackson thought Mujib the more likely to make concessions since he needed the SG and his influence (especially regarding the continuance of UNROD) more than the SG needed him, and that the next step was to try to persuade him to drop his precondition for meeting Bhutto. Jackson, ever hopeful, suggested to Waldheim how this could be done:

> He should exploit the PM's dependence on him to generate political support to get UNROD continued until the end of 1973, and simultaneously generate support for it from friendly governments, but this would take time. He should then send a personal representative to the Prime Minister – '<u>at the right time</u> and most carefully briefed' – in the hope that he would agree to drop his precondition for a meeting.[28]

It seems that Waldheim couldn't wait and the honour of being sent as his personal representative fell to Roberto Guyer, who saw the Prime Minister on 13 November.

> 13 November, 2300: Roberto had a lousy reception from Mujib. He's done his best but he does not know (a) Mujib and (b) the sub-continent. KW furious, making Brian terribly upset, feeling that Roberto had been placed in an impossible position (did anyone think of me three weeks ago?) Thus he (BU) was up and down to me most of the day and so I saw KW at 1800 and then again at 1945 and produced my final face-saver. God only knows if it will do anything but KW saw quickly that it left him in a strong position and Brian realised that Roberto was protected.

When Chandler arrived it was already clear that the monsoon had failed throughout south-east Asia and that the *aman* harvest would be poor; his immediate estimate was a shortfall of a million tons. Given the urgency Jackson made an appeal on 14 November on behalf of the Secretary-General for 700,000 tons to be delivered during the first three months of 1973.[29] (Most of the 1 million tons for which he had appealed on 31 May had by then been provided.)

Umbricht tried to persuade Jackson not to visit Dacca in November, since he would not be there, but it was fortunate that he did, for he learnt directly from Chandler the findings of his survey. They were very bad: because of shortage of fertiliser and heavy attacks by pests the harvest in Bangladesh was even poorer than in the rest of south-east Asia. The *aman* crop would be almost 1.5 million tons less than in a normal year. Given the low level of government stocks it was clear that over 2.5 million tons would have to be imported in 1973 – more than in 1972.

> Sunday 26 November, Palam Airport [Calcutta]: Friday night was one of the worst I can remember. I've never been frightened of work in my life before – and this coming week seemed impossible. I forced myself through yesterday and evolved a food policy for '73. I don't know if it's good, bad or indifferent – but <u>it is a course of action</u>. The Government will buy it, so will Waldheim; can I sell it to friendly governments on Friday? We'll see. Bangladesh will need about 2,500,000 tons of grain next year. Can we <u>get</u> the grain for them? If so can we get the <u>shipping</u> – probably even more difficult. If we can get the grain in ships to Chittagong and Chalna in time can the Government distribute it reasonably well? The most difficult task of all. <u>But</u> UNROD <u>must</u> turn over operational responsibility at some point – and I reckon 1 April is reasonable. Then a UN Special Mission for nine months. Then finish.
>
> Victor will be furious that all this has happened in his absence, but he went off to this stupid advisory committee of UNIDO (the UN Industrial Development Organisation) against the advice of all his staff. I foresaw things would cascade as soon as Chandler had come to his conclusions about the present big harvest. I had his basic ideas by Friday night. I revised my plan of sleeping at Calcutta airport tonight, and Air India are making a bunk for me in a Jumbo which is due to leave at midnight for Frankfurt. With luck I can give two to three hours of dictation [in Geneva] by lunchtime – talk to NY at 1500 and then sleep.
>
> Harold Caustin [a former UNRRA colleague helping him draft his report to the General Assembly] is due with the second half of the report, which I want to get into the machine on Monday 4 December. Tomorrow a summary of Chandler's report will be cabled to Geneva and added to Harold's Part II. Then I'll add my proposed policy – to be approved by KW on Thursday 30th. If the meeting with governments goes OK on Friday 1st I can finish the draft over next week-end.
>
> It was the <u>prospect</u> of all this that frightened me on Friday night. Now I feel I can get through this coming week – anti-biotics are helping my voice. Subhas very good and as reliable and affectionate as ever.[30]

Jackson realised that d'Astugues might find it difficult to inform Umbricht about his visit, so before leaving Dacca he had told him to cable Umbricht in Vienna telling him simply that he (Jackson) would tell Umbricht about it over the phone. D.Astugues said he appreciated Jackson's thoughtfulness. When Jackson arrived in Geneva Erik Jensen, the *Chef de Cabinet* at the *Palais des Nations*, showed him a cable from d'Astugues to Umbricht. It had been sent in code, but because UNIDO's office in Vienna had no decoding equipment it had come via Geneva, and after reading it Jensen had refused to relay it. It gave a totally distorted account of Jackson's visit, inciting Umbricht to get the Secretary-General to over-rule his policies.

> In short it was a crude attempt to get himself made head of any post-UNROD organisation, simultaneously playing on Umbricht's vanity who wants a nonentity to follow him. (Umbricht, as you may recall, has been pushing this line for weeks.) I sent d'Astugues a cable that will scare the pants off him. At 1430 (when I could hardly speak) Victor returned an earlier call of mine from Vienna, all sweetness and light.[31]

He could have done without all that. The week in New York which he had been so much dreading went as planned and had a satisfactory ending.

> 1 December: Meeting with governments said to be a personal triumph. I have far more money for a mini-UNROD in 73 than I could ever use. Even HMG toss in $1m on a 'personal basis'. We had quite a chorus: US / Canada / Scandinavia / Japan (amazing!) / Australia / NZ / EEC – France and so on. USSR even nodding their heads. Mujib is far luckier than he should be, but that does not mean that millions may not die in 73. I've given B'desh a policy for 73; I've given friendly governments a realistic strategy. My main objectives are thus achieved. Dacca informed.

The following week Umbricht was in New York discussing with Waldhem what sort of mission should succeed UNROD. Umbricht wanted something small which would not steal his limelight; Waldheim wanted something bigger and was proposing to write to Mujibur making a stronger commitment than donor governments would agree to. Jackson, in the nutcrackers as usual; had to persuade Waldheim to go easy.[32] He also had to host 'a terrible cocktail party' for Umbricht; it was a success, but emotionally draining. As if that wasn't enough he then had to host one of his staff lunches.

Jacko's weekly staff lunches had become an institution: he held them on most Thursdays when he was in New York, paying for them himself and often helping to prepare the food; fruit salads were his speciality. They were light-hearted occasions and all sorts of people would turn up – lift operators, ambassadors, ministers, USGs, security men; occasionally Kofi Annan, on one occasion U Thant's Astrologer![33] Brian Urquhart thought them much the most enjoyable lunches he had at the UN, but they were more than that: they brought together the people who were helping him at whatever level and showed them that they were part of a team doing an important job. As for the members of his team in the field, he cared about them too, understood their personal problems and saw to their needs, and they responded with intense loyalty.

Then it was Liberia's turn. He already had the impression that President Tolbert's brother, the Minister of Finance, resented any outside influence, and when he arrived he heard that moves were afoot to destroy him; he wasn't worried. The President still wanted his advice, and during the next day three constructive lines of policy were adopted as a result of his influence. He knew that his visits were useful and that his unobtrusive advice was genuinely welcomed, but he also knew that in the Third World generally the foreign expert adviser was becoming less and less welcome.[34]

In Accra there were problems between Ghana and the VRA on the one side and Kaiser's on the other, with faults on both; presumably the issue was the price of electricity. He would try to help but he doubted that he could achieve much.

13 December, New York: This bloody awful UNROD report will kill me. Harold has done all he can; about 80% OK but the real KICK is missing. A postscript to a bad 48 hour stretch: letter of four lines from B, 'To let you know that Ronald will commence his cancer tests on me from Tuesday 19 December. I expect they will take two or three days.'

He spent Christmas with Joan near Bath. It was an unhappy time; her mother was dying and her funeral took place on New Year's day. And he had dreadful 'flu. The UNROD report[35] tells the story from the cyclone of 1970 to the end of 1972. However hard it was to write, as a record of the operation straight from the horse's mouth it should be read by any student of humanitarian relief. UNROD was the largest, most difficult and ultimately – thanks to Jackson – the most successful UN relief operation since UNRRA. Apart from the fact that he was not given the administrative support he needed it provided a model of how such operations should be carried out in future. One sentence deserves to be quoted here:

> To this end the ACC accepted the Secretary-General's invitation that the specialised agencies should harmonise their individual efforts with UNROD, so that the system might speak with one voice and act as one.

For him that should have been a satisfying echo of his exhortation to the ACC twenty-five years ago: 'We're all in the same boat and we've just got to get together so row, row, row!' (see page 134) But was it? He had always seen Bangladesh as a cold intellectual challenge to his own thinking and methods; while failure would have destroyed him success meant nothing. This was child's play compared with MESC and UNRRA, but where were the young to whom he cold pass on his experience?[36]

It now looked as if there would be a poor *boro* (dry season) harvest, so Jackson, unsure of what further aid would be forthcoming, made the painful recommendation that the government should spend its reserves of foreign currency in order to ensure a steady flow of grain through 1973. By the end of January he could see the outlook for the year and decided not to tell Mujibur until Umbricht had left. 'Then I'll bloody well ram it down Mujib's throat'. He had lost patience with him and 'saw no reason why people should die because of politicians' vanity and ambition'.[37]

February started with 'a stinking cable from Victor and Wheeler [working for the World Food Programme] which was so intellectually dishonest that both Pierre Sales and Nicky Beredjick blew their tops'. It gave basic information for his next meeting with governments and tried to conceal the seriousness of the food situation by implying that headquarters had deliberately misinterpreted their figures in the past. The truth was that for four months New York had queried their figures again and again because they just didn't make sense. 'Subhas Dhar – bless his courageous heart – has clearly put his head on the chopping block and fought Victor and Wheeler and obviously demonstrated their own miscalculations to them. Thank God, we <u>have</u> been giving governments the true position.'[38]

> 7 February: Events in B'desh unfolding as I feared. This is a case where it is hateful to be right. Lacking experience, VU and Co. all believed things couldn't get worse. They have. The rains have now failed for the next – boro – harvest. The import need for grain will now exceed 3,000,000 tons. Both naturally furious that the Old Man of the Sea saw further. I've played everything factually and low key, but it doesn't help. Thank goodness VU – who <u>has</u> contributed a great deal, even if my patience is exhausted – will leave in seven weeks. It's so sad – but so human – that he wants to convey the public impression that so long as he was there all was well. The crunch will be June onwards unless someone can work miracles. I lay no claims.
>
> 16 February: Cry for help from Dacca for 'quite unexpectedly there's a tremendous bottleneck of ships arriving'. <u>Now</u> (1730 on a Friday night) he asks us to charter six more vessels IMMEDIATELY and it's the Washington Birthday long weekend.

At this point he heard from his lawyers that, as he expected, an action for divorce <u>would</u> be contested on grounds of domicile, so would fail; an action for judicial separation would not be contested. Dining with Edith Lehman – now a widow of 82 – he admired a large bowl of yellow freesias in the Governor's study. 'Oh, they're a gift from Barbara.' He endured two hours of pleading to take no legal action of any kind. He was very angry, not with Edith, but with Barbara for trying to get at him through one of his dearest and closest friends; he pointed out how she had virtually conceded to Anna the role of mother, and how her life as well as Robin's and his own had been affected for all these years. He took his leave as lovingly as ever and his determination to proceed was all the stronger.[39]

Barbara wrote asking him to defer legal action: her US doctors thought she had cancer of the intestine; then a different American doctor thought she had a tumour on her liver; a fortnight later a minor operation showed that there was none. Her plea not to proceed was rejected.

The task for the next Chief of Mission would be different from Umbricht's; he would not direct the relief operation, but oversee its gradual handover to the Bangladeshi authorities and the specialised agencies. In his second rôle as the Secretary-General's Special Representative (which Umbricht was not) he would endeavour to promote normal relations between India, Pakistan and Bangladesh.

A diplomat was called for. Accordingly Waldheim appointed Francis Lacoste, formerly France's permanent representative to the UN, Ambassador in Belgium and Canada and Resident-General in Morocco. There was still a stalemate, with two particular problems unresolved: what to do about the prisoners of war and the Biharis – an Urdu-speaking minority of Indian Muslims who had found themselves left in East Pakistan following partition. They were believed by Bangladesh to have sided with the Pakistan Government during the war, and were held in camps protected by the ICRC and supplied and fed by UNROD. Like the POWs they wished to go to Pakistan.

7 March: Francis Lacoste seems OK. Clearly very intelligent and experienced. Appalled at the famous letter from KW last April which VU has always interpreted as making him King of UNROD. 'However have you been able to conduct an operation with that impossible document to contend with?' He may well ask!!

15 March: I do NOT like Mujib's politics after the great victory. [The Awami League had just won 291 seats out of 300.] The well-deserved criticism of his handling of the POWs and Biharis is now snowballing in the West. I'm sympathetic to the plight of the people of Bengal but I am NOT attracted to Mujib.

I was told that the meeting went like a bomb. I don't know. All here more than kind to me. [This was a meeting with donor governments, evidently another of Jackson's great days.] We got (a) the 175,000 tons from EEC and individual promises from some of the member states, (b) 100,000 tons from Australia, (c) $2.5m in cash from US; Washington didn't want to reveal more than $2.5m so as not to take pressure off other countries to contribute cash, but [gave] personal commitment that I can have more cash whenever I need it; (d) most important of all – at the Development Conference to be held in Dacca on 31 March and 1 April two or three countries will give Bangladesh cash for grain imports to offset costs incurred by the government in buying grains earlier this year.

I am now concerned that we may have achieved too much too soon for Mujib. He is to make a Great Policy Speech next Sunday. I don't trust him one inch. With KW's agreement I've sent him a message he won't like, i.e. that world opinion is increasingly turning against B'desh because of (a) detention of POWs against Geneva Convention and (b) threat to expel

Biharis (where?) who have not accepted B'desh citizenship.

Tonight I am for the first time in '73 'cautiously optimistic' (monsoon permitting) we can bring B'desh through this year. If so, it will be a real triumph for UN. After I'd cabled the results to Dacca I composed a fruit salad for fourteen. Francis [Lacoste] obviously intrigued – I think he'll be OK. He'll leave with much, much more ammunition in his pocket than I'd hoped for: (a) good small compact staff of 30 professionals (b) all money needed for shipping ops etc until 31 December and (c) more promising grain situation. Quit at 1840 feeling that perhaps I'd done a little for UN but, above all, faith in human beings reinforced.

17 March: Would you believe it – three pages of code from VU – STILL trying to oppose my transport policy, while *en clair* he cries out [that] his lightering position is desperate. OK I can last. Lacoste will be there in ten days. Nothing will be conceded.

Back in February Zambia had been faced with severe economic problems resulting from Rhodesia's closing of their common border. No-one could find 'the Jackson 1967 Report on Zambia'. He knew that President Kaunda had one copy and U Thant the other, which he couldn't find, and now Zambia needed more help.

19 March: Tony Gilpin and John Saunders to lunch. Zambia meeting with Philippe. [Gilpin was UNDP's Regional representative for Southern Africa, Saunders Deputy Director of its Regional Bureau for Africa, Philippe de Seynes USG for Economic Affairs.] Why waste words. I gave them a policy – the only one possible. So the boys will write a position paper for the Great Leader on his return next Saturday. At the end I said to Philippe 'I've suggested how you might build a focal point for ops around Tony, but how will you handle it here in NY?' 'But Jacko' – and this with a gentle smile – 'when I talked to the Secretary-General it was assumed that you would create a smaller B'desh team'. Am I in cloud-cuckoo-land?

Despite being in a lot of pain he went to Accra for a meeting of the Volta River Authority. He thought it worth the effort, for it had been his life for over twenty years. Then he intended to surrender to the doctors in New York. Waldheim was worried about his health, but wanted to talk to him about Zambia at his convenience. When they met that evening he asked Jackson to take charge of the Zambia Aid Programme, UNZAP.

His need for a Deputy was now irrefutable, so Waldheim asked Anstee if she would agree to a secondment from UNDP starting in June. She was not keen to go to headquarters because she loved working in the field; and with political trouble brewing in Chile felt it her duty to be there; but knowing, too, how much Jacko needed her and that overwork was threatening his health, she felt unable to refuse. UNDP agreed on the understanding that the arrangement would last only seven months and that she would retain her post as resrep in Chile. President Allende also agreed, provided she returned to Chile for two weeks in every two months.

On 30 March his petition for judicial separation was listed among the undefended cases to be heard in London. Joan welcomed this as a first step in the right direction; Jacko remained deeply depressed. 'I'm convinced I've nothing left to offer you either personally or professionally. My long letters about personal and professional life are only meant to try to protect you because I love you with all of me.'[40] His long letters also revealed his growing doubts about the prospects of them ever having a future together, and a sense of having failed her in not going all out for a divorce. His decree of separation from Barbara was issued on 23 July.

On 31 March UNROD was formally wound up, to be succeeded by UNROB – the UN Special Relief Office, Bangladesh. 'The mission had achieved, if not miracles, at least more than could reasonably have been expected and more than any comparable United Nations operation had done',[41] to which we may add 'or has done ever since'. Aid to the tune of more than $1,300 million had been mobilised and more was still to come. As Jackson put it 'the umbrella was folded and the crutches replaced by a walking stick'.

He thought that the situation in Bangladesh was now under control. Japan had just sent 100,000 tons of rice and Belgium $1 million; the EEC had paid him the compliment of giving Bangladesh the largest grant in its history, 'confident that UNROB would ensure that the Government would use it wisely'. All should be well provided that the weather did not fail and Mujib did not make a fool of himself.[42]

On 11 May the planned clearance of wrecks at Chalna was completed, four days ahead of contract. The government then had the face to demand $1.9 million in taxes on the operation. 'Christ! Help the bastards – and then pay taxes! Mujib won't know what has hit him – but Lacoste will relay precisely what I've sent him.'[43] Two other wrecks remained which Searle had not considered hazardous but which the Government wanted removed. The lifting equipment was still there so it was now or never, and Sweden offered $2 million to get the job finished.

It was becoming increasingly difficult to move grain around the world at this time; there was not enough equipment (elevators, wagons, ships). The result was that by May the quantities reaching Bangladesh were less than the ports could handle. By early June Mujibur was alarmed that stocks of grain were running so low that the current ration was at risk, and wrote to President Brezhnev asking for urgent help. UNROB checked the estimates and Lacoste confirmed that the request was justified. The Soviet Union agreed to provide 200,000 tons of wheat, but in view of its own uncertain harvest made this a loan, to be repaid in March 1974.[44]

In May Jackson went to Zambia; in June Anstee joined him in New York as his deputy for both UNZAP and UNROB. Their visits to Zambia in July are described in the next chapter.

On 28 August, thanks to Lacoste, an agreement was reached in New Delhi between India, Bangladesh and Pakistan for a three-way repatriation: the return to Pakistan of 90,000 POWs and civilian internees held in India, the return to Bangladesh of something like 200,000 Bangalees held in Pakistan, and the transfer of the Biharis from Bangladesh to Pakistan. Numbers still had to be agreed and some means of funding the operation, likely to cost more than $14 million, would have to be found. On 5 September Jackson and Sadruddin Aga Khan, the UN High Commissioner for Refugees, met Waldheim at Zurich airport, where he approved their proposals for ensuring a co-ordinated response to requests for financial assistance to implement the New Delhi agreement; on 13 September he made the appeal.

Anstee was now doing her second stint as Jackson's deputy. On 11 September she was at PIPPINS *en route* for Dacca when Gabriel Valdés, her UNDP boss, phoned to tell her that there had been a military coup in Chile. She left at the crack of dawn the next day. Maria saw her at London Airport to break the news that

Allende had been found dead in his palace, and Joan flew back to New York. She briefly saw Jacko who was furious with both Valdés and her because he had not been consulted before the decision was made that she should return to Chile. Not only was he angry, he was worried that she would be in danger, as indeed she was. She had missed her flight to Santiago and Chile's frontiers were now closed. She eventually entered the country on a hair-raising flight from Buenos Aires over the Andes in a tiny military aircraft at night.[45]

In early October she returned to New York to resume work for Jacko, planning the resettlement operation; as usual both of them were working very long hours. Jacko spent three days in Bangkok and made a final brief visit to Dacca, returning to New York on 11 October, completely worn out. A few days later he collapsed in a restaurant and Joan rushed him to hospital. He was clearly a very sick man, and it proved virtually impossible to identify the cause of his illness.

20 November: Dearest Maria and James, Whatever virus started off my misfortunes was very tough, and to the scientists, a new boy. I was hit hard: the more so because I went to Asia tired out and vulnerable. The University Medical Centre in NY is a most remarkable institution. They cleared my lung (the danger area) in six days; X-rays every 6 hours! That involved so many drugs that the balance of my blood was thrown out. It's now nearly in balance again. If all goes well I hope to be permitted to fly again by early December. I realise that I've been very lucky in several ways and I am most grateful. Joan, of course, did two jobs simultaneously: ran the office like a bomb and monitored me continuously.

I was let out about 6 November. The doctors wanted me to go away immediately but compromised on half time (in theory) for eight or nine days, followed by ten days out of New York. So on Friday last [16 Nov] we set out by train and bus to Williamsburg; Joan returned on Sunday evening.

Bangladesh finishes (successfully I think) on 31 December. What then? Joan has done a wonderful job on Zambia, but officially returns to UNDP at the end of the year. Waldheim and his wife had us to dinner before I left NY and was very appreciative of 'our' work, but it is very hard to see where we go from here.

If I can fly again, it's Africa from 9 to 22 December. Then Robin and Xmas.

I feel my own inadequacy greatly – it is a bad period. Too many strains in the past, too many crises and disappointments in '73, clearly too much work for two people to compete with, the sheer unpleasantness of living in NY. I want so much to give her comfort and understanding – but it is here that my own resources seem to be so limited, and I do not go about things as I should. Sometimes I feel that some of my own wounds have not healed.

As always, my dearest love goes to you all. Jacko.

The Secretary-General was able to report to the Security Council that although further reports would still be necessary, Bangladesh would start the new crop year with a substantial carry-over of food grains for the first time since the emergencies of 1971-72.[46]

On 31 December, as UNROB closed its doors, Subhas Dhar remembered the day in April 1972 when Sir Robert (he could never bring himself to address him as Jacko, despite repeated entreaties to do so) had asked him to join UNROD.

Dear Sir Robert,

UNROD/UNROB has given me an opportunity to serve the land (and its people) where I was born and brought up. More importantly, a part of mankind, who desperately needed outside assistance and under-standing, got it at the right time and, I believe, in right measure. I need hardly say that, but for your outstanding leadership and constant vigilance, this vast – and successful – humanitarian effort would have been impossible.

I have nothing more to add today except to thank you once again most sincerely for the opportunity you have given me and for your confidence in me. It would indeed be a pleasure to work with you again on some other project in any part of the world.

With warm personal regards, yours sincerely,

Subhas.

Zambia isolated

16 Africa and Indo-China

THE PROBLEMS FACING ZAMBIA had very little in common with those of Bangladesh. There had been no natural disaster, there was no immediate crisis, no risk of starvation, at least not yet, but they too were the result of a double whammy, which in Zambia's case resulted from the actions of one man: Ian Smith, the Prime Minister of Rhodesia, which had been a British colony until 1965 when he made a unilateral declaration of independence (UDI). The UN Security Council thereupon imposed mandatory sanctions on Rhodesia which inevitably bore on Zambia too.[1]

Jackson was sent there in February 1967 to see what UNDP might do to help. In Lusaka he stayed with Antony Gilpin, UNDP's regional representative for Southern Africa. The problems mainly concerned transport and power, and his mission was essentially technical.

Gilpin was fascinated to see him at work: his professionalism was an inspiration to his colleagues, though there were occasional awkward moments: 'one would feel a stab of embarrassment when, in speaking with Africans, he would refer to a mythical 'Bongo-bongoland'. Jacko's light touch was sometimes a bit heavy, but his sincerity and devotion to the people of Africa, as well as to the objectives of the UN, shone through radiantly.'

Unfortunately the Zambian government saw his mission primarily as political, intended simply to increase aid, and refused to provide the expert advice for which Jackson asked. He was not prepared to let UNDP be used as a political lever, so nothing came of his mission. The politicians felt let down, though President Kaunda understood his position. When UNDP later persuaded the government to obtain the expert advice which he had recommended it proved of considerable value. If action had been taken on some of the proposals in Jackson's 1967 report (which nobody could find) Zambia would have been in a much stronger position to deal with the problems that would arise six years later, when the second blow fell.[2]

In 1973 Smith closed Rhodesia's northern border with Zambia, but made an exception for Zambia's exports of copper, which went by the Rhodesian Railway to the Mozambique port of Beira. Copper was a major source of Zambia's revenue, but this seemingly helpful gesture was not entirely altruistic. Rhodesia's rail-freight charges must have been a valuable source of income at that time, and Kaunda saw that in continuing to use the Rhodesian Railway he would have been providing support to the Smith régime. Determined to demonstrate Zambia's practical support for the UN sanctions and its opposition to the white rulers of Rhodesia and South Africa, Kuanda spurned Smith's 'offer'. To emphasise his determination he closed his own border posts on the northern bank of the Zambesi.

At Gilpin's suggestion the Zambian Government appealed to the Security Council, invoking for the first time Article 50 of the UN Charter. This enables a state facing economic difficulties resulting from measures taken by the Security Council against another state to consult it regarding a solution. When Gilpin went to UNDP headquarters in New York he found that Jackson had arranged for him to see the Secretary-General (who, having asked him how to pronounce his name, continued to address him as Mr Jilpin!).

Gilpin explained to Waldheim why he thought the UN should assist Zambia: the border closure constituted a confrontation between two weakened economies; without aid Zambia could well go under, with aid it could survive and the effects of the tightened sanctions might topple the Smith régime. He was over-optimistic; Kaunda's high-principled stand increased Rhodesia's difficulties – no more, no less -and at crippling cost to Zambia over the next five years.

After sending a mission to assess Zambia's needs the Security Council passed a resolution (329) appealing to all member states under Article 49 for immediate assistance to Zambia to enable it to maintain its normal flow of traffic and help it to implement the sanctions policy. (Article 49 requires member states to assist each other in carrying out measures decided upon by the Security Council.) It asked the Secretary-General to organize assistance to enable Zambia to carry out its policy of economic independence from the racist regime of Southern Rhodesia and it asked ECOSOC to consider the matter periodically.[3] On 27 March Waldheim asked Jackson to take charge of the Zambia Aid Programme – UNZAP.

He went there briefly in May, saw that the immediate need was to provide alternative transport and supply lines to maintain Zambia's external trade. In practice this meant making the best possible use of the existing roads, other railways and ports. Dar es Salaam in Tanzania was accessible by road, and there was a rail link to Lobito, 1000 miles away on the coast of Angola. That was all.

He arranged for Anstee to go there in June to make an estimate of the economic cost to Zambia of the border-closure, which would form the basis of appeals to governments for assistance, and joined her there on 5 July. Always on the lookout for any sign of sanction-breaking, he kept his eye on the shelves in the shops. Some bottles of French liqueurs aroused his suspicion, but a closer look revealed a thick layer of dust suggesting that they had been standing there for years!⁴

They planned to go to the Victoria Falls one week-end to write their report, then Jacko heard that Kaunda <u>might</u> wish to see them again. Conscientious to a fault, he cancelled the plan, infuriating Joan. Needless to say no call came from Kaunda until the following week.

In July Jackson reported to ECOSOC: by closing the border, he said, Zambia had made more sacrifices than any other member state to implement the UN policy of sanctions against Rhodesia; it was for him, on behalf of the Secretary-General, to ensure that all member states were made aware of the great cost to Zambia of its courageous stand; they had a clear responsibility to share the burden. The government was doing its best to use its resources, particularly its infrastructure, with maximum efficiency and to ensure that any assistance from abroad was limited to essentials; it was a policy based on self-help with the UN doing all it could to assist. The Secretary-General, he said, would do all in his power to generate further support from the UN system, and would maintain small offices at Lusaka and HQ; the IMF and IBRD were keeping the situation under continuous review; UNDP had already created five additional key posts and was prepared to provide further technical co-operation. The Secretary-General, however, had no financial resources to allocate to Zambia. Only other member states could decide whether or not effective action would follow. It would be unjust to leave Zambia to carry its great financial burden alone; assistance, bi-lateral or multi-lateral, should be provided as soon as possible; the adoption of Resolution 329 was unprecedented. The additional costs to Zambia resulting from the border closure [estimated by Anstee] were likely to be $64 million in 1973.[5]

The Secretary-General had not set up a central UN fund as he had for UNROD, but asked that donations be made direct to the Zambian government, and this was not a desperate situation for which Jackson's strong-arm tactics, so successful there, would be appropriate. All he could do was exhort and apply discreet pressure behind the scenes, which he went on doing for five years, writing a new variation on the same theme each year as donors' enthusiasm waned. Gilpin reckoned that if Zambia had taken more trouble to tell donors how their gifts were being used, as he had suggested, they might have responded more generously.[6]

By July 1974 the deficit had risen to $154.6 million; assistance received was $62.4 million. World-wide inflation was increasing the cost of all forms of transport, and by the end of 1975 it was likely to be around $300 million. The Zambian delegate to ECOSOC reaffirmed Zambia's commitment to the total liberation of peoples and territories still subjected to colonialism, *apartheid* and foreign occupation. Jackson said that the Secretary-General fully shared President Kaunda's view that the programme of assistance should be regarded as a response on the part of the world community to a cause that should command the support of all who believed in human freedom; nations providing assistance should see it not as financial support for Zambia but rather as affording mutual assistance in carrying out the measures decided upon by the Security Council in accordance with Article 49.[7]

Year by year Zambia's problems grew: the price of copper fell, exports and imports were hampered by congestion in Dar es Salaam; agricultural production was hit by bad weather; political unrest in Angola put the rail link to Lobito out of action. In January 1975 the Government imposed severe import controls; in June Kaunda demanded austerity and self-reliance to meet the country's economic difficulties.

The only good news Jackson could give ECOSOC that year was that the track of the new Tan-Zam Railway linking Lusaka with Dar es Salaam had been laid and it would be brought into operation in October. (The railway was built by China to counter the influence of the West and, more particularly, Russia; it was China's answer to the Aswan Dam.) More than ever, he said, Zambia was bearing a disproportionate share of the burden arising from the UN policy of sanctions against Rhodesia; member states had a clear obligation to do much more to share it.[8]

When he landed at Livingstone in June 1976 the red carpets were out again; all passengers were asked to remain seated until a very important mission from the United Nations had disembarked. Seeing four nuns in white sitting in front of him he discreetly suggested to the Mother Superior that they might like to join the United Nations. She was happy to oblige and with her three daughters led them out of the plane with great dignity.

This was a difficult visit: Zambia was looking to the UN in the mood of 1967 and '73, and what they wanted him to say (and he would have liked to say) went far beyond what Waldheim could accept. There had been a steady pressure from government representatives arriving week after week and ready to give, but Zambia, alas, was apparently not organised to receive. Jackson had a long meeting with Kaunda, and another with the Minister of Economic and Technical Co-operation at which Subhas Dhar was also present.

> The Minister, a lady of about 35, first class, was disconcerted when Subhas – in the most charming and courteous manner – started putting the tough questions. She tried to slap him down, but he, even more courteously and charmingly, didn't yield an inch. 'You see, Minister, your government will have to answer my questions if we, your friends and allies, are to fight for you. Your present application to be classed as 'Most Seriously Affected' must fail as it stands, etc. etc.' Suddenly she realised that he meant exactly what he said, scrapped another meeting and got down to business with him. I left them to it.[9]

Zambia's financial burden seemed likely to reach $650 million by the end of 1976, and possibly $800 million by the end of 1977; assistance from the international community was around $100 million. Jackson could only repeat the same message: the Secretary-General would do everything in his power to mobilize support from every possible source, but ultimately it was only other nations that could help Zambia to solve its problems.[10]

Reporting to ECOSOC in July 1977 for what turned out to be his final time he said that Zambia's record in responding to the UN sanctions policy was unsurpassed; the lives of its people had been disrupted for 11 years and it had not received assistance commensurate with the cost. The need for other nations to share its burden was obvious, but unfortunately, just as with natural disasters, aid tended to diminish after the first reactions.[11]

A resolution was passed requesting the Secretary General to continue UNZAP until the situation in relation to the minority racist regime of Southern Rhodesia was resolved satisfactorily.[12] Jackson wrote telling the Prime Minister that this would provide a good foundation for mobilising further support for Zambia.[13] The PM replied expressing the sincere appreciation of President Kaunda, the government and the people of Zambia, for his untiring efforts to woo support from UN member states. 'Although the response has declined as years have gone by, you have nonetheless managed to keep the case alive in the minds of Member States of the United Nations.'[14] Increasing inflation and unemployment led to public discontent and in October 1978, largely as a result of heavy pressure from both the people and the IMF to relax its principled stand, Zambia reopened its southerly trade link through Rhodesia in order to increase copper exports and permit vital fertilizer to be imported in time for the planting season. Tanzania and Mozambique, its allies in the struggle against white domination, were dismayed. It was a sad ending to a noble enterprise.

*

Jackson's illness in October 1973 after his final trip to Bangladesh had left him very weak, nevertheless by December he was off again to Monrovia, Accra and Lusaka. After a quiet Christmas in London with his family and a few days in New York, he joined Joan in Santiago.

Her house, VILLA CLARA ROSA, was a few miles outside the city, hidden in a valley in the foothills of the Andes, with a large and beautiful garden filled with roses and shrubs, dropping down to the river Mapocho, then in full spate as the snow melted in the mountains. It was an idyllic spot – or had been until it was invaded by Pinochet's secret police in October, just after Joan had returned to New York. They were searching for Carlos Altamirana, the only prominent supporter of Allende to have escaped capture, whose sister-in-law, a Venezuelan communist millionaire, was the owner of the Villa. They took away the Allende government's development plan – 'subversive literature' – as well as Joan's parents' letters – suspect because written in English – and ransacked her bedroom. This invasion of what was technically UN territory caused Waldheim to protest vigorously, and Joan received a personal apology from the Chilean *chargé d'affaires* in New York. No lasting harm was done, but the idyll was shattered. Her career in UNDP had also taken a knock on the grounds that she had been 'too close to the Allende Government', so that by the time Jacko arrived she was temporarily without any official responsibility there, frustrated but free to enjoy with him the garden, its flowers, its fruit and its swimming pool.[15]

> 1 February 1974, Villa Clara Rosa: I have loved every moment of my time here. These three weeks will never be forgotten – your primary objective of recapturing the magic of Trélex has been accomplished in full. We both know that we have stopped our world for three weeks and gotten off it. We may have turned our backs on the reality of what lies outside this most beautiful garden and on the unpleasantness of UN/UNDP – but we faced beauty all the time and have given each other, I believe, complete companionship and devoted love. I think we have a sensible plan of action for 1974. New York is the phase to which I do NOT look forward. We recognise NY and the official UN/UNDP atmosphere for the threat it represents – a threat more subtle because we love both institutions. The institutions do not threaten us but some of their inhabitants do. Let us be guided accordingly.

His contract expired at the end of March; his new one was 'limited to service on assignment with UNROB', which no longer existed, and made no mention of UNZAP! There were times now when he had little solid work to get his teeth into and he felt that he was gradually losing interest. He was fed up with the UN as it was; he carried on because he knew it could be so much better.

As he was about to leave for Liberia in June Waldheim spoke to him about a possible internal survey of the UN structure for handling economic and social matters, something on the lines of the Capacity Study, but on a much smaller scale. Jackson could see the need for this (just as he had in 1948!) but said that if asked to do it he would need a first class assistant – preferably Anstee. He would not commit himself until Waldheim made him a formal proposal. The matter was clumsily handled in the ACC, 'where it caused much fireworks', and in ECOSOC. Not surprisingly, it raised some hackles in the higher reaches of the UN Secretariat, and in October Jackson wrote a 'strategic withdrawal' statement for Waldheim to put to the ACC calling off the whole idea.[16]

Having been appointed Deputy Director of UNDP's Regional Bureau for Latin America Anstee was now based in New York, so she decided to take an apartment at Waterside Plaza, within walking distance of the UN building. Jacko was on the point of taking the adjacent one, but got cold feet at the last minute and lost his deposit. This was a difficult time for them both; Joan wanted to make firm plans for their future together and to know where they stood, so before he set off for Africa at the end of August she placed the ball firmly in his court. For the next six days (in Monrovia and Accra) he thought of little else. Back in London he wrote saying that he was unable to commit himself so long as he was unsure of his future work. He felt that he had failed her, indeed that he was incapable of making a genuine and lasting human relationship, even wondering if he was responsible for the breakdown of both his marriages. Yet he loved her, and would continue so to do.[17]

On his way to Bangkok at the end of September he ran into Umbricht in Geneva, just back from a meeting in New York with Waldheim and Mujibur.

> He said that he was surprised I wasn't there, but KW had said I was now fully occupied with 'the inter-UN organisation restructuring'!! My guess is that Mujib asked KW for Victor's attendance, whoever else was there, because he (Mujib) knows him better and believes him to be more sympathetic to Bangladesh than I am. According to Victor the meeting did not make much progress. I'm genuinely sorry if that is the case, for the sakes of the people of Bangladesh, but, for what my judgement is worth, it would require exceptional political skill to regenerate effective support. Most governments, I fear, have written off both Mujib and Bangladesh. If Victor thought he might stir some feeling of jealousy in me he was talking to the wrong man!![18]

He was on his way to a meeting of the Mekong Advisory Board. The Indicative Basin Plan of 1970 had been well received internationally and resulted in an upsurge in funding for the project at the time. 'But once again regional events conspired to frustrate the committee's development efforts'[19] – regional events being the war in Vietnam which had now spilled over into Laos and Cambodia; nevertheless the advisory board soldiered on.

Later in 1974 he decided to take the other apartment at Waterside and opened a doorway linking it to Joan's. On the 37th floor, with splendid views over the East River, this became their base for thirteen years where they entertained colleagues, ambassadors and friends. A second visit to Villa Clara Rosa for Christmas and the New Year brought them both much happiness.

In early March 1975 North Vietnam launched a large-scale offensive against the South. This marked the beginning of the end of the twenty-year war. Waldheim had long realised that a relief operation in Indo-China would be needed and at one point in 1972, when it had looked as if the war might soon end, he had told Jackson that he counted on him to take charge of it. At that time Jackson had quite enough on his plate, and knowing that other people were keen to get their hands on it he took care not to get involved. As the war continued Waldheim blew hot and cold about what should be done and who should do it, at one point designating someone other than Jackson.

On 31 March, in response to desperate appeals from UNICEF and UNHCR in Saigon, Waldheim launched an appeal for $100 million. By 10 April $9 million had been received, the largest contributions being from Australia, Sweden and Canada.[20] On 17 April he asked Jackson to coordinate an emergency programme; on the same day the Khmer Rouge led by Pol Pot entered Phnom Penh and overthrew the Cambodian government. On 30 April South Vietnam surrendered to the communist North.

Australia offered UNICEF the use of a *Hercules* transport aircraft to bring food and medical supplies, but for the government of the Democratic Republic of Vietnam this was unacceptable because the plane and crew were military, wearing the insignia and uniforms of the Royal Australian Air Force. Raymond Aubrac, a friend of Jackson's who was in Hanoi at the time as the Secretary-General's Special Representative, immediately cabled him in New York, and Jackson, speaking as an Australian, repeated the offer in the name of the Secretary-General, but that too was no good; he suggested painting UN markings on the plane, and using a civilian crew wearing UN armbands – but still the government would not agree, 'so the concentrated milk and medicines waited somewhere in the hangars in Thailand or Laos while the sick and starving children fled from the bombardments'. On his return to New York on 8 May Aubrac was asked by Waldheim to 'prepare the first international actions with Sir Robert Jackson'.[21]

The previous day a draft resolution appealing for all states to assist in reconstruction of Indo-China had been adopted by ECOSOC without a vote.[22]

Some delegates said that they had already responded to the appeal; others merely expressed support for the resolution. China said that the South Vietnamese and Cambodian peoples had recently won great historic victories of world significance and extended to them its warmest congratulations.

Of the three nations comprising Indo-China, Laos had suffered least destruction, but needed food and medical supplies; Cambodia had suffered much, but the new government of Democratic Kampuchea refused all offers of international aid. Clearly most of the fund would be used for Vietnam, especially the South, which urgently needed food, medical supplies, clothes and agricultural tools. The US delegate was the last to speak: for his country the situation in Indo-China was complex … He was constrained to note that his Government would not provide any economic assistance for the rehabilitation of North Vietnam and had expressed elsewhere its uncertainty about the position with regard to South Vietnam. It must see what kind of government there would be there and would view with care and compassion requests for aid from responsible authorities in South Vietnam.[23]

The response to Waldheim's appeal was therefore small; no further mention of relief to Indo-China was made in ECOSOC and Jackson never went there at that time. In August 1977 he reported to Waldheim that the operation was in the process of being wound up and urgent medical supplies for Laos were still being provided.[24] By then the only bi-lateral assistance going into Indo-China was from the USSR, some socialist states and Sweden.[25]

His contract was extended for 1976 as co-ordinator of UN Assistance Programmes (unspecified). He was very unsure about his future, and neither he nor Anstee liked New York.

> 20 June, Accra: We are both of us much better in the field – NY is simply bureaucracy, working hard to prevent mistakes, nearly as hard to rectify them, and plagued by personalities. I only need to get away from New York to feel the change – to realise there are different ways to live. But it's crystal clear to me that UN and UNDP are now controlling our lives; is that what you want? Or do you now want to live your own life – decide your own destiny? Basically it's more your decision than mine. I'm certain – if you want us to stick together, as I do – that we'd be miles healthier and happier if we got out soon and LIVED. I'm nearly 65.[26]

22 June, Accra: All in all VRA in pretty good shape; we can still get a bit more from Kaiser (justifiably) for our power – the subsidiary aspects, fishing, inland water-transport, resettlement etc all very impressive. Like you and La Paz, I was home again. Mostly very good memories of Ghana.[27]

He never went there again.

His next mission was to a very small state – Cape Verde, a group of islands some 300 miles off the western tip of Africa. Formerly a Portuguese colony, it was admitted to membership of the UN after becoming independent in 1975 when it was already suffering the consequences of seven years continuous drought. The Secretary-General had appealed to member-states to provide assistance and authorized the release of $500,000 from the UN Emergency Operation Fund. A good harvest early in 1976 improved matters, but only temporarily, and in November he sent Jackson there on a mission. On his return the General Assembly adopted a resolution appealing to Member States and the Secretary-General to mobilise assistance, and proposing that Cape Verde, already classified as Most Seriously Affected should be given the benefits enjoyed by Least Developed Countries.[28] Jackson also visited Guinea Bissau on the mainland where economic problems were the result of eleven years of a war of liberation.

São Tomé and Principe comprise an even smaller state than Cape Verde. The larger island, São Tomé, on the equator 200 miles west of Gabon, is about 400 square miles in area (slightly bigger than the Isle of Man); tiny Principe is 90 miles to its north. As a Portuguese colony it had produced exclusively for export, importing almost all its food, but following independence Portuguese ships going to Angola no longer called there; the islands were now isolated from the mainland and from each other; the only air link was to Luanda, the only telephone to Lisbon.

In December 1976 the General Assembly, deeply concerned at their serious economic and social situation, requested the Secretary-General to mobilise assistance, particularly from the developed countries, and recommending that São Tomé and Principe should be classified as Most Seriously Affected.[29]

In June 1977 Jackson went there to review the situation with the government and ascertain its needs. He saw at once what assistance was required:

(1) training in administration and management, especially of the former cocoa plantations, and in certain technical disciplines;

(2) communications: a small aircraft was needed immediately to operate between the two islands and to provide a link with the mainland; a small ship was also needed for the movement of exports and supplies of food and equipment; a telephone link with the outside world was essential.

The government, having already consulted other advisory bodies, produced a detailed list of its needs costing about $13 million.[30]

By mid-August Jackson considered that the food situation in Cape Verde was under control until the end of the year, but that further assistance would be needed in 1978. The government had asked him to return in October/November, when the new harvest could be assessed. Support for São Tomé and Principe was being mobilised and there too the government had asked him to return as soon as possible for a longer visit to discuss the main problems confronting the country.[31] But those were two more member states he would never visit again.

In July he and Joan had spent a week in Nyon on the shore of Lac Léman, visiting their old haunts in Trélex, walking up through the wood to St Cergue, picnicking in the Jura, and doing the classic boat tour of the lake on a day of pouring rain. They looked around for a house where they would both live, but without reaching any decision; then he left for Zambia to prepare his final report to ECOSOC.

After that he learnt that he urgently needed an operation on his right eye and told Waldheim that this would make it difficult for him to fit in all his commitments before the end of the year. If Waldheim could say how he envisaged handling these matters in 1978 he could make plans to avoid official dislocation. 'If you wish me to carry on next year, I should be honoured to do so; alternatively, if you desire to make other arrangements I should perfectly understand.'[32]

Waldheim replied:

> You know how much I have appreciated your willingness to serve the Organization on a number of most delicate and important assignments during these last few years. You have discharged your responsibilities with great credit and have earned the respect and admiration of those who were privileged to work with you. You can also be justly proud of the confidence that you gained of the Governments with which you had worked so closely.
>
> I have decided to re-organize the arrangements for co-ordination of assistance to various countries in Africa as of the beginning of next year.

I am, therefore, grateful for the assurance of your understanding in this matter. I know that even after you have left your present position I can continue to count on your availability for any assignments for which your long experience and strong commitment to the Organization would make you the obvious choice. I am heartened by this knowledge.

I very much hope that the operation will be a success and I extend to you my very best wishes for a speedy recovery.

Warm personal regards, Kurt Waldheim.[33]

Urquhart was shocked by Waldheim's letter: 'It seems to me an incredible way of dealing with people, especially someone of your calibre, but I have no doubt it did not surprise you and I must say it did not surprise me.'[34]

Anstee reckoned that 'the whole sorry game was KW's politicking in order to get votes through appointments to ensure his re-election. Geographical representation also came into the picture, irrespective of competence. Jacko was in the middle of helping Zambia, Cape Verde and São Tomé; he did not want to let them down or let them think he was abandoning them; they respected and relied on him and very much wanted him to continue'.[35]

He sent messages to the Presidents and Prime Ministers of Cape Verde and São Tomé offering to help them in a personal capacity if they needed him.[36] The difference in the scale of assistance needed in these small islands and in Bangladesh could not have been greater, but small nations were no less important to him than large ones and his distress at being taken off the job before it was finished no less too.

After his eye operation he came to stay at Petersham. He found it very frustrating not being allowed to read. Despite his depression he soon displayed his customary good cheer, writing daily comments of encouragement to us in the kitchen diary:

19 September – Jacko arrives. 'Oh, dear!'
20 'Give us strength, we beseech thee, Oh Lord.'
26 'Heavens above! Still here!!!'
28 'Count-down – day 7'
4 October 'FREEDOM !!!!! (TEMPORARY) BLAST OFF!!!'

He wrote to Joan:
> Maria is wonderfully patient with me mooning about the establishment. ... For the last two weeks I have been spoiled in every conceivable way. On Monday evening [3 October] James and Maria and I lowered a bottle of medicine to celebrate their Release (alas, only temporary!).[37]

Back in New York he found that nothing had been done about Cape Verde, where the crops had totally failed. He urged that the Secretary-General should assign whoever would be concerned with African affairs in 1978 to take charge of a mission there as quickly as possible.[38] Shortly afterwards Waldheim transferred responsibility for assistance to Cape Verde and São Tomé and Principe to A A Farah, the African ASG for Special Political Questions.

In November he returned to 'The Royal Convalescent Arms' for a few days to see his eye specialist and get his new contact lenses fitted. He also saw Barbara, who had finally agreed to a divorce. Robin then announced his engagement, whereupon she declared that his marriage and his father's divorce could not both take place in the same year.

> 15 November, Brussels: Dearest Maria and James, on many occasions I've tried to tell both of you how much all your love and affection have meant to me, but there has been a special quality in the last, and this visit extended over weeks during which I have been absorbed into your family at a time of physical discomfort made more difficult by distasteful developments on the official side. All being well you will read this on your Silver Wedding Anniversary as I – to my regret – fly away to Baghdad, Bangkok and on to Australia.[39]

He gave us a silver ash-tray with a Silver Jubilee crown-piece at its centre, and an inscription round the rim signed with his squiggly **J**.

He was on his way to Melbourne to join Alan and Bett in celebrating their golden wedding anniversary and Alan's recovery from a serious illness. Under doctors' orders himself, he stopped for two days in Bangkok. He called at the Mekong office and saw his blind secretary; Chulikorn Thaisanguanvorakul, Angela for short. In 1969 he had paid for her to go to Kuala Lumpur to learn braille shorthand – a typical example of his generosity to members of his staff with personal problems. His concern for her did not end there: whenever there was a new Executive Agent she felt insecure. 'Sir Robert always approached my boss to discuss my future like a father'.[40]

He found Melbourne a strain; he knew he had been right to go there, but he felt he was on parade all the time and would have liked a day off. It was five years since his last visit; many of his friends had died and the Australian way of life seemed to have changed. In many ways he felt a stranger in the land. People seemed to think that he had cheered Alan up, but the prognosis was still not clear. On his last day he collected Sheila (whose husband was working in Melbourne) and took her to YARALLA where Alan still lived. Before going out for a farewell lunch they sat under two magnificent silky oaks, 80 feet high and covered with deep orange flowers – the ones he had planted as a small boy.[41]

After he got back to New York in December his friends in the UN wanted to give him a party, but he didn't want any fuss made, preferring to slip away quietly. Waldheim of course gave him a farewell luncheon at which he paid him due tribute.

He spent Christmas and the New Year with Joan in Jamaica. Negril, on the western tip, had a long and deserted white beach, where they stayed in an isolated bungalow, a far cry from the hotels of OPERATION COOLOFF. Food was scarce except for the fish sold on the beach every morning, to which Jacko remained allergic, so they lived largely on tinned food brought from New York. They spent their time swimming, relaxing and crawling about on all fours to find his new contact lenses every time he dropped them.

It was another happy interlude for them, but they both knew that they had reached a professional and personal watershed. Jacko's long innings with the UN seemed to have reached its end while Joan's was still in its ascendancy; it seemed inevitable that their paths would continue to diverge.

17 Back to UNDP

UNDP TURNED TO HIM ONCE MORE: Bradford Morse, who had succeeded Rudolph Peterson as Administrator in 1976, invited Jackson to resume his appointment as Special Adviser in order to look into two matters: (i) ways of using retired senior executives to increase UNDP's capacity for technical co-operation activities, (ii) pre-investment follow-up activities.[1] The appointment would last for two years and he would retain the rank and status of Under Secretary-General. Jackson was happy to do this and would not take any salary, just expenses. The tasks would not be onerous, and the arrangement gave him the continuity of employment which enabled him to remain in the USA. During April he visited Brussels, Geneva, Paris, Stockholm and The Hague.

The appointment also helped maintain his link with the Mekong. The committee had ceased to exist when the new governments of Laos, Vietnam and Kampuchea (formerly Cambodia) failed to appoint members in 1976, but the advisory board had continued to meet once or twice a year. At the beginning of 1978 Laos, Vietnam and Thailand agreed to establish an Interim Mekong Committee, which UNDP formally recognized so that it could finance its projects in the region. Jackson offered to assist it for a few days a month, chiefly to help mobilise resources, and was given the title 'Counsellor'.

A visit to Petersham nearly put an end to his travels: one evening during dinner we heard footsteps above us and assumed they were our children's – until we saw a pair of legs dangling outside the window. A cat burglar had shinned up a drainpipe and was now running off with his haul: nothing of any financial value, but all Jacko's travel documents, his passport and his UN *laissez-passer* with its precious G4 visa enabling him to live and work in the USA. It was very embarrassing, but he moved fast to get replacements; to his and our great relief he was able to return to New York as planned on 7 May.

Joan joined him there and they spent eighteen happy days together, even if he thought too many evenings were given over to entertaining! 'It was a good period, and a contrast to the earlier part of the year. I think that both of us underestimated the thinness of the ice over which we travelled.'[2]

The question of whether Joan should go to Robin's wedding was exercising them both; even Jacko was not greatly looking forward to it, for he could foresee four or five encounters with people who were 'for Barbara' right or wrong, and he was worried that 'she might try to cart him around' to give the impression that they were not really separated.[3] The young couple wanted Joan to be there; they were both very fond of her, and saw her as Robin's future step-mother. She dreaded the thought of going and resented the event as an obstacle to her and Jacko's happiness. Had they been married her position would be clear; as it was it would be anomalous. She wanted the occasion to be an opportunity for them to show that they were together, with heads held high. During the church ceremony Jacko would clearly have to be at Barbara's side, but Joan insisted that throughout the reception he must be seen with her. On that understanding she accepted the invitation.[4]

Joan, Maria, James and Jacko at Petersham, summer 1978.

Maria and I were also invited. The wedding was on 15 July, a lovely summer's day, at St. Edward's Church in Stow-on-the-Wold, a pretty Cotswold town in Gloucestershire. Whatever emotional undercurrents there were, all went smoothly. Afterwards the four of us drove back to Petersham, stopping on the way for dinner, to which Jacko had also invited Sheila and her husband. We had often heard Jacko talk of 'Sheila Collins, his faithful secretary', but were unaware of their relationship during the 1940s. Jacko usually kept the various parts of his life in watertight compartments and it clearly never crossed his mind that these two were better to remain so. Not that the occasion was in any way disagreeable for us, but Sheila was distinctly frosty towards Joan. She was by now Barbara's staunch ally and we were the enemy. (Years later, when I approached her about this book I was still regarded as the enemy and repulsed accordingly, but she soon relented and we became good friends.)

Alan had died unexpectedly on 16 June, so after visiting Bangkok in August Jackson went on to Melbourne to see Bett and Tam (Andrew, their son). They were still in shock and Bett was getting frail, but Tam was taking good care of her. Jackson was glad to have seen them and shared their sorrow, but a few days in Canberra left him in low spirits, only too conscious of the mess he had made of his life. He could see where he had gone wrong, but it was too late to put things right. He was conscious of his age and wondered if he could find something to do which was moderately useful; he felt that a year of his life had gone for very little.[5]

7 September, Manila: I have thought very much of us today – much happiness in the past; still hope for the future. For the last ten years you've been the only person in my life, the only person I've wanted to be with. And you have given me more than anyone else.

8 September: I went to the UNDP office and spent about four hours there; they talked very sensibly and were helpful over the 'retired executives' scheme – my mind is a little less murky than before.

His travels never ceased as he continued his consultations for UNDP: Tokyo, Bangkok, Dacca, Delhi, Teheran, Istanbul, Rome, Geneva; then a month's holiday with Joan at PIPPINS, and on to Dublin, New York, Ottawa and Toronto.

At the end of the year he was asked by the United Nations Industrial Development Organisation (UNIDO, based in Vienna) to undertake an appraisal of its Senior Industrial Development Field Advisers programme (SIDFA). UNIDO's purpose is to promote industrial development and help accelerate the industrialisation of developing countries. A SIDFA was a member of a resrep's team who advised a developing country on industrial matters. This task meant yet more travel, and after spending Christmas with Joan and making his customary New-Year visit to Petersham, he set off on yet another round of the usual capitals in the Far East, taking in a meeting of the Mekong Interim Committee in Hanoi. He also went to Latin America, one of the few parts of the world where he had never worked, visiting Buenos Aires and Lima for the first time.

At the end of March he delivered his report on SIDFAs, recommending that:

(1) UNIDO should be transformed into a specialized agency, independent of the UN.

(2) UNIDO and UNDP should determine which countries needed full-time SIDFAs and which could share, and review the effectiveness of present resreps and SIDFAs, and (3) UNIDO should consider appointing up to 50 SIDFAs of the requisite quality by the end of 1980. All the governments he had consulted stressed the importance of quality.[6]

> 5 May, Vienna: Naturally the report was referred to as masterly, excellent, 'why can't all UN reports be written like this?', elegant (try that for size!!), lucid and concise, brilliant etc., I was suitably moved, knowing that it meant damn all.
>
> The only two [at the meeting] who cheered me up were the Sudanese who said that I could come and live there any time I wanted to, and a charming youngster from Trinidad & Tobago who spoke at the very end: 'Mr President, I was going to say a very great deal about SIDFAs, but now that I've read Sir Robert's report it would be like turning up for church on Monday!' That brought the house down.
>
> As for reality, BH [Bruce Harland, head of UNIDO's Technical Advice Division] has lobbied continuously to ensure that it gets nowhere in the governing council – apparently emphasising that the developing countries would be fools to take a stand on such a small matter and that they'd lose far more in other directions. He's naturally played as hard as he can on 'no more UNDP funds for this nonsense' etc., and emphasised the political appointments. Probably quite a good wrecking job. It's all pretty depressing – echoes of the Capacity Study. The governments really are behind this small report – it <u>could</u> have important effects IF UNIDO/UNDP put <u>good</u> SIDFAs and resreps on the ground – an essential step if <u>good</u> project identification, etc. is to be expanded to absorb available funds.[7]

Five years later UNIDO was transformed into a specialised agency, as he had recommended.

Jackson continued working on his UNDP assignments, travelling mostly in Europe. In November he was in Nairobi, *en route* to Tokyo to finish his report on pre-investment, when he had a phone call from Rafeeuddin Ahmed, Waldheim's

Chef de Cabinet: the Secretary-General was facing a new problem in Kampuchea: 'Would Jackson allow his name to be put forward among others as prepared to take it on?' 'Forget me' he replied – 'when people want me to do a job they ask me to do it. I'm on my way to Delhi'.[8] Waldheim would never have approached Jackson in such terms; perhaps that was Ahmed's idea; no sooner had Jackson arrived in Delhi than he rang again to say that the Secretary-General wanted him to return immediately.

In New York Waldheim told him in great detail of his various problems: hostages in Teheran, independence for Namibia, and the problems in South-east Asia; this took a good two hours. At the end he said 'I've just asked a few questions and of course I'm delighted that you'll do it'. 'Under our usual understanding?' (that he would delegate his entire powers to Jackson) 'Of course'. As they walked to the door Waldheim put his arm around Jacko's shoulders. 'By the way,' asked Jacko, 'which of the three jobs do you expect me to do?' 'Oh yes – South-east Asia'.[9]

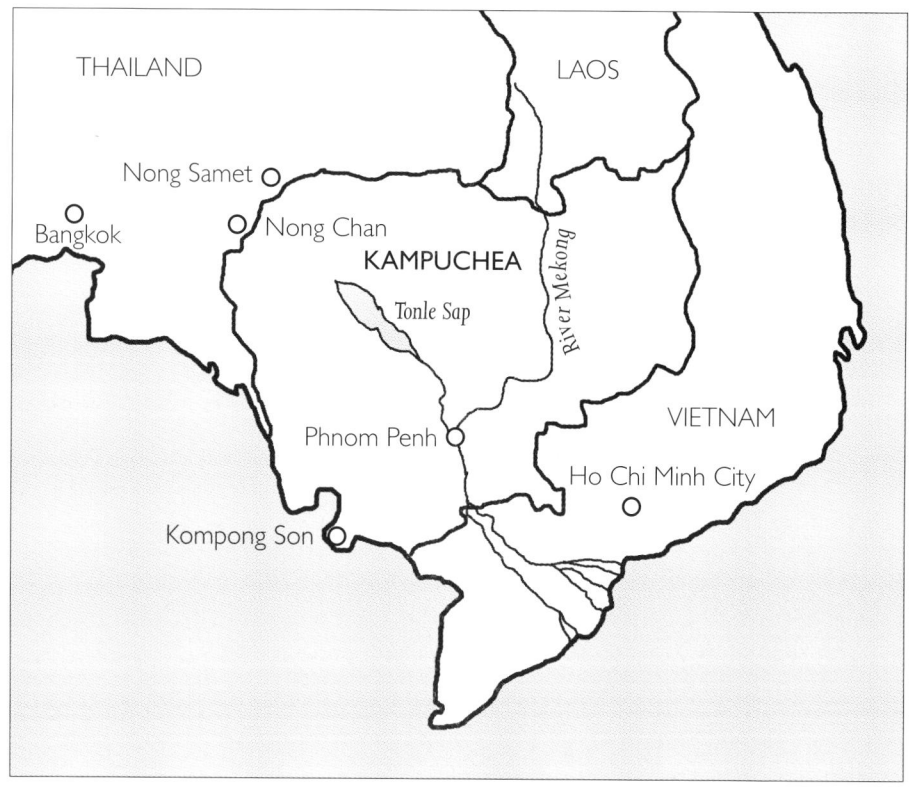

Kampuchea

18 Kampuchea

KAMPUCHEA WAS TO BE JACKSON'S last relief operation. For all his seemingly nonchalant agreement to Waldheim's request, he must have had some idea of the problems he would face. The logistical skill and personal dedication he had demonstrated first in UNRRA and later in Bangladesh had succeeded against great odds and achieved results beyond the reach of more conventional UN bureaucrats. Now he would face different problems: with the cold war at its height, humanitarian considerations became increasingly subordinated to political concerns and the conflicting national interests of member states. This he would find hard to stomach.

When the Khmer Rouge entered Phnom Penh, the capital of Cambodia, in April 1975 they emptied it at gun-point, forcing the entire population – skilled workers, old men and women, invalids and children – out into the country to work in the fields. The Democratic Republic of Kampuchea had arrived.

This nightmare was ended by an invasion by Vietnam, whose massive air and ground assault swept through the lightly armed Khmer Rouge forces and entered Phnom Penh on 7 January 1979. But this was not so much liberation as domination, and by Cambodia's traditional enemy. Many Khmers Rouges, including Pol Pot himself, were still at large and fled north-west together with thousands of other Khmers towards the border with Thailand.

The People's Republic of Kampuchea (PRK), as it now called itself, shut itself off from the world. Despite the terrible conditions inside the country the President, Heng Samrin (a former Khmer Rouge officer who had defected to Vietnam), disregarded offers of aid from UNICEF and ICRC (the two organisations whose mandates allow them to assist nations not recognised by the UN). Not until July, when he claimed that two million people were starving, did he let it be known that one representative of each would be welcome. They arrived in secret, bearing suitcases of medicines, and were only allowed to stay for two days, but saw enough to convince them that predictions of widespread disaster current in the west must be taken seriously.

As arrangements for a relief operation were suggested the PRK authorities raised one objection after another, demanding in particular that all aid, including any for the border area, must enter Kampuchea via Phnom Penh. This was unacceptable to UNICEF which on principle had always supplied aid to children on both sides of a conflict. Having established by a discreet survey that there were thousands of mothers and children there in desperate straits, UNICEF decided to pass supplies quietly across the border. Some of these inevitably reached members of the Khmer Rouge, which Heng Samrin eventually accepted, but he insisted that supplies passed across the border must not exceed those entering via Phnom Penh.[1]

The new regime, like Vietnam itself, had few supporters among the member states of the UN, with the result that after three days' discussion in September the General Assembly gave Kampuchea's seat to the murderous Khmer Rouge rather than to the *de facto* government – a bitter pill for the PRK to swallow. This decision was a furher indication of difficulties ahead and it shocked Jackson profoundly.

As the Vietnamese army pursued the remaining Khmer Rouge forces during September the numbers of refugees on the border grew to several hundred thousand. The Thai Government told the Secretary General that if the UN would undertake to provide for their sustenance Thailand would open its doors to them. Waldheim agreed and asked WFP (the World Food Programme, a subsidiary of FAO) and UNICEF to do all they could to comply with this request.[2] He had already designated UNICEF as lead agency for the relief operation, so WFP supplies would be able to enter Kampuchea under UNICEF's umbrella. On 17 October Thailand allowed refugees to enter, and the UN High Commission for Refugees (UNHCR) set up holding centres for them inside the border.

On 19 October Waldheim launched an appeal on behalf of UNICEF and ICRC, which were already operating a Joint Mission in Phnom Penh. Nations were shocked by the plight of Kampuchea, and responded generously, pledging $210 million, but once again Waldheim had not set up a central fund, so donors could give to any of the five organisations involved: UNICEF, ICRC, FAO, WFP and UNHCR.

By 21 November, when Jackson agreed to take on Kampuchea, it was far too late to ask for 'one voice', he therefore went immediately to Washington, hoping to persuade the US Government to make its contribution directly to the Secretary-General, but the White House, for all its respect for Jackson as a master-operator, preferred to decide for itself exactly where its money should go – or not go.[3] So with one hand tied behind his back he set off for Geneva and Rome to see the heads of ICRC and FAO, and thence to Bangkok. He had a second, though temporary, handicap to contend with: Harry Labouisse, the Executive Director of UNICEF, was due to retire at the end of the year, and Waldheim, having designated UNICEF as lead agency, was anxious not to hurt his feelings. He had therefore not yet announced Jackson's appointment; consequently Jackson could only explain his presence in Bangkok by saying that 'his name was Jackson and he had been sent there to help'.[4]

On 1 January 1980 James Grant succeeded Labouisse. He had worked for UNRRA in China and spent much of his life with USAID, later becoming President of the Overseas Development Council in Washington, where he had urged the US Administration to contribute generously to Kampuchean relief. At first alarmed at the extent to which UNICEF's resources were being consumed by that operation, after visiting Phnom Penh and the border his enthusiasm for it was unbounded.

The following day Jackson's appointment was announced as 'the Secretary-General's Special Representative to coordinate humanitarian programmes in Kampuchea'. One was based in Phnom Penh to provide relief inside Kampuchea, the other in Bangkok to assist the refugees on both sides of the border. It was not a promising combination.

On his return to Bangkok on 13 January Jackson called a meeting of the agencies to agree objectives and policies; knowing their sensitivities he never took the chair himself, inviting them take it in turn. All agreed on the importance of playing down the UN's role on the border so as not to provoke Hanoi and Phnom Penh. These meetings would continue throughout the operation, co-ordinating activities as far as possible and ensuring that at least in Bangkok they spoke to the

Thai Government and to the voluntary agencies with one voice, though there were occasional lapses.

UNICEF had appointed John Saunders, recently retired from UNDP, to head the Joint Mission in Phnom Penh. He found the authorities very uncooperative on account of their anger that WFP, a UN organisation, was providing aid to the Khmer Rouge on the border.

By March donors were beginning to doubt whether Kampuchea's infrastructure had the capacity to deliver supplies on the scale required, and an informal meeting raised only $24 million of the $260 million needed; Jackson knew the importance of convincing them that their supplies would be efficiently distributed, and this setback strengthened his hand when he met the Kampuchean authorities. The problem wasn't so much the infrastructure as their failure to make better use of it.

Since the UN itself had no outpost with its own Head of Mission, Jackson visited Bangkok more frequently than he had Dacca, often staying for five weeks at a time at the Erawan Hotel, sending daily reports in coded cables to UN headquarters:

8 April 1980: For reasons as yet unknown, attitude of authorities in Phnom Penh towards the international agencies has suddenly deteriorated at the very moment when their cooperation is essential. Increasingly they are failing to give international officials the facilities that are essential for them to do their job.[5]

Jackson addressing donor governments in New York, 26 March 1980, William Buffum by his side.
UN 143,499 Y Nagata

Before visiting Phnom Penh he went to Hanoi to tell the

Prime Minister of Vietnam of the difficulties facing the Joint Mission. The Prime Minister said that his government regarded the assistance being given by WFP to the Khmer Rouge as a cancer which would be tolerated with great reluctance provided that every effort was made by the UN to play it down, and so long as an important programme of international assistance was being provided for Kampuchea. On that understanding his government would intercede with the authorities in Phnom Penh in an effort to eliminate the Mission's difficulties.[6]

In Phnom Penh Jackson, Saunders and Jean Hoefliger of ICRC met most key ministers, (Heng Samrin was away) and listed their immediate concerns: for example nearly 80,000 tons of food, largely Russian, was sitting in warehouses at Kompong Som awaiting distribution to the provinces where it was urgently needed; the long round-about air route from Bangkok to Phnom Penh was costly; a Swedish medical team in Bangkok had been awaiting clearance from Phnom Penh for two months. Jackson left them in no doubt that the ability of the international agencies to mobilise further assistance would be decisively influenced by their own efforts over the next six weeks to improve the distribution of food, make better use of the truck links and infrastructure, and remove impediments to the relief operation.[7]

Moscow, like Hanoi, was exasperated at Phnom Pen's long delays in admitting medical teams from Eastern Europe. Jackson suggested that the Soviet Red Cross might provide helicopters to move supplies and seed rice inside Kampuchea, and it was agreed that Phnom Penh should approach the USSR direct.[8]

At least the governments which could most influence the situation (Kampuchea, Vietnam and the USSR) were now fully aware of the facts and how he thought they could best help to remove difficulties; he would be able to brief donors accurately at their next meeting in May.[9]

There were three men in Phnom Penh on whose judgement Jackson relied: Saunders, Hoefliger and Malcolm Harper, the local Director of OXFAM.[10] OXFAM was the largest of the 34 voluntary agencies working in Phnom Penh. Like the Joint Mission they all lived and worked in the Samaki Hotel, in constant touch with each other, and they had formed a committee which met weekly under Harper's leadership..

When Saunders and Harper were immersed in discussion one day Grant

(UNICEF) and Hocké (ICRC) looked in. Grant, as usual, was bubbling over with enthusiasm: 'You're doing a great job here, John and Malcolm; you guys, you're really fantastic'. When Harper suggested that possibly they weren't doing such a great job and began mentioning problems he was brushed aside: 'We're problem-solvers in UNICEF, don't you worry.' Harper and Saunders both thought that Grant was living in a dream world and that their recommendations to headquarters were not being taken seriously enough.[11]

Saunders was on friendly terms with the Soviet Ambassador and thought Jacko would find it helpful to meet him in order to thank him for his assistance so far and explore other possibilities, such as using Soviet helicopters to distribute supplies. He invited them both to tea. The Ambassador was young, good humoured, well travelled, and spoke excellent English. Saunders recalled their encounter:

> As I had expected, the Ambassador and Jacko got along very well. Jacko soon relaxed into that friendly machine-gun conversational style he liked, mixing five different subjects plus jokes in as many minutes, and at intervals swooping back on each topic exactly where he had left it. One of his concerns was to explain the many and various problems in trying to overcome the resistance of member governments to giving more funds and support for the work in Cambodia.
>
> As time went by I began to be conscious that explanations were called for; one needed a lot of net practice to score boundaries, varying the length and spin couldn't always persuade the ball past the defensive bat, you could try to get him leg before wicket, *in extremis* there was the possibility of a googly …. What can only be described as the trace of a hunted look began to appear on the face of the attentive Ambassador. Occasionally he gave an interrogatory glance at me. I decided that discretion was the better part of valour. Trying to explain would have succeeded in simultaneously demonstrating that the Ambassador's English was not as good as he thought, and that Jacko was not explaining himself clearly enough. Later I conveyed to the Ambassador, through another channel, those points which may have been lost on the field of play.[12]

Using cricketing metaphors was one of Jacko's endearing eccentricities, though the uninitiated, from Trygve Lie onwards, did not always find them helpful!

Despite Saunders' hopes, when Charles Egger, the Deputy Director of UNICEF, went to Moscow in June to pursue the question of helicopters he was directed to Aeroflot who saw the matter in purely commercial terms, with payment in dollars, not roubles.[13]

By early May the régime in Phnom Penh had made only minimal concessions to keep the Joint Mission sweet; the staff were very gloomy, and given the reception Grant had received, Saunders advised Jackson to delay his next visit until July. Rational discussion with the authorities had become almost impossible and they needed time to cool down.[14]

The good news was that donors felt that they were now being given more accurate reports by the Joint Mission and pledged $116 million, reaffirming their commitment to the whole relief operation.[15]

Problems on the border were different: much of the donors' support was going to UNHCR, while WFP, UNICEF, and ICRC were living from hand-to-mouth. There was fighting between the camps, some of which were controlled by the Khmer Rouge; people were being killed daily and it was a miracle that ICRC staff were unharmed.

Some 400,000 people inside Kampuchea were being fed via a 'land bridge' at Nong Chan, where lorry-loads of rice were unloaded, carried across the border into Kampuchea and re-loaded onto family ox-carts or bicycles for the long trek home; farmers obtained seed to raise their first crop for several years.[16] The scope for this, however, was limited because seed sent over the border must not exceed the amount being sent into Kampuchea direct; the Foreign Ministry in Phnom Penh had issued a mighty blast at the imperialistic agitators, claiming that much more international assistance had gone to Thailand and the border area than to Kampuchea itself. Though not correct, this was effective propaganda, and not helpful for fund-raising.[17]

> 5 June: Taxes, taxes, taxes, or charity begins at home: Vietnam claims taxes for our aircraft flying over their airspace; Kampuchea claims landing taxes for relief aircraft; Thailand claims three or four taxes on WFP rice exports; could include 14% for exports to communist countries; Thailand also trying to levy yet another tax on FAO rice seed exports. This bunch of bananas is

high on my agenda for Siddhi. [Siddhi Savetsela, the Thai Foreign Minister.] Time now of essence but rice is political dynamite in terms of internal Thai politics. Happy days.

6 June: Thai open door is virtually closed; signs of pressure from Thai supreme command to push all existing camps across border into Kampuchea. UNICEF and ICRC made it clear to supreme command that this would virtually bring present programme to an end. ... From start of UN involvement on border nasty skeleton in our closet. About 5% of WFP food deliveries is handed over direct to Thai army which supplies it to certain camps undoubtedly occupied by armed elements of Khmer Rouge. Nothing to do with UNICEF or ICRC, but I am sure Hanoi and Phnom Penh know of this and do not draw nice distinctions about which UN agencies are responsible. Pro tem we let this sleeping dog lie.

Jackson always believed, and claimed that Waldheim also did, that WFP had no alternative but to provide food for those armed elements, although it violated UN principles. Not to have done so would have meant great suffering and almost certain death for large numbers of women and children.[18]

Though UNHCR was doing a good job in running its refugee camps in Thailand, it never discussed its intentions with anyone else.

13 June: This was dramatically illustrated at this morning's inter-agency meeting when it became clear that UNHCR in Bangkok has been discussing repatriation with the Thai Government for the last three months without informing any of the other agencies, with the result that the announcement of the repatriation plan has led to violent political reactions from Hanoi, even more so from Phnom Penh, all of which has a direct effect on the joint mission.[19]

Attacks by Vietnamese forces on the border soon put paid to Thailand's attempts at repatriation.

After a week in New York a weekend with Joan at PIPPINS was just what Jacko needed before returning to Bangkok.

'They were 46 exceedingly good hours even if I had to shout in order to be let in! ... All too brief – but one of the best visits ever, my beloved. A good memory to live on for five weeks. I'll go flat out to be back by the end of the first week in August. Everything was what it should be – weather, garden, beef et al. And you!'[20]

At the end of June it was WFP's turn to incur Jackson's wrath: without any prior consultation it had decided to reduce its rate of shipments to the border. Evidently this was revealed in a cable sent by UNICEF on 30 June, which to Jackson's dismay had not been encoded. The Thai Government reacted violently, protesting that the Secretary General had broken the agreement made with the Prime Minister in October 1979; Siddhi threatened to stop all UN operations through Thailand.[21] Headlines in the press, probably government inspired, warned 'Thailand may cut Phnom Penh supply line' – 'Major relief groups stop aid on border'.[22]

There never had been any formal agreement between Thailand and the UN, so Jackson immediately signed one to the effect that no change would be made in arrangements on the border without prior consultation and agreement on the part of all concerned.[23] He also gave Siddhi Waldheim's assurance that he had no intention of terminating the humanitarian operations on the border so long as he was directed by the General Assembly to carry them out and funds were made available. At present these should last until the end of the year.[24]

WFP's reason for reducing supplies had been the cost of demurrage, which could be $4,000 a day per ship. Jackson told them that large deliveries of food were essential to provide a continuous supply, and that the presence of waiting ships would hasten the rate of unloading; in any case these costs were insignificant compared to the overall cost of the operation and were the responsibility of the Joint Mission, not WFP. Wherever he went his message to anyone organising supplies was to ship them as soon as possible.[25]

A visit to Phnom Penh in July convinced him that the most important element of the whole operation was getting aid to the people inside Kampuchea; the worst aspect so far was FAO's failure to deliver the critically important final 15,000 tons of seed rice.[26]

> 21 July: Grant arrived in Bangkok too late for last night's meeting. I therefore met with him and Egger at 7 o'clock this morning. He is completely unaware of the political volcano which now exists; I think I managed to convince him of the basic political dangers both here and in Phnom Penh, but we will

need to keep our fingers crossed. Fortunately Egger is now well briefed, fully understands the political dangers and is sensible.

Saunders was very conscious of tension between Jacko and Jim Grant, once describing it as 'their strong mutual dislike'; his own friendship with Jacko certainly soured his relationship with Grant, but they were both big men who spoke their minds and there was scope in plenty for treading on toes. Jacko was often maddened by Grant's impetuosity, and Grant was doubtless frustrated by Jacko's restraining hand, but underneath they remained good friends. Once at a UNICEF staff meeting in New York Jackson cut Grant off with the words 'amateurs – you have no idea of how to run this operation', but Grant seems to have borne no grudge.

Saunders was posted to New York in June to direct the UNICEF operation at headquarters. Kurt Jansson, his successor in Phnom Penh, was a Finnish administrator and former ASG, who like him had been brought out of retirement. Saunders's frustration with the authorities had been understandable; Jansson, starting afresh, saw that further complaint would be pointless.[27] He concentrated on monitoring distribution and was able to allay fears that most of the food provided was being consumed by the Vietnamese Army.[28]

He was struck by Jackson's single-mindedness, which at times bordered on fanaticism, and found his attitude towards Heng Samrin and Hun Sen, the Foreign Minister, somewhat patronising: one of his standard remarks was that what really mattered was what one had in one's head and in one's wallet, patting his forehead and back pocket. Seeing that this did not go down well Jansson suggested that he drop the habit – but to no avail! He found Jacko friendly though rather impersonal, and invariably appreciative; he was not the only colleague to receive a parting gift with an inscription signed with his typical **J .**[29]

By August the Phnom Penh authorities' relations with the Joint Mission had improved; at last they seemed to recognise the importance of demonstrating that they could handle the assistance being provided. On the border efforts were being made to reduce direct support to three Khmer Rouge camps and both

Phnom Penh and Hanoi appeared to accept that everything possible was being done to preserve a delicate political balance in a very difficult situation.[30]

Jackson had now made the journey from New York to Bangkok and back six times, and visited Tokyo, Moscow and Canberra. He was due for a rest. The monsoon had begun and the maximum possible amount of food and seed had been delivered to Kampuchea. He was able to spend most of September with Joan at PIPPINS.

In Phnom Penh the picture continued to improve, and by October he was confident that the basic objectives of the 1980 operation would be achieved. The Kampucheans, though not well fed, were in much better shape than a year ago; there might be small pockets of malnutrition, but there was no likelihood of famine. Existing stocks and cargoes of rice in ships now *en route* would provide ample supplies until the main harvest in December. Despite all the political difficulties, the strategy evolved at his first meeting in Bangkok in December 1979 should have succeeded by the end of 1980. Some assistance would be required in 1981, and the case for this would be presented to donors on 19 November. For the first time ministers displayed genuine appreciation of the efforts of the international organisations, and expressed Kampuchea's gratitude to the Secretary-General personally.[31]

> Thanksgiving Day, New York: There is no doubt that 'Events' certainly changed both of our lives. I don't think either of us could possibly have imagined what the next twelve years held in store for us, but as I look back the pluses and the happiness far, far outweigh the minuses and the unhappy times. So it is natural that I should say 'Thank you for all that you have brought into my life'. Whatever you may think, I love you more deeply, and more wisely than ever before – and (perhaps vainly) I believe that that love is reciprocated. (How many men can stroll around in superb $2000 pullovers, soon to be followed by a magnificent $3000 job?). [They had been knitted by Joan, and were priced on the basis of the hours she spent on them!] So many, many memories – most of them to be treasured – on which to look back. I shall be a fortunate man if we are given more time together; if not, I shall have been more fortunate than most, and enriched by twelve years of special companionship and shared interests.[32]

Two days later he went to London for a minor operation at 'Sister Agnes' (King Edward VII's Hospital for Officers in London, often called Sister Agnes after its founder). A quiet Christmas at PIPPINS completed his convalescence. Once again he and Joan stayed at Petersham before setting off in different directions at the beginning of January, she to New York, he to Bangkok.

He could look back on 1980 with at least a modicum of satisfaction; the danger of famine in Kampuchea had been averted by relief via Phnom Penh, most of which was provided by western countries, some by the USSR. 'No mean achievement,' wrote Joan, 'when one knows something of the almost insuperable logistical, financial, political and, alas, institutional obstacles.'[33]

But without 'one voice' and a single fund which he could allocate solely on the basis of humanitarian need, his hand was weaker than it had been in Bangladesh. The political problems were of a different order, and would eventually determine the course of the two operations.

Most of the problems in 1981 would be on the border; he was clear that the decisive element in the relief programme would be the timely delivery of rice seed, and feared that FAO would repeat its inefficient performance of 1980.[34] The fact that all its invitations for tender were being called from Rome and none from Bangkok[35] did not augur well, and delivering the seed via the land-bridge was still problematic.

In January UNICEF advised that this method should be suspended as soon as possible, but in a manner which would not provoke unfavourable reactions from the Thai Government.[36] No such luck: the Thai National Security Council had a new secretary, Prasong Sansouri, who saw himself as Thailand's hawk and was doing his best to impede any attempts to help Kampuchea. He insisted on re-opening the land bridge as a condition for agreeing to the export of any rice.

> It is futile and academic to talk about reopening the land bridge until we can see positive results emerging from FAO's efforts to purchase seed in Thailand, which have still not started. Furthermore any proposal to reopen the land bridge would require the most careful preliminary consultations with authorities in Phnom Pen and Hanoi – a point made exceedingly clear to me in Hanoi yesterday. As to Phnom Pen, all concerned would be inviting a political explosion if rice seed passed into Kampuchea over the border before supplies had already begun to arrive at Kompong Som.[37]

Vietnam's *chargée d'affaires* complained later in New York that the land-bridge was functioning again and warned that this might have undesirable consequences. She was told that Sir Robert was doing his best to keep land-bridge deliveries down to a minimum but his concern was also to deliver a maximum quantity of rice seed to Kampuchea before the monsoon which would soon start. It was necessary to ship some through the bridge if the desirable quantity was to reach Kampuchea in time.[38] There were no undesirable consequences.

In May Jackson called an informal meeting of donors in New York to ensure that they were fully informed about conditions in Kampuchea, and could not claim later that they had not been; he reminded them that while the Secretary General and the agencies could propose what should be done, it was for governments to dispose, and they alone bore the responsibility for what would happen there.

He also categorically rejected criticisms made at a previous donors' meeting (when he was in hospital) that agencies had wrongly used their funds for 'development' and 'reconstruction'. These criticisms had never been substantiated by specific examples and he challenged governments to give them. He spoke with some force: there would be no hope of mobilising the funds required if governments were able to create inaccurate and dishonest impressions about the use of funds. There was silence.[39] At this point a slip of paper was passed to him across the table:

> Jacko: 4-5 pm today is another one of your finest hours – to be treasured by your friends. Jim Grant.[40]

According to Jansson Jacko did not much like routine diplomats. He could be quite rude and even condescending when chairing donors meetings in New York. He was particularly hard on those from countries that for political reasons questioned everything that was reported about the relief operation. One, from an EEC country that contributed little, who posed long-winded questions at every meeting, was cut off with the words 'when your country contributes its fair share to the programme we will listen to you'. With that he turned to the next speaker.[41]

The Thai Government was now delaying UNHCR's repatriation efforts in Thailand, and making other difficulties for them. Its cooperation with international organisations in Bangkok was non-existent. This was all part of its very hard anti-Vietnam policy.[42]

By June the scene in Bangkok was worse: UNICEF's delivery of fuel was already two months late, and the border situation had become more dangerous. Political confrontations between the various Khmer factions were increasing; armed clashes were the order of the day and night, bringing an inevitable toll of dead and wounded; China had sent 25,000 new automatic weapons to the Khmer Rouge and the area was thick with armed pick-up vans manned by totally irresponsible youths.[43]

The flow of refugees from UNHCR holding centres to the border was continuing, but very few seemed to have gone on to Kampuchea itself. Financial provision had been made for 160,000 rations, but the border population was already 177,000 and another 4,000-5,000 could be expected each month; border clashes led to more costs, consequently a total of $25 million would be needed for the second half of 1981. There was also the possibility of more Kampucheans coming to the border following a bad monsoon. WFP was providing rations for 97,000 Thai villagers (displaced from their homes by the refugee camps), well above the figure on which estimates had been based, and an additional $1 million would be required for the second half of the year.[44]

On 31 May Barbara died after a long illness. The two of them had made their peace in December, bringing comfort to Robin as well as to themselves. He saw her again in May shortly before she slipped into her final coma.

By the end of June he was worried that the operation was not being run effectively, partly because the five agencies all had staff problems and were too often acting independently. UNICEF was seriously short-handed in Bangkok and Phnom Penh; the standard of ICRC staff had dropped during the past year, and the morale in the Joint Mission was low. At this stage it would be extremely difficult to stimulate the agencies into real action, or for them to consider appointing new staff.[45]

UNICEF's Board of Directors now wanted it to cease acting as lead-agency and reduce its commitment in Kampuchea to its normal role by the end of 1981. Jackson saw no difficulty with this inside Kampuchea, but the border was another matter; a UN mission of comparable size to UNICEF's would be needed.[46]

Joan had official business in Bangkok at the beginning of July, so to celebrate her birthday Jacko arranged that they would spend the weekend at Hua Hin, a quiet resort on the eastern side of the Gulf of Thailand, two hours' drive away. They were so busy talking that it was an hour and a half before they noticed that they were passing the same large pagoda for the third time. Their driver clearly had no idea of how to get to Hua Hin and spoke no English, so they bought a map at a petrol station. Having passed the pagoda for the fourth time they reached Hua Hin after five hours of travelling in great heat and humidity. 'Third time round the pagoda' would now denote for them a total mess; 'fourth time round' would indicate that salvation was in sight! But Jacko's back collapsed and he had to lie flat for the whole week-end.[47]

The US Ambassador, Morton Abramowitz, left Bangkok on 7 July; he had been particularly helpful to Jackson, but his espousal of the refugee cause was not to the liking of the new hard-line Reagan administration. His successor, John Gunther Dean, announced on arrival that he would be 'Ambassador to Thailand, not to the refugees'![48]

By mid-July the border population had already reached nearly 200,000 and could grow further if the monsoon was bad. Of the 97,000 rations being provided for Thai villagers, he guessed that roughly one third ended up with the Khmer Rouge. For him this was the most unsatisfactory element in the entire operation; it always requiring careful handling with Thai Government officials, who were extremely sensitive about it.

Funds for 1981 were still some $16 million short, chiefly because support from the EEC had dropped by two-thirds. At this rate the border operation would be bankrupt by the end of October. He had to be sure of getting that $16 million by the end of September. The management of the operation had also become very fragile; it was only held together by a small group of officials in Bangkok. The attitude of most of the agency headquarters was a combination of disinterest and inefficiency.[49]

Once again he had been overdoing things, and at the end of August he went back to Sister Agnes for a check-up. Nothing was seriously wrong, and as usual he was told to take things quietly for a while. He spent most of September at PIPPINS with Joan – one of the few times that year when they were able to be together. Long periods of separation had always been a feature of their relationship, and one of its strengths was their intense interest in each other's work, expressed in their daily letters, which were still as loving as ever. But their times together were now under a new strain: Barbara's death had made their marriage possible, yet Jacko absolutely refused to discuss this, to Joan's dismay and deep hurt.

In October he had a visit from the ASEAN group – the Association of Southeast Asian Nations (namely Indonesia, Malaysia, the Philippines, Singapore and Thailand. The group's main purpose was to prevent the spread of communism in the area.) They told him that they expected Kampuchea to receive no further assistance unless they, the ASEAN Governments, could be convinced that conditions inside Kampuchea still posed a direct threat to the lives of the people. They thought that enough had been done and Kampuchea should now be treated as one more developing country. Could the ASEAN countries say that he – Jackson – and the UN Secretariat shared their views? Jackson reminded them that it was for governments to determine policies and for the Secretariat to implement them as best they could; thus no view could be attributed to the UN Secretariat at that stage.

It was just as he had expected: the ASEANs wanted to introduce political considerations into the future conduct of the humanitarian operations. When he turned the conversation to the potential financial burden which Thailand could face in the future, their dilemma became clear: they wanted a humanitarian operation in 1982 which would relieve Thailand of any financial burden while at the same time denying any assistance to Kampuchea. He replied with his usual tact: 'such an arrangement would in his view create difficulties for many donors'. The meeting ended in a relaxed atmosphere.[50] That it should have done so is a measure of Jackson's patience and forbearance. Much as he deplored and resented this cynical attitude, which was spreading, towards an operation which he continued to see as humanitarian and nothing but humanitarian, as the Secretary-General's Special Representative he would never allow a hint of his own feelings to show.

Waldheim sent him a telegram on his 70th birthday; he himself was due to retire at the end of 1981:

> This is a particularly fitting opportunity for me to express my sincere gratitude for the very distinguished contribution you have made to the work of the United Nations in so many fields of its endeavour. I have indeed relied on your wide experience and invaluable assistance and have especially appreciated our close personal association over the years. My wife joins me in wishing you every happiness and further success in the years to come. Warm personal regards, Kurt Waldheim.

There had indeed been a warmth in their relationshhip, and at times a touch of love-hate. With his successor, Pérez de Cuéllar, warmth was unlikely; he was a bit of a cold fish.

The success of the operation in 1981 inevitably made it harder to keep up the pressure for assistance in 1982. He had to prepare reports for the next donors' meeting in February conveying the sense of urgency which the situation demanded. Drafts provided by FAO and WFP lacked punch; he was tempted to rewrite them himself, but knew that this would cause resentment at their headquarters (especially FAO's) and do more harm than good. He was worried that donors might not respond adequately to Kampuchea's emergency needs; this could result in malnutrition and the consumption of locally grown rice which should be kept for seed, leading to an even worse situation in 1983.

He knew that it would now be virtually impossible to mobilise direct support for Kampuchea in Washington, but he also knew that the State Department recognised two reasons for maintaining some kind of programme: (i) to avoid aggravating the general political situation, and (ii) to avoid causing more Kampucheans to move to the border. He therefore spent a day giving officials in the administration information to use in briefing members of Congress.[51]

The problem was even wider: western governments generally were sceptical about WPF's recent estimates of food deficits and were now looking to the socialist countries to take responsibility for providing for a substantial proportion of Kampuchea's needs. The USSR was reacting adversely to this;[52] furthermore, they were trying to persuade Kampuchea that the UN was responsible for providing all relief supplies and that they, the USSR, would concentrate on 'development' which the UN had publicly refused to undertake.[53] Jackson decided to hold separate meetings with socialist governments in future on the day after the main (western) donors' meetings.

9 May: All present indications are there will not be sufficient food exports into Kampuchea during the next three months to meet major deficits in certain provinces from the end of August until new harvest is available November/December.

While they continue in their efforts to apply pressure on Socialist countries to provide their fair share, certain of our donors recognise that a genuine emergency may well arise about September and that they may be forced to act. For our part we must ensure that they are kept fully informed and be prepared to act very quickly if they give us the funds; FAO inputs remain of decisive importance and here we remain seriously under-funded.

Jackson briefing press after donors' meeting on 26 July 1982.   UN 150,056 Y Nagata

The ASEANs, afraid that the Khmer Rouge might lose Kampuchea's seat in the General Assembly, were pressing the other two external political parties to combine with them. These were the Khmer People's National Liberation Front led by Son Sann (a former Prime Minister of Cambodia, now old and frail), and Moulinaka, a smaller party led by Prince Norodom Sihanouk (who had ruled Cambodia for 25 years, and now claimed the loyalty of a tiny force just inside Kampuchea's border). On 22 June they reluctantly agreed to combine with the Khmer Rouge to form the Government of Democratic Kampuchea. Sihanouk became President, and Son Sann Prime Minister. Pol Pot had by now withdrawn into the background and his successor, Khieu Samphan, became Vice President. Sihanouk was merely a figurehead and the so-called government an unhappy partnership, nevertheless the coalition secured Kampuchea's seat by an increased majority.[54]

By the end of May the transfer of operational responsibility on the border from UNICEF to WFP was complete, and the WFP team led by Winston Prattley, the resrep in Thailand, was making steady progress in securing greater rationalisation of the operation over the whole length of the border. Having stressed from the start that the border operation should be conducted with as low a UN profile as possible, Jackson was not pleased to find the operation calling itself WFP-UNBRO (UN Border Relief Operation). Some title was needed, but he was angry at not having been consulted. Not that he blamed Prattley; the title probably emanated from Headquarters. To find WFP's official cars flying the UN flag was even worse![55]

Hanoi still saw the border operation as 'a cancerous growth', and reluctantly accepted aid to the Khmer Rouge as the political price of assistance for Kampuchea itself, so long as aid was also provided inside Kampuchea.[56] Unfortunately, given the current attitudes of donors towards Kampuchea, that was becoming increasingly difficult.

After a brief holiday with Joan at PIPPINS and a week in Geneva Jackson returned to Bangkok on 11 October. Gunther Dean, just back from Washington, assured him that the balance of $4.5 million promised by the USA would be made available very soon. He said he hoped that existing arrangements would continue in 1983 and that no organisational changes would be made. He emphasised the importance of having in Bangkok someone from UN who could keep all the agencies in line, and also anticipate the political dangers and defuse them.[57]

The formation of the Sihanouk coalition had increased the polarisation of the various groups on the border and intensified political differences within them; consequently political assassinations were now taking place as the struggle for military and political power and control of black market operations intensified.[58]

> 27 October to Secretary General: In 1983 even-handedness in the execution of these operations will be if anything more important and also more difficult than in the past. Much skill and patience will be required to mobilise funds for Kampuchea, but for both humanitarian and political reasons every effort must be made to do so. At the same time it will require equal skill to ensure that the border operation, now operating with increased smoothness, is not disturbed by the inevitably more complex political situation that is already evolving as a result of the Sihanouk coalition.

Jackson's contract ran until the end of the year. He was well aware that there were some in the secretariat who wanted to get rid of him. His concern was not so much for himself, as for the thousands who depended on the operation being directed with the dedication and skill that it required. Gunther Dean's hopes that existing arrangements would continue showed that the US administration shared that concern, and may possibly have led to the intervention of Arthur E Dewey, Deputy Assistant Secretary of State in the Bureau for Refugee Programs, to press for the renewal of Jackson's contract for 1983. As leader of the US delegation to the donors' meetings in New York he usually met Jackson (and sometimes Grant too) for lunch on the previous day; he reckoned him 'the premier role model for international crisis management and humanitarian leadership'.[59] He knew that there were those in the Secretariat (eunuchs he called them) who whispered in de Cuéllar's ear that Jackson, who was nearly 71, had to go. Their concern was not that he was too old; they felt insecure and uncomfortable around him because he was too good. 'The eunuchs may have been among the heaviest crosses Sir Robert had to bear, but they became our crosses in the US Government as well. We made it clear that any attempt to marginalize Jacko was also an attempt to marginalize the United States.'

Dewey approached de Cuéllar through William Buffum, the Under Secretary-General responsible for General Assembly and Political Affairs (to whom many of Jackson's cables were addressed).

> I suspect he used the method which a few other senior people in the know would use with de Cuéllar. Bill would probably slip past the *chef de cabinet* to catch him alone; whatever the business it was always done with more dispatch if one caught the Secretary-General alone.

Dewey reckons that his intervention to convey the United States's strong wish that Jackson's contract be renewed was one of his greatest contributions to the cause.[60]

> 27 January 1983 to Secretary General: Mr Shustov of the Soviet delegation called on me yesterday; the Russians are worried that all the humanitarian assistance is going to the border or the holding centres and only a trickle of aid is going to Kampuchea itself. He said that his government appreciated my personal efforts to mobilise further support for Kampuchea, but he knew that I would understand if it were forced to adopt a different official posture towards these operations if the present imbalance in what has always been regarded as an 'even-handed' operation was not redressed. As always our meeting was held in a very agreeable atmosphere and Mr Shustov went out of the way to emphasise that the information recently provided about USSR assistance to Kampuchea had been made available as a gesture of support for my own personal efforts.
>
> 25 February: Just received long and depressing letter from Everest [UNICEF's special representative in Phnom Penh]. The atmosphere in Phnom Penh is increasingly anti-UN, the authorities there feel that donor governments are now discriminating against them and favouring Khmers outside the country who are hostile to them; this attitude of course is understandable; Everest is of the opinion that the authorities may ask all UN personnel to leave the country with the possible exception of the UNICEF mission, which of course continues to execute its regular program. There is no doubt that the political temperature is rising steadily; I look forward to my approaching visit with interest.

In mid-February a refugee camp at Nong Chan had been destroyed and evacuated as a result of conflicts between the parties to the coalition; between 20 and 30 people were killed. The Thai Government allowed about 20,000 former occupants to move to two sites further from the border, but were insisting on them moving back to Nong Chan or another site; either way the cost of providing fresh accommodation would be about $650,000; increasing the food reserve would cost another $250,000.[61]

About a week later the Government moved them to Nong Samet, a camp further north which, they said, was on Kampuchean territory and therefore liable to attack by the Vietnamese Army. They said, too, that the Vietnamese Army had the right to help the Heng Samrin regime by attacking any refugee camp on Kampuchean soil, because they contained resistance soldiers in addition to civilians, all of which Jackson saw as directly related to the uneven-handedness of the operation.[62]

His visit to Phnom Penh in March was timely; the authorities were increasingly irritated by the endless international squabbling over Kampuchea and dismayed at the great reduction in the scale of assistance it could now expect, while assistance on the border and in Thailand continued on the same scale. It was not surprising that they wanted numbers of international staff reduced to a minimum.[63]

Jackson, by now very much *persona grata* in Phnom Penh, was invited to dine with the Foreign Minister, Hun Sen. Their relations were cordial and correct, but the young Minister, still in his twenties, was not sure how to address his guest. Like many foreigners he felt that 'Sir Robert' was possibly over-familiar, but Jacko assured him that it was correct. 'Even better,' he said, 'call me Comrade Sir Robert'![64]

A day spent inspecting the border operations convinced Prattley that things would become even more difficult: the three factions of the coalition were all armed to a greater or less degree, fighting each other and among themselves. Much of the area was now a stinking mess with obvious and urgent problems of sanitation, which could only be resolved if conditions returned to relative stability.[65]

On 24 May the donor governments met in New York. As always, Jackson took great care to protect the Secretary General's position so that he could not be blamed for failures by governments of member states; all his reports to donors fulfilled the General Assembly's request that the Secretary General should <u>keep them fully informed</u> of the essential humanitarian needs of Kampuchea. Any failure to meet them would be their responsibility, not the Secretary General's.

> Throughout the discussion on Kampuchea representatives of the ASEAN countries endeavoured to score minor political points, and in so doing reflected one of the least attractive aspects of the UN when genuine needs of people who have endured terrible suffering are subordinated to third rate political bickering. It is significant to my mind that a discussion of this

nature could never have taken place during the days of UNRRA or indeed at any time during the following 20 years or so. Very little in the way of new assistance was provided; there is no doubt that this uneven-handedness will increase the disfavour with which the socialist countries now regard these operations.

The political cynicism which developed during the Kampuchean operation as national interests overrode concern for suffering people would become the norm for all subsequent humanitarian operations.[66]

Pledges were made which Jackson thought sufficient to continue the border operation until October, after which he urged governments to consider how the operations should be handled the following year. The Secretary General would, he said, be put in a very difficult position were he to be asked to assist only Khmers on the border (above all Khmer Rouge) and to do nothing for those in need within Kampuchea itself.[67]

His meeting with representatives of the Socialist countries the following day revealed their deep dissatisfaction with the extreme imbalance of the programmes, nevertheless the USSR and Vietnam went out of their way to emphasise their great appreciation of the work of the Secretary General and his staff during the last three years and of their continuing efforts to mobilise essential humanitarian assistance despite the hostile attitude that now existed among many donors.[68] Evidently they too were worried that they might lose the benefit of his services.

Jackson very soon saw that, pledges notwithstanding, the border operation was running short of money; for once he had been over-optimistic. No funds had been provided for rice except for a small contribution from Italy, none for the health services recommended by WHO, or for the cost of moving and rehousing nearly 100,000 Khmers recently uprooted by border incidents. He doubted if WFP would have enough to continue beyond the end of August and suggested holding a small informal meeting of key donors on 12 July.[69]

Until late 1982 it had been possible to monitor the distribution of food supplies on the border, and thus remain accountable to donors. After the dry season offensive by Vietnamese troops in January 1983 many encampments which had been attacked were abandoned, and many of the settlements which replaced them were virtually armed encampments where the military mixed freely with civilians, frequently intervening in the process of food distribution and other efforts to provide relief. This was creating an intolerable situation for UNBRO.

Jackson and Prattley raised the matter with senior officers in the Thai Supreme Command, pointing out the situation which could arise if member states were to ask questions about UN's involvement in providing assistance to armed elements in the border camps, contrary to its principles. At their suggestion Prattley wrote to the Thai Commander, General Riem, asking him to intervene personally to ensure that armed elements were removed from the camps and other areas in which UN personnel were involved, so that UNBRO's authority was maintained.[70] Prasong undertook to do what he could to help, and at the end of June Supreme Command assured Prattley that appropriate action was being taken to separate the armed civilian elements and was expected to be completed within the next two or three weeks.[71]

On 23 June Jackson called a meeting of representatives of donor governments in Bangkok, principally to explain WFP's cash flow problem and urge them to use their charms with their Foreign Ministers in order to generate the necessary financial support.

After his usual three weeks leave with Joan he returned to Bangkok in August to find that the shortage of cash for the border operation was even more serious. Despite all his meetings with donor governments since May, no new pledges had been made at the donors' meeting on 12 July. Expenditure was immediately cut down to absolute essentials and water supplies were reduced substantially.

He immediately informed donors' representatives, arranged to meet them again on 1 September and to see Ambassadors in Geneva before the next formal donors' meeting in New York on 16 September.

One thing was very clear in Bangkok – they could not continue with this hand-to-mouth existence; if the voluntary agencies were unable to pay their staffs they would disperse and it would be virtually impossible to get them back.[72] A week later the voluntary agencies were told they would have to take in another notch in their operational belt because of the financial situation. No doubt they would run to their embassies, which should help efforts to mobilise funds.[73]

A report from WFP that the Japanese Government (more sympathetic than others towards Kampucheas needs) would contribute $12.7 million to the Kampuchean operation turned out to be premature, for when the Thai Government heard of it they prompted the ASEANs to block it, and the proposed contribution was now being reconsidered in Tokyo.

Finding it difficult to restrain himself from criticising this political intervention, Jackson provided the Japanese Ambassador with extensive notes of the current situation in Kampuchea which could be of use to his government if it decided to resist pressure against its Kampuchean contribution. The Ambassador said he expected it to be a matter of deferment, not cancellation.[74]

An analysis of available funds showed that by taking in every reef in UNBRO's sails the remaining cash could be made to last until the end of September. Savings by WFP of $600,000 from their present resources plus $250,000 expected from West Germany and $125,000 from Norway should cover October. A meeting with American Embassy officials brought a reassuring message from Dean: the US intended at the donors meeting on 16 September to announce a contribution which should cover November and December. In that case the border operation would be financed on a bare-bones basis until the end of the year. A pledging conference would be needed in November to obtain funds for 1984.[75]

Asked what his own feelings were about what the relief operations had achieved Jackson said that they were a mixture of sadness and despair:

> The fundamental objective of preserving the lives of the people has been achieved, but much more could have been achieved if the humanitarian operations had not been subjected continuously to political pressures. ... Inside the country, the aid has been far less than the scale of destruction warranted. As for the refugees, one can take partial satisfaction in resettlement – repatriation to a peaceful Cambodia would have been far better. As for the border, it's sheer, unending, bloody tragedy.[76]

On the evening of 22 September Jackson and senior members of the Secretariat attended a meeting with the Secretary General. Two current issues were discussed – the likely crisis in November when it would be necessary to mobilise fresh funds for the border operation, and the threat of a new food emergency within

Kampuchea in 1984. Jackson said that in his view continuity of staff who thoroughly understood the operation was essential and in that connection the services of two key officials required urgent action. (He possibly meant Prattley on the border and Everest in Phnom Penh.)

> The Secretary-General then enquired about my own position. I replied that my services remained at his disposal and if I was needed during the transitional period covering the two approaching crises, I was ready to assist. The Secretary General then explained that he did not wish to continue the appointment of a Special Representative for these operations beyond the end of this year and that I was too senior for the future arrangements that he had in mind. He therefore did not feel that he would require my services beyond the end of this year. In response I emphasised the importance of having in Bangkok someone with sufficient status who could hold together the staffs of the international organisations and voluntary agencies etc., and who could do his best to prevent adverse political developments.[77]

His note for the file, impersonal as ever, concealed deep feelings. He cannot have been surprised when the blow finally fell, but that did not lessen the hurt caused by being taken off the job before it was finished, or his concern about how well his successor would handle it. That de Cuéllar should have told him this in the course of a meeting with others present, rather than privately, passes belief.

By now the authorities in Phnom Penh had become very unhelpful; their inability to make decisions was creating a major administrative problem.

> The understandable ignorance on the part of the regime – it lives in near isolation – of the outside world and how the UN system operates adds greatly to the difficulties of those who wish to assist them. The Prime Minister asked me … to convey to the Secretary General personally their great gratitude for all he has done, also their complete reliance on him and faith in him to deal successfully with the approaching food crisis.[78]

Knowing that Jackson's appointment was at an end, donors were concerned about future administrative arrangements, not only for humanitarian reasons, but also because of their accountability to their legislative bodies, which was directly linked to fund-raising, and because as matters stood no staff would be available after 31 December. (It was now 10 November)

Above all, they wished to ensure that the new coordinator would have the standing, contacts and other qualifications to do the job successfully, and that they would be fully consulted before any appointment was made. They did not think that the post should be down-graded as proposed and were concerned that no provision was being made for the critically important function of fund-raising; nor for the travel funds which that would require. Past experience had shown that if a food crisis developed in Kampuchea, which Jackson thought inevitable, the coordinator would be unable to discharge his or her responsibilities effectively if limited to only four visits to Bangkok each year.[79] He was convinced that developments on the border together with the deteriorating situation in Kampuchea would make 1984 more difficult than 1982 or 83.[80]

When his departure was announced Jackson received many tributes, of which that from the Thai Ambassador to the UN was particularly gracious: 'He had helped the Cambodian people to survive, not only as individuals but as a nation, through the years of famine. Hundreds of thousands of lives had been saved through his inspired leadership.'[81]

His contract was renewed for another three months. He went to Bangkok in January, and again in February when he also visited Hanoi and Moscow, gathering information on which to base a strong case for Kampuchea at a donors' meeting on 1 March. Senior officials in both capitals were realistic enough to realise that political considerations would over-ride humanitarian needs and they expected him to have a rough farewell passage at the meeting.

He was also preparing the way for future management by his Japanese successor, Tatsuro Kunugi, a former ASG. Anstee believes that his appointment was 'not unconnected with Japan's recent generous contributions of aid for Kampuchea'.[82] Jacko, whatever he thought, being Jacko, naturally went out of his way to help Kunugi and ensure a smooth hand-over, even offering to carry on until June without any official title. (He was given a contract for a further three months 'on special assignments' and made his final visit to Kampuchea in May.)

Early on the morning of the donors' meeting on 1 March Gene Dewey was sitting in the US Mission to the UN when he realised that nothing had been planned to mark the end of 'one of the greatest *tours de force* in the annals of the UN'; the

Secretariat had probably decided, conveniently, that there was no call for the Secretary-General to put in an appearance. He called Bill Buffum immediately and asked him to try to get the Secretary-General to make an appearance with some appropriate remarks. Buffum said it was a bit late, but he would see what he could do. Dewey was there:

> 'An hour and a half later, as Sir Robert was delivering his opening speech from the dais, the door behind was opened and out strode the Secretary-General followed by an overly large entourage from the Secretariat. De Cuéllar sat down, read verbatim Bill Buffum's well crafted remarks, got up, turned on his heel and with the curious entourage still in his wake, strode out of the chamber by the door by which he had entered.
>
> 'Sir Robert, who had barely taken note of this abrupt interruption, harrumphed before saying, as the door was closing, 'now that that's over with, we can get down to business'. De Cuéllar was clearly annoyed at having been shamed into doing the right thing, and Jacko, not knowing or caring how all this came about, was even more annoyed at the interruption and unappreciative of the mouthpiece that had heaped these generous accolades upon him.'[83]

19 The last lap

A UN CONTRACT AS SENIOR ADVISER enabled him to continue as Counsellor to the Mekong Interim Committee. Again he took no salary, but he still had his little office on the 29th floor and his UN *laissez-passer* permitting him to work in the US.

After the strains of Kampuchea he was looking forward to spending August with Joan at PIPPINS, but when he got there he was unable to relax. Tired and listless, not at all his usual self, he didn't want to go out or see anyone. Maria and I were invited for a week-end, and quite failed to raise his spirits. Despite glorious weather they spent a miserable month.

By rights he should have been relaxing and enjoying a sense of achievement, instead of which he was overcome by a sense of failure. Something inside him seemed to have snapped, and he had lost his self-esteem. The fact that he felt incapable of embarking on a new chapter of his life with Joan cast a lengthening shadow over their relationship.

In fact he was not well, and on his return to London he was found to have pericarditis. After an operation to remove the fluid from his lungs he was kept in hospital for tests to try to establish the cause of his illness. The doctors finally concluded that it must be some strange Asian virus, like the one he had picked up in Bangladesh.

In early November he was allowed to return to New York, where he spent Christmas with Joan, feeling better physically than he had for a year.[1]

In January 1985 they both went to Hanoi for a meeting of the Mekong Interim Committee, Anstee because the UN Department of Technical Cooperation, of which she was deputy head, was funding many of its projects. They departed from Bangkok early one morning on a chartered plane taking the delegates and secretariat to Hanoi for the meeting, or so they thought until they realised that there were no delegates from Thailand on board. It was only after they had flown

600 miles to arrive in a freezing Hanoi that they were told the reason: the Thai Government had decided at the last minute to boycott the meeting because of its exceptionally strained relations with Vietnam, whom it accused of crossing into Thailand in pursuit of Khmer Rouge forces. This was regrettable, since all three member states had until then seen the committee as a technical body representing economic interests which overrode their political divisions. The two delegations present decided to defer discussion of any important matters until a later date and returned to Bangkok.

Their journey was not entirely wasted: Anstee made a brief official visit to Ho Chi Minh City, after which they bought enough material in Bangkok to re-upholster all the sofas in the apartment, in a pattern which Jacko knew from the Erawan Hotel, virtually his second home by now. He returned to New York where he spent most of the year, except for his usual spell in England in the summer.

This was a time when Jackson was often asked to give talks and lectures. The first of these was in April when he was invited to speak at a symposium on macro-engineering at the Massachusetts Institute of Technology (MIT). This was a subject in which his interest had recently been aroused by Dr Frank P Davidson (brother of Alfred, UNRRA's General Counsel) who was Co-ordinator of MIT's Macro-Engineering Research Group. The subject of the symposium was tunnelling and underground transport, and he explained how the tunnels in Malta had been the key factor in protecting personnel and equipment.

Later in the year he chaired a seminar on 'The Problems of the Sahel and Macro-Engineering Options'. Various ways were considered of arresting the southward spread of the Sahara desert and improving local food production: how to bring water to this vast area – how to recharge the aquifers, or alternatively how to create a massive new storage and transport system. Either way, where would water come from and how?

One option was quickly disposed of: towing an iceberg to the African coast! Filling oil tankers with water when they returned to Africa was eliminated on the grounds that the quantities would be too small to make it worthwhile. Three other ideas were considered: (1) diverting the Niger or Ubangi river and building aqueducts; (2) pumping water north from the Congo River, or across the Atlantic from the Amazon through under-sea plastic pipes; possibly cheaper than (1); (3)

building de-salinization plants off the coast and digging a canal inland.

Jackson, forthright as usual, wound up the conference by declaring that the central problem was 'BBC – 'bell bloody cat'' [to bell the cat – to undertake the leading part in any hazardous enterprise]. What he meant was – 'how can this project proceed from a general outline to a specific, workable plan? How can that plan acquire a driving and coordinating force that will push it through subsequent phases? And how can it be presented to potential backers, allies, opponents, and constituents so as to win necessary support?'[2] The voice of realism at last!

In January 1986 he gave the BROCK CHISHOLM MEMORIAL LECTURE in Geneva. He had been asked to talk about the origins of the UN system and 'the founding fathers', of whom Chisholm was one, having been largely responsible for the creation of the World Health Organisation in the late 1940s.

Once again he recalled the war: how the health of the local population had been one of his major concerns in Malta, MESC and, above all, UNRRA – an organisation which had greatly influenced Chisholm's thinking because he had seen it as 'an action organisation made up of people who were in a hurry'.

He quoted Chisholm's words in the preamble to WHO's constitution: 'Health is a state of complete physical, mental and social well-being, and not merely the absence of disease or infirmity', and referred to his courage in refusing to allow the US Government authorities to trespass on his headquarters or intervene in his operations at the time of the McCarthy witch hunt in 1947. Chisholm thought that fighting off the FBI was probably the most important thing he did, for it changed the attitude of the American Government. The record of the United Nations itself at that time, said Jackson, was a very sad affair when compared to Brock's superb conduct and leadership of WHO.[3]

In February he was shown some draft chapters of a forthcoming history of UNICEF – THE CHILDREN AND THE NATIONS, by Maggie Black, which he thought gave all the credit to Dr Ludwik Rajchman, whereas in his opinion UNICEF had no single founding father, being the result of the efforts of many people. He recognised that Rajchman had played an important part, but there were others, including Lehman and LaGuardia. The text was slightly amended and Jackson was invited to write a foreword. Most of its fourteen pages described the work of UNRRA, concluding with his main point: 'there would never have been a UNICEF if there had not been an UNRRA, a fact in which many of us who lived through the post-war UNRRA experience feel a special kind of pride.'

His foreword was acknowledged by UNICEF as 'a very important additional dimension to the book',[4] but when a shorter edition was published in 1987 it was omitted, much to his dismay; he thought he might have been informed and even invited to produce a shorter one.[5]

In the summer he was asked to write an article for a London quarterly magazine on 'Disasters and the United Nations – International Operations, Science and Politics'. This gave him a lot of trouble.

> July 8, New York: 'I am a Disaster' has gone to London; I haven't the least idea whether [they] can use it. I'm quite prepared, despite a lot of work, to see it end up in the WPB. It was a Cow to write – Disasters / Science / Politics really demand three separate articles – they are not (at least to me) three flavours of ice cream that go easily together.[6]

How could they not use it? No-one but he could have written it with such authority, for it described what much of his life had been about: disasters caused by natural forces, and those resulting from man's political actions. Prevention of and preparation for natural disasters were criticised as insufficient because of lack of foresight by governments; as for the UN's response to man-made disasters, the relief measures taken by the specialised agencies were often hampered by insufficient support from member governments. The mobilisation of funds was always a crucial element. He cited UNRRA's efforts to mitigate the aftermath of World War II and the insufficiency of aid after the Kampuchean auto-genocide as examples of the impact of national politics on disaster relief.[7]

Again he spent most of August at PIPPINS. This time his health was fine but the weather was terrible; it rained nearly every day and was bitterly cold. He stayed for a week with Robin and his family in London, returned to New York, and set off for Australia in mid-October.

On the way he stopped in Hawaii for a few days to give talks about the UN at the University's Institute for Peace; the so-called 'International Year of Peace' had just begun. Speaking at a dinner sponsored by the United Nations Association on 24 October, the 41st anniversary of the founding of the UN, he wondered if the last 40 years would come to be regarded as the Age of Fear. In that time over 20 million people had been killed as a result of armed conflict, so it was not surprising that the reputation of the UN was at an all-time low. In his opinion governments had not used the organisation as had been intended; when they failed to resolve their own conflicts they passed the buck to the UN and then blamed it for failing to do better; governments also went to enormous lengths to get their nationals appointed to positions in the organisation and all too often the people forced on the Secretary General were unsuitable. As for the mass media – they were not interested in good news about the UN and many of their criticisms were unjustified or inaccurate; the situation, he said, was not as bad as they made out. UN's activities in the political field (which attracted most of the criticism) accounted for less than 10% of its budget; the other 90% was used in the economic and social fields through its subsidiary agencies such as UNDP. He referred to UNRRA and finally to UNICEF, 'the organisation that meant most of all to him personally'. And not only to him: Betty Jacob, Co-Director of the Institute for Peace, who had invited him to speak at Hawaii, had been very active drumming up support for UNICEF in its early years.

He flew on to Christchurch, staying for a few days with Relda, 'the person he loved above all for 53 years',[8] who was now a widow with a grown-up daughter. He wrote daily to Joan.

> 1 November: I've always believed New Zealand to be the most beautiful country in the world and I now begin to wonder if Christchurch is not the most beautiful city, with its superb parks, wonderful trees and wide streets, all immersed in an ocean of colour. ... But it is remote. So far all has gone well with this trip. I miss you, but not New York.
>
> 7 November, Melbourne: The Head of Interviews at Radio Australia is a nice woman, and clearly intelligent, but how can the young ask thoughtful questions about wars and their aftermath, and horrors (Kampuchea) they've never seen? Anyway, they wanted 15/20 minutes and went on for about 80. One programme now looks like four or five. They seemed satisfied.
>
> 9 November: Just as well 75 years celebrations only come once! Very pleasant dinner with Patricia Guest and friends. Robin wormed out of her that her birthday was the same as mine and the party somehow rolled on until midnight when he and Patricia's son drank our joint healths. We've been friends for 40 years and never knew we shared a birthday. A happy

occasion for us all, and your health was drunk as well. Bed at 0100. NOT my routine!

Robin hired a car for the purpose of 'Operation Nostalgia'. We found Tam at home (at Black Rock, 10 km south of Melbourne) and all three of us were very happy to be together; at their last encounter Tam was nineteen and Robin six. Not surprisingly they clicked immediately and forged an alliance against the Old Man of the Sea. Robin then drove along the Beach Road to Mount Eliza where we succeeded in finding ALLAWAH, the cottage where we had stayed 24 years ago. And so on to Mornington, where I regained my sight in 1922/23 [see page 2]. A delightful outing for which I was genuinely grateful to Robin.

His father's 75th birthday was not the only reason for Robin's presence in Australia at this time. In the Queen's Birthday Honours in June he had been appointed Companion of the General Division of the Order of Australia (AC) for services to international relations, and Robin had come for the investiture. Jacko had told Joan nothing about this, not even the fact of his high honour. Evidently this trip down memory lane, into the compartment of his life labelled Australia, was for family only, but her feelings were badly hurt.

The Investiture, 13 November 1986

14 November: Yesterday the heavens remained open all day and Sydney was awash. However we got to Admiralty House (the Governor-General's NSW residence) on time and the investiture business proceeded satisfactorily. I liked the G-G [the Rt. Hon. Sir Ninian Stephen] and his large friendly and maternal wife. Essential protocol observed but the atmosphere that of a home. I was informed (charmingly) by the Official Secretary that with a labour government Companions are top of the list; Knighthoods suppressed. AC takes precedence (to my surprise) over Companions of Honour and all Knighthoods. So it's all quite respectable.

15 November: Yesterday, my last day with Robin, seemed to disappear: in the morning a bunch of media people – press/radio/TV – a kind of 'no holds barred' round table in the UN office. I did my best but found it very tiring. Lunch with 500 – 600 members of the Institute of Directors – very kind to me but I only got one modest slice of meat and two bits of broccoli.

Now that I'm 75 Robin has decided that I am to be allowed the title 'Venerable' or 'Very Venerable' which I like very much!

Back to UN till about 1500.

Robin left early the next day. The Union Club, where Jacko was staying, was being renovated, and he now had it to himself. After buying provisions and some presents for friends and colleagues he went out in search of fruit, but – where to find a fruiterer? A friendly taxi driver told him 'None in the city these days, mate, just barrows and none of them at weekends'. They found one at King's Cross, the red light district. He asked the owner where he came from.

Owner: 'Malta.'
Venerable: 'Where?'
Owner: 'A little island; you wouldn't know.'
Venerable: 'Where IN Malta? Valletta – Sliema – Marsa – Mdina – Verdala – where? CITTA VECCHIA?'
Owner: (thunderstruck) 'CITTA VECCHIA, Sir!'
Venerable: 'In the old walls.'
Owner, putting his arms round the Venerable, to the surprise of the other customers: 'Yes Sir.'

The price of the fruit he selected – pineapple, passion fruit, rock melon, bananas, grapefruit etc., etc. – was $14.95. '$12 to you, Sir.'[9]

16 November: I paddle along – busy, but also time to myself. Naturally many memories of 50 years ago and reflections on the past. I never made any major decisions about my so-called career. Jobs just came. I didn't ask for them. Anyway, I do know that my love and thoughts remain with you.

19 November: Don't ask me where Monday and Tuesday went. All I know is that I arose each day about 0715 and didn't finish until the early hours of the next. … I decided to make today a non-day. It has been a wise decision – I needed to regain my breath.

20 November: Gradually bringing this Sydney operation to an end.

21 November: General conclusion is that all my media mutterings and meetings in high places have put UN more on the map in Australia than for the last 20 years. If so, good.

22 November: I think I'm now over the worst of the work. My love and thoughts are with you and I wish you all the luck in the world both personally and professionally.

He stayed for a few days in Brisbane with Denise Conroy, a friend of Joan's whom he had taken over in his usual way. She drove him around parts of Queensland and spoilt him thoroughly. Surfers' Paradise was unrecognisable; where once there had been miles of deserted beaches with a scattering of cottages such as KITAWAH there now stood rows of 40-storey apartment blocks. Further inland the countryside was unspoilt; there was fruit of every kind going for a song, and they found some excellent chops for him to barbecue. 'Sad / sad / that you weren't here.' Despite the relaxed days he wasn't sleeping well; too many thoughts were chasing around. All the same it was a very happy break.[10]

30 November, Bangkok: Endless happy memories of this room (446) in the Erawan come back to me. It is a mass of beautiful flowers from friends (and the management, with the usual card 'Welcome Home, Sir Jackson') and a great basket of fruit. The memories here go back 30 years, and so it is with Melbourne and Sydney and Queensland and, above all, with those I love.

1 December: Kylin Cahor [a Cambodian colleague who had also worked for Anstee] had about a dozen of my friends to dinner. It was a charming gesture and a great success. Several toasts were made, and he made sure that we all drank to your health and success in Vienna. [Anstee had just been promoted to Under Secretary-General – the first woman – and appointed

Director-General of the UN Office at Vienna]. I'm glad that I embarked on this sentimental journey. My love and thoughts are with you. Roll on 18 December!!!

It wasn't all sentimental: there was important Mekong Committee business to be done. Largely on account of his suggestions on this and previous occasions a major review of the project's future was initiated. Knowing it could have important political and economic effects he decided to continue as Counsellor until it was completed. His contract as Senior Adviser was at last bearing fruit, and was renewed until September 1987, enabling him to complete 25 years' involvement with the Mekong.

On 26 March he gave the first BRUNEL LECTURE for the macro-engineers at MIT, describing some of the creations of the great nineteenth century British engineer, Isambard Kingdom Brunel: the London Tunnel under the River Thames, the Clifton Suspension Bridge over the River Avon, the Great Western Railway with its Royal Albert Bridge at Saltash linking Devon to Cornwall, and his three steamships – the GREAT WESTERN, which plied between Bristol and New York for 20 years, the GREAT BRITAIN, which made 32 voyages to Australia, and the GREAT EASTERN, which for many years laid cables across the Atlantic.

> Today, if Brunel were alive he would, I am sure, seize on every advance in the future of science and technology – and they have been limitless – and marry them to his fertile imagination. That being done, he would proceed to attract public attention and support until capital to execute the project materialized.

What was currently lacking, he suggested, was neither imagination nor capital, but a marriage between engineering and diplomacy. Great and imaginative macro-engineering projects were already on the drawing boards, and the technical means to carry them out were at hand, yet they languished because, unlike Brunel, so few of their architects possessed the diplomatic and negotiating skills necessary to convince governments and people that they should be brought to life. It was the same point he had made two years ago – 'bell bloody cat'.[11]

The macro-engineers now looked on Jackson as their 'patron saint'. After he died they presented his portrait in bas-relief, by the Parisian sculptor Joseph Erhardy, to MIT.

Unable to decide where to live – New York, London, Geneva? – in April he accepted an invitation to lecture at the University of Hawaii for eight months as a Distinguished Visiting Scholar, starting in October.

> 12 June 1987, New York: Dearest Hodge, good to hear your voice yesterday. There's really no news here. For me, UN is moribund; on all sides I hear cries of distress from decent officials who find it hard to get results in an atmosphere which has increasingly become 'couldn't care less'. Sad.

Having shifted the contents of his apartment into Joan's he met her in London on 1 July. They drove first to PIPPINS, which she was selling, and then to THE WALLED GARDEN at Knill. This was a large property on the Welsh borders which her Aunt Christina (Chris) was buying, which was also to be Joan's new base in the UK. The main house was in the throes of major alterations, so they stayed in OWL COTTAGE adjacent to it. Maria and I joined them there for a week-end; we went for a walk in the hills with Joan and got lost on the way home. When we eventually arrived back it was to find Jacko looking as black as thunder. He had been unable to get a fire going for the barbecue; poor man, he was using off-cuts of roofing timber which had been treated – very effectively – to make them fire-resistant! He found some other wood and the steaks were up to his usual standard, but the incident took the edge off our enjoyment of what turned out to be the last of his barbecues. We drove him back to London the next day.

Although on the surface he remained cheerful he was now deeply unhappy. He and Joan both realised that their relationship was not what it had been. The good times had been when they were working together to achieve something they both believed important: the Capacity Study had brought them together, they had collaborated in Zambia and Bangladesh; now there was nothing, though each sought the other's advice about whatever they were doing. He rejoiced in Joan's success as she went from strength to strength, but he was conscious of his age and very unsure of himself and his future. The professional side of their partnership had come to an end, and the personal part alone was not strong enough to sustain it. He knew he would never marry again, but he also knew that Joan was still the most important person in his life, and still hoped that she would want their love, companionship and shared interests to continue.

Joan had despaired of him ever taking a decision about their making a home together, and had given up trying. Not prepared to end up foot-loose like him, she had decided to join Chris at Knill. She made it clear to Jacko that he would always be welcome there, as he had been at Pippins, but he could see that Knill would be <u>their</u> home, and knew that whatever Joan said he would feel out of place.

He was still bitterly hurt by 'the contemptible treatment' that he had received from Pérez de Cuéllar in 1984, even more so than by Trygve Lie's double-crossing in 1948,[12] and this spilt over into his personal feelings; the fact that Joan was necessarily on civil terms with the Secretary-General (with whom she usually conversed in Spanish) cannot have helped.

He stayed with her in Vienna for a few days in September.

> It is excellent to see you batting so exceedingly well and confidently at the Vienna wicket. As to which I have only two points. First, don't bat longer than you need in order to demonstrate your quality as a Test Batsman. (I know that you are – all that remains is to go on as you are and convince the onlookers.) I am a prime example of how not to bat. I should probably have closed my innings after the Capacity Study when I was physically fit enough to do the things I'd always wanted to. Now, as you see, I've left it far too late. You must have <u>plenty</u> of time to enjoy Knill and your beloved Bolivia and to write.
>
> In your own interests (which are also UN's) you should never be away from New York and P de C <u>for longer than eight weeks. Never forget.</u>
>
> Thank you for all your kindness and hospitality here. It has been very good to be with you again. This is a tough patch, but, speaking for myself, I'm still just afloat.
>
> My love as always. WHEB.[13]

Then he went to Bangkok for his final Mekong Committee meeting. The Erawan Hotel was due to close on 31 December, to be pulled down and rebuilt; another chapter in his life was about to end.

> 12 September: The consulting firms [engaged by the Mekong Committee] have worked hard in responding to their terms of reference; no new ground broken, but they have gone over the last 17 years since the first Indicative Basin Plan was prepared. In one sense they've done work that the Secretariat should have done, particularly in the last 8-9 years. In short all my criticisms at the

time are now confirmed. By midnight on my first day I was sure that much material had been assembled, but NOT in the shape of a Basin Plan, and full of political stupidity. All next day with Kamp [the Executive Agent], who was totally receptive. Sunday pm: Kamp and key advisers and my three colleagues – all first class. Thursday night worked until 0330 and prepared new outline for consultants' Indicative Basin Plan. Friday Kamp appeared somewhat more than grateful for my homework; when I've read the next draft Indicative Basin Plan draft in November I reckon I can close my innings.

30 September, New York: In a few hours I shall leave UN. No regrets, only sadness that governments and weak men have reduced it to such a shambles. No leadership / no imagination / no courage / no training of the staff / an administrative and financial mess. I did what I could, but it was a pitiful business after the exhilaration of UNRRA. Now I'll potter until 28 October, then a necessary paddle round the world and then perhaps I'll be able to work out something else.

One thing I must add. There were some good patches in the last 25 years and the best were when we were working together. Thank you! My love and thoughts are with you as always. WHEB.

Before he began his paddle round the world he stayed for a few days with Robin and Carlie in Putney. On the night before he left, 10 November, Joan stayed with us in Petersham and the six of us had dinner together at a local restaurant, partly to celebrate his 76th birthday, partly to wish him *bon voyage*. It proved to be anything but a celebration; it was a highly embarrassing occasion, and for Joan deeply distressing. If there is one characteristic which Jacko had always displayed, it was courtesy. On that evening it deserted him; he seemed a different man.

The most likely explanation for such untypical behaviour is that he suffered a slight stroke. The following morning he was his usual self and set off as planned, evidently unaware of his strange behaviour the previous evening. Throughout the trip he wrote his usual daily accounts of his activities, which he posted to Joan in weekly batches.

Back in room 446 at the Erawan he was overwhelmed with kindness, but there was an air of sadness among the staff as the date of its closing approached, when they would lose their jobs. He gently declined the management's offer of a dinner service for 18 and settled for six cups and saucers decorated with the Erawan's three elephants. He needed 35 presents to take to Melbourne, Sydney, Brisbane, Christchurch, Wellington, Auckland, Honolulu, New York and London, and so far had bought 27, mostly at DESIGN THAI[14] (the shop where over the years he had bought, among other things, lengths of silk for Maria and ties for me).

On 17 November he reached Melbourne. Staying at the Melbourne Club he came across a copy of a biography of Viscount Bruce which brought back vivid memories.[15]

> If I had listened to his advice in 1947 I'd have had – I believe – a much happier life. 'Useless to go to UN. Lie is hopeless. UN will never cease to need reform. You will be able to do nothing. Join John [Boyd Orr] and follow him. We'll see to that. If Whitehall doesn't like the idea, resign. Above all, do <u>not</u> trust <u>those</u> gentlemen.' How wise, and alas, how correct. Ah well! It all led to many interesting developments, despite the wreckage of what [might] have been a useful career. However, I am exceedingly grateful for many very happy experiences – if that's the right word – in the subsequent 40 years, in which you have formed the centrepiece.[16]

The last lecture he had given before leaving Britain, indeed the last lecture he ever gave, was the LORD BOYD ORR MEMORIAL LECTURE at the Rowett Research Institute in Aberdeen, which Boyd Orr had founded. 'As the moving spirit behind the creation of FAO,' he said, 'Boyd Orr was, like Brock Chisholm, one of the founding fathers of the UN system.' He ended his lecture by saying that in a long and varied life his greatest regret was that circumstances had deprived him of the privilege and honour of working for John Boyd Orr.[17]

He spent a week-end with his old friend Elisabeth Murdoch, now Dame, at her home, Cruden Farm, near Frankston, 30 miles south of Melbourne. 'I wished greatly that you could have been with us – hers is one of the most beautiful gardens in Australia.' On his way back to Melbourne he stopped off to spend a very happy day with Tam, to whom he was more devoted than ever.[18]

Joan was in Bolivia, where she was planning to build a house on the shores of Lake Titicaca. 'Very glad that you should now be in your favourite part of the world. Hope everything goes <u>very</u> well there, particularly Lake T. Project. My love and thoughts are with you.'[19]

In Brisbane Denise Conroy looked after him again, just as she had the previous year. He was tired and taking things very quietly, but at least he was feeling really relaxed for the first time in many months.[20] Joan was planning to visit Australia the following year, possibly bringing Chris, and he and Denise discussed how they might spend their time. Jacko wrote to her, setting out the pros and cons of this and that, and, as usual, virtually planned an entire itinerary for them – but 'it was ONLY A SUGGESTION!!!'[21]

The next day, 2 December, a letter from Joan arrived, which must have been written about a week after the dinner party. He wrote back later the same day:

> I am greatly saddened that you feel that the bottom has dropped out of your life, and I realise all too well that you also feel that I am responsible for your distress.
>
> I have done my best to explain my own problems, but I'm afraid that I've failed to convey them to you in such a way that you could understand them. ... I wonder if you will find some moments of happiness in Bolivia? ... Your letter speaks of your feelings all too clearly. You will understand my reaction. ... My love remains for and with you. WHEB.[22]

The daily letters he had been writing for her now seemed pointless; he would send them, but couldn't write any more. He spent a week in Christchurch with Relda, and a few days in Hawaii, arriving back at the apartment in New York on 18 December.

20 Epilogue

HIS MINOR STROKE AT THE RESTAURANT had been a warning of worse to come. The circumstances in which this befell him could not have been more unfortunate. When Joan rang him from Vienna on the day of his return to New York he sounded cheerful enough. She had arranged for the housekeeper to cook his lunch in the apartment on the next day, Saturday, and for Valentina Lim ('Nena' – a devoted friend and colleague whom they had both known for many years) to visit him. Because he had meetings that day he cancelled both arrangements and arranged for Nena to come on the Sunday evening.

He had promised to phone Joan on the Saturday evening. When he had not called by midnight (Vienna time) she phoned him and got no reply. Her half-hourly calls throughout the Sunday produced the engaged signal. When Nena arrived at the apartment at seven in the evening she could hear his groans and called a colleague from the floor below – Luis Maria Gomez – who broke the security chain on the door. They found him lying on the floor. Evidently he had tried to answer Joan's calls, but could not lift the receiver. Later he had managed to ring the emergency services, but his speech was so slurred that they assumed he was drunk; after that he was unable to replace the receiver. He must have lain there for forty hours, helpless but conscious. Paralysed on his left side and hardly able to speak, he was rushed to hospital.

He kept calling for Joan, and when she arrived he clung to her hand as she sat at his bedside each day. His one wish was to be taken back to England and Sister Agnes, and as soon as he was strong enough she and Robin escorted him on a flight to London, with ambulances and stretchers arranged at both airports.

After a month in hospital he was moved to a rehabilitation centre at Unstead Park in Surrey, where he stayed for the next eight. Joan went there for weekends whenever she could. Wheeling him round the gardens in April I tentatively suggested that he might come and spend a day with us in Petersham. To my delight he said he would like to, and we fetched him several times. He was getting stronger and his speech and writing were nearly back to normal; he was allowed to write five short letters a day, and even appeared in a BBC television programme about Kampuchea.

Robin found a ground floor flat for him in Roehampton, close to his own home, and Jacko moved there in October. He was looked after by a succession of housekeepers; Thérèse, a pretty and very efficient young actress, 'resting', was his favourite, but she could only stay for a month. He liked having visitors, and walked round the garden most days; what he most enjoyed was watching the cricket on television. Joan phoned him daily and visited him when she could. Weak though his body was, she found his mind as sharp as ever; he was still up to the minute on political affairs.

By then we had moved from Petersham to a first floor flat just outside the gates of Richmond Park, and we wondered if he would be able to climb the spiral staircase leading to it. Luckily it had strong hand-rails on both sides, and by gripping them firmly he managed it confidently and was able to pay us a few more visits.

During 1989 he remained much the same, but in early 1990 he had a bad fall following a blackout, and during the second half of the year he gradually went downhill.

One of his visitors was Bess Manisty, his friend from Malta days. When clearing out his belongings in the apartment he had come across a piece she had written about Roger the cat, and sent it to her. Shaken as she was (see page 31), she had invited him to her house in Sussex, where he visited her twice during the summer of 1987. Like him, she had become a Catholic, and seeing him now so frail was concerned for his spiritual well-being and asked a priest whom she knew to visit him. Fr Eric Flood did not get very far, for Jacko would keep dropping names, particularly that of his old friend Jackie Heenan, who had been Cardinal Archbishop of London.

On New Year's Day 1991 Joan and her Viennese housekeeper, on their way back from Knill to Vienna, had a splendid dinner party with Jacko and his housekeeper at Roehampton. He was in good form, drank champagne and laughed and reminisced as of old. On 12 January his condition suddenly deteriorated, and he was given absolution. He called repeatedly for Joan, but alas, for once she could not be contacted quickly, and arrived too late to say goodbye.

His Requiem Mass took place at St Simon's Roman Catholic Church, Putney, on 21 January at ten o'clock in the morning, when the few regulars at Monday Mass found themselves surrounded by about 60 strangers. John Saunders gave the address and I played the organ.

Saunders had known Jacko for many years, and their friendship had deepened when they were both working on the Kampuchean operation. Jacko was glad to find a soul-mate to talk to in Phnom Penh and later in New York, and John would listen, fascinated. 'Jacko was always concerned,' he said, 'that the help actually reached the people who needed it, the poor widows in the fields, rather than with the technical accomplishment, great though it was, of the tonnages passing from ship's tackle to dock side. The movement of ships, trains and planes were simply a means to the all-important human end. Despite his pre-occupations at the highest levels of international life, Jacko also had a concern for the well-being of friends and colleagues. He would always find time to help.'[1]

The Requiem Mass was followed by a cremation service conducted by Fr Flood, at which Robin and Carlie, Joan, Maria and I were present. As the coffin disappeared part of Smetana's MaVlast was played – the piece that he had broadcast in Athens in 1944. Afterwards came the final irony: Fr Flood, having no idea where Joan fitted into the picture, asked her: 'And are you one of the family?'

Three days later tributes were paid at the UN by his former colleagues, including (at Joan's insistence) Pérez de Cuéllar. Brian Urquhart said that Jacko was not only a wonderful leader, but a wonderful boss if, of course, the people working for him met his high standards. 'He was extraordinarily kind and considerate. He never failed to call families of people who were out in the boondocks somewhere doing a difficult job; he always remembered children's birthdays and things like that and it wasn't phoney, it was genuine. He was a very affectionate and kind man.'

Yet despite his great triumphs Jacko also had a strong sense of failure. Saunders had always been aware of this; it seemed to stem almost entirely from his dismissal by Lie in 1948. Jacko had only spoken to him about it once, saying how his entire world had seemed to crumble about him; it was as if that traumatic event, coming after three brilliant successes – Malta, MESC and UNRRA – had blighted whatever prospects he had cherished, and after that nothing had ever come right. There were other factors too: the Capacity Study (which Saunders reckoned one of the best reports ever produced about the UN and development) for all its excellence did not achieve everything he had hoped; had it been written in more diplomatic language it would, he thought, at least have been discussed more calmly and possibly accepted more readily. Though Jacko always denied wanting to succeed Hoffman, directing UNDP was something he could have done supremely well in happier circumstances. The UN would never have the political power to co-ordinate the specialised agencies, but in Saunders's view Jacko's understanding of what was needed, combined with his powers of persuasion, could have achieved much. As it was his skills were only called upon in emergencies, and though he had the rank of Under Secretary-General and a small office at UN Headquarters he never had his own department and was not accorded the status he must have hoped for, and deserved. Even the completion of the Volta dam was in some ways an anti-climax. The golden sunrise of African independence, of which that was the first ray, soon gave way to dirty weather. The fact that Jacko would not talk about the events that followed Nkrumah's fall from power suggested that he had a sense, if not of failure, of disappointment that the scheme had not led to a greater future for Ghana.[2]

Writing to Saunders Jacko had once quoted the words of a French Abbé of the Middle Ages: "There is only one sadness; not to be a Saint. It is necessary to hate oneself – but gently.' Having encountered a few saintly men and women in my lifetime – generally in some modest occupation – has made me realise again and again how frail and inadequate most of us are, how we fail to make the best use of the life that has been given to us. So I understand something (in the sense of failure) of what the good Abbot means.'[3]

He was replying to a letter from John and his wife, congratulating him on his Australian award. That letter, I think, is the one with which to end this book:

> 'In this pioneer service no-one has served with such distinction for so long and at so high a level as you have. Your work for the Kampuchean people was simply the most recent in a long roll of achievements for the poor and suffering of the world. Perhaps even more vital in the long run was the

demonstration of a UN role which was positive and yet different from that of any single power or group of governments. More striking still in the end was the trust placed in the United Nations by governments of strongly differing views, and in some cases actively at war with each other. You showed courage and insight in leading the way forward, hacking a UN path through the political, organisational and security jungle. You brought more distinction to the United Nations than anyone else involved in that long and immensely difficult campaign. Since settlement is still far away I would add that progress would be more significant were you still at the centre of the enterprise.

'Despite your preoccupations at the highest levels of international life you have always shown a concern for the well-being of colleagues, whatever their role and place, and are perceptive about needs and sensitive to ways of bringing help. Only after knowing you for a long time did I begin to have some idea of the extent of that personal generosity, because you are so modest and uncommunicative about what you do.

'This is a rare opportunity to try to say to you however inadequately what your example means to those who work for a more civilised world, and who are sorely in need of encouragement in these times. You will be the first to insist that an immense amount remains to be done. Yet what may come can only be built on the firm foundation hewn out of harsh reality by a small band of pioneers of which you are a leading and most distinguished member.'⁴

Acknowledgements

I am especially grateful to Andrew Jackson, Sir Brian Urquhart and the late Sheila Collins and John Saunders for their helpful advice over many years; also to all those whom I have consulted at various times, some of whom are no longer alive: Raymond Aubrac, Jacques Beaumont, Nicky Beredjick, Maggie Black. Léonce Bloch, William Buffum, Joan Burch, Joan Clark, Harlan Cleveland, Myer Cohen, Anna Colebrook, Denise Conroy, Alfred Davidson, Frank Davidson, Adrienne de Donker, Arthur E Dewey, Philippe de Seynes, Subhas Dhar, John Duthie, Charles Egger, Alan Everest, Fay Garcia, Antony Gilpin, Norma Globerman, Nina Grima, Patricia Guest, Philomena Guillebaud, Malcolm Harper, Eric Hayward, Julia Henderson, Patricia Hutchinson, Pamela Jensen, Robert Rhodes James, Kurt Jansson, Andrew Joseph, Margaret Howard, Betty Jacob, George Lansky, Houston Kenyon, Jane MacGowan, Peggy Manisty, Ruben Mendez, James Moxon, Max Nicholson, Dame Elisabeth Murdoch, Erica Powell, Una M Pollard, Robert Raymond, John Reedman, Garth Ap Rees, Bruce Rohrbacher, J-P B Ross, Alexander Rotival, Pierre Sales, C Hart Schaaf, William Searle, William Shawcross, Mano Sivasankhar, Dame Mary Smieton, David Smith, Admiral Sir Victor Smith, Maurice Strong, Richard Symonds, Douglas Williams and Richard Woodman. If there are others whom I have failed to mention I beg their pardon. Finally I thank Sinclair Goodlad for his helpful editorial advice.

I am grateful to the staffs of Churchill Archives Centre, Cambridge, the Lehman Suite at Columbia University, National Archives (formerly the Public Record Office), Georgetown University Library, National Australian Archives, National Library of Australia, Norwegian National Archives and the United Nations Archives for their helpful cooperation.

The extracts from the Cadogan Diaries in Chapter 7 are reproduced with the kind permission of the Trustees if Sir Alexander Cadogan's Will Trust.

The photograph of the *Ohio* in Chapter 3 is reproduced by permission of the Imperial War Museum.

The cartoon by LOW in Chapter 5 is reproduced by kind permission of Solo Syndication / Associated Newspapers.

The photograph of Barbara Ward by Dorothy Wilding in Chapter 5 is reproduced by kind permission of the Estate of Tom Hustler/National Potrait Gallery, London.

End-notes

Most of Jackson's official papers and letters whose location is not given below, as well as some of his personal correspondence with Sheila Collins and Barbara Ward, are held by the Bodleian Library, University of Oxford, MSS. Eng. c. 4676, fols. 158-323; c. 4677; c. 4678, fols. 1-137; c. 4733, items 1-4.

Abbreviations used in end notes.

ADM	British Admiralty papers held at National Archives in London (NA),
CAB	British Cabinet papers held at NA.
CCL	Churchill College Library, Cambridge.
ECOSOC	Economic and Social Council of the United Nations.
ERP	European Recovery Plan (the Marshal Plan)
FAO	Food and Agriculture Organisation
FO	Foreign Office papers at NA.
GA	General Assembly of the United Nations.
GUL	Georgetown University Library, Washington, DC.
HMSO	Her Majesty's Stationery Office, London.
IBRD	International Bank for Reconstruction and Development, The World Bank.
IMF	International Monetary Fund
MT	Ministry of Transport papers held at NA.
NA	National Archives (British) in London, formerly Public Record Office.
NAA	National Australian Archives.
NLA	National Library of Australia.
NNA	Norwegian National Archives
OH1	Jackson's oral history interviews in March/April 1978 held in the Lehman Papers at Columbia University, New York City.
OH2	Jackson's oral history interviews for the UN held between 29 November 1985 and 21 February 1986.
SC	Security Council of the United Nations.
SG	Secretary-General of the United Nations.
SR	Summary Record (of a meeting).

Endnotes

Prologue

1 Urquhart: A GLOBAL AFFAIR – AN INSIDE LOOK AT THE UNITED NATIONS, 1995.

PART ONE — ONE SUCCESS TOO MANY

Chapter 1 — Wilbur

This chapter is mainly based on information provided by Andrew Jackson, son of Alan, Robert Jackson's elder brother.

1 Testimonial from Superintendent of hospital.
2 Jackson to HM Treasury, 29 June 1945.
3 OH2, 29 November 1985, p 1.
4 See James Rundle: AGAINST ALL ODDS, a History of Mentone Grammar School, 1991.
5 Tonkin to Kathleen Jackson, 10 April 1929.

Chapter 2 — All at sea

This chapter is largely based on conversations and correspondence with Andrew Jackson and Peggy (née Dick), also Lady Knight who had known Peggy and 'Jacks' at the time and Joan Burch, a friend from his childhood.

1 Jackson talking impromptu to James Rundle (author of AGAINST ALL ODDS) in Melbourne, 23 November 1987.
2 THE MENTONIAN, June 1929.
3 Records of Department of Defence (Navy Office), Canberra.
4 See ^{1}.
5 Admiral Sir Victor Smith, interview, Canberra, 14 February 1993.
6 See ^{1}.
7 See ^{3}.
8 Jackson to his brother Alan, 3 December 1946.

Chapter 3 — The man who saved Malta

Main sources for Chapter 3: Jackson's notes on the SWISSAIR notepads – 'Notes, 1987', and his first Oral History memoir of 1978 – 'OH 1'; Playfair et al: THE MEDITERRANEAN AND THE MIDLE EAST, HMSO 1964, and Woodman: MALTA CONVOYS, John Murray, London 2000.

1 Jackson to his mother, 16 October 1938.
2 See RA Watson-Watt THREE STEPS TO VICTORY, p 187, ODHAMS 1957.
3 Notes, 1987.
4 Ibid.
5 Jackson to his brother, 7 June 1939.
6 CAB5/9, JDC 506-C, 20 July 1939.
7 CAB2/9, CID 370th Meeting, 27 July 1939.
8 ADM116/4061. 1 March 1940.
9 Macintyre: THE BATTLE FOR THE MEDITERRANEAN, Pan Books, 1964, page 17.

10 Jackson to his brother, 7 September 1939.
11 Francis Gerard: MALTA MAGNIFICENT, Cassell 1943, pp 125-7. Peggy Manisty was also called Bess. To avoid confusion with Jackson's first wife, the latter name is used here.
12 Manisty: personal journal.
13 Manisty interview, 1992.
14 OH1, pp 7 & 16.
15 Notes 1987 and OH1 p 10.
16 OH1, pp 10-15.
17 Cunningham: A SAILOR'S ODYSSEY, Hutchinson, London, 1951, p 297.
18 See Woodman, Op.cit., page 117.
19 See Playfair and Woodman, Op. cit. on which are based the accounts which follow of the progress of the war and the convoys.
20 Notes, 1987.
21 See Micaeleff: WHEN MALTA STOOD ALONE, Interprint, Malta, 1981, and Boffa: THE SECOND GREAT SIEGE, St Joseph's Home, Malta 1970.
22 Mrs Nina Grima, interview, Hobart 1 February 1993.
23 Dobbie to Ford, 22 August 1941.
24 OH1, pp 30-35.
25 CAB 65/19.
26 CAB 65/23.
27 Jackson to his mother from Cairo, 28 November, 1941.
28 OH1, p 32.
29 See [12].
30 Dobbie to Jackson, 5 November, 1941.
31 Ford, Report on Jackson to Admiral Cunningham, 20 December 1941.
32 Edward Jackson to Robert Jackson, 29 November 1941.
33 Dobbie to Jackson, 17 February 1942.
34 Based on a talk given by Edward Jackson in December 1943 in Cyprus.
35 MacIntyre, Op.cit., page 192.
36 Note by Andrew Cohen (assistant to Sir Edward Jackson) dated 'about 20 August 1942'.
37 Macintyre: Op.cit., page 14.
38 For Gallantry: MALTA'S STORY BY A NAVAL WIFE, published in Ilfracombe in 1956.
39 Stewart Perowne: THE SIEGE WITHIN THE WALLS, Hodder & Stoughton, 1970, pages 34 and 115.

Chapter 4   The Middle East Supply Centre (MESC)

1 Foreword to index of FO922 files. .
2 Max Nicholson, interviews, May 1992.
3 Martin W Wilmington: THE MIDDLE EAST SUPPLY CENTRE, State University of New York Press, 1971, page 41. Wilmington, American, began studying MESC for a doctoral thesis in the early 1950s, consulting Jackson among others. He completed it in 1960, but died in 1964. After editing by another hand the book was published in 1971 with a Foreword by Jackson

ENDNOTES

in which he expressed his approval of the book.

4   See [2].
5   Sheila née Collins, interview, 1992.
6   Ibid.
7   OH1, pp 40-41.
8   See [5].
9   Casey Family Papers, NLA, MS 6150, 20 March 1942.
10 E M H Lloyd: FOOD AND INFLATION IN THE MIDDLE EAST, Stanford University Press, 1956, pp 86-87.
11 Wilmington: Op. cit., p 45.
12 WJ Hudson, CASEY, OUP Melbourne, 1986, p 140.
13 Ibid., p 139.
14 OH1, p 111.
15 Lloyd, Op. cit., p 87.
16 Ibid., pp 99-101.
17 Wilmington: Op. cit., pp 57-8
18 Nicholson to Jackson 15 September 1942, MT59/1170.
19 Lord (Keith) Murray of Newhaven, interview, April 1992.
20 Wilmington:Op. cit., p 84.
21 Government Publicity Note, 11 November 1942, MT59/1170.
22 Brief for Minister of War Transport, 19 December 1942, MT59/1173.
23 Note of Cabinet Meeting 14 July 1943, MT59/1173..
24 THE ECONOMIST 13 March 1943; see also 20 February and 3 April.
25 Jackson to O'Neill, 4 May 1943.
26 MT59/1170, 3 November 1942.
27 Jackson Memorandum, Spring 1943
28 Jackson to Nicholson, 17 April 1943.
29 Jackson to Nicholson, 14 June 1943.
30 See [2].
31 THE ECONOMIST, 4 September 1943.
32 See [22].
33 Jackson to Nicholson, 1 October 1943.
34 Jackson to Nicholson, 4 November 1943.
35 See Lloyd, Op. cit., Chapter 31
36 Jackson to Establishments Officer, MWT, 10 January 1944.
37 See [2].
38 Wilmington, Op. cit., p 164.
39 Wilmington, Op. cit., p 82.
40 Jackson to Nicholson, 28 May 1944.
41 Jackson to Nicholson, 26 September 1944.
42 Jackson to Nicholson, 2 October 1944
43 See [19].

44 OH1. P 90.
45 Harold Macmillan: War Diaries 1943-1945, Macmillan, 1984.
46 OH1. p 86.
47 Note by Hasler, 29 January 1945, FO371/51333.
48 Jackson to FO, 12 February 1945.
49 Wilmington: Op. cit., Jackson's Foreword, p x.
50 US Department of State, Bulletin 13 (30 Sept 1945) p 494, quoted by Wilmington (p 5) and by Jackson in his Foreword (p ix).
51 Wilmington, Op. cit., p 167-8.
52 Nicholson to the author, 31 March 1992.

Chapter 5   UNRRA – the first UN organisation

1 Woodbridge: UNRRA Official History, Columbia University Press, 1950, Vol I p 3.
2 Ibid. Vol I, p 88.
3 Ibid. Vol I, p 150.
4 Ibid. Vol I, p 39.
5 Lt-Col JPB Ross (later a senior UN official) to the author, 17 July, 1992.
6 Jackson to Edward Jackson, 13 July 1945.
7 Note by Hasler 19 April 1945, FO371/51336.
8 See [6].
9 Jackson: Memorandum to William Shannon 31 August 1954, p 10. Shannon was writing a biography of Lehman, but did not complete it.
10 Note by Rendel, 25 April 1945, FO371/51336.
11 Note by Hasler, 27 April 1945, FO371/51336.
12 Memorandum to Shannon, p 11.
13 Ibid., p 12.
14 The copy of this note in Jackson's papers is unsigned and unaddressed; it appears to be written by Hasler and intended for Law, though not sent.
15 Note by Rendel, 30 May 1945, FO371/51337.
16 Eden to Stettinius, June 1945, FO371/51337.
17 Law to Anderson, 16 June 1945, FO371/51337.
18 Cable to Foreign Office, late May 1945, FO371/51336.
19 See [6].
20 Woodbridge: Op.cit., Vol I pp 178, 240.
21 Law to Lyttelton, March 1945 FO371/51335.
22 OH1, pp 166-168.
23 Jackson to Noel-Baker, 25 November 1945.
24 Memorandum to Shannon, pp 19-29.
25. Hasler to Jackson, 28 November 1945.
26 Jackson to Hasler, 11 December 1945,
27 See letter from Jackson to Noel-Baker, 17 December 1945.
28 US Congressional Records – Senate, 14 December 1945, pp 12050-51.

ENDNOTES

29 Hasler to Jackson, 21 December 1945.
30 Hasler, note, 4 January 1996, FO371/58031.
31 Memorandum to Shannon, p 13.
32 OH2 pp 218-9; also Memorandum to Shannon p 31.
33 Note of meeting between Lehman and Jackson, 13 December 1945.
34 Halifax to Foreign Office, 4 January 1946, FO371/58031.
35 Morgan to Gale, 10 January 1946, FO371/58031, Cable 362.
36 Rendel & Hasler to Jackson, 10 January 1946, FO371/58031.
37 Noel-Baker to Rendel & Hasler, 11 January 1946, FO371/58031.
38 Hasler to Jackson, 12 January 1946.
39 Jackson to Rendel and Hasler, 21 January 1946.
40 Lord Halifax to FO, 30 January 1946, FO371/58031.
41 Jackson to Ward, 10 February 1946.
42 OH1, p 220
43 Alfred Davidson interview, 17 April 1992.
44 Ibid.
45 OH2, 6 December 1985, pp 6-8.
46 Jackson, 'Fragment of a Memoir', August (?) 1986.
47 Memorandum to Shannon, p 36.
48 OH1, p 230.
49 Memorandum to Shannon (conclusion).
50 Hasler to Jackson, 23 April 1946.
51 Thomas J Mayock: Preliminary Monograph to Woodbridge, June 1947, p 35.
52 Jackson to his brother Alan, 4 May 1946.
53 Jackson on tape recording in archives of Snowy Mountains Hydro-Electric Authority.
54 OH2, 29 November 1985, p 62.
55 Edward Jackson to Collins, 25 July 1946.
56 British Legation to the Holy See to FO, 23 July 1946.
57 Reported in New York Times, 27 July 1946.
58 Woodbridge: Op.cit Vol I, p 46.
59 See [43].
60 Note by Jackson, 30 August 1946.
61 Mayock: Op.cit., pp 60-61.
62 Jackson to Ward, 3 August 1946.
63 Jackson to Ward, 1 September 1946.
64 Collins, interview, 1993.
65 Ibid.
66 Jackson to his brother, 23 September 1946.
67 See [64]
68 Betty Jacob, interview 1992.
69 Jackson to Ward, 29 September 1946.
70 See Mayock, op.cit., pp 61-66.

ENDNOTES

71 See [43].
72 Bridges to Jackson, 10 December 1946.
73 Jackson to his brother, 3 December 1946..
74 Jackson to his brother, 30 January 1947.
75 Jackson to his brother, 4 February 1947.
76 UNRRA Operational Analysis Paper No 53, April 1948, p 10.
77 Harlan Cleveland interview, 7 December 1992.
78 Ibid.
79 O J Todd CHINA'S YELLOW RIVER, September 1947.
80 See [77].
81 Jackson to Bridges, 10 June 1947.
82 Bridges to Jackson, 10 June 1947.
83 Jackson to Bridges, 19 June 1947.
84 Bridges to Jackson, 20 June 1947.
85 Rooks to Inverchapel, 20 June 1947.
86 Jackson to Bridges, 23 July 1947.
87 Bridges to Jackson, 29 July 1947.
88 Note by Jackson, 11 June 1947.
89 Collins to Alan Jackson, 8 July 1947.
90 Jackson to Noel-Baker, 25 August 1947.
91 THE STORY OF UNRRA, issued by the Office of Public Information, 15 February 1948.
92 Jackson to Yasushi Akashi, UN Department of Information, 1 November 1985.
93 Jackson to Bridges, 30 September 1947.

Chapter 6   Operation Cool-off

1 Jackson to his brother, 12 October 1947.
2 Jackson to Bridges, 5 November 1947
3 Cabinet Paper (47)114, 28 March 1947, FO371/67564.
4 See [2].
5 Jackson to Bridges, 7 November 1947.
6 Jackson to Bridges, 9 November 1947.
7 Jackson to his brother, 21 November 1947.
8 Bridges to Jackson, 24 November 1947, FO371/72645.
9 FO to Minister of State, 24 November, FO371/72645.
10 Bruce to Jackson, 24 November 1947.
11 Ward to Collins, 2 December 1947.
12 Jackson to Collins, Saturday [13 December] 1947.
13 Lie to Jackson, 16 December 1947.
14 The carbon copy of Collins' letter is undated, but Jackson's to her of 24 December appears to be his reply.
15 Jackson to Cadogan, 3 January 1948..
16 Jackson to Lie, 3 January 1948.

ENDNOTES

17 Diaries of Sir Alexander Cadogan, 5 January 1948, CCL.
18 Hall-Patch to Cadogan, 6 January 1948, FO371/72645, Telegram No 61.
19 Cadogan to Hall-Patch, 6 January 1948, FO371/72645.
20 Jebb to Cadogan, 7 January 1948. .
21 Note of SG's 107th Private Meeting, 7 January 1948, UN Archives, series DAG 1/1.3.1-1.
22 McNeil, Memorandum, 29 January 1948, FO371/72645.
23 Jackson to Collins, 10 January 1948.
24 Alan Bullock, ERNEST BEVIN, FOREIGN SECRETARY, Heinemann, 1963.
25 Hall-Patch, 17 February 1948, FO371/72645, UN 385/10/78.
26 Jackson to Collins, 17 March 1948.
27 Mason, Brief for Bevin, 1 April 1948, FO371/72645.
28 Hall-Patch, Further advice, 2 April, 1948   "   "
29 McNeil to Secretary of State and Sir Orme Sargent, (Parliamentary Under-Secretary) 3 April 1948, FO371/72645, XC18942.
30 Jackson, Note, 5 April 1948.
31 Jackson to Lie, 8 April 1948.
32 FO to Washington, 9 April 1948, FO371/72645, XC18942.
33 Jackson to Lie, 10 April 1945. UN Archives.
34 Jackson to Lie, 14 April 1948. UN Archives.
35 THE SPECTATOR, 9 April 1948.
36 Urquhart: A LIFE IN PEACE AND WAR, Weidenfeld & Nicholson, 1987, p 116.

Chapter 7   Disaster at Lake Success

References to UN Archives in this chapter are to the series DAG 1/1.3.1-1.
1 Record of 113th Private Meeting in SG's office, 22 April 1948. UN Archives.
2 Urquhart: to the author, 2 October 1992.
3 Jackson: Draft memorandum to Lie, undated.
4 Jackson: Memorandum, 30 April 1948.
5 Jackson: Summary of discussions in Washington, undated.
6 GA Resolution 181 of 29 November 1947.
7 GA Resolution 186 of 14 May 1948.
8 This account of events is based on Luard: A HISTORY OF THE UNITED NATIONS, Vol I, Chapter 10, Macmillan 1982.
9 Jackson: Memorandum, 17 May 1948.
10 Cadogan to FO, 17 May 1948, FO371/68553 No 1515.
11 Cadogan: Diaries, 16 May 1948. CCL
12 Jackson: memorandum to Lie, 17 May 1948. .
13 Cordier, note on contacts made with State Department, 15-17 May 1948, Papers of Trygve Lie, NNA.
14 FO to Cadogan, 17 May 1948, FO371/68553, No 2112,
15 Cadogan: Diaries, 17 May 1948, CCL
16 Ibid., 18 & 19 May 1948.

ENDNOTES

17 Cadogan to Bevin, 19 May 1948, FO371/72676, No 1530
18 Mason to Jebb, 21 May 1948, FO371/72676, UN1046/G
19 Jackson to Lie, 26 May 1948..
20 Ibid.
21 See [18].
22 Makins: Record of conversation, 21 May 1948, FO371/68650, E7866G
23 Urquhart to Jackson, 20 May 1948.
24 Note by Jackson, 21 May 1948, FO371/72676; XC 8997.
25 Note by Jackson, 5 April 1948.
26 OH2, 6 December 1985, p 39.
27 Jackson to Cadogan, 26 May 1948.
28 See [19].
29 Note by Wright, 21 May 1948, FO371/68650
30 See [19].
31 Ibid.
32 Ibid.
33 Urquhart to Lie, 'Points from Commander Jackson', undated.
34 Foreign Office to Cadogan, 25 May 1948, FO371/68650, Telegram No 2265
35 Cadogan to Jebb, 27 May 1948, FO371/72676.
36 Bridges to Jackson, 1 June 1948.
37 Alan Bullock, ERNEST BEVIN, Politico 2002.
38 Jackson to Lie, 28 May 1948.
39 Jackson to Lie, 2 June 1948.
40 Lie's copy of [38], NNA.
41 Jackson to the eight ASGs, 2 June 1948.
42 Record of 115th Private Meeting in SG's Office, 4 June 1948.
43 Lie's comment is on a copy of [41].
44 OH2, 6 December 1985, p 33.
45 Urquhart, interview and correspondence, October 1992.
46 Ibid.
47 SC Resolution 50 (1948), 29 May 1948.
48 Jackson to Lie, 5 June 1948.
49 Urquhart to Jackson, 21 June 1948.
50 Urquhart to Jackson, 22 June 1949.
51 Bernadotte: TO JERUSALEM, translated Bulman, Hodder and Stoughton 1951, p 133.
52 OH2, 6 Dec 1985, p 43.
53 Urquhart: Bunche papers, kindly made available by the author...
54 Diary of Houston Kenyon, with whom Barbara usually stayed when in New York.
55 Jebb to Bevin 8 July 1948, FO371/72677
56 Roberts to Jebb and Sargent, 15 July 1948, FO371/72677,
57 Record of Proceedings, 14 July 1948, COORD-PREP/58/Rev.1.
58 Julia Henderson, interview 29 June 1992

ENDNOTES

59 See [45].
60 Jackson to Vaughan, 15 July 1948
61 SC Resolution 54, 15 July 1948.
62 Jackson: Memorandum, 22 July 1948, UN Archives
63 See [53].
64 Ibid.
65 Bernadotte: Op.cit. p 194
66 Ibid p 191
67 Jackson, Fragment of a Memoir, UN Staff Recreation Council, Journal of the Society of Writers, December 1986.
68 See Maggie Black: THE CHILDREN AND THE NATIONS, Unicef, 1986 pp 64-65.
69 Report in New York Times, 24 April 1948.
70 Note by Jackson, 14 April 1948, UN Archives.
71 Jackson to Ording, 14 July 1948, UN Archives.
72 Jackson to Cordier, 11 August 1948, UN Archives.
73 Lie to Jackson, 12 August 1948, UN Archives.
74 Jackson to Lie, 12 August 1948, UN Archives.
75 See [78].
76 Jackson: Memorandum to Cadogan, 20 August 1948.
77 Cadogan Diaries, 20 August 1948, CCL
78 Jackson described the events of Friday 20 August again in a Personal and Confidential Memorandum dated 23 August which he gave to Cadogan 'in substitution for his rough and ready notes' of 20 August. FO371/72645.
79 Ibid., conclusion.
80 Jackson to Cadogan, 25 August 1948, enclosing draft of [81], FO371/72645. .
81 Lie to Jackson, 28 August 1948, FO371/72645.
82 Jackson to Lie, Thursday [26 August 1948], Lie papers, NNA.
83 Note by Mason, 28 August, FO371/72645.
84 McNeil to Lie, 28 August 1848, FO371/72645.
85 Lie to McNeil, 29 August 1948, FO371/72645
86 UN Press Release, 9 September 1948.
87 Lie papers, NNA.
88 OH2, 6 December 1985, p 59.
89 Jackson to Collins, 16 October 1948.
90 Note by Rundall, 2 September 1948, FO371/72645
91 Casey Family Papers, 20 November 1951, NLA, MS 6150.
92 See Wilmington, op.cit., page xi.

PART TWO   WHAT NEXT?

Chapter 8   Odd job man

1. Bridges to Jackson, 6 January 1949.
2. Jackson to Bridges, 7 January 1949.
3. Bridges to Jackson, 18 March 1951.
4. Nicholson to Sir Ben Lockspeiser (Secretary to the Privy Council Committee for Scientific and Industrial Research), 29 March 1949.
5. Records of Tribunale del Lazio, Rome.
6. Jackson to Collins, 9 December 1949.

Chapter 9   Casey to the rescue

1. Casey to Essington Lewis, 11 Jan 1950. NAA, Series M1142/1.
2. Jackson to Casey, 6 February 1950.
3. Edward Jackson to Robert Jackson, 13 April, 1950.
4. Draft of Cabinet paper by Casey, March 1950, NAArchives, Series M1142/1
5. Based on a paper Jackson wrote for Spooner (Casey's successor) in May 1951.
6. Ward to Jackson, 5 August 1950.
7. Jackson to Dunk, 21 July 1950.
8. See [5]
9. Dunk to Jackson, August 1950.
10. Cabinet paper – final draft
11. Casey to Bridges, 23 October 1950.
12. Jackson to Casey, 7 November 1950.
13. Casey to Bridges, 22 November 1950.
14. Bridges to Casey, 28 November 1950.
15. WJ Hudson: CASEY, OUP Melbourne, 1986, p 208.
16. Report `in the hospital newspaper, 10 October 1950.
17. Andrew Jackson, interview, March 1993.
18. James Merralls, interview, March 1993.
19. McNeil to Jackson, 28 March 1951.
20. Ward, draft article, November 1951.
21. The Countess of Albemarle, Interview 1992.
22. Casey to Bridges, 28 May 1951.
23. Jackson to Bridges, 20 October 1951.
24. Jackson to Bridges, 31 January 1952.
25. Casey, Diary for 16 November 1951; NAA
26. Hall-Patch to Casey, 17 December 1951.
27. Jackson to Ward, 5 March 1952.
28. Ward to Jackson, 28 and 29 March, 1952.
29. Jackson to Ward, 30 March and 6 April 1952.
30. Jackson to Ward, 1 April 1952.

31 Jackson to Ward, 4 April 1952.
32 Jackson to Minister (Casey), 15 April 1962.
33 Notes for Minister dictated before Jackson left Delhi.
34 Jackson to Casey, 12 April 1952.
35 Casey to Bridges, 23 April 1952.
36 Here and in the next chapter I have drawn on VOLTA – MAN'S GREATEST LAKE by James Moxon, Andre Deutsch 1969. Formerly a District Commissioner, Moxon joined the Information Service in 1948 and knew Jackson well.
37 Jackson to Bridges, 24 September 1952.
38 Ibid.
39 Jackson to his brother, 31 October 1952.
40 Ibid.
41 Jackson to Walter Ward, 7 November 1952. GUL
42 Ibid.
43 Jackson to Walter Ward, 19 November 1952. GUL
44 Eden to Casey, 29 December 1952.
45 Bridges to Jackson, 28 November 1952.

Chapter 10   The Volta River Project

1   James Moxon, interview 1992.
2   Volta River Aluminium Scheme, November 1952, Cmd. 8702, HMSO.
3   Jackson to Mrs Ward (BW's mother) 5 July, 1953
4   Moxon, Op.cit., pages 73-74.
5   Jackson to Lady Murdoch, 9 December 1953.
6   Jackson to Lady Murdoch, 5 March 1954.
7   Robert Raymond: BLACK STAR IN THE WIND, Macgibbon & Kee London 1960. Raymond was Press Officer of the VRP.
8   VOLTA RIVER PROJECT: PREPARATORY COMMISSION REPORT, HMSO London 1956.
9   Mrs Anna Colebrook, interview, 1993.
10 Jackson to Bridges, 7 June 1956
11 Jackson to Ward, 2 August 1956.
12 Jackson to Ward, 5 August 1956.
13 Jackson to Ward, 22 October 1956.
14 Jackson to Ward, 28 November 1956.
15 Jackson to Winnifrith, 2 January 1957
16 Duthie to the author, 16 December 1997
17 Jackson to Winnifrith, 14 March 1957
18 Winnifrith to Jackson, 20 March 1957
19 Moxon, who was with Nkrumah in India, interview, 1992.
20 Jackson to Collins, 7 March 1959.
21 OH2.
22 Jackson, in the Unilever quarterly PROGRESS, No 282, 1964.

ENDNOTES

23 Jackson to Moxon, 1 February 1987. Moxon was revising his book and had asked Jackson for his reminiscences.
24 Jackson to Nkrumah, 24 February 1960
25 Jackson to Burke Knapp, Vice-President of IBRD, 27 February 1960.
26 Jackson to Nkrumah, 2 March 1960
27 Jackson to Nkrumah, 5 April 1960.
28 Urquhart: A LIFE IN PEACE AND WAR, Weidenfeld and Nicolson, London 1987, p 146.
29 Jackson to Nkrumah, 28 July 1960.
30 Jackson to Nkrumah, 27 August 1960.
31 Moxon: Op.cit., pp 16-17.
32 PANDORA'S BOX, directed by Daniel Reed, BBC Television, 1992.
33 Mahoney: JFK: ORDEAL IN AFRICA, Oxford University Press, New York, 1983, p 159. Mahoney was US Ambassador to Ghana, 1962-65.
34 Ibid., pp 165-6.
35 Jackson to Nkrumah, 2 March 1961.
36 Moxon: Op.cit., p 109.
37 Mahoney, Op.cit., p 169.
38 Jackson to Nkrumah, 25 March 1961.
39 Jackson to Nkrumah, 22 April 1961.
40 Memorandum No 2266 (undated) by Minister of Finance for Standing Development Committee.
41 Jackson to Nkrumah, 18 June 1961.
42 This account of these events is based on a note by Jackson: *Developments in Relation to the Volta River Project*, 10 July 1961.
43 Jackson to Nkrumah, 4 July 1961.
44 The Minister for Presidential Affairs, Mr T Adamafio, to Jackson, 21 September 1961.
45 Jackson, in a draft appreciation of Nkrumah, undated but probably 1972. See also Mahoney, Op. cit., p 175.
46 Mahoney, Op. cit., p 177.
47 Adeane to Jackson, 20 November 1961
48 Jackson to Sir Norman Brook, Cabinet Secretary, 1 December 1961
49 Kennedy to Ward, 28 December 1961, quoted by Mahoney, Op. cit., page 179.
50 Moxon: Op.cit., p 114
51 See [23].
52 See [32]

PART THREE   BACK TO THE UN

Chapter 11   Not forgotten

1. The Mekong Committee – a Historical Account (1957-89), 1989, Bangkok, p 25.
2. Ibid., p 39; comment by the first Executive Agent, C Hart Schaaf.
3. Jackson to President Tolbert (Tubman's successor) 19 August 1971.
4. Jackson to his brother, 25 September 1962.
5. President Tubman to Jackson, 22 October 1962.
6. Jackson to Tubman, 23 October 1962.
7. Hoffman to Jackson, 1 November 1962.
8. Paul-Marc Henry interview, 27 August 1992.
9. Anna Colebrook interview, 1992.
10. OH2, 10 February 1986, p 4.
11. Ibid. p 5.
12. This brief account is based on an unpublished HISTORY OF TECHNICAL ASSISTANCE written by Tom Oliver in 1978 and approved by Jackson, with additional comments by Anstee.
13. Jackson to Anstee, 19 May 1968.

Chapter 12   The Capacity Study

1. A STUDY OF THE CAPACITY OF THE UNITED NATIONS DEVELOPMENT SYSTEM, United Nations Publications DP/5.
2. Ibid, Vol II pages 423/4.
3. Ibid., page 426.
4. Ibid., page 427.
5. Jackson to his brother, 28 June, 1948
6. Myer Cohen, interview 2 October 1992.
7. Jackson to Hoffman, 1 December 1968
8. Anstee, NEVER LEARN TO TYPE, Wylie, Chichester, 2003, p 264.
9. Hoffman to Jackson, December 1968.
10. Jackson to his brother, 14 December 1968.
11. Ward to Dame Elisabeth Murdoch, 16 December 1968.
12. Jackson, address to UNDP governing council, January 1969.
13. Jackson to Hoffman, 29 January 1969.
14. Hoffman to Jackson, 24 February 1969.
15. Jackson to Hoffman, 1 March 1969.
16. Comment by Anstee, 2006.
17. See [6].
18. Jackson, address to UNDP governing council, 18 June 1969.
19. Hoffman to Jackson, 18 April 1969.
20. Anstee, op. cit., page 251.
21. Ibid., page 252.
22. CV Narasimhan: THE UNITED NATIONS AT 50: RECOLLECTIONS, Konark, New Delhi, 1995.

ENDNOTES

23 Told to the author by Richard Symonds, to whom Jackson had made the remark.
24 Hoffman to Jackson, 16 December 1969.

Chapter 13   The Consensus

1. Capacity Study, page 429, para 15(c).
2. Comments of the IACB, DP/6, 6 February 1970
3. Comments of the Consultants, DP/8, 24 February 1970
4. Report of the Administrator: DP/7, 20 February 1970
5. Rotival to the author, 4 October 1993.
6. DP/SR. 190 – 206
7. DP/L128, 27 March 1970
8. Ibid.
9. Jackson to his brother, 3 April 1970.
10. Jackson to Anstee, 14 April 1970.
11. DP/L 134.
12. Rohrbacher to Jackson, dated 25 May but sent a week later.
13. Narasimhan, Op.cit.
14. OH2, 10 February 1986, pp 18-19.
15. Cohen interview, 2 October 1992.
16. DP/SR 211 – 239.
17. DP/SR 216.
18. DP/SR 239.
19. Jackson to Anstee, 21 July 1970.
20. Strong to Jackson, 4 August 1970.
21. Capacity Study, Chapter 1, para 159.
22. Stephen Browne, FOREIGN AID IN PRACTICE, Pinter, 1990
23. The Capacity Study, Chapter 1, final paragraph.

Chapter 14   The Fountain

1. Jackson to Anstee, 4 July 1970.
2. Jackson to Anstee, 2 January 1971.
3. Jackson to Anstee, 6 January 1971.
4. Jackson to Anstee, 13 January 1971.
5. Jackson to Anstee, 31 January 1971.
6. Jackson to Anstee, 1 February 1971.
7. Garth Ap Rees interview, 4 November 1998.
8. Jackson to Anstee, 24 March 1971.
9. Jacksonto Anstee, 29 March 1971.
10. Jackson to Anstee, 22/23 April 1971.
11. Jackson to Anstee, 25 April 1971.
12. Jackson to Anstee, 11 July 1971.
13. Jackson to Anstee, 23 July 1971.

14 Jackson to Anstee, 31 August 1971.
15 Jackson to Anstee, 3 September 1971.
16 Washington Post, 1 September 1971.
17 Jackson to Trend, 17 September 1971.
18 Jackson to Anstee, 29 November 1971.

PART FOUR — THE GREATEST OF OPERATORS

Chapter 15 — Bangladesh

1 See Oliver: THE UNITED NATIONS IN BANGLADESH, Princeton University Press, 1978.
2 Report of the SG to the GA and SC, 15 February 1972.
3 Urquhart, A LIFE IN PEACE AND WAR, Weidenfeld & Nicholson, London, 1987, p231
4 Jackson to Anstee, 5 April 1972.
5 Jackson to Anstee, 9 April 1972
6 Jackson to Anstee, 12 April 1972.
7 Ibid.
8 Jackson to Anstee, 21 April 1972.
9 Anstee to the author, February 2000.
10 Jackson to Anstee, 25 May 1972.
11 Jackson to Umbricht, 25 May 1972
12 Jackson to Anstee, 25 and 27 May 1972
13 Anstee to the author, date
14 Jackson to Anstee, 21 May 1972.
15 Jackson to Anstee, 16 June 1972.
16 Oliver, Op. cit., page 147
17 Jackson, memorandum, 17 August 1972.
18 Subhas Dhar, interview 6 October 1992.
19 Based on Jackson's note of the meeting, 19 August 1972.
20 Jackson to Anstee, 26 August 1972
21 WF Searle UN HARBOR CLEARANCE IN BANGLADESH.
22 Anstee to the author, February 2000.
23 Jackson to Anstee, 18 September 1972.
24 Jackson to Anstee, 9 September 1972.
25 Jackson to Anstee, 13 and 14 September 1972.
26 Jackson to Anstee, 12 November 1972.
27 Personal Note by Jackson, 23 October 1972
28 Personal Note by Jackson, 26 October 1972.
29 Oliver, Op. cit. page158.
30 Jackson to Anstee, 26 November 1972.
31 Ibid.
32 Jackson to Anstee, 4 December 1972.
33 Antony Gilpin to the author, 2004.

ENDNOTES

34 Jackson to Anstee, 6-9 December 1972.
35 UN Document S/10853 and Add.1, 1 January 1973.
36 Jackson to Anstee, 9 September, 1972.
37 Jackson to Anstee, 31 January, 1973.
38 Jackson to Anstee, 1 February, 1973.
39 Jackson to Anstee, 23 February 1973.
40 Jackson to Anstee, 2 and 3 April 1973.
41 Oliver, Op. cit., page 164
42 Jackson to Anstee, 4 April 1973.
43 Jackson to Anstee, 16 May 1973.
44 WF Hughes, RELIEF AFTER DISASTER, unpublished report, August 1980, page IX/12. Hughes was IMF representative in Bangladesh at the time.
45 See Anstee, Op. cit. page 314 ff.
46 UN Document S/10853/Add.4, 6 December 1973

Chapter 16   Africa and Indo-China

1 SC Resolutions 216, 12 November and 217, 20 November 1965.
2 Antony Gilpin memoirs, unpublished.
3 SC Resolution 329 of 10 March 1973.
4 Anstee to the author, 21 December 2000.
5 489th meeting of ECOSOC, 17 July 1973, SR.
6 See [2].
7 1913th meeting of ECOSOC, 15 July 1974, SR.
8 1972nd meeting of ECOSOC, 23 July 1975, SR.
9 Jackson to Anstee, 26 June 1976.
10 2028th meeting of ECOSOC, 2 August 1976, SR.
11 2079th meeting of ECOSOC, 25 July 1977, SR.
12 Resolution 2093 (LXIII), 2080th meeting of ECOSOC, 26 July 1977.
13 Jackson to Mainza Chona, Prime Minister of Zambia, 26 July 1977.
14 Chona to Jackson, 31 August 1977.
15 See Anstee: NEVER LEARN TO TYPE, pages 325-329.
16 Jackson, letters to Anstee between July and October 1974.
17 Jackson to Anstee, 2 September 1974.
18 Jackson to Anstee, 30 September 1974.
19 THE MEKONG COMMITTEE – A HISTORICAL ACCOUNT, page 46.
20 UN Archives, S 0364-0004 and 0009.
21 Aubrac: OÙ LA MÉMOIRE S'ATTARDE, Editions Odile Jacob, Paris. 1996, pp 323,332.
22 Draft Resolution E/L.1660; Resolution 1944 (LVIII), 7 May 1975
23 1950th meeting of ECOSOC, 7 May 1975, SR.
24 Jackson to Waldheim, 16 August 1977.
25 OH2, 14 February 1986, p 32.
26 Jackson to Anstee, 20 June 1976.

ENDNOTES

27 Jackson to Anstee, 22 June 1976.
28 GA Resolution 31/17, 24 November 1976.
29 GA Resolution 31/187, 21 December 1976.
30 Letter from the SG to Member States etc., A/32/220/Add.1, 19 July 1977.
31 Jackson to Waldheim, 16 August 1977.
32 Ibid.
33 Waldheim to Jackson, 1 September 1977.
34 Urquhart to Jackson, 7 October 1977.
35 Anstee to the author, 21 December 2000.
36 Jackson to resreps in Guinea-Bissau and Gabon, 5 September 1977
37 Jackson to Anstee, 5 October 1977.
38 Jackson to Raffeeudin Ahmed, Executive Assistant to the SG, 20 October 1977.
39 Jackson to Gibsons, 15 November 1977.
40 Chulikorn Thaisanguanvorakul to the author, 5 April 1993.
41 Jackson to Anstee, 2 December 1977.

Chapter 17   Back to UNDP

1 Morse to Jackson, 1 January 1978.
2 Jackson to Anstee, 29 May 1978.
3 Jackson to Gibsons, 30 May 1978.
4   Anstee to Jackson. June 1978
5 Jackson to Anstee, 2 September 1978.6   UNIDO document ID/B/228, 11 April 1979.
7 Jackson to Anstee, 5 May 1979.
8 OH2, 14 February 1986, p 55.
9 Ibid., p 57.

Chapter 18   Kampuchea

Jackson's cables and other papers quoted or referred to in this chapter which are not otherwise identified are in UN Archives, Series S-0536/0007-0013.

1 For a fuller account of these events in 1979 see Maggie Black's history of UNICEF – THE CHILDREN AND THE NATIONS, Unicef, 1986.
2 Jackson, letter to Ingram, Executive Director of WFP, 9 May 1983.
3 See Shawcross: THE QUALITY OF MERCY, André Deutsch, London 1984, p 221.
4 OH2, 14 February 1986, p 58.
5 Jackson to UNHQ, 8 April 1980.
6 See [2].
7 Jackson to UNHQ, 21 April, 1980.
8 Jackson to Saunders, 7 May 1980.
9 See [7].
10 Jackson to SG, 21 April 1980.
11 Malcolm Harper, interview 17 March 1992.
12 Saunders to the author, 6 March 1992.

ENDNOTES

13 Shawcross, Op.cit., page 279.
14 Saunders to Jackson, 8 May and 3 June 1980.
15 Shawcross, Op.cit., pages 277-8.
16 Shawcross, Op.cit., page 230
17 Jackson to SG, 17 April 1980.
18 See [2].
19 Jackson to UNHQ, 13 June 1980.
20 Jackson to Anstee, 30 June 1980.
21 See [2].
22 Jackson to UNHQ, 8, 9 and 11 July 1980.
23 Jackson, Note for the file 9 July 1980.
24 See [2].
25 Shawcross, Op.cit., page 280.
26 Jackson to UNHQ, 17 July, 1980
27 Shawcross, Op.cit., page 278.
28 Black, Op.cit.,. page 404.
29 Jansson to the author, 27 September 1992 .
30 Jackson to UNHQ, 25 August 1980.
31 Jackson to UNHQ, 13 October 1980.
32 Jackson to Anstee, 27 November 1980.
33 Anstee, Christmas letter, 6 December 1980.
34 Jackson to UNHQ, 30 January 1981
35 Jackson to UNHQ, 9 January 1981.
36 UNICEF cable to its HQ, 12 January 1981.
37 Jackson to UNHQ, 5 February 1981.
38 Jackson, note for the file, 22 May 1981.
39 Ibid.
40 Grant to Jackson, manuscript note of 6 March 1981.
41 See [29].
42 Jackson to UNHQ, 20 April 1981
43 Jackson to UNHQ, 16 June 1981.
44 Jackson to UNHQ, 16 and 17 June 1981.
45 Jackson to UNHQ, 29 June 1981.
46 Jackson to SG, 2 June 1981.
47 Anstee, Christmas letter, November 1981.
48 Shawcross, Op.cit., page 411.
49 Jackson to SG, 17 July 1981.
50 Jackson to SG, 15 October 1981.
51 Jackson to SG, 26 February 1982.
52 Jackson to UNHQ, Reflections on a Sunday morning, 15 March 1982.
53 Jackson to UNHQ, 20 March 1982; this was the view of Alan Everest, UNICEF's Special Representative in Phnom Penh.

54 Shawcross, Op. cit., page 340.
55 See 2. Jackson's letter to Ingram was headed "Acronyms".
56 Jackson to UNHQ, 20 August 1982, after visiting Hanoi.
57 Jackson to UNHQ, 16 October 1982.
58 Jackson to UNHQ, 18 October 1982.
59 Dewey to the author, 14 May 2000.
60 Dewey to the author, 15 July 2000.
61 Jackson to UNHQ, 16 February 1983.
62 Jackson to UNHQ, 28 February, 1983.
63 Jackson to UNHQ, 7 March 1983.
64 Everest to author, July 2004.
65 Jackson to UNHQ, 5 May 1983.
66 Comment by Anstee, July 2004.
67 Jackson to SG, 24 May 1983.
68 Jackson to SG, 25 May 1983.
69 Jackson to UNHQ, 8 June 1983.
70 Prattley to General Riem, 10 June 1983.
71 Jackson to UNHQ, 29 June 1983.
72 Jackson to UNHQ, 11 August 1983.
73 Jackson to UNHQ, 17 August 1983.
74 Jackson to UNHQ, 23 August 1983.
75 Jackson to UNHQ, 25 and 30 August 1983.
76 Shawcross Op.cit., pages 414-5.
77 Jackson, Note for the file, 22 September 1983.
78 Jackson to UNHQ, 14 October 1983.
79 Jackson to SG, 11 November 1983.
80 Jackson to UNHQ, 2 December 1983.
81 Report by Ted Morello in Far Eastern Economic Review, 22 December 1983.
82 Anstee to the author, December 2001.
83 Dewey to the author, 15 July 2000.

Chapter 19   The last lap

1 Anstee, Christmas letter, December 1984.
2 Report of Seminar on The Problems of the Sahel and Macro-Engineering Solutions held at the Rensselaerville Institute, New York State, November 1985.
3 Jackson, Brock Chisholm Memorial Lecture, Geneva, January 1986.
4 Jack Charnow (UNICEF) to Jackson, 15 July 1986.
5 Jackson to Grant, 26 May 1967.
6 Jackson to Anstee, 8 July 1986.
7 Jackson: Foreword to "Disasters and the United Nations", Interdisciplinary Science Reviews, Volume 11 No 4, 1986, JW Arrowsmith Ltd., London.
8 Jackson to Gibsons, 12 November 1986.

ENDNOTES

9   Jackson to Anstee, 16 November 1986.
10 Jackson to Anstee, 22-28 November 1986.
11 Jackson, Brunel Lecture at MIT, 26 March 1987.
12 Jackson to Anstee, 27 August 1987.
13 Jackson to Anstee, 2 September 1987.
14 Jackson to Anstee, 14 November 1987.
15 Edwards: BRUCE OF MELBOURNE, Man of Two Worlds, Heinemann, London 1965.
16 Jackson to Anstee, 20 November 1987.
17 Jackson, Lord Boyd Orr Memorial Lecture, 6 November 1987.
18 Jackson to Anstee, 14 November 1987
19 Jackson to Anstee, 23 November 1987.
20 Jackson to Anstee, 29 November 1987.
21 Jackson to Anstee, 1 December 1987.
22 Jacksson to Anstee, 2 December 1987.

Chapter 20   Epilogue
1   John Saunders, address at Jackson's Requiem Mass.
2   Saunders, interview 27 February 1992.
3   Jackson to Saunders, 1 October 1986.
4   John and Winifred Saunders to Jackson, 23 September 1986.

Index

Where a name appears frequently in the text the index gives the pages between which it may be found, or the chapter number in bold type. The name may not be found on every page of the section or chapter.

A

Abramovitz, Morton, 317
Acheson, Dean, 75
Adeane, Sir Michael, 193
Ahmed, Rafeeuddin, 300, 301
Alexander, Field-Marshal, 59
Allende, President, 275, 277, 286
Altamirana, Carlos, 286
Anderson, Sir John, 67
Annan, Kofi, xi, 270
Anstee, Margaret Joan, vii-ix, 200-208, **12, 13, 14, 15**, 283-293, 298-289, **18, 19, 20**
Ap Rees, Garth, 240
Arden-Clarke, Sir Charles, 171, 174
Ataturk, Kemal, 18
Attlee, Clement, 86, 112, 127
Aubrac, Raymond, 289

B

Bailey, Dr EE, 43, 57
Ball, JA, 2
Barron, Colonel EC, 25
Beredjick, Dr Nicky, 262, 263, 271
Bernadotte, Count Folke, 131-136
Bevin, Ernest, 103-106, 111, 113-1134, 122-127, 132-3, 143
Bhutto, President Zulfikar Ali, 247-249, 252, 256-257, 263, 266-267
Black, General, 238
Black, Maggie, 333
Blewitt, Captain Kit, 251, 252

Blickenstaff, David, 240
Bloch, Léonce, 210
Bodley-Scott, Dr Ronald, 162, 242-244, 263, 270
Bolton, Bill, 19
Bouton, Dr WK, 1, 11
Brezhnev, President, 276
Bridges, Sir Edward, 30, 69, 92-99, **7**, 147, 155-167, 178, 181, 241, 264
Brown, Ernest, 65, 66
Bruce, Viscount, 102-104, 343
Brunel, Isambard Kingdom, 339
Buffum, William, 322, 330
Bunche, Ralph, 131, 136

C

Cadogan, Sir Alexander, 108-110, 120-121, 126, 141, 143
Cahor, Kylin, 339
Campaigne, Curtis, 240
Cannon, Congressman, 94
Cargill, Peter, 252, 253, 255
Casey, Richard, **4**, 101-102, 136, 145, **9**
Caustin, Harold, 86, 268, 270
Chalmers, Captain WS, 78
Chamberlain, Neville, 15
Chandler, Professor Robert, 264, 267, 268
Charteris, Sir Martin, 184
Chatfield, Admiral of the Fleet Lord, 20
Chifley, Ben, 84
Chisholm, Brock, 333, 33
Chou en-Lai, 261

375

INDEX

Chulikorn Thaisanguanvorakul (Angela), 294
Churchill, Randolph, 29
Churchill Mrs, 70, 71
Churchill, Winston, 23, 28, 40, 42, 66, 70-71
Clark, Joan, 263
Clayton, William, 84, 89
Cleveland, Harlan, 94
Cohen, Andrew, 23
Cohen Benjamin, 102, 140
Cohen, Myer, 200, 206-208, 211-224, **12**, 228, 232, 237-238, 253
Collins, Sheila, vii, **4, 5, 6**, 135 144, 147, 148, 183, 202, 242, 255, 295, 298, 299
Conroy, Denise, 338, 344
Cooper Brothers & Co, 173
Cordier, Andrew, 117-121, 137-139
COSUP, 24, 36
Creal, Eric, 9-12
Cripps, Sir Stafford, 122-126
Crotty, John, 5
Cunningham, Admiral Sir Andrew, 24-25
Curtin, John, 40

D

Dalglish, Rear-Admiral RC, 8, 9
d'Astugues, Marcel, 253, 269
Davidson, Alfred, 79, 85, 90, 332
Davidson, Dr Frank P, 332
Dean, John Gunther, 317, 321, 322, 327
de Cuéllar, Pérez, 319, 322, 328, 330, 341, 347
de Gaulle, President, 191
de Seynes, Philippe, 274
Deloitte, Plender, Griffiths & Co., 95
Deshmukh, Sir Chintaman, 162-167
Dewey, Arthur E, 322, 329-330
Dhar, Subhas, 254, 258, 262, 268, 271, 278, 285
Dick, George, 93
Dick, Mrs, 10, 11, 93
Dick, Peggy (Mrs Jackson), 10-21, 83-93, 149, 158
Dixon, Owen, 158, 161
Dobbie, Lieutenant-General Sir William, **3**
Douglas, Lewis, 125-132

Dunk, William, 154, 155
Durnford, Captain, 15-19, 39
Duthie, John, 180

E

Eden, Anthony, 58, 167
Edgerton, Major-General Glen, 94
Egger, Charles, 309-312
Eisenhower, General, later President, 73, 182
English, Joanna (Anna), 178-183, 194, 200-203, 238, 242, 272
Erhardy, Joseph, 340
European Recovery Plan (ERP), 96, 118, 120, 122-125
Evans, Rear-Admiral ERGR, 7
Evatt, HV, 102, 137-138
Everest, Alan, 323, 328

F

Farah AA, 294
Fitzgerald, Dr, 103
Flood, Fr Eric, 346-347
Ford, Rear-Admiral WRT, 9, **3**

G

Gale, Lieutenant-General Sir Humfrey, 69-80
Gbedemah, KA, 181-182, 192
Ghandi, Mrs, 249, 256-257
Gibson, James, 277, 294, 298, 331, 340, 343, 347
Gibson, Mary (Maria), vii-viii, 13, 216, 259, 276-277, 294, 298, 331, 340, 343, 347
Gilpin, Antony, 274, 281-284
Gomez, Luis Maria, 345
Grant, James, 305-322
Grigg, Sir James, 59
Guest, Patricia, 335
Guyer, Roberto, 245, 250, 257, 259, 267

H

Hagen, Toni, 250-251
Halcrow, Sir William & Partners, 165, 195
Hall-Patch, Sir Edmund, **6**, 122-129, 161

INDEX

Hammarskjold, Dag, 213
Harding, William, 240
Harland, Bruce, 300
Harper, Malcolm, 307-8
Harriman, Averill, 118
Hasler, William, 58-59, 67, 71-78, 82
Hassan, Said, 162
Hayden, Senator, 7
Heenan, the Very Reverend JC, 97, 157, 346
Hendrickson, Roy, 59, 60, 64-66
Heng Samrin, President, 303-307, 312, 323
Henry, Paul-Marc, 206-208, 12, 228, 230, 237, 248-249
Heppling, Sixten, 210
Hitler, Adolf, 15, 22, 25, 27
Hocké, Jean Pierre, 308
Hoefliger, Jean, 307
Hoffman, Paul, 118, 200-208, 12, 229-233, 14, 253, 255, 264, 350
Hoo, Victor, 102, 118
Hoxha, President, 64
Howell, Harry, 80, 95
Hun Sen, 312, 324
Huyser, Jan, 241

J

Jackson, Alan (Bill), 1, 4, 11, 21, 83, 93, 96, 157-161, 175, 183, 200, 202, 210, 213, 294-299
Jackson, Andrew (Tam), 158, 200, 299, 336, 344
Jackson, Archibald, 1-5
Jackson, Beryl, 2
Jackson, Bett, 158, 175, 183, 294, 299
Jackson, Carlie (Robin's wife), 342, 347
Jackson, Sir Edward, 23, 32, 56, 84, 93, 133, 147, 150-157
Jackson, Audrey, 56, 333, 147, 150-157
Jackson, the Rev James, 1
Jackson, James Dunlop, 8
Jackson, Kathleen, 1, 4, 5, 11, 22
Jackson, Robert Ward (Robin), 178-183, 200, 202, 231, 242-3, 253, 263, 272, 277, 294, 298, 316, 334-342, **20**

Jackson, Wilbur Kenneth, 1, 11
Jacob, Betty, 335
Jansson, Kurt, 312, 315
Jebb, Gladwyn, 101-111, 122-126, 133, 143
Jensen, Erik, 269

K

Kahn, Richard, 39, 40, 43
Kaiser, Edgar, 183-196, 291
Kai-shek, Generalissimo Chiang, 94
Kaldor, Professor Nicholas, 191-192
Kamp [Mekong], 342
Katzin, Alfred, 70-73, 116
Kaunda, President, 274, 281-286
Kennedy, President JF, 189-194
Kerno, Ivan, 102
Keynes, JM, 39
Khieu Samphan, 320
King George VI, 33
Kirk, Alexander, 42, 54
Kraczkiewicz, Karol, 210-211
Kunugi, Tatsuro, 329

L

Labouisse, Harry, 305
Lacoste, Francis, 273-276
LaGuardia, Fiorello, 79-98, 113, 121, 132, 333
Lampson, Sir Miles, 42
Landis, James, 54-57
Langer, Senator, 75-6
Laugier, Henri, 102, 117, 130
Law, Richard, 59, 65-69
Leathers, Lord, 57
Lehman, Herbert, 53, 59, 60, 63-80, 82, 85, 92
Lehman, Edith, 66-7, 77-79, 272, 333
Leith-Ross, Sir Frederick, 65-67
Lewis, Major-General Richard, 73
Lie, Trygve, 80, 101-115, **7**, 147, 165, 167, 264, 308, 341, 343, 347
Lim, Valentina (Nena), 345
Lovett, Robert, 114, 118, 120

INDEX

Lumumba, Patrice, 189
Lyttelton, Oliver, 29, 30, 38-41, 168

M

Macduff, See Jackson, Robin
MacDuffie, Marshall, 43, 48, 50
Macintyre, Donald, 21, 35
Macmillan, Harold, 58, 193-194
Makins, Sir Roger, 123
Manisty, Peggy (Bess), 21-2, 26-31, 346
Marshall, George C, 96, 120-126
Mason, Philip, 113, 122, 143
McCormick, Congressman, 74
McDiarmid, John, 240, 257
McNamara, Robert, 239, 252
McNeil, Hector, 102-103, 111-114, 133-144, 158
Menzies, Robert, 149, 153
Mills, Christina (Chris), 340-341, 344
Milton, Robert, 193
Molotov, V, 91
Montgomery, General Bernard, 42
Montini, Monsignor, 155
Morgan, Lieutenant-General Sir Frederick, 69, 76-78, 138
Morse, Bradford, 235, 297
Moxon, James, 190
Moyne, Lord, 136
Mujibur, Sheik Mujibur Rahman, **15**, 288
Murdoch, Dame Elisabeth, 173, 343
Murdoch, Sir Keith, 173
Murdoch, Rupert, 173
Murray, Keith, 43, 49, 53-58

N

Narasimhan, CV, 215-6, 223-225, 228, 231-232
Nasser, Colonel, 182
Neame, Elizabeth & Humphrey, 88
Nehru, President, 183
Nerfin, Marc, 210-211, 233, 238, 241
Newall, Air-Chief-Marshal Sir Cyril, 20
Nicholson, Max, **4**, 147
Nina, 15, 22, 26

Nixon, President, 243
Nkrumah, Kwame, **10**, 261
Nkrumah, Fathia, 185
Noel-Baker, Philip, 71, 90, 97
Norman, Mrs, 36

O

Olds, Glenn, 231
Ording, Aake, 137-9
Orr, John Boyd, 102, 104, 343
Osagyefo, See Nkrumah
Owen, David, 102-110, 117-8, 129-144, 204-208, 210, 215

P

Pearson, Lester, 214, 225
Pelt, Adrian, 102, 117
Perowne, Stewart, 36
Peterson, Rudolph, 243, 253, 259, 297
Pillau, Sir Raghavan, 167
Pinochet, General, 286
Pio, Padre, 12-13, 132
Pius XII, Pope, 73, 112, 155
Pol Pot, 289, 321
Popov, 251
Pound, Admiral Sir Dudley, 16-20, 32
Powell, Erica, 174
Prasong Sansouri, 314, 326
Prattley, Winston, 321-328
Price, Byron, 117-118, 132, 140, 144

Q

Queen Elizabeth II, 184, 193-194

R

Rajchman, Dr Ludwik, 333
Rawlings, Flight-Lieutenant Jerry, 196
Relda, 13, 84, 201, 245, 335, 344
Riem, General, 326
Roger, 15, 27, 31, 38, 40
Rommel, Field-Marshall, 27, 42
Rooks, Major-General Lowell, 71, 80, 92-96

INDEX

Roosevelt, President, 53, 72
Ross, Lieutenant-Colonel JPB, 64
Rotival, Alexander, 230
Rountree, William, 43-44, 57
Rusk, Dean, 118, 121

S

Sadruddin Aga Khan, Prince, 276
Sailer, Dr Erna, 249-254
Sales, Pierre, 253-254, 262, 271
Salter, Sir Arthur, 63-4
Sargent, Sir Orme, 123
Saunders, John, 274, 306-312, 347-348
Scobie, General, 58
Searle, Captain William, 262, 276
Shustov, Mr, 323
Siddhi Savetsila, 310-311
Sihanouk, Prince Norodom, 320-322
Smith, Ian, 281-282
Smith, Victor, 9
Sobolev, AA, 117-118, 129, 144-5
Somerville, Vice-Admiral Sir James, 24
Son Sann, 320
Spooner, William, 159
Stalin, Joseph, 85-86, 90-91
Stephen, Sir Ninian, 337
Stevens, Major-General JES, 155-159
Stokes, Richard, 93
Strong, Maurice, 233, 238
Sutherland, Duke and Duchess of, 111

T

Talleyrand, 2, 115
Thibodeaux, Ben, 43-44
Tito, President, 64
Tolbert, President, 243-244, 270
Tonkin, HL, 3-5
Truman, President, 72, 74, 83-90, 112
Tubman, President, 201-2, 206, 241-243
Turing, Alan, 148
Thant, U, 237-238

U

Umbricht, Victor, **15**, 288
UNICEF, 219, 289, 304-323, 333-335
Urquhart, Sir Brian, xi, 117, 123, 125, 130-134, 144, 247, 257, 259, 267, 270, 293, 347

V

Vaidyanathan (Vaid), 240
V$_{ALCO}$, 185-188
Vandenburg, Senator, 75
Vaughan, David, 134-5

W

Waldheim, Kurt, 245, 249-253, 259-269, 273-276, 292-296, 300-316, 321, 323
Ward, Barbara, 51, 53, **6**, 116, 130-136, 147, **9**, **10**, 200, 202, 213, 231, 238, 242-244, 254-255, 260-264, 272, 275, 294, 298-299, 316, 318
Watson-Watt, Robert, 16
Wavell, General Archibald, 25-29
Wheeler (WFP), 271
Wheeler, General, 262
Wilmington, Martin W, 44, 60-1
Wilson, Harold, 204
Winant, Frederick, 43-44, 48, 51, 56, 70
Winant, Gil, 70
Winnifrith, John, 181
Wright, Michael, 123-125